_ML_ Binding

This textbook has an ML-BINDING designed for exceptional durability and long lasting use. The ML-BINDING is distinguished by:

Extensive Testing for Durability

The ML-Binding has endured highly sophisticated testing that approximates the wear and tear of heavy classroom use.

Reinforced Stress Points

A specially designed reinforced endsheet assembly strengthens the joint area and relieves stress on the first and last signatures. This also enables the book to stay open easily.

Maximum Cover Adhesion

Latex-impregnated kraft liners are the strongest available providing superb adhesion to the backbone and cover of the book.

Flexible Spine for Ease of Use

Tubular liners add strength and also enhance flexibility at normal stress points on the spine of the book.

The ML-BINDING exceeds the Manufacturing Standards and Specifications set forth by the National Association of State Textbook Administrators.

McDougal, Littell
English

Dear Student,

You are entering a challenging and exciting period of your life. Your view of the world is becoming more mature and more complex. The textbooks you use should reflect this growth. They should encourage you to think new thoughts and explore new ideas. Most of all, your textbooks should help you discover and develop your own special talents and skills.

McDougal, Littell English was created to help you achieve these goals. The photos, fine art, and literature selections were chosen to fire your imagination and expand your knowledge of the world. The text was designed to appeal to your interests and abilities while at the same time challenging you to improve your writing and speaking skills.

We hope you will enjoy working with the images and ideas in this book. More important we hope that using the book will give you confidence in your abilities and an eagerness to try out new ideas. In the process, you will discover that language can be lively, exciting, and even fun.

The Editors

"*Your* world is as big as you make it."

Georgia Douglas Johnson

McDougal, Littell
English

Gold Level

ML

McDougal, Littell & Company

Evanston, Illinois
New York   Dallas   Sacramento   Raleigh

Authors

Kathleen L. Bell, Assistant Director of Composition, Department of English, University of Miami, Coral Gables, Florida

Kraft and Kraft, Developers of Educational Materials, Stow, Massachusetts

Susan Duffy Schaffrath, Consultant in Educational Materials for the Elementary and Middle Grades, Chicago, Illinois

Mary Ann Trost, Former Elementary Teacher, East Cleveland City School District, East Cleveland, Ohio

The Editorial Staff at McDougal, Littell & Company

Consultants

Deborah Kay Bossmeyer, Middle School Team Leader and Language Arts Teacher, DuValle Middle School, Louisville, Kentucky

Patricia Brackenrich, Principal, White Sulphur Elementary School, White Sulphur Springs, West Virginia

Ann E. Davis, Assistant Superintendent, Washington County Education Service District, Portland, Oregon

Karla J. Dellner, Coordinator of Staff Development, San Juan Unified School District, Carmichael, California

Joy C. Fowles, Ph.D., Coordinator for Secondary Education, Clear Creek Independent School District, League City, Texas

Susan Vignes Hahn, Assistant Superintendent for Instruction, Archdiocese of San Francisco, San Francisco, California

Nana E. Hilsenbeck, Language Arts Supervisor, Volusia County School District, Daytona Beach, Florida

Bobbi Mulholland-Mahler, Coordinator of Curriculum, Irvine Unified School District, Irvine, California

James W. Reith, Program Coordinator for Language Arts, Foreign Languages, and Libraries, Scottsdale School District, Phoenix, Arizona

Acknowledgments: See page 607.

Cover Photography: Craig Aurness—West Light/Masterfile

Cover Quote: From "Your World" by Georgia Douglas Johnson (1886–1966).

ISBN: 0-8123-5732-9

2 3 4 5 6 7 8 9 10 11 12 13 14 15 / 92 91 90

Composition

Beginning with You

Developing Writing Skills

Resources and Skills

Featured Writers

Peter Abrahams

Maya Angelou

Mary Austin

James A. Baggett

Henry Beston

Truman Capote

Lucille Clifton

Dorothy Cottrell

Emily Dickinson

Carlota Cárdenas de Dwyer

Elizabeth Enright

Ernest Hemingway

Juan Ramón Jiménez

Melissa Kim

Edward Lear

Henry Wadsworth Longfellow

Marianna Mayer

Ogden Nash

Christina Georgina Rossetti

Mildred Taylor

William Carlos Williams

William Wordsworth

Longer Literature Selections

Composition

Beginning with You

Developing Writing Skills

Writing for Different Purposes

People in all times and places have searched for ways to give form to their thoughts, feelings, and ideas. Early Native Americans expressed themselves in these rock carvings. Writers of today use the printed word to communicate with others.

1

The Writer's World

Good writing ideas don't have to come from exotic adventures. Sometimes the most interesting ideas come from ordinary experiences, such as learning a new skateboarding stunt or talking to a grandparent or friend.

When you are trying to grow as a writer, the best place to start is with your own ideas and experiences and the writing you do without direction from a teacher or textbook. This chapter will show you how to record your personal experiences in a journal. You will also learn how to observe and how to use precise sense words to make your writing lively and descriptive.

1
Starting a Journal

Focus Use a journal to record private thoughts and to gather ideas for writing.

As you grow older, you grow more complex. New ideas and information are all around you. Your world becomes larger, more fascinating, and sometimes more confusing.

One way to sort out new ideas is to write about them in a journal. A journal is a notebook or folder used for personal writing. It is a place where you can write about anything you want in any way you want.

Journal writing is like thinking on paper. It is done by people of all ages and all professions. Most people use journals to record their experiences and observations. Here is how one student, Anthony, used his journal to express his feelings.

> My dad is in the Navy. In the last ten years we've lived in California, Rhode Island, Hawaii, and the Philippines. It's fun to see new places, but I hate, hate, hate moving around. I have to start all over every time, making new friends. Then just when I'm getting used to everything, we have to move again. It isn't fair.

As you can see, your journal can be a private place for private thoughts. However, it can also serve another purpose. It can be a Writer's Idea File. Here are two ways to make your journal work as an idea file.

> Find a place in your journal to list writing ideas. When you see, read, hear, or experience something that might be a good writing topic, jot it down in your journal.

Use a section of your journal like a scrapbook. Collect articles, pictures, programs, and other things that interest you. These, too, can supply ideas for writing.

Whenever you need a writing topic, look in these two parts of your journal. Also check the section of your journal where you do your personal writing. Your thoughts and experiences are valuable sources. For example, Anthony's journal entry on page 6 offers several possibilities. Anthony could report on one of the more unusual places he has lived. He might decide to describe the difficulty of making new friends. Or he might remember and write about something funny that happened during one of his moves.

The more you use your journal, the more confident you will be about your writing abilities. Journal writing will also give you practice in expressing yourself more clearly.

Writing Activities Keeping a Journal

A Choose one of the topics below or one of your own. Write a journal entry in which you explore your thoughts.

> Let me introduce myself . . . .
> My most unusual dream
>   was . . . .
> A perfect day for me
>   would be . . . .
> Here's the real story . . . .

B Use parts of your journal for a Writer's Idea File and Writer's Scrapbook. Add at least two writing ideas each day for the next five days.

2
The Senses of Sight and Hearing

Focus Use precise sight and sound words to make your writing more lively.

How do you change the notes in your journal into a finished piece of writing? The first and most important step is to become a good observer. A good observer pays special attention to what he or she sees, hears, touches, tastes, and smells. A good writer searches for precise words to describe what he or she observes.

Try this experiment. Look around the room for a few moments. Then close your eyes. Try to recall what the room looks like. Form a picture in your mind. Who is sitting on your left? What is he or she wearing? What does the top of your desk look like? What color are the walls of the room?

Now open your eyes and study the room. How accurate were your observations? Choose one item in the room and try to think of some specific words to describe what you see.

Most writers rely heavily on the sense of sight. Read the description that follows.

Literary Model

Her grandparents' house smelled cool and sweetish. There was a bowl of white and pink stocks on the hall table, and her grandmother's green linen parasol leaned in a corner among the pearly company of her grandfather's canes.

In the shaded living room, Fiona saw her mother knitting and her grandmother at the piano playing the same kind of music she always played, with the loose rings clicking on her fingers.

From "Nancy" by Elizabeth Enright

Notice that the writer does not just list the objects and people in the room. She uses details that help the reader see them in a fresh way. The flowers are *white and pink*. The parasol is *green linen*, and it leans near the grandfather's *pearly* canes. The living room is *shaded*.

The writer also describes the sounds in the room. The grandmother is at the *piano playing*. As she plays, her loose rings are *clicking on her fingers*.

To understand how important sound is in your world, try the following experiment. Cover your ears tightly. Do you suddenly feel isolated and removed from the activity around you? Try to remember what the room sounded like before. Were classmates moving in their seats or rustling papers? Were there voices in the hall? Was someone coughing?

Now uncover your ears and listen carefully. What words could you use to explain the sounds around you?

Here is how one writer describes the sound of the sea. What "sound" words does he use?

Literary Model   . . . hollow boomings and heavy roarings, great watery tumblings and tramplings, long hissing seethes, sharp rifle-shot reports, splashes, whispers, the grinding undertone of stones . . . .

From "The Headlong Wave" by Henry Beston

Writing Activity Using Your Eyes and Ears

Imagine you are at one of the places listed below. You must describe this place to a friend who has never been there. Write a paragraph about the sights and sounds you observe. Try to use words that will let your friend "see" and "hear" the experience.

a carnival	a sporting event	an airport
a farm	a beach	a camping trip
a traffic jam	a crowded bus	a shopping mall

3
Touch, Smell, and Taste

Focus Using precise sense words can make your writing more descriptive.

When you watch a football game on television, you use the senses of sight and hearing to experience the action. Yet you are missing other important sensations.

Think about how the experience would be different if you were at the game. You would feel the brisk autumn breeze on your face. You would sense the rumble when the fans begin to cheer. You would taste the hot chocolate and smell the hot dogs sold at the concession stands.

We sometimes take for granted the senses of touch, taste, and smell. However, they are extremely important tools for writers. To see how a writer uses touch words, read this description of a donkey named Platero.

Literary Model

Platero is small, downy, smooth—so soft to the touch that one would think he were all cotton, that he had no bones. Only the jet mirrors of his eyes are hard as two beetles of dark crystal.

From *Platero and I* by Juan Ramón Jiménez

Can you imagine what it might feel like to run your hand over Platero's coat? This feeling occurs because Jiménez uses touch words such as *downy, smooth, soft,* and *cotton.* In contrast, Platero's eyes are described as *jet mirrors, hard as beetles,* and *dark crystal.*

The senses of taste and smell are closely related. Think about smells you like or dislike. Do you associate particular tastes with those smells? Have you ever tasted a new dish because you liked the way it smelled?

To use the senses of taste and smell effectively in your writing, you need to be specific. How many "smell" words can you find in the following passage about Chut, an orphan kangaroo?

Literary Model

> Chut's wounds healed. The men were good to him. He learned the new smells of firesmoke and potatoes roasting in ashes; the mellow smell of coffee and the sharp tang of tea, the odors of frizzling bacon and grilling chops; of tobacco smoke by a campfire under stars; and the sneeziness of raw flour and the smells of men.
>
> From "Chut, the Kangaroo" by Dorothy Cottrell

Now read about a picnic. Can you almost taste the food? How many "taste" words can you find in the passage?

Literary Model

> On the barbecue pit, chickens and spareribs sputtered in their own fat . . . . Orange sponge cakes and dark brown mounds dripping chocolate stood layer to layer with ice-white coconuts and light brown caramels. Pound cakes sagged with their buttery weight and small children could no more resist licking the icings than their mothers could avoid slapping the sticky fingers.
>
> From *I Know Why the Caged Bird Sings* by Maya Angelou

Writing Activity Making a Sensory Word List

In your journal or writing folder, begin your own list of sensory words. Put each of the following headings at the top of a separate piece of paper: *Sight, Sound, Touch, Taste, Smell*. Write as many sense words as you can under each heading. Add to the list throughout the year and refer to it when you write. Here are some words to get you started.

Sight	Sound	Taste	Touch	Smell
green	yelp	bitter	prickly	fragrant
scramble	crash	sour	cool	smoky
sneak	stutter	juicy	gritty	fresh
dash	giggle	sweet	slippery	rotten
chubby	sigh	buttery	fuzzy	burnt
dented	rumble	bland	sticky	musty
frilly	hiss	mild	rough	stagnant
sparkling	rustle	spoiled	velvety	aromatic
spotted	thud	dry	clammy	
tiny	whine	tangy	itchy	
round	shrill	spicy		
slink		sugary		
bronze		fishy		
lumpy		salty		
gloomy		burnt		
fragile		fruity		

Read the Starting from Literature selection that begins on the following page. As you read, look for sensory descriptions. Find words and examples that show the observation skills of the author.

Starting from Literature

from *My Prairie Year*

Brett Harvey

The following selection is based on a young girl's journal. The girl was Elenore Plaisted. Her journal described her life on the Dakota prairie during the 1890's. In 1985 Elenore's granddaughter turned the journal into a book.

O ne night in the fall I awoke to find Mother shaking me urgently. "Get up, Elenore, quickly, now, and help me with the children." As we woke Marjorie and Billy and wrapped them in blankets, I *(Sense of sight introduced)* saw that the room was lit by a red glare from outside the windows. Mother hustled us downstairs and out the door to the cellar. We stood in the doorway for a moment, transfixed by the column of fire towering in the black sky. It was a prairie fire—still far away but being blown toward our place by high winds, and coming closer all the time. Sparks were sailing through the air and dropping onto the barns, the granary, and on the grass around us. We saw the silhou- *(Sense of touch introduced)* ettes of the men against the red sky, beating out the sparks as they fell, and dragging wet blankets up ladders to the barn roof. Mother tucked Marjorie and Billy safely in the cellar and then she whirled away to join the men. I stationed myself outside the cellar door to guard the children and, using a piece of old carpet, beat out any sparks that fell too close.

By now clouds of sparks were falling everywhere. The men were working feverishly and shouting, the horses in the barn were snorting and stamping with fear, and the oxen were being driven in from the coulee[1] where they had been staked out for the night.

Suddenly Mother was beside me, her face grim in the crimson light, her hair and shawl whipping around her. She grabbed me and pulled me against her smokey-smelling body and, as we clung together, we felt a great wave of intense heat and suddenly the wall of fire seemed to be all around us, roaring and crackling. We stood still, too terrified even to scream, waiting to be swallowed up by flames. But the wall of fire swept past us with incredible speed, and then it was gone.

The next morning I looked out on a prairie that was charred black as far as the eye could see. Wisps of smoke curled up here and there where small fires were still smoldering. But standing in the middle of a great yellowish square of ground were our house and barns—scorched, but safe. That square patch of land had been ploughed early in the summer while the grass was still green. It had saved us from being burned.

In the winter the snow was so deep and the cold so terrible that we sat around the enormous cylindrical stove which was red hot, swathed in blankets, overcoats and woolens. We had to put the butter on the stove so that it would melt enough to cut. I cried because of the cold, standing on my soapbox with my arms in the steaming dishwater.

At first the snow looked just the way it had back in Maine. But soon it was coming down so fast and thick we could see only white outside our windows. Daddy said it looked like a blizzard and that it might

[1]coulee: a deep gulch, streambed, gully, or ravine that is usually dry in the summer

go on snowing for days. He went out and stretched a strong rope from our front door to the door of the barn. The wind was howling like wolves and the snow kept coming down so heavily that you couldn't see more than a few inches in front of you. Daddy would push the door open with all his might, letting in a great blast of icy, snowy wind, and feel his way blindly along the rope to the barn to feed and water the animals.

The winter days stretched out long and cold and dark and boring. I thought spring would never come.

Then one day a box arrived from Aunt Addie, Mother's sister back in Maine. We unpacked it on the big pine table, exclaiming at all the treasures. There were jars of real *fruit*—apples, oranges and lemons— wools and cottons for new clothes, toys, and best of all, books and magazines. I was starving for something to read. I drank in the smell of fresh new pages and printer's ink.

Trying Out Sensory Writing Choose one of your earliest memories. Did you feel happy, sad, silly, frightened, or some other way? Describe this memory in your journal. Remember to use all of your senses to make your memory seem as real as the day it happened.

Creative Writing

A Have you ever noticed that excitement can sharpen your senses? Think of an athlete walking on to a field before a big game. Or think of a musician walking on stage before a cheering audience. At such exciting times, a person is often more alert and more aware.

Recall a moment in your life just *before* an important event. Try to relive the moment in your mind. In your journal, write down vivid sense details that describe what you experienced. List the details under the following four categories: 1) sight, 2) hearing, 3) touch, and 4) taste and smell. Use your details to write a description of your experience in your journal.

B Write a story about a true or imaginary incident that involves an animal. Describe the incident from the animal's point of view. Use sense details to make your story lively and colorful. The following examples may give you ideas for writing.

1. An elephant at the zoo views you with curiosity.
2. A mosquito lands on your arm ready for a tasty treat.
3. A cat watches with envy as you eat a fish dinner.
4. A tiny puppy tries to understand your commands.

Application and Review

A Identifying the Senses Identify the sense (sight, hearing, smell, touch, or taste) you associate with each of the following words.

1. sweet
2. sticky
3. yelp
4. slim
5. tart
6. shout
7. smooth
8. perfumed
9. sting
10. blond
11. piney
12. clap
13. smoky
14. yellow
15. salty

B Using Sensory Words Write a description of each of the following items. Use at least two different senses in each description.

1. a pickle
2. a basketball
3. a rose
4. a motorcycle
5. a flute

C Using a Journal Choose one of the topics listed below and write a journal entry about it. Use sensory words to make your writing come alive.

Describe your room at home.
Describe a favorite relative.
Describe an incident that happened this week.
Describe an incident that happened when you were
    younger.
Describe the cast party you went to.
Describe an exciting sporting event.
Describe your neighborhood.
Describe an autumn day.

2
Using Thinking Skills to Find Ideas

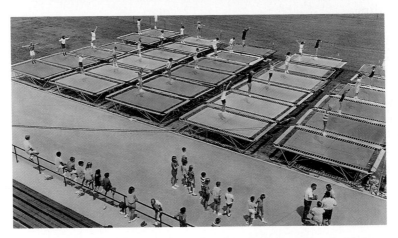

The high-flying fellow in the photo at the right is George Nissen, inventor of the trampoline. How do you suppose he ever thought of such an idea?

Like many creative thinkers, Nissen turned something ordinary into something brand new. One day while he was daydreaming about his childhood, he remembered how much fun he'd had bouncing on the bed. Then a thought struck him. "Why couldn't grown-ups have the same kind of fun?" Before long, Nissen (with the help of a friendly kangaroo) was demonstrating the world's first trampoline.

You can be a creative thinker, too. This chapter will help you stretch your imagination and learn to look at old things in new ways.

1

Reflecting

Focus You can find ideas for writing by *reflecting,* or exploring your own thoughts.

Where do ideas for writing come from? Some of the best ideas are as close as your own thoughts. **Reflecting** is a thinking skill you can use to examine your inner world—your knowledge, memory, and imagination.

Reflecting may help you to find out what you already know about a subject or how you feel about it. When you reflect, you can also relive past events. You may even explore your imagination or discover new ideas. The following techniques will help you search for writing ideas within yourself.

Brainstorming This technique involves thinking of as many ideas as possible in order to solve a problem. Begin by thinking about one general idea or topic. Then list any words or phrases that come to mind. Keep adding to your list until you run out of ideas. Review the list and underline a word or phrase that might be a good idea for writing.

Freewriting This requires that you write nonstop. Start with any topic and write whatever comes to your mind. Write without stopping for two or three minutes. Do not judge the value of your ideas. Just keep writing.

Jesse started with the topic of race cars. He used freewriting to explore his ideas.

> The engines are roaring, crowds yelling. Race tracks are always exciting, crowded. How do they get the cars here? How does someone become a race car driver—I wonder if I'd be scared behind the wheel. Or brave? Like a stunt driver. How do you get a job like that?

Clustering This technique helps you to explore and organize your ideas. As with freewriting and brainstorming, all you need is a piece of paper and a pen or pencil. Then follow these steps.

1. Begin by writing your topic, or starting point, in the center of your paper. Circle it.
2. Think about other ideas associated with your topic. These ideas may be the main parts of your topic or simply related thoughts. Circle these new ideas and link them with lines to your topic.
3. Think about additional ideas that are related to the new ideas you found. Write them down near the ideas they relate to. Circle the additional ideas, and connect them to the related ideas.

Alicia used clustering to generate a number of ideas for a report on California.

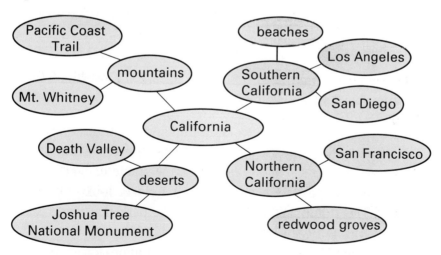

Writing Activity Using Reflecting

Use brainstorming, freewriting, or clustering to generate ideas about one of the subjects listed below.

your earliest memory   a hero   the Civil War   holidays

2
Observing

Focus You can find ideas for writing by *observing* the world outside yourself.

You have just studied ways to look within yourself to explore ideas. You also can explore ideas by **observing**— paying close attention to what is around you.

One way to explore ideas is to list the features of the people, places, and things you encounter. Here are some of the features you can look for.

size	parts	sound
shape	quantity	taste
color	condition	duration
weight	depth	function
height	width	importance
age	feel	value

Notice how David used observing to take a closer look at a familiar object in the example below.

David had seen the statue hundreds of times as he walked through the park. Yet he had never paid any attention to it. Today, however, the statue caught David's eye. He decided to take a closer look.

The statue was in a corner of the park that was overgrown with weeds. Its top was hidden by the branches of a nearby tree. As David approached, he noticed the statue was about six feet tall, with a brick base. Standing on the base was a soldier with a musket in his hand. He was wearing a three-pointed hat. He was gazing into the distance. The statue was made of some sort of metal, but over time it had taken on a green color. In places the surface was rough and pitted with age.

David looked at the base and saw a small plaque that was mostly covered by the weeds. When he pulled back the weeds, he was able to read the plaque. It stated that the statue had been erected to honor the town's soldiers who fought in the Revolutionary War.

David realized that he had found a fascinating topic for writing. He would go to the library and find out more about the soldiers who participated in the Revolutionary War. He might investigate the specific battles in which men from his town had participated.

Minuteman statue, Concord, Massachusetts.

By using his powers of observation, David was able to see a familiar object much more clearly. What are some of the features David examined as he observed the statue?

Writing Activity Using Observing

Choose a partner and select an interesting object in your classroom, your school, or your neighborhood. Observe the object closely, using the list of features on page 22 as an aid. Each partner should create a list of details that describe the object. Then compare lists to see who was a better observer.

3
Asking Questions

Focus *Inquiring,* or asking questions, is another useful way to get ideas for writing.

In addition to observing the world around you, you can explore ideas by asking questions, or **inquiring**. This is the method reporters use when they cover a news story. They frequently ask questions that begin with the words *who, what, when, where, why,* and *how.* These questions can be applied to any type of writing.

After seeing a documentary about Rome, Rachel decided to find out more about the Roman Colosseum. She asked these questions as she explored the subject.

Who built the Colosseum?	The Romans under Emperor Vespasian
What was the Colosseum?	An outdoor arena that could seat about 50,000 spectators
When was it built?	It was completed and dedicated in A.D. 80.
Where was it built?	Rome
Why was it called the Colosseum?	A large statue, *a colossus,* was built near its entrance.
How was it used?	Mock naval battles, combat between gladiators, battles between men and wild animals, and other public events were held there.

The six questions helped Rachel to identify the information she needed. They also helped her to think of other *who, what, when, where, why,* and *how* questions, such as the ones listed below.

> How were mock naval battles held?
> Who were the gladiators?
> Why were battles between men and wild animals held?
> What was the purpose of the colossus?

By asking questions, Rachel decided that she was most interested in the events held at the Colosseum. She decided that would be the focus of her paper.

Writing Activities Asking Questions

A Think of a real or imaginary person you would like to interview. It could be a rock star, an actor, a character in a book, a historical figure, or anybody you find interesting. Then use the reporters' method to make a list of questions you would like to ask this person.

B Study the photograph below. Think of questions that you would like to have answered, then list them.

4
Creative Thinking

Focus *Creative thinking* involves looking at things in unexpected ways.

You may think that only people such as artists, musicians, poets, and inventors are "creative." Yet creativity is important to everyone. Anyone can be creative by turning off the part of the mind that evaluates and criticizes and by thinking of new ways to look at things. Here is how one student used creative thinking to come up with an original idea.

A few weeks ago Darcy's next door neighbor, Mr. Colburn, was called out of town unexpectedly. He asked Darcy if she could take his dog for a walk every day while he was away. Shortly after that, another neighbor, Mrs. Curtis, became ill. She had seen Darcy walking Mr. Colburn's dog. Mrs. Curtis asked Darcy to walk her dog until she got better.

Darcy enjoyed the walks, and she especially enjoyed playing with the dogs. She thought to herself, "What if I offered to walk dogs on a regular basis? I could even charge a fee and make some spending money."

Darcy wrote a flier offering her services as a dog walker. She gave the fliers to all the dog owners in the neighborhood. Soon, she could be seen daily, surrounded by a half-dozen neighborhood dogs, walking down the street.

Darcy used creative thinking by asking herself a question beginning "What if?" She discovered a way to do something she enjoyed, provide a service, and make money. You can use the same process by following the steps on the next page.

1. Do not block your creativity by trying to judge every idea right away. Instead, let your mind freely play with new thoughts, new possibilities. Remember that great ideas, such as the laser beam, were first regarded as impossible and foolish.
2. Use observing, as you learned in part 2. Look for new or unusual details in the world around you. Try to find new connections between things.
3. Use your imagination. Spur your thoughts by asking yourself questions that begin "What if?" Here are examples of the types of questions you might ask.

   - What if I combined two things that do not usually go together? (Music videos are a combination of records and television.)
   - What if I used this object in a new or unusual way? (The frisbee was originally a pie tin.)
   - What if this person, place, object, event, or idea did not exist? (What would the world be like without television?)
   - What if I changed just one part of this? (What would happen if cars could run on water?)
   - What if the relationships between things were different? (What if parents had to do homework?)

Writing Activity Creative Thinking

Creative thinking may lead to new uses for old things. The telephone was originally designed to send voice messages. Now telephones allow computers to talk to one another. They even send pictures from one city to another. Use "What if?" questions to come up with new uses for radios.

Creative Writing

A The following poem by Henry Wadsworth Longfellow praises young people by using a **metaphor**. A metaphor is a comparison between two unlike things that have something in common. Longfellow uses a metaphor when he describes young people as "living poems."

> *To Young People*
> You are better than all the ballads
>   That ever were sung or said,
> For you are living poems
>   And all the rest are dead.

Write a short poem that uses a metaphor to describe a person you know. First, use freewriting to think of things that you associate with that person. Then create a metaphor that compares the subject of your poem to one of those things. Use your metaphor as the starting point of your poem. You may wish to begin your poem with the words *You are*.

B E. M. Forster once wrote a story about a young boy who found a bus behind his house that traveled to paradise. Imagine that you have found a similar bus that can travel to the land of dreams. Create a story about such a bus. Explore ideas for your story by inquiring, that is, by asking the *who, what, when, where, why,* and *how* questions.

Crossroads

English and Math

You use the thinking skill of seeing relationships in math. Numbers and shapes may be grouped in many ways. For example, you know that some numbers are even and some numbers are odd. You also know that some numbers are whole numbers and some are fractions. You are also able to see sequences in numbers. For example, you know that in the sequence *5, 10, 15* . . . the next number is *20*. Finally, you can identify parts and wholes. All of these tasks require you to use thinking skills.

Activities

A. The numbers in the following lists are arranged in special order. On your paper, write the number that will complete each sequence.

1. 3, 6, 9, 12, 15, _____, 21, 24
2. 2, 4, 7, 11, 16, 22, _____, 37
3. 896, 448, 224, 112, 56, 28, 14, _____

B. Look at each group of figures. Write the letter of the figure that is different from the others on your paper.

Application and Review

A Using Reflecting Below is the beginning of a cluster chart. Use your clustering skills to continue filling out the chart. Your focus is music.

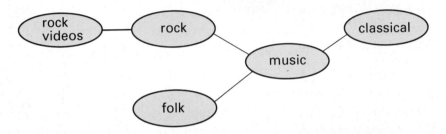

B Using Observing Think about what you were doing at exactly 1 P.M. yesterday. Use your observing skills to remember as many details as possible. Then write a paragraph describing what you observed.

C Using Inquiring Use inquiring to develop a list of questions about one of the following story topics: a young person mysteriously ages ten years in one night, huge animal footprints are found at the local park, or a woman in colonial clothes knocks on your door asking for help. Then answer the questions.

D Using Creative Thinking The following passage shows how an inventor used creative thinking. Read the passage and then write the "What if?" questions the inventor may have answered.

> Hans Lippershey was a Dutch man who made eyeglasses. One day in 1608 he peered through two glass lenses at once. He noticed that doing so magnified the image. So he mounted the lenses at both ends of a tube. He invented the telescope.

Starting Points

Ideas for Writing

Starting Points provides pictures and quotations to help you find ideas for writing. Although the pictures and quotes are grouped by the four types of writing, feel free to browse through all of *Starting Points* when you are looking for ideas.

To use *Starting Points,* jot down your thoughts as you look at a picture or read a quotation. The following questions may help.

Pictures

1. *Description* How could I describe this picture? Does the image remind me of anything else I could describe?
2. *Narration* What feelings, memories, or ideas does the picture make me think of? What story could I tell about this picture?
3. *Explanation* What process does the picture show? What things or ideas could be explained in a composition?
4. *Persuasion* What issue does this picture point out? How do I feel about the issue?

Quotations

1. *Description* How can I expand on this quotation?
2. *Narration* Does this quotation make me think of a real or imaginary event or person?
3. *Explanation* How does this quotation apply to my own life? Can I think of an example that supports the quotation?
4. *Persuasion* What is the main point of the quotation? Do I agree or disagree with it?

Starting Points

Description

From childhood's hour I have not been
As others were—I have not seen
As others saw.

Edgar Allan Poe

GRAND CANYON 7

He could throw a lamb chop past a wolf.

Bugs Baer
describing
baseball
pitcher
Lefty Grove

Flamingo Boats, Stephen Rosser, 1988.

Sail—
boats on the sea:
white butterflies, winging
across a watery meadow of blue.

Carlotta Cárdenas de Dwyer

Narration

How sorry we would
be if many of our
wishes were granted.
Aesop's Fables

When in doubt,
tell the truth.
Mark Twain

And that is what life's
all about—changes
going on every
minute, and you
never know when
something begins
where it's going to
take you.
Joan Blos

Explanation

There is nothing new under the sun, but there are lots of old things we don't know.

Ambrose Bierce

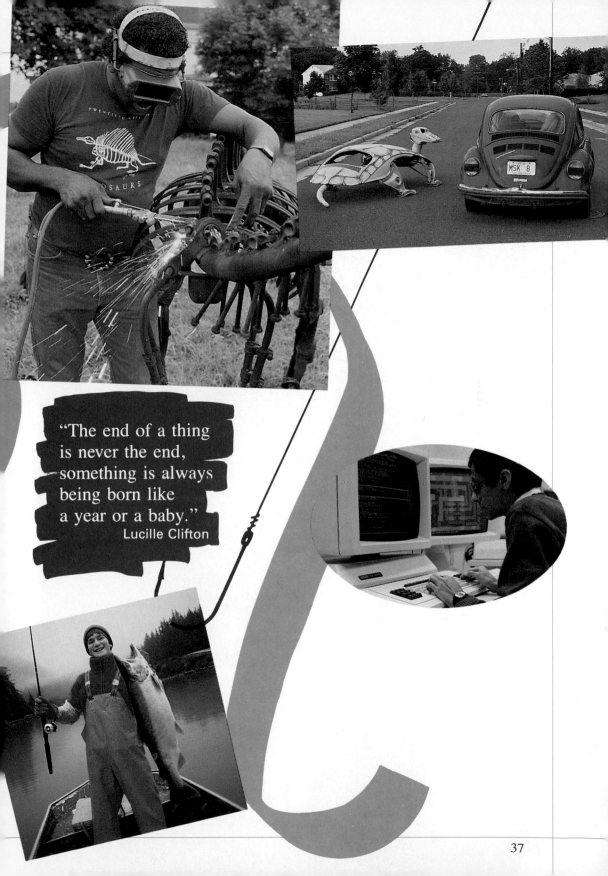

"The end of a thing
is never the end,
something is always
being born like
a year or a baby."
Lucille Clifton

Persuasion

Volunteers clean an oil-soaked bird.

Senior citizens demonstrate for health care benefits.

Join Smokeys Campaign
PREVENT FOREST FIRES!

It is television's primary damage that it provides ten million children with the same fantasy, ready-made and on a platter.

Marya Mannes

Sell a country! Why not sell the air, the clouds and the great sea, as well as the earth? Did not the Great Spirit make them all for the use of his children?

Tecumseh, Shawnee Chief

3
Choosing a Writing Process

"Anyone for anchovies?"
"Extra cheese on mine, please!"

Everyone makes pizza a little differently, although the basic steps and ingredients remain the same. Just as there are different ways to create a pizza, there are many ways to write. The route through the four basic writing stages—prewriting, drafting, revising, and presenting—is a flexible one. Each writer must make individual choices, creating his or her own special recipe for writing. As in pizza making, the important thing is to create an end product that is—delicious!

1
The Writing Process

Focus The *writing process* is a thinking process that has four stages.

To write clearly, you must think clearly. But writing, like thinking, is different for each person. There is no one correct way to write, just as there is no one way to think. The skills that you learned in Chapter 2 will help you to think clearly, to identify the problems you will face in your writing, and to solve them. Nothing will be more valuable to you as a writer.

The Stages in the Writing Process

Most writers go through four stages in the writing process. These stages are 1) prewriting, 2) drafting, 3) revising, or editing, and 4) publishing and presenting.

The four stages in the writing process are not like the four bases in a baseball game. If you were to return to an earlier base in baseball, you would never score a run. In the writing process, however, you are free to go back and forth among the four stages until you are satisfied with your writing. The choices in each stage make the process a little different for every writer and for every type of writing.

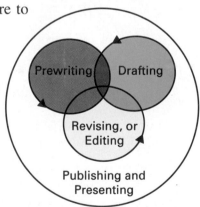

Prewriting During prewriting, you find ideas for your writing, choose and limit a topic, and consider your purpose and audience. You also gather information to support or explain your topic. In addition, you may create a writing plan to help organize the details for your writing.

Drafting At this stage you write a first draft, using your writing plan as a guide. You may need to write two or more drafts of your paper. Getting words on paper is the main task. Changes and corrections can be made later.

Revising, or Editing When you revise or edit your paper, you improve your draft. You may ask a classmate to be a peer editor for your draft. After you are sure that your paper is clear and effective, you must carefully proofread it for errors in grammar, spelling, and punctuation.

Publishing and Presenting In the final stage of the writing process, you share your writing with an audience. When you share your writing in its written form, it is called *publishing*. When you share your writing orally, it is called *presenting*.

You may want to experiment with the writing process until you find what works best for you. Every writing assignment presents a slightly different problem, however. The writing process can help you find solutions.

Writing Activity Thinking About Writing

Think about how you write. Then answer the following questions about your writing process.

1. How do you get ideas for writing?
2. What prewriting activities have you tried? Which ones have worked best?
3. Do you write your first draft slowly or quickly?
4. Have you ever asked another classmate to read and comment on your draft? Were the comments helpful?
5. Did you follow any of your reader's suggestions?
6. What method do you use for proofreading?
7. What are some of the ways you have shared your writing with others? Can you think of any other possibilities?

2
Prewriting: Choosing and Limiting a Topic

Focus Choose a general subject that interests you. Then limit the subject to fit your assignment.

To find your own topic, use the methods that you studied in Chapters 1 and 2. Try a few different methods until you find an idea that interests you.

After you have chosen a general subject, or topic, your next step is to narrow or limit it. This means you must make your subject more specific—very specific if you are writing just one paragraph. A composition, on the other hand, is several paragraphs about one topic. Topics for compositions can be broader than topics for single paragraphs.

How can you make your subject specific? Use the same methods that you used to discover writing ideas. You might brainstorm to find several smaller ideas that tie in to your general subject. Then you can ask questions about that specific idea until you discover a limited topic.

One student, Jennifer, began limiting her subject, pets, by brainstorming. She listed everything that came to mind.

the neighborhood pet shop   canaries that sing
caring for a pet   tropical fish
animals that make good pets   talking parrots
my pet chameleon   what to do with pets if
cocker spaniels   you are not at home

After looking over her list, Jennifer decided to write about her pet chameleon. To narrow her topic even more, Jennifer asked herself the questions at the top of the next page.

Who?	my pet chameleon, Houdini	**How?**	escapes from cage
What?	causes problems, always in trouble	**Why?**	doesn't like cage; may be bad-tempered
When?	all the time	**Where?**	at home

The answers to these questions helped Jennifer narrow her topic. She decided to write about Houdini's frequent escapes from its cage. This topic is specific enough to cover well in a single paragraph.

Purpose and Audience

After you have limited your topic, you must consider your **purpose,** or reason for writing. Is it to tell a story or to describe a person, place, or thing? Do you want to give instructions or explain an opinion? Then you must consider your **audience,** or readers. Will they be students, your aunt, or the editor of your local newspaper? Answering these questions will help you choose the best information and the right kind of language for your readers.

Writing Activities Limiting a Subject

A Imagine that your teacher has assigned a paragraph on the subject of *magic*. Limit this subject so that it can be covered well in one paragraph. Use brainstorming and questioning to limit your subject. Write your purpose and tell who your readers will be. Share your specific topic with your classmates.

B Writing in Process Choose one topic. If you need ideas, try Starting Points on pages 31–39 or select a topic from the Ideas for Writing in the Writer's Handbook, pages 547–549. Limit your choice so that it can be easily covered in one paragraph. Decide on your purpose for writing and tell who your audience will be. Save your notes in your writing folder.

3
Prewriting: Developing a Topic

After limiting your topic, you must develop it. The first step is to gather information that supports or explains it.

There are several ways to gather information. You can talk to others, look through your journal, or brainstorm. You might also browse through the library, or simply observe your subject. You might analyze a situation. That is, you break down a problem into its parts. You might look at the causes and effects of a situation. You might look at the steps in a process, or at the important features of a new invention.

At times, it will be necessary to use more than one method of gathering information, depending upon your purpose for writing. The following will help you decide what kind of information you need and how to gather that information.

Sensory details appeal to the five senses of sight, sound, smell, touch, and taste. For a review on using your senses, refer to Chapter 1, pages 8–12. You can gather sensory details through observation, memory, or imagination.

Stories tell about real or imaginary experiences. A brief story, or **anecdote,** can help your readers understand an idea. A story can come from your experiences, from talking to others, from reading, or from your imagination.

Examples help to develop a general idea. Imagine that you are writing a composition about your school's intramural sports program. You might give examples of the different sports that are included. Examples can come from your own experience, observation, reading, or research.

Facts and Statistics can support an opinion or add important information to a report. Suppose you were writing a report about a famous hockey player. You might use facts and statistics to show how the player's performance compares to that of other hockey players. Facts and statistics can be proven true. Gather facts in reference books, such as encyclopedias, atlases, and almanacs. You will learn more about facts and opinions in Chapter 9, pages 157–158.

Reasons are explanations that tell why you think your ideas are right. Reasons are often used to support an opinion or tell why something happened. Look for reasons in your experience, reading, and research.

Writing Activities Developing Details

A Read the following list of topics. Decide on the types of details that could be used to develop each topic. These include sensory details, stories, examples, facts, statistics, and reasons. Then choose one of the topics and list several details you might use to develop it.

> Why girls should play Little League
> baseball
> A bakery in my neighborhood
> How I met my friend from
> Japan
> Why a certain television show
> should be canceled
> Famous musicians of the 1980's

B **Writing in Process** Gather information and develop the details for the topic you selected in part 2. Use the methods presented in part 3 of this chapter and in Chapter 2. Choose details that fit your purpose for writing. Save these notes in your writing folder.

4
Prewriting: Organizing Ideas

Focus Look over your details and arrange them in a logical order. Then make a writing plan.

Organize Your Details

The final step in the prewriting process is to organize your information. Read your list of details and cross out any that do not support your main idea. Add any new ideas to improve your writing and put the details into a logical order. You can organize ideas in several ways.

Chronological Order Details are arranged in the order in which they did or should happen. Use chronological order to tell a story. Also, use it to explain a process. See page 112.

Natural or Spatial Order Details are arranged in the order in which you see them. This might be from side-to-side, top-to-bottom, or far-to-near. Arrange details in natural order to describe a person, place, or thing.

Order of Importance Details are arranged from the least to the most important idea, or from the most to the least important idea. Use order of importance to arrange reasons or to plan descriptive or persuasive writing. For more help in organizing your writing, see pages 93–95.

Make a Writing Plan

After you decide on an order for your details, make a writing plan. Include your topic, audience, and purpose. Also, show your details in the order in which you plan to write them. Look at Jennifer's writing plan on the next page.

topic		my pet chameleon
purpose		to tell about the problems my pet causes
audience		classmates
details	2	My chameleon is an escape artist.
	3	leaps off high tables
	4	travels fast
		~~eats only live prey, such as crickets~~
	5	keeps trying to escape
	6	I bought him a heat lamp.
	7	My chameleon doesn't do much except sit on a rock.
		~~Frogs are also difficult, unrewarding pets.~~
	1	chameleon's name—Houdini

I should number these details in the correct order.

These details aren't important to the story.

As you organize details, you may find that you have more than one main idea. In that case, you will write a composition. A composition is several paragraphs about the same topic. Each paragraph consists of several sentences that have the same main idea. You will learn more about paragraphs in the next chapter, pages 62–71.

When you write a composition, first decide what the main idea of each paragraph will be. Then group together the details that support each main idea. Next, organize the ideas in each paragraph and then put the paragraphs in a logical order.

Writing Activity Making a Writing Plan

Writing in Process Make your own writing plan. Use the details and topic you developed in part 3. Save your plan in your writing folder.

5
Drafting

Focus Let your writing plan guide you as you put
your ideas into sentences and paragraphs.

Now that you have finished planning your writing, you are
ready to begin drafting. Write down your details in the order
you want to present them. Use your writing plan as a guide.

Do not be afraid to make changes or add new ideas. Be
sure that these new ideas support your topic. Take out any
unnecessary details as well. Try different ways of organizing
your details until you find the best type of organization to
express your ideas.

Do not try to express your ideas perfectly in the first draft.
In the drafting stage you are free to cross out, change
wording, add or reorganize details. You may even write
several drafts before you are satisfied.

Choose a Drafting Method

No two people write in exactly the same way. Everyone
develops his or her own writing style. Some people start
drafting and don't stop until they have all their ideas on paper.
Others write a sentence or two and stop. They read over what
they have written and make corrections. Then they continue
writing. Still others combine these two methods. Use whatever
style is most comfortable for you.

Use the Right Language

As you write, choose language that suits your audience.
However, always use standard English. **Standard English**
follows all of the rules of good grammar. It is understood by
everyone who speaks the English language.

Standard English can be formal or informal. **Informal English** is the language of everyday speech. It is casual. It includes simple sentences and simple vocabulary. **Formal English** often uses longer sentences and an advanced vocabulary. Use informal English when writing to a friend or classmate. Use formal English in all serious writing, such as class papers, essay contests, and business letters.

A Sample Draft

Jennifer followed her writing plan as she wrote the first draft of her paragraph. Notice her thoughts as she wrote.

I got more than I asked for when I received

~~I felt very lucky when I got~~ a chamelon for my

That's when

birthday. I decided to name him Houdini. I had figured

such a small pet

that a ~~chamelon~~ would be no trouble. I was wrong. A

leaped

chamelon is an escape artist. He ~~jumped~~ out, jumped off

the table, and went under a radiator. It took me a long

time to catch him. From that time on, he has tried to get

out every time I feed him. I tried to make him feel

better. I bought him a new cage and a lamp. It didn't

help Houdini just sits on his rock all day, looking for

the nearest exit.

> My topic sentence should be more interesting.

> I'll use this idea later.

> I need a more specific verb.

Writing Activity The First Draft

Writing in Process Write a draft of the paragraph you have been planning. Keep your audience and purpose in mind. Follow your writing plan but remember that you can make changes as you write. You may need to write more than one draft. Save your work in your writing folder.

6
Revising, or Editing

Focus Revise to improve your writing. Proofread to correct mechanical errors.

You are now ready to begin the third stage of writing, **revising,** or **editing**. When you revise, you improve what you have written. You might add or take out details. You might also change the way you have organized your details. You add precise nouns, strong action verbs, and descriptive adjectives and adverbs. When you proofread, you look for mistakes in grammar, capitalization, punctuation, and spelling.

Try to plan writing assignments so that you have time to put your draft away for a few days. At least put it away for an hour or two. When you look at it again, you may see mistakes that you missed the first time. Another way to find mistakes is to read your draft out loud. You can also ask a friend or parent to read your draft and to offer suggestions. Follow these guidelines when you revise.

Guidelines for Revising

1. Do all the sentences in each paragraph tell about one main idea?
2. Are the details specific? Should any be left out? Should any be added?
3. Are the details arranged in logical order?
4. Are the sentences in the best possible order? Should any sentences be moved?
5. Does my writing accomplish my purpose?
6. Does my language suit my audience?
7. Do I like what I have written? Will others enjoy reading it?

Peer Editing

Sometimes it is difficult to find the weaknesses in your own writing because you know what you mean in each sentence. You may think that everyone else will also.

Peer editing gives you another point of view. In peer editing, you share your writing with a classmate. This person becomes your first audience. He or she can point out both the strengths and weaknesses in your paper.

A peer editor can give written comments on your paper or just talk to you about them. There are two ways to do peer editing. The first is for you and another classmate to exchange papers and to edit them. A second way is to do peer editing with a small group of your classmates. In this case, each person would look for only one type of problem.

When you are peer editing, follow these guidelines.

Guidelines for Peer Editing

1. Give at least one positive comment about the paper. Be as specific as possible. For example, instead of simply saying you liked your class-mate's paper, say, "I like the way you described the old man. I could almost see him."
2. What could be improved in this paper? Once again, be as specific as possible. For example, you may feel that the paper has a dull beginning or a weak ending.
3. Is any part confusing? Why is it confusing?
4. Use the Guidelines for Revising on the previous page. Give your answers to each of the seven items.

After you have received your peer editor's comments, think about them carefully. You may not agree with the comments, and you do not have to do everything that a peer editor suggests. If you agree, however, you may be able to improve your paper by making the suggested changes.

Proofreading

Checking for mistakes in grammar, capitalization, punctuation, and spelling is called **proofreading**. Proofread your writing several times before making a final copy. Use the proofreading symbols found at the bottom of this page to make corrections on your draft. Follow these guidelines.

Guidelines for Proofreading

1. Look for errors in grammar and usage. Use the grammar chapters in this text for help.
2. Be sure you have capitalized correctly. For further help, see Chapter 26, pages 498–515.
3. Punctuate your writing correctly. If you are not sure when to use a comma or other punctuation marks, refer to Chapter 27, pages 516–543.
4. Check your work for spelling errors. Check the spelling of proper nouns, especially the names of people you have mentioned. Refer to pages 568–573 in the Writer's Handbook, or look up the word in a dictionary.
5. Check the correctness of any dates or other figures you have used in your writing. Be sure your facts are stated clearly and accurately.

Symbols for Revising and Proofreading

Use the following symbols for revising and proofreading.

Symbols for Revising and Proofreading

∧ Add let*t*ers or words.   — or ⌿ Take out a letters or

⊙ Add a period⊙   w*o*ords.

= capitalize a letter.   ¶ Begin a new paragraph.

/ Make a capital Letter   ↷ Then add a comma.

    lowercase.   ∽ Trade the position of

                               letters or wrods.

A Sample Revision

Here is how Jennifer revised and proofread her paragraph. Notice her thoughts as she wrote. Also notice the kinds of errors she found as she proofread.

I got more than I asked for when I received a chamelon for my birthday. I had figured that such a *Little did I know that* small pet would be no trouble. ~~I was wrong.~~ A *When I opened the door to his cage,* chamelon is an escape artist. He leaped out, jumped off *raced* the table, and went under a radiator. It took me *an hour* ~~a long~~ time to catch him. That's when I decided to name him *make a getaway* Houdini. From that time on, he has tried to ~~get out~~ *more content* every time I feed him. I tried to make him feel ~~better. I~~ *by buying big heat* bought him a new cage and a lamp. It didn't help Houdini just sits on his rock all day, looking for the nearest exit.

> **I should say what he leaped out of.**

> **I should use stronger verbs.**

> **This should be two sentences.**

Writing Activity Revising and Proofreading

Writing in Process Carefully read over the draft of your composition. Check the content and organization. Add or take out details as necessary. Improve your word choice. Use a revising partner to help you find weaknesses in your draft. Follow the Guidelines for Revising and Guidelines for Peer Editing in this part.

When you are satisfied with the content and organization of your draft, it is time to proofread your writing. Use the Guidelines for Proofreading on page 54 in this part to help you locate your errors. Use proofreading symbols to make corrections on your draft.

7

Publishing and Presenting the Final Copy

Focus Make a neat final copy of your writing. Find a way to share it with your readers.

Writing the Final Copy

When you are satisfied with your writing, begin your final copy. First, choose a good title for your writing. Center your title at the top of the page. Leave a one-inch margin around your writing. Indent each paragraph.

When you have finished writing, proofread your final copy one more time. If you find a mistake, correct it neatly.

Publishing Your Writing

Now you will share your writing with your readers. There are several ways to share your work in its written form.

Writing Booklets Making writing booklets is another way to share your work. You and your classmates might make booklets on a single theme, such as "Our Hobbies."

Bulletin Boards and Posters Display your writing on the bulletin board in your room or on the school bulletin board. You might also make a poster to display your descriptive writing. Glue a neat copy of your writing on a piece of posterboard. Use photographs or drawings to illustrate your topic.

Contests Enter your writing in contests or send it to newspapers or magazines. Ask your teacher for details.

Presenting Your Writing

You may also share your writing through an oral presentation. Here are three ways to present your writing.

Oral Presentations Read your work out loud to the class, or give oral presentations in small groups.

Skits Plan a skit to dramatize a narrative. You might also record your story on a cassette tape.

Models For a report on how something works, you might make a model of that object. To demonstrate the use of wind as an energy source, you might make a model windmill.

Compare Jennifer's final copy with her first draft.

My Escape Artist

Student Model
I got more than I asked for when I received a chameleon for my birthday. I had figured that such a small pet would be no trouble. Little did I know that a chameleon is an escape artist. When I opened the door to his cage, he leaped out, jumped off the table, and raced under a radiator. It took me an hour to catch him. That's when I decided to name him Houdini. From that time on, he has tried to make a getaway every time I feed him. I tried to make him feel more content by buying him a big new cage and a heat lamp. It didn't help. Houdini just sits on his rock all day, looking for the nearest exit.

Writing Activity Presenting a Final Copy

Writing in Process Make a final copy of your work. Write as neatly as possible and include a title. Indent each paragraph. Leave a one-inch margin around your writing. Proofread your final copy one last time and decide on a way to share your writing.

Speaking and Listening

You know that you can get information for a report by reading, doing research, and brainstorming. Another good way to gather information is by talking to people.

In order to get the right information, you must ask the right questions. To discover the right questions, follow these steps.

1. Ask yourself what you want to know about a subject.
2. Make a list of this information.
3. Turn each item on your list into a question. Some questions might have more than one part.

Suppose you were interviewing someone about his or her career. You might ask some of these questions to learn specific details about the career.

> What type of education is required?
> Is there a special training program?
> What is the salary range in this career?
> What hours do you work?
> Do you work alone or with other people?
> What is the most enjoyable/challenging part of your career?

Activity

First, choose a career you would like to learn more about. Then choose a person to interview about the career. Do enough research to determine what kinds of questions you would like to ask.

Interview the person. Listen carefully to what he or she says. Take notes and ask questions if you do not understand something.

Creative Writing

A According to the *Guinness Book of World Records*, the tallest person on earth in 1985 was Muhammad Aalam Channa, from Pakistan. He was 8 feet, 3 inches tall. Imagine that you are the tallest person on earth. How would your life be different from what it is today?

List the advantages and disadvantages of being 8 feet, 3 inches tall. Write a paragraph that tells whether your life would be easier or more difficult if you were that tall. Include reasons from your list to support your opinion.

B Have you ever thought about being an architect? An architect designs buildings. If you were to design your own house, what would it look like? Make a list of all the special features that would be in your house. List the different rooms and the colors you would use to decorate each room. List the furniture you would put in each room. Finally, decide where your house would be located. Would it be on a farm in North Dakota? Would it be in a high rise in New York City? Then, in a few paragraphs, describe your house.

English and Other Subjects

The writing process is really a thinking process. First, you identify what you want to write about. Then you consider and try different methods. Whenever you solve a problem, you use a similar process. First, you identify the problem. Next, you think about the choices. Third, you decide upon a solution and try it. Then you evaluate the results and, finally, adjust your solution as necessary. Look at how Tim solved a problem.

Problem My cat just gave birth to four kittens. There is not enough room in our apartment to keep them. What can I do?

Choices Put an advertisement in the newspaper.
Give them to friends. I know Lisa wants a kitten.
Give them to my cousin who lives on a farm in Iowa.
Take them to a shelter.

Find a Solution I think I'll give them to friends. Then I can see the kittens whenever I want.

Try Out the Solution and Evaluate the Results Only two friends actually want kittens. I have four.

Adjust I let Lisa and Washington pick out the kittens they wanted. Then I asked my mom if we could keep the other two until we visit my cousin this summer. My mom agreed.

Activity

Read the following problems. Choose one and tell how you would solve it. Use the five-step process for problem solving.

1. You'd like a new skateboard but do not have enough money.
2. You hear classmates planning to cheat on a test.
3. Your class is working on gymnastics equipment. You are afraid.

Application and Review

A Limiting a Topic Look over the general subjects that are listed below. Choose two of them. Then limit each topic so that it can be covered in a single paragraph.

food   hobbies   animals   robots   cars

B Organizing Details Look over the following details about the praying mantis. Write the words *Appearance* and *Actions* at the top of two columns. Put the details in the proper column.

Sits and waits until its victim is within reach
Lashes out and impales its victim on sharp spines
Claw at the top of each forelimb
Powerful forelegs
Small jaws and mouth
Eats nothing but live food
Wide-spaced, bulging eyes
Becomes the color, shape, and texture of its prey
Prayerful posture
Eats mostly insects such as bees, butterflies, and crickets
Cannibalism in the species is common.

C Identifying Parts of the Writing Process Look at the following list of writing activities. Tell whether each activity is most likely *Prewriting, Drafting, Revising,* or *Publishing and Presenting*.

1. correcting errors in spelling
2. gathering information
3. recording your story on tape
4. writing your ideas in paragraph form
5. brainstorming
6. changing the order of details in your draft
7. working with a revising partner

4
Learning About Paragraphs

Have you ever played on a winning team or been part of a group that worked together to get something done? If so, you know what teamwork is all about.

The sentences in a paragraph are like players on a team. Just as team members cooperate to win a game, the sentences in a paragraph work together to explain the main idea of the paragraph.

This chapter will show you how to achieve your writing goals by building winning paragraphs. You will learn to write sentences that work together as a team to form an effective paragraph.

1
What Is a Paragraph?

Focus A *paragraph* is a group of sentences that all tell about one main idea.

A writer expresses ideas in sentences. The sentences are arranged in paragraphs. In a paragraph, all the sentences work together to tell about one main idea. Read this paragraph.

Literary Model

> There was no price that could be put on Sounder's voice. It came out of the great chest cavity and broad jaws as though it had bounced off the walls of a cave. It mellowed into half-echo before it touched the air. It was louder and clearer than any purebred's voice. Each bark bounced from slope to slope in the foothills like a rubber ball. It was not an ordinary bark. It filled up the night and made music.
>
> From *Sounder* by William Armstrong

The first sentence of the paragraph says that Sounder's voice was special. This is the main idea of the paragraph. All the other sentences tell about the main idea. They talk about the things that kept Sounder's bark from being ordinary.

Notice that the first line of the paragraph is indented. It begins a few spaces to the right. The first sentence in a paragraph is always indented.

The group of sentences below only looks like a paragraph. It is not really a paragraph at all. See if you can tell why.

> Pigeons are good at living in the city. Some pigeons are brown, some are gray, and some are black. Once my brother caught a pigeon and tried to train it. Carrier pigeons have flown thousands of miles.

This group of sentences has four main ideas. Each sentence could be the main idea of a separate paragraph.

Now see how the paragraph could be improved.

> Pigeons are good at living in the city. They can live in just about any sheltered place—under railroad tracks, tucked under the edges of roofs, in gutters, in garages. Loud city noises don't scare pigeons a bit. The honking of car horns or the roar of trucks simply doesn't bother them. People don't frighten them, either. In fact, they like living near people because people often feed them.

Remember that a good paragraph has only one main idea. It is made up of complete sentences. All these sentences work together to tell about the main idea.

Writing Activity Studying Paragraphs

Read the following paragraphs. Use what you have learned to decide if each is a good paragraph. Explain your reasons.

1. Baseball is truly an international sport. The major U.S. leagues include two teams in Canada. The sport is popular in many Latin American countries. It is also a major sport in Japan, where games sometimes attract more than 30,000 fans.

2. Flapjack has strange habits for a parakeet. She likes to sleep late in the morning. I like to sleep late too, but Mom always wakes me. Flapjack's crabby all day if someone wakes her before ten. Last Saturday morning, I was crabby. I had to get up early and mow the lawn. Flapjack settles down after her usual breakfast of a pancake spread with peanut butter.

3. Snack-sized pizzas are easy to make. First, toast and butter half an English muffin. Spread a thin layer of spaghetti or pizza sauce on the muffin. Add extras such as cooked hamburger, onions, olives, and mushrooms. Put mozzarella cheese on top. Broil three to five minutes or until the cheese is melted.

4.   Wearing braces on your teeth has some good points. Three students in Mr. Chen's math class got braces the same week. New metals and ways of putting on braces mean that braces work better in a shorter time. People with braces often feel shy about them at first. My mom says it's better to have braces for a few years than to have crooked teeth your whole life.

5.   The removal of the Cherokees from Georgia during the winter of 1838–39 is known as the Trail of Tears. That winter U.S. troops forced seventeen thousand men, women, and children to march through snow and bitter cold. Most were barefoot. All were hungry. One famous Cherokee named Sequoya invented a system for writing the Cherokee language. The California redwood trees are called sequoias in honor of this leader. Almost a fourth of the Cherokee people died on the Trail of Tears.

The Trail of Tears, Robert Lindneux, 1942.

Good Topic Sentences

Focus A *topic sentence* presents the main idea of a paragraph.

The sentences in a paragraph work together to explain one idea. The main idea of a paragraph is often stated in a topic sentence. Usually the topic sentence is the first sentence in a paragraph. It lets the reader know what the rest of the sentences are going to be about.

Read the following paragraph. What is the topic sentence of this paragraph? What main idea does it express?

Professional Model　　Pluto is far out in the solar system, and it is small—only about 3,000 kilometers in diameter, even smaller than the Moon. Because it is small and distant, Pluto is a dim object beyond the range of even most larger telescopes. It was discovered in 1930 by Clyde Tombaugh, who studied thousands of sky photographs that had been taken over a long period of time. Decades had been spent searching for an image that shifted slightly among background stars. In that year, Tombaugh was certain he had found the elusive planet.

From *Mysteries of the Satellites* by Franklyn M. Branley

Writing Good Topic Sentences

A good topic sentence states the main idea of a paragraph. The topic sentence must also catch the reader's attention. Read the following topic sentences. Do they make you want to read more of the paragraphs that they begin?

I'm going to write about Samantha, who was good at solving mysteries.
This story is about a werewolf.

Each of these topic sentences states the main idea of a paragraph. However, neither of them is interesting enough to catch the reader's attention. A good topic sentence never begins with such words as "I am going to write about . . ." or "My paragraph is about. . . ." An interesting topic sentence is written so that the reader wants to read on.

Look at these revised topic sentences.

Samantha was a super sleuth.
Part wolf, part man, the werewolf howled at the
full moon.

These topic sentences present the main ideas and interest the reader. The reader wonders, "What mysteries has Samantha solved?" and "What will the werewolf do?" The reader wants to read the paragraphs to find the answers to these questions.

Limiting the Topic

As you write a topic sentence, think of it as an umbrella. It is one sentence that covers, or takes in, all the other sentences in the paragraph. However, be sure that the main idea expressed by the topic sentence can be covered in one paragraph. If necessary, narrow the main idea of a topic sentence. You should be able to tell about the idea in just one paragraph.

Guidelines for Writing a Topic Sentence

As you write topic sentences, keep the following important points in mind.

1. A topic sentence should tell what the paragraph is about.
2. A topic sentence should be interesting enough to catch the reader's attention.
3. A topic sentence should present an idea that is narrow enough to be covered in one paragraph.

Writing Activities *Good Topic Sentences*

A Read the topic sentences below. Tell which sentences are interesting and which are not. Then rewrite the dull sentences to make them more interesting.

1. Frightened and injured, the only survivor made his way through the thick jungle.
2. I'm going to tell you about my best friend.
3. *Incredible* is the only word to describe Michael Jordan.
4. I taught my dog some tricks.
5. Coral, which comes in unusual shapes and delicate colors, is actually a type of skeleton.
6. This paragraph is about camping.

B Here are three groups of sentences. Make them into paragraphs by writing a topic sentence for each group. Be sure that each topic sentence tells what the other sentences in the group are about.

1. _____ . The food of Mexico has become popular in all parts of the country. Many Mexican words have become part of the English language. Mexican music has influenced American music. Mexican designs have been used in American houses, especially in the Southwest.

2. _____ . His coat and mane were soft gold. He stood, straight and proud, looking over the grasslands. He gave a long, powerful roar. He was the master of the kingdom.

3. _____ . Long ago the people of East Africa used jewelry as weapons. The Aztecs of Mexico used it to show a person's place in society. Jewelry has been worn for its magical powers and as a way of remembering people. For example, in the 1800's some British women wore bracelets made of the braided hair of dead relatives.

Crossroads

English and Health

Most Americans today are very concerned about their health. They exercise and try to eat healthy foods.

Advertisers and health groups have noticed this attitude. They are developing ads that teach people more about health. Often, these ads are catchy slogans that capture the main idea about a food or product. Here are some examples.

Have more milk 'cause milk does more.
The incredible, edible egg.

Activity

Look for the topic sentence in each paragraph below. Then read the rest of the sentences to see what information each adds about the main idea. Write the topic sentence of each paragraph. Then rewrite the topic sentence as a catchy slogan.

1. A study done in Britain shows that eating cheese after a meal may be good for your health. Scientists have found that cheese may fight bacteria in your mouth that can cause cavities. Even if eating cheese does prevent tooth decay, the study warns that eating cheese will never replace brushing your teeth.

2. Drinking milk is a habit that will keep you healthy throughout your life. Milk keeps your bones strong while you are growing. Scientists studied women who drank milk regularly as children and teenagers. The bones of these women were stronger than those who did not drink as much milk. In addition, scientists noticed that some women continued to drink milk as adults. These women kept the good bone structure they had as children.

Application and Review

Studying Paragraphs Use these two paragraphs to answer the questions below.

Pueblo boys learned many things from their fathers. They learned to grow corn, squash, and beans. The Pueblos lived on the desert lands of the West and Southwest, especially in New Mexico. The boys learned to weave beautiful designs into cloth. Also, the craft of painting designs on pottery was handed down from one generation to another. Boys learned to weave baskets for harvesting corn. They also learned to make silver jewelry and carve wooden dolls. Pueblo men taught the boys *kachina dances* that were often performed in underground rooms called *kivas*.

One howl shows that a wolf wants to "talk." Another type of howl signals a warning that danger is near. When the members of a pack gather to begin a hunt, they greet each other with howls. Then, a much wilder, more primitive howl signals the beginning of the hunt. Wolves usually howl very loudly when other packs are near. This warns the other wolves to keep out of a pack's territory. A wolf howls sadly when a loved one dies or is injured. You can also tell the age of a wolf by the pitch of the howl. Very young wolves have a much different sound than adolescent wolves or fully grown adult wolves.

1. What is the main idea of paragraph 1? of paragraph 2?
2. Which paragraph does not have a topic sentence?
3. What is the topic sentence of the other paragraph?
4. Write a topic sentence for the paragraph that does not have one.
5. Which paragraph has a sentence that does not tell about the main idea? Write the sentence.

5
Revising and Combining Sentences

Largest ball of string on record. Collected by Francis A. Johnson, 1950–78.

What kinds of things can you string together—
laundry, lights, beads, victories? Some people even
string together string!

In writing, however, stringing too many thoughts
together in a sentence is confusing. This chapter will
show you how to avoid stringy and run-on sentences.
You will also learn how to revise sentences to make
your meaning clear and how to combine related ideas
within a sentence.

1

Avoiding Run-on and Stringy Sentences

Focus Avoid run-on and stringy sentences.

Each sentence that you write should express a complete thought. However, if you put too many thoughts into a sentence, you have written a **run-on sentence** or a **stringy sentence**.

Avoiding Run-on Sentences

> The skywriter had too much to write *he ran out of gas*.

The example above contains two complete thoughts. There is no period at the end of the first idea. There is no capital letter at the beginning of the second idea. The example is a run-on sentence. It should be written as two separate sentences.

> The skywriter had too much to write.
> He ran out of gas.

Avoiding Stringy Sentences

> We read about planets and the next day we watched a movie about Venus and Mars and then we went to the planetarium.

The sentence above strings too many ideas together with the word *and*. The result is a stringy sentence. Each complete thought in a stringy sentence should be a separate sentence.

We read about planets. The next day we watched
a movie about Venus and Mars. Then we went to
the planetarium.

Notice that *and* joins two sentence parts that are alike,
Venus and *Mars*. Sometimes it is correct to join sentences and
sentence parts with *and*. You will learn how to do this in part 2.

Writing Activities Improving Sentences

A Identify each sentence by writing *Run-on, Stringy,* or *Correct.*

1. Beth found her library book and she finished reading the
   story and then she went to bed.
2. Chris uncovered the treasure he jumped for joy.
3. Alan and Zoe learned how to cast a fly rod today.
4. Doug ate a large pizza for lunch he was still hungry.
5. Some herb tea contains cinnamon and nutmeg.
6. We made popcorn and told ghost stories.
7. Sunday, we played soccer my team won.
8. The wind howled outside and an owl hooted in the
   distance and the boards in the old house creaked.
9. Jake thought the animal was an alpaca it was a llama.
10. Emma uses a computer and she wrote a program to draw
    pictures and she prints the pictures in color.

B Rewrite these run-on and stringy sentences as separate
sentences.

1. The doorbell rang Mr. Montrose was at the door.
2. I had a dream about *Alice in Wonderland* and I thought I
   was Alice and I chased the White Rabbit.
3. Last January was the coldest month of the year there were
   twenty-two days of below-zero weather.
4. The koala is not a bear it is a marsupial.
5. Blue smoke rose from the chimney and light glowed from
   the windows and we could smell supper cooking.

2
Combining Sentences and Sentence Parts

Focus You can join sentences and sentence parts with *conjunctions.* The words *and, but,* and *or* are conjunctions.

Sometimes you will want to join ideas that are related. Conjunctions join related sentences and sentence parts.

Joining Complete Sentences

Two sentences may often contain ideas that are alike. These related sentences can be joined by a comma and the word *and.*

> Arthur wrote the story. Anna illustrated it.
> Arthur wrote the story, **and** Anna illustrated it.

Sometimes two sentences are on the same topic but contain ideas that are different. These sentences can be joined by a comma and the word *but.*

> The pea soup looked terrible. It tasted delicious.
> The pea soup looked terrible, **but** it tasted delicious.

Two related sentences can show a choice between ideas. These sentences can be joined by a comma and the word *or.*

> Is the tire inflated? Does it need air?
> Is the tire inflated, **or** does it need air?

Joining Sentence Parts

Sometimes ideas in two sentences are so closely related that words are repeated. By combining such sentences, the repeated words can be left out.

And is used to join sentence parts that show ideas are alike.

> Brian plays the drums. *Brian plays* the guitar.
> Brian plays the drums **and** the guitar.

When sentences contain ideas that are different, the related parts can usually be joined by *but*.

> Chris will write the music. *He will* not *write* the words.
> Chris will write the music **but** not the words.

Sentence parts that show a choice between ideas can usually be joined by *or*.

> Should I buy the tape? *Should I* borrow it?
> Should I buy the tape **or** borrow it?

Writing Activities *Combining Sentences*

A Join each pair of sentences. Follow the directions in parentheses.

1. Leroy is afraid. He won't admit it. (Join with **, but**.)
2. Will Kathy help us? Is she too busy? (Join with **, or**.)
3. Thunder rumbled in the distance. The sun was shining here. (Join with **, but**.)
4. Jesse wanted to buy the album. He didn't have enough money. (Join with **, but**.)
5. Michael planted the rosebushes. Becky watered each one. (Join with **, and**.)

B Join the related parts of the sentences. Leave out words in italics.

1. Adam watched the eclipse. Meg *watched the eclipse*.
2. Jane can leave on Friday. *She can leave on* Saturday.
3. The stove is old. *It is* reliable.
4. Steve nodded to the catcher. *He* pitched the ball.
5. We carried sleeping bags. *We carried* cooking utensils.

3
Adding Words to Sentences

Focus You can combine two related sentences by adding an important word from the second sentence to the first sentence.

Sometimes the main ideas of two sentences work together, but one idea is more important than the other. There may be only one word in the second sentence that is really important. Read this example.

Sam dropped the pan. *The pan was* hot.

You can add the important word, *hot*, to the first sentence. Drop the rest of the second sentence. The new sentence is a shorter, better way of presenting the idea. Notice that the words in italics were left out.

Sam dropped the **hot** pan.

You can sometimes combine several sentences this way.

The bus was full of commuters. *The bus was* creaky.
    The commuters were tired.
The **creaky** bus was full of **tired** commuters.

The motorboat rocked on the water. *The motorboat was*
    sleek. *The water was* choppy.
The **sleek** motorboat rocked on the **choppy** water.

Sometimes you will have to use a comma when you add more than one word to a sentence. Notice where the comma is added when the following sentences are combined.

Mrs. Gómez stroked the kitten. *The kitten was*
    frightened. *The kitten was* shivering.
Mrs. Gómez stroked the **frightened, shivering** kitten.

Adding Words That Change

Sometimes you must change the form of the word before you can add it to another sentence. For example, you may have to add -*y* to the end of a word.

> Please repair those faucets. *They* leak.
> Please repair those **leaky** faucets.

Sometimes you will have to add -*ing* or -*ed*.

> I like to hear the thunder. *It* crashes.
> I like to hear the **crashing** thunder.

> Vera replaced the plate. *It had a* crack.
> Vera replaced the **cracked** plate.

Sometimes you will have to add -*ly*.

> We painted the porch furniture. *We were* careful.
> We **carefully** painted the porch furniture.

Sometimes the word ending in -*ly* can go in more than one place in the sentence.

> Ryan picked up the lizard. *Ryan was* fearless.
> Ryan **fearlessly** picked up the lizard.
> Ryan picked up the lizard **fearlessly**.

When you make changes in the form of a word, check the dictionary to see that you have spelled the word correctly.

Writing Activities Combining Sentences

A Combine each pair of sentences. Follow any instructions in parentheses. Leave out words in italics.

1. The watch ran on a battery. *The battery was* tiny.
2. Around the turn came the horses. *They* galloped. (End the important word with **-ing**.)

3. The puppy scampered along the beach. *The puppy was* frisky. *The beach was* deserted.
4. The mare nuzzled the colt. *The colt was* small. *The colt was* wobbly. (Use a comma.)
5. Please oil those hinges. *They* squeak. (End the important word with **-y**.)
6. Deanna opened the door. *She opened it* cautiously.
7. The child held tightly to the bear. *The bear was* worn. *The bear was* tattered. (Use a comma.)
8. I bandaged my brother's ankle. *It was* sprained.

B Combine the sentences in each group. Add the important words from the second and third sentences to the first. You may have to change the endings of some words.

1. Ken used markers to make the signs. The markers were green. The signs were for the pep rally.
2. One boy sat in the waiting room. The boy was small. The waiting room was huge.
3. Barbara skated over the ice. The ice was smooth. She was graceful.
4. Danielle slipped into the hall. She slipped silently. The hall was empty.
5. The raccoons were able to open the garbage cans. The raccoons were clever. The garbage cans were covered.
6. The campers ate the bread. The bread was crusty. The campers were hungry.
7. The clown put on the makeup. The clown put it on skillfully. The makeup was sticky.
8. The lock snapped open. The lock had rust on it. It snapped suddenly.
9. The fire spread to the warehouse. The warehouse was abandoned. The fire spread quickly.
10. Sophie cut the fabric. The fabric was red silk. Sophie cut it carefully.

4
Combining Sentences by Adding Groups of Words

Focus One sentence may contain a group of words that can be added to another sentence.

Sometimes a group of words in one sentence can add important information to another sentence. The two sentences may be combined. Here is an example.

> We tossed coins. *We tossed them* into the fountain.
> We tossed coins **into the fountain**.

Sometimes the group of words in the second sentence tells about a person or a thing in the first sentence. These words should be added near the name of that person or thing in the first sentence.

> The bruise was painful. *It was* on my shoulder.
> The bruise **on my shoulder** was painful.

> The boy practiced for weeks. *The boy is* playing the violin now.
> The boy **playing the violin now** practiced for weeks.

When the group of words describes an action, place the group of words near the words that tell the action.

> My dog was waiting. *She was* at the end of the driveway.
> My dog was waiting **at the end of the driveway**.

Sometimes the group of words may be put in more than one place in a sentence.

> Our electricity went off **at ten o'clock**.
> **At ten o'clock,** our electricity went off.

Sometimes, however, words can be added to only one place to make a sensible sentence. Study these sentences.

Mom asked me to wash the dog *three times today*. (Did she want you to give the dog three baths?)

As I looked, I saw a plane fly *out the window*. (Did the plane crash through the window?)

After you combine two sentences, always read the new sentence carefully. Be sure it is clear and makes sense.

Writing Activities Adding Groups of Words

A Combine each pair of sentences. Add a group of words from the second sentence to the first sentence. Leave out the words in italics. Write the new sentence on your paper.

1. The arrow is Matt's. *The arrow is* in the target.
2. Jane spotted a wallet. *It was lying* under the car.
3. The band was playing. *It was playing* a march.
4. All the wood is cut. *It is* by the fireplace.
5. The snow was two feet deep. *It was* blocking our door.

B Combine each pair of sentences. Add the important words from the second sentence to the first sentence.

1. Those footprints are important clues! The footprints are in the mud.
2. There is a new box of cereal. It is in the cabinet.
3. The wind blew the dust. It blew into my eyes.
4. Jamie hit a long fly. It went deep into center field.
5. My favorite was the fish. It was cooked on the grill.
6. Uncle Jack phoned. He phoned before we left.
7. Our group collected the syrup. The syrup was from sugar maple trees.
8. The sunburst design was hand-painted. The sunburst design was on the new tray.

Application and Review

A Correcting Run-on and Stringy Sentences Rewrite each of the following stringy and run-on sentences as two or three sentences. Use correct capitalization and punctuation.

1. We climbed that steep hill we weren't even tired.
2. Steve got out the rake and he looked for his gloves and then it started to rain.
3. Brent started to walk to Kathy's house and he stopped to talk to Charlie and he stayed for a game of checkers.
4. Arlyn's head ached she had the flu.
5. Dorothy unwrapped the yarn she put it slowly into the dye.

B Combining Sentences Join each of the following sets of sentences. Leave out any words in italics. Follow any directions in parentheses.

1. My friends and I saw a movie. *It was* scary. *My friends and I saw the movie* yesterday.
2. The watchdog snarled. *The snarl was* fierce. (End the important word with **-ly**.)
3. New Jersey is small in size. It has a large population. (Join sentences with **, but**.)
4. An object landed in the sand. *The object had a* glow. (End the important word with **-ing**.)
5. You can buy the book at Anderson's Bookstore. You can borrow it from the Edgewater Library. (Join sentences with **, or**.)
6. The fingerprints are evidence. *The fingerprints are* on the cane.
7. Today I decided to buy the seed. *I decided to* plant the garden. (Join sentence parts with **and**.)
8. Mugs of soup warmed the skiers. *The mugs were* big. *The soup was* steaming.

6

Writing a Description

*In the long summer afternoons . . . I went down
to the river. . . . Often I jumped from stone to
stone on the broad bed of the shallow, clear, fast-
flowing river. Sometimes I found little pools of idle
water, walled off by stones from the flow. I tickled
long-tailed tadpoles in these. The sun on the water
touched their bodies with myriad colors. . . . And
sometimes I lay on my back on the green grass on
the bank of the river . . . watching thin, fleecy
white clouds form and re-form . . .*

From *Tell Freedom* by Peter Abrahams

Have you ever had a perfect summer afternoon in
a special place and then tried to describe it? Vivid
description makes any story, letter, or report more
interesting. In this chapter you will learn how to
make strong description a part of all your writing.

Detail, *Reflections,* Ken Danby, 1970.

1
Thinking About Descriptive Writing

Focus A good descriptive paragraph paints a picture with words.

In your speaking and writing, you often describe people, places, and things. You use **sensory details** that tell how things look, sound, taste, feel, and smell. Imagine that you are writing a letter. You want to describe the costume you wore to a Halloween party. What would you write?

Read and Think Maggie wrote this paragraph in a letter to her cousin. Look for vivid words and phrases as you read.

Student Model

My hobo costume was outstanding. No one recognized me behind my dirt-smudged face. I even pulled a bashed-in old felt hat over my head so that no one could see my hair. I wore one of Dad's old corduroy suits. The ripped, patch-covered jacket hung down to my knees. Underneath the jacket was a bright red sweatshirt. I held the baggy pants up with a frayed rope. From the rope hung a tin plate and cup that clinked when I walked. Old army combat boots provided the final touch.

Think and Discuss Carefully reread the paragraph. Then discuss the following questions with your classmates.

1. What are some of the details that help the reader know what the costume looks like?
2. Can you describe how Maggie has arranged the details in her paragraph?
3. Which senses does Maggie appeal to in this description?
4. Why are sensory details important in descriptions?

Read and Think In this paragraph, the writer describes a Christmas memory about baking fruitcakes. What descriptive words and phrases does he use to create a vivid picture?

Literary Model

The black stove, stoked with coal and firewood, glows like a lighted pumpkin. Eggbeaters whirl, spoons spin round in bowls of butter and sugar, vanilla sweetens the air, ginger spices it. Melting, nose-tingling odors saturate the kitchen, suffuse the house, drift out to the world on puffs of chimney smoke. In four days our work is done. Thirty-one . . . cakes bask on window sills and shelves.

From "A Christmas Memory" by Truman Capote

Think and Discuss Discuss these questions in class.

1. What sensory details does this paragraph include? To which senses do they appeal?
2. Which sense does Truman Capote appeal to first? second? third?
3. What descriptive verbs does the author use?

Follow Up You have looked at and thought about two descriptive paragraphs. Both use vivid words and phrases to create a picture for the reader. The details in each paragraph are organized in a logical order. Keep these features in mind as you read the following literature selection.

Description in Literature

from *M.C. Higgins, the Great*

Virginia Hamilton

What is this mysterious place called the "Mound"? Is the Kill-burn clan who lives there as crazy and dangerous as everyone says it is? Mayo Cornelius Higgins (M.C. for short) has been told to stay away from the Mound, but Ben Killburn is M.C.'s best friend. In this excerpt, M.C. visits Ben's homeplace. With M.C. is his new friend, Lurhetta. Notice how beautifully Newbery Award winner Virginia Hamilton uses sensory details to describe the visit.

They entered an area behind the farthest house, where there was a fenced space for chickens. Beyond the fence was a barn and an open side door into a small, dark room where the chickens roosted. As they came around to the front, M.C. could tell that the whole of the large barn had been white-washed once, long ago. But now it was faded silver like all of the other outbuildings. It was then he noticed that every object on the Mound could appear suddenly to shimmer. Houses, barns, hard outlines wavered at any moment.

Sense of sight introduced

Because sunlight can't soften, he thought. No trees. No shade at all.

There was just burning light beating down on everything and going through everything in shimmering waves of heat.

They entered through identical barn doors, one of which was open to air and light. Inside, the barn was a massive, two-story shell. Walls and roof and one great oak crossbeam spanning the height. Hanging from the beam was an abundance of drying things, thick as fur.

Details arranged in natural order: top to bottom

Simile

Not vegetables, but thousands of herb weeds and
dried mushrooms. On the walls from top to bottom
hung gourds, their range of colors so bright, they
looked painted. There were vertical rows of field
corn on lengths of heavy twine hanging down the
walls. M.C. did recall seeing corn rows far off at the
other end of the Mound. As the corn aged, it
changed colors from yellow to orange, red and some
black.

The floor of the barn was dark, packed earth. It
had an odor of pungent coolness. Its full width and
length had been dug out into pits some five feet
across. Each pit was lined with chicken wire and
shaped like hollow pyramids standing on end. Some
pits were full of vegetables and covered with a net of
vine. Some were empty or only partially full, with
their nets rolled back. Bushel baskets of produce
lined one side of the floor, their contents ready to be
sorted and put into the pits.

"For goodness sakes!" Lurhetta said, and abruptly
was still. There was room between the pits to walk
around them. There was cool light in the barn from
the open door and from cracks in the walls and roof.
M.C. noticed one small, closed door to their right as

Sense of
smell
introduced

they entered; behind it, the muffled sound of
chickens clucking.

In the midst of the stillness—the muted stripes of
light, the yawning pits—sat an ancient, shriveled
woman on a green folding chair. She took cabbages
from a bushel basket and rolled them like rubber balls
into a pit, whispering furiously at the heads all the
while. She did not cease her slow, rhythmic work as
they came near. But she grinned quite pleasantly at a
cabbage head.

"Hi you, Grandymama," Ben said. "It's my grandmother," he told Lurhetta. Skirting the pits, he went
up to the old woman and placed his hands lightly on
her shoulders. . . .

"This is Lurhetta—see, Grandy?" Ben said.

Lurhetta came near. She leaned around Ben to see
the woman dressed in a length of gray flannel. A long
nightgown.

"Hello there, Grandy," Lurhetta said. Uncertainly,
she held out her hand.

Grandymama tore off a cabbage leaf. Swiftly she
rolled it tight in trembly hands and smiling, gave it to
Lurhetta.

"Now she don't want that thing," Ben said.

"It's all right." Lurhetta took the leaf. "Should she
be in here all by herself?"

"It's her place to be," Ben said.

Silently then, Lurhetta made her way down the
length of the barn. They followed, fanning out behind
her, hearing at their backs the cabbages in their
rhythmic roll and plop into the pits.

Trying Out Descriptive Writing Describe your own or a
friend's home at mealtime. What does the kitchen look like?
Who would be there and how would they be acting? What
sounds would you hear? What food would be cooking? How
would it taste and smell?

2

Prewriting: Gathering Details

Focus When writing a description, use details that appeal to the senses.

Using Sensory Details

You experience the world through your senses. For example, when you eat an orange, you taste the tangy juice. You also see the bright orange color and smell the special fragrance. You feel the smooth pulp on your tongue.

Whenever you write, use sensory details like these that appeal to sight, hearing, taste, and smell. Let the reader experience what you are describing. Refer to Chapter 1, pages 8–12, for more information on using your senses in writing. Read the following sentences. Sensory details have been added to the second sentence in each set.

> The girl wore a sweater over her dress.
> The frail girl wore a faded sweater over
>   her crumpled dress.

> Carmen bit into the apple.
> Carmen crunched into the tart, cold apple.

Gathering Details

Sensory details are the building blocks of descriptive writing. You can gather the details you need in three ways.

First, you can **observe** your subject carefully. For example, imagine that you are watching a lion at the zoo. Study him closely. Is he yellow, golden, or the color of wheat? Does he walk, swagger, or prance? Is his mane woolly or silky? How would you describe his roar?

Sometimes details can be gathered from your **memory**. Suppose that you want to describe your first camping trip. Searching your memory can provide details of itchy insect bites, a cool mountain lake, and the smoky smell of a campfire.

Your **imagination** is another good place to find details. In your imagination, anything can happen. You can create new and unheard of details such as purple zebras, chocolate-covered broccoli, bells that hum, and ice-cold petals.

Creating a Mood

Mood is the feeling the reader experiences when reading a story or poem. To create a mood in your writing, you need to use descriptive details. For example, imagine that you want to create a calm, relaxed mood in a description of a woodland setting. You might use phrases like *filtered sunlight, leaves ruffled by a gentle breeze,* or *the still pond.* To create a feeling of noisy confusion as you describe a thunderstorm, you might use phrases like *the crack of thunder* or *hail pounding the canvas tent.* You could help the reader see *wind beating saplings to the ground* and feel *the driving force of the rain.*

Writing Activities Gathering Details

A Imagine that you are at an amusement park or carnival. Collect a variety of sensory details for a description of this scene. What would you see, smell, and hear? What textures can you tell about?

B Writing in Process Create an imaginary place. You might refer to Starting Points, pages 31–39, or Ideas for Writing, page 548 in the Writer's Handbook. Brainstorm with some classmates to think of descriptive details. Record ideas on a chart. Write each of the five senses (sight, hearing, taste, touch, smell) across the top of a paper. Under each heading, list details suggested by brainstorming. Save this chart.

3
Organizing and Drafting

Focus Make your descriptions clear by organizing details in a logical order.

The first step in writing a description is to make a list of sensory details. Next, you must arrange them in a logical order. This will help your readers clearly picture what you are describing. There are many ways to organize a descriptive paragraph. Here are some of them.

Natural Order

Often, you arrange details in the same way that you would notice them. Then you are using **natural order.** Natural order is sometimes called **spatial order.** Natural order is one of the most common ways to arrange details. For example, you might look at a skyscraper by starting at the bottom and working your way to the top story. When you look at a room, you might notice the things in the room from left to right. These are natural orders. Read the paragraph on the next page. The details are arranged in natural order, from side to side.

The cotton field ran to within a hundred feet of the house and was bordered with a barbwire fence which continued to the back of the house and the garden gate. Past the fields was the lawn, long and sloping upward to the house. On its western edge a dusty driveway cut from the road to the barn. Beyond the lawn and the drive lay the west fields where hay, corn, soybeans, and sugarcane were planted each spring.

From *Let the Circle Be Unbroken* by Mildred Taylor

Order of Importance

Another way to organize your description is either to begin or end with the detail that impressed you the most. This is called the order of importance. For example, if your waitress at a restaurant had green hair on St. Patrick's Day, you might want to begin describing her with that striking detail. However, some details are more powerful if they are left for the end of a description.

Grouping by Senses

A third way to organize a description is by describing with one type of sense detail at a time. Notice how the details in this description are grouped by senses.

*Writing
Model*

Confusion reigned in the restaurant kitchen. The counters overflowed with food in various stages of preparation. Bright red tomatoes and deep purple cabbages were stacked next to dozens of freshly-washed lettuce heads. Partly-husked ears of corn revealed sparkling white rows of kernels. The strong odor of boiled corned beef and cabbage fought with the garlic of the spaghetti sauce. The rich, heavy odor of roasted duck completed a menu of aromas. Huge kettles were banged against steel counters. Above all the noise, chefs shouted to each other in several different languages. In the background was the steady whack, whack of a butcher knife hitting the cutting block.

Grammar in Action   Like adjectives and adverbs, prepositional phrases can help you add descriptive details to your writing. These phrases are especially helpful when you want to show *where* something is or *how* an action is performed. Note the use of prepositional phrases in the following descriptive passage. For more information on prepositions, see Chapter 24, pages 462–468.

> *Into the clearing* came the monster. Its green scales dripped *with swamp water*. The eyes bulged *from the giant head*. The powerful tail dragged *over the gravel*. *With ease*, the monster smashed *through the back door*. Now, *in the middle of the kitchen*, the thing halted momentarily.

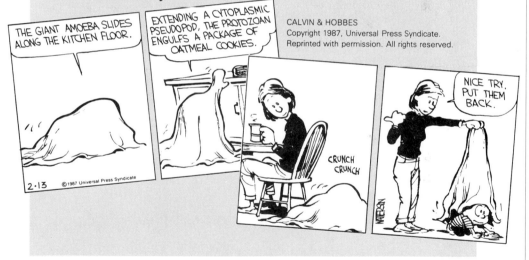

Writing Activity Writing a Description

Writing in Process   Use the details you wrote for either Activity A or B in part 2, page 92, to write a descriptive paragraph. Use natural order, the order of importance, or grouping by senses to arrange the details. Then write a draft of your descriptive paragraph.

4
Revising and Presenting

Focus Improve description by carefully revising your writing.

Using Adjectives and Adverbs

Adjectives describe nouns and pronouns. Adverbs describe verbs, adjectives, and other adverbs. Use adjectives and adverbs to make your writing more vivid.

As one student, Helena, reread her draft, she added adjectives and adverbs so her readers would see the house as she did.

> The house was alone on the block. The paint was
> *slowly rusty Broken*
> coming off, and the door moved ˄ on ˄ one ˄ hinge. ˄ Pieces of
> *green and clear   sagging*
> ˄ glass lay on the ˄ front porch. Weeds were growing
> *cracked*
> through the ˄ sidewalk.

Helena added only enough descriptive words to make her paragraph more interesting. A paragraph can be difficult to understand if too many descriptive words are used.

Using Strong Verbs and Precise Nouns

Action verbs are words such as *galloped, chase,* and *laughs.*
State-of-being verbs and **linking verbs** are words like *is* and *became.* Try to use action verbs in your writing. Action verbs are stronger and more exact than state-of-being verbs. For more information on verbs, see Chapter 20, pages 364–397.

Also pay special attention to the nouns in your descriptive writing. Replace general nouns such as *shoes, flower,* and *dog* with more precise nouns like *sneakers, tulip,* and *collie.* To learn more about nouns, see Chapter 19, pages 346–363.

As Helena continued to revise, she replaced weak verbs with strong action verbs and made some nouns more precise.

The house ~~was~~ *stood* alone on the block. The paint was ~~coming off~~ *peeling* and the front door ~~moved~~ *swung* slowly on one rusty hinge. Broken pieces of green and clear glass ~~lay~~ *glittered* on the sagging front porch. ~~Weeds were growing~~ *Ragged dandelions struggled* through the cracked sidewalk.

Using Similes and Metaphors

Similes and metaphors are another way to brighten your descriptive writing. A **simile** is a comparison that uses *like* or *as*. A **metaphor** also compares one thing with another. However, a metaphor does not use *like* or *as*. A metaphor says that one thing *is* another.

> *Simile*   Life is like a journey.
> *Metaphor* Life is a journey.

Now read Helena's revision. Notice the simile she added.

Student Model

The empty house stood alone on the block. The paint was peeling, and the front door swung slowly on one rusty hinge like an autumn leaf about to fall. Broken bits of green and clear glass glittered on the sagging front porch. Ragged dandelions struggled through the cracked sidewalk.

Writing Activity The Language of Description

Writing in Process Revise the description you wrote in part 3, page 95. Replace weak verbs with strong action verbs and general nouns with precise nouns. Add adjectives and adverbs for detail. Add a simile or metaphor if it fits. Make a final copy and share it with your classmates.

Speaking and Listening

In a world filled with noise pollution, it is easy to tune out some sounds. However, sound is important to description. To describe accurately, writers must listen carefully to the sounds around them. In fact, writers often carry notebooks so that they can record sense details anytime and anywhere. In this way, a writer can build a storehouse of sense impressions. This is the raw material the writer uses to create similes, metaphors, and other descriptive images.

Activity

Spend one morning carefully listening to the sounds around you. Begin as you awake. Try to hear and absorb every sound. Tune in to each separate sound. As accurately as you can, write down what you hear. Ask yourself what a certain sound might be compared to. In this way, you may create similes or metaphors. For example, you might describe the horn of a large truck on the highway as a trumpeting elephant. After your listening session, write a sentence that describes each sound with the details you recorded. Your morning of listening should produce many sentences.

Creative Writing

A Imagine that you own a restaurant. Plan a new menu. Write a brief description of four menu items that would make your customers' mouths water. Remember, too many adjectives can spoil a description. Choose your adjectives carefully.

B Use the following "recipe" to write a description in the form of a poem.

1. Write a noun.
2. Write two words describing the noun.
3. Write three words ending in *-ing* telling what the noun does.
4. Write two more new words describing the noun.
5. Write a synonym for the noun.

Look at this example.

> dragon
> fiery, hungry
> roaring, lunging, crunching
> ornery, scaled
> monster

Crossroads

English and Geography

One way to describe a place is to draw a map of it. Different kinds of maps can show different types of facts. One kind of map, a topographical map, shows what the surface of the land is like. Usually, colors are used to show the various features. Green areas are low, yellow areas are higher, and brown areas are very elevated or mountainous. Other geographic details such as rivers and lakes are shown on this kind of map, too.

Activity

Study the topographical map of Italy shown below. Use the details on the map to write a description of what the country looks like.

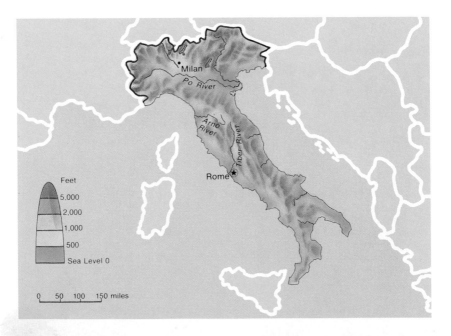

Application and Review

A Analyzing a Description Read this paragraph. Then answer the questions that follow.

> The bull ring or Plaza de Toros was a big, tawny brick amphitheatre standing at the end of a street in an open field. The yellow and red Spanish flag was floating over it. Carriages were driving up and people were getting out of buses. There was a great crowd of beggars around the entrance. Men were selling water out of big terra cotta water bottles. Kids sold fans, canes, roasted salted almonds in paper spills, fruit, and slabs of ice cream. The crowd was gay and cheerful but all intent on pushing toward the entrance. Mounted civil guards with patent leather cocked hats and carbines slung over their backs sat their horses like statues, and the crowd flowed through.
>
> From *Bull Fighting: A Tragedy* by Ernest Hemingway

1. List the descriptive words and phrases in this paragraph that help you get a clearer picture of the scene.
2. What comparison did the author use?
3. Describe the order used in this description.

B Using Descriptive Language Improve these sentences. Add the kinds of words described in the parentheses.

1. The shark ate the smaller fish. (Use a stronger verb and better adjective.)
2. The Halloween costume was unusual. (Use a stronger verb and an adjective.)
3. The bank president looked at the empty safe. (Use a stronger verb; add an adjective and adverb.)
4. The pillow was soft. (Use a simile or metaphor.)
5. The nurse walked quietly down the hall. (Use a stronger verb and an adjective.)

7
Writing a Narrative

What if . . . you were sitting on a red velvet couch suspended seventy floors above the street? An event such as this—whether real or imaginary—could certainly be the starting idea of a great story.

Two photographers, Kevin Clarke and Horst Wackerbarth, spent four years traveling across America, taking pictures of their red couch in unusual settings. The adventures they had could form many chapters in a long narrative. How did they balance the couch on a canoe in a glacial lake? How were people persuaded to pose?

You may not have a red couch to write about, but you have many stories waiting to be told. When you write a narrative, you will have to choose characters, a setting, and a plot, and decide how you will present them. This chapter will show you how.

1
Thinking About Narrative Writing

Focus A *narrative* is a story based on real or imaginary events.

Imagine that your class has just returned from a field trip to a nearby aquarium. Your teacher asks you to write a story about a sea creature. What would your story be like?

Read and Think Jorge based his story on a real event. Read Jorge's story to learn about an unusual sea creature.

Student Model

The water of Santa Rosa lagoon was bright blue. My friend Maria and I decided to go snorkeling. We wanted to find an angelfish for Maria's aquarium. We put on our fins and masks and began to search underwater. Suddenly, a large sea monster swam toward me. It was shiny black, with two arms and two long flipper legs. There were two silver humps on its back and one large eye in the middle of its face. As it swam, thousands of bubbles came out of its silver humps. I came to the surface and ripped off my mask.

"Maria," I screamed. "Get out of the lagoon! There's a horrible sea monster!"

As I reached the shore, I heard Maria's laughter. I turned around to see Maria standing with the horrible creature. I began laughing, too. My sea monster turned out to be our neighbor, Mr. Velásquez, who had gone scuba diving.

Think and Discuss Read Jorge's story again. Then discuss the following questions with your classmates.

1. Who are the characters in Jorge's story?
2. Which sentence tells you where the story takes place?
3. What happens first in the story? How does the story end?

Read and Think Here is another example of narrative writing.

Literary Model

. . . In time a greater danger, a sadness, came to the forest. . . . The serpent . . . lay waiting. . . . Suddenly he coiled and struck the unicorn from behind like a whip. . . . Fear gripped the animals as they watched the battle. The serpent wound himself like steel bands about the unicorn's hind legs. A fierce war-cry came from the unicorn as he struggled to free himself. His nostrils flared, and he reared up with his forelegs thrashing. Sharp cloven hooves came crashing down upon the serpent, whose strong hold began to weaken. The unicorn was gigantic in his mighty splendor. His spirit was ruthless, and his mane flowed like windswept flames. Over and over he screamed and struck until the viper was overwhelmed and powerless.

Whirling around, the unicorn drew back and faced his enemy. Then his blue eyes caught the serpent's, and the evil one felt shame pierce his cold heart for the first time. He slithered away in fear, knowing that one of his own kind would have never spared his life.

From *The Unicorn and the Lake* by Marianna Mayer

Think and Discuss Think about these questions. Discuss your ideas with your classmates.

1. What is the setting of the story?
2. Who are the characters in this narrative?
3. How are the events of the story arranged?
4. Is the story based on a real or an imaginary event?

Follow Up Now you have read narratives based on both real and imaginary experiences. Each story has a set of characters, a setting, and tells the events in the order they happened. Try to identify these elements as you read the following selection about a magician and his tricks.

Narration in Literature

"The Sleeve Trick"

Stephen Leacock

Sometimes things are not what they seem to be and sometimes things don't happen as expected. Notice how Canadian humorist Stephen Leacock weaves the unexpected into the following narrative.

First main character introduced

"*L*adies and gentlemen," said the conjurer[1], "I have shown you that the cloth is absolutely empty. Now I will proceed to take from it a bowl of goldfish. Presto!"

Setting

All around the hall people were saying, "Oh, how wonderful! How does he do it?"

Second main character introduced

But the Quick Man on the front seat was nobody's fool. He said in a big whisper to the people near him, "He—had—it—up—his—sleeve."

The people nodded brightly and said, "Oh, of course." And everybody whispered around the hall, "He—had—it—up—his—sleeve."

Plot events arranged in time order

"My next trick," said the conjurer, "is the famous Hindu Rings. You will notice that the rings appear to be separate. At a blow they all join (clang, clang, clang). Presto!"

There was a buzz of amazement. Then the Quick Man was heard to whisper. "He must have had another lot—up his sleeve."

Again everybody nodded and whispered, "The rings were—up his sleeve."

The conjurer frowned.

"I will now," he went on, "show you a most amusing trick, by taking any number of eggs from a hat.

---

[1] conjurer: a magician

Will some gentleman kindly lend me his hat? Ah, thank you. Presto!"

He took seventeen eggs from the hat. For thirty-five seconds the audience began to think he was wonderful. Then the Quick Man whispered along the front bench, "He has a hen—up his sleeve."

The egg trick was ruined.

The Quick Man went on whispering as the conjurer performed more tricks. According to him, the conjurer must have concealed up his sleeve a loaf of bread, a doll's cradle, a live guinea pig, and a rocking chair—in addition to the fishbowl, the rings, and the hen.

The conjurer could tell that everybody was losing faith in his tricks. So he rallied for a last try.

"Ladies and gentlemen," he said, "I will now present to you the famous Japanese Trick recently invented by the natives of Ireland." He turned toward the Quick Man. "Will you, sir, kindly lend me your watch?"

It was passed to him.

"Have I your permission to put it into this mortar and pound it to pieces?" he asked savagely.

The Quick Man nodded and smiled.

The conjurer threw the watch into the mortar and grasped a sledgehammer from the table. There was a sound of violent smashing.

"He's slipped it up his sleeve," whispered the Quick Man.

"Now, sir," said the conjurer, "will you kindly pass me your derby hat and allow me to dance on it? Thank you."

The conjurer made a few quick passes with his feet and showed the hat completely crushed. The Quick Man beamed. This time the real mystery of the thing fascinated him.

"And will you now, sir," said the conjurer, "take off your tie and permit me to burn it with a match? Thank you, sir. And will you allow me to smash your glasses with my hammer? Thank you."

By this time the Quick Man was beginning to look puzzled. "This thing beats me," he whispered. "I don't see through it a bit."

There was a great hush upon the audience. The conjurer gave the Quick Man a withering look. Then he said, "Ladies and gentlemen, you can see that I have—with this gentleman's permission—broken his watch, burned his tie, danced on his hat, and smashed his glasses. If he will give me the further permission to paint green stripes on his overcoat, I shall be delighted to entertain you. If not, the show is at an end."

Amid a burst of music from the orchestra, the curtain fell. And the audience went home knowing there are some tricks, at any rate, that are not done up the conjurer's sleeve.

Climax

Conclusion

Trying Out Narrative Writing You have read some examples of narrative writing. Now try writing a brief narrative of your own. First, think about how to get started. Where will you get a story idea? Who will your characters be? What details will you include? Then write your narrative.

When you have finished your narrative, think about what worked well and what parts were troublesome. What would you do differently next time? This chapter will help you develop and improve your narrative writing skills.

2
Parts of a Narrative

Focus All narratives have three parts: a *setting,*
characters, and a *plot.*

Although every story has a setting, characters, and a plot, how the writer of each story handles these elements may vary greatly. One narrative may emphasize plot, while another might concentrate on characters or setting.

Setting The setting of a story tells where and when the action takes place. A writer may choose a real setting or create an imaginary one. A writer usually describes the setting early in the story so the reader can picture each part of the action as it is happening.

Characters are the people or animals that the story is about. Characters may be based on real people, or they may come from the writer's imagination.

Plot The events that happen in the story make up the plot. The writer usually tells about these events in the same order that they occurred. The story builds until the most exciting part, or **climax,** of the story is reached. After that, the author directs the details toward the end, or **conclusion**.

Writing Activity Analyzing Narratives

Examine a narrative you have read recently. Answer the questions below about the story.

1. What is the setting of the story?
2. Who are the characters?
3. Briefly describe the plot of the story.

3
Prewriting: Finding and Developing Ideas

Focus Ideas for stories may come from your experiences. They can also come from what you read or from your imagination.

Finding a Topic

All stories start with a writer's ideas. Look at the world around you. Explore your imagination for ideas.

Finding Story Ideas in Your Experience You can discover ideas for stories in your own life. There may be a story in the first time you rode a horse, or your first day at dance class. You can also write about people you know. Think about the time your friend thought he saw a ghost, or the summer your neighbors found a family of raccoons in their attic.

Looking for Ideas When you Read A friend's letter about a fishing trip may contain a story idea. A newspaper or magazine article may suggest something to write about. An entry in your journal could be developed into a story.

Thinking Creatively Sometimes your imagination is the best place to begin a story. Ask yourself "What if . . . ?" What if the apples in an orchard were magical? What if you ate one? Think of other times, other worlds, or unusual people.

Exploring Your Ideas

Your first brainstorming session may not give you all the ideas you need. For example, you may have an idea for a terrific character or an unusual setting. However, that may be all you have. Now you must help this idea grow into a story. Ask yourself some questions to make your idea grow. Ask *Who? When? Where? What happened? Why?* and *How?*

Write down all your questions and several possible answers for each one. Then choose the answers you like best. These will become part of your prewriting notes.

One student, Ellen, remembered a deserted cabin that she had seen on vacation. The cabin seemed like a good setting for a story. Now Ellen had to come up with the other elements for her story. After Ellen asked her questions, she put the answers into the form of an idea chain. Here is how the chain looked. The answers she chose are marked with a star.

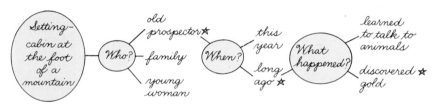

Next Ellen will decide how the prospector looked. Then she will ask herself what happened after he found the gold.

Writing Activities Working with Story Ideas

A Think about something you have always wanted to be, such as an explorer, the President, or a composer. Join a group of three or four other classmates. Brainstorm and share ideas for a story that tells about your one day as a _____ . Write a list of the ideas that you like. Choose the best idea to develop further. Save the other ideas in your notebook.

B Writing in Process Use the idea you chose from Activity A, or find an idea in Starting Points, pages 31–39. You might also look at Ideas for Writing, page 547, in the Writer's Handbook. Ask questions to develop your idea. Begin with an idea chain similar to the one on this page. Include many details.

4
Prewriting: Organizing a Story

Focus Writing a *story contract* and a *plot outline* will help you focus on and organize the ideas in your story.

The answers to your prewriting questions have provided details for your story. The next step is to make a story contract. Then you must decide how to organize your ideas.

Making a Story Contract

A **story contract** is a brief statement of who your characters are, what will happen in the story, and where the events will take place. Making a contract helps you focus ideas.

Look at the questions and notes you wrote as you developed your story idea. Sum them up in one or two sentences.

Here is how one student, Jill, wrote her story contract.

Student Model   I will write a story about trying to solve a mystery. It will take place in my neighborhood. Mrs. Hayes and I will be the characters.

Making a Plot Outline

Next, you will need to organize the events in a story. You can do this by making a **plot outline**. In part 2, you learned that a plot is the series of events in a story. A plot outline lists these events in the order in which they happened or will happen. In other words, they are listed in **chronological order**. The first event is listed first. The second event is listed second, and so on.

Jill wrote a plot outline as she prepared to write her story. Jill listed the events in chronological order. She studied her plot outline. Note her thoughts as she made changes.

1. My neighbor, Mrs. Hayes, comes home on the bus.

   (happens every Monday)

2. I'm curious about the package she carries.

   3. She always carries a box wrapped tightly with string.

3. I follow her to her house.

   I forgot to tell about the package.

4. I fall in the bushes.

   These two ideas are out of order.

5. I try to look in her window.

   This has nothing to do with my story.

6. Mrs. Hayes comes out and yells at me.

7. There are many interesting people in my neighborhood.

When Jill studied her outline, she saw that she had left out some information. She had listed two events in the wrong order and included an unnecessary detail. Before you begin to write, be sure to check your outline for any needed changes.

Writing Activities *Organizing Story Events*

A Imagine that you are writing a story about training your dog. The plot outline of your story is shown below. Write the items below in correct time sequence.

> He got away and rolled in a mud puddle.
> My dog, Alfie, was a dog in need of training.
> Then I tried to teach him to roll over.
> Instead of shaking hands, he jumped on me.
> As I gave Alfie a bath, I decided that maybe he was
>   better off not trained.
> First, I tried to teach him to shake hands.

B Writing in Process Choose one of the story ideas you developed on page 111. Make a plot outline for it. Remember to study your outline and make changes if you need to.

5
Drafting a Narrative

Focus During drafting, expand the ideas in your plot outline into sentences and paragraphs. Write an introduction, body, and conclusion for your story.

Drafting Your Story

Now you are ready to draft your story and put your ideas into sentence and paragraph form. Your narrative should have an introduction, a body, and a conclusion.

A story begins with an **introduction.** This is usually where the author introduces the characters and describes the setting. The action of the story may also begin in the introduction.

Most of the action takes place in the **body,** or the middle part of the story. It is in the body of the story that the action builds to the **climax,** or most exciting part.

The writer then brings the story to an end, or **conclusion.** At the conclusion, the loose ends are tied up and the story is brought to a close. Some narratives are only a paragraph or two. Others must be longer to tell the story. Your plot outline will help you decide how long your story should be.

Paragraphs in Your Draft Your plot outline can also help you break your story into paragraphs. A paragraph has one main idea. Your introduction may be a paragraph by itself. Each main event in your plot outline can also become a main idea for a paragraph. Then write your conclusion.

A New Direction Sometimes as you draft a narrative, you may find your story going off in unexpected directions. New ideas may come to you that are better than those in your plot outline. Do not be afraid to try to use these new ideas.

Jill began to draft her story. She made some changes in the introduction as she wrote. Her thoughts are shown in blue.

> I always thought there was something mysterious
> *Maybe it was the long black cape she wore.*
> about Mrs. Hayes. Every Monday she came home on
>
> the four o'clock bus. She carried a big brown box
> *had to know*
> wrapped tightly with string. I ~~wish I knew~~ what was in
> *package*
> that ~~box.~~

I need to tell why she was mysterious.

The last sentence is boring.

Jill thought carefully as she worked on her draft. You will see later how she made further improvements.

Using Time Words

A writer uses time words and phrases to make events flow smoothly from one to another. These time words help the reader to follow the events in a story.

Jill's introduction contains the time phrases "every Monday" and "four o'clock." These tell you when Mrs. Hayes appeared. Here are some other time words.

Time Words and Phrases for Narrative Writing

first, next, always, once, long ago, every summer, the first time, by morning, after lunch, that evening, soon, later, in a while

---

Writing Activities Drafting a Story

A Look at Jill's plot outline on page 113. Explain how you would break her ideas into paragraphs.

B Writing in Process Using your plot outline from Activity B on page 113, develop an introduction, body, and conclusion. Use time words to make the events flow smoothly.

6

Using Description and Dialogue

> **Focus** Description and dialogue make a narrative come to life.

Using Description

Writers use description to help the reader picture, feel, hear, taste, or smell what is happening in a story. Realistic description makes the reader feel as if he or she is part of the story.

As Jill worked on her draft she wrote this.

> Mrs. Hayes lived in the house next door.

Jill realized that her readers could not tell much about Mrs. Hayes's house, so she added some description.

Student Model

> Mrs. Hayes lived in the house next door. It was an old white house with peeling paint. Its shutters creaked whenever the wind blew. Tall, scraggly bushes grew beneath each window.

Jill's descriptive details make the house seem mysterious. Readers feel that something spooky may be about to happen.

Using Dialogue

When characters talk together, their conversation is called **dialogue.** Dialogue keeps the action moving in a story. It is a more interesting way of showing what is happening than just telling about the action. You can also use dialogue to help your readers learn about a character. Writers reveal what a character is like by showing what the character says and how he or she talks. Before you use dialogue in your story, refer to the following **Grammar in Action.** It will show you how to punctuate and capitalize dialogue correctly. Notice that a new paragraph begins each time the speaker changes.

Grammar in Action   When you write dialogue, use quotation marks to enclose the exact words of a speaker.

"I think someone is following us," Maia said.

If the quotation is interrupted by explanatory words such as *she said,* enclose both parts of the quotation with quotation marks. Look at the following example. Note that commas separate the quotations from the explanatory words.

"The problem," she said, "is that we're out of time."

When you need to combine other punctuation marks with quotation marks, remember these rules. 1) Periods and commas always go *inside* the quotation mark. 2) If a question mark or exclamation point belongs only to the quotation, place the end mark *inside* the quotation mark. If the question mark or exclamation point belongs to the entire sentence, place the end mark *outside* the quotation mark.

Juan asked, "Why are you worried?"
Did Juan say, "I'm worried"?

For more information on the punctuation of dialogue, see pages 533–534.

As Jill continued drafting her story she wrote this.

I could hear Mrs. Hayes talking to someone inside her house. But Mrs. Hayes lived all alone!

Jill saw that if she added dialogue she could make her readers feel some uneasiness about Mrs. Hayes. She changed her draft to read:

Inside, Mrs. Hayes was talking. I could hear her raspy voice as she said, "And how are you today, my little ones?" Who could she be talking to? Mrs. Hayes lived alone!

Now Jill's readers can hear Mrs. Hayes for themselves.

Writing Activities Using Description and Dialogue

A Rewrite the statements below as dialogue. (See answers in margin.)

1. I told Ron that I couldn't help him. He was angry.
2. Ruth said that we must put mushrooms on the pizza. Eric told Ruth that he didn't like mushrooms.
3. The lifeguard shouted at us to get off the pier. We said we would.
4. Julie asked Carlos to hang a picture. He told her that he would do it if he could find a hook.
5. Sue wanted to know where Nancy was. Denise told her that Nancy had an appointment with the dentist.

B Writing in Process Carefully study the draft of your story. Add description and dialogue where needed.

7
Revising a Narrative

Focus Before making a final copy, consider what changes would improve your story. Revise your story to include these changes.

Put the draft of your story aside for awhile. Think about it. Then reread it carefully. Decide what changes would make your story more enjoyable. Here is Jill's draft.

Last Monday,

I hid under those bushes. I was determined to

I didn't tell when.

discover what was in the mysterious package.

Inside, Mrs. Hayes was talking. I could hear her

croaked

raspy voice as she said, "And how are you, my little

ones?" Who could she be talking to? Mrs. Hayes lived

alone!

I can use more powerful verbs.

peek

As I stood up to look in Mrs. Hayes's window, I

tumbled

went backward.

Mrs. Hayes came out and asked what had happened.

She was angry, but what she said explained the mystery

of the package.

I felt silly that night.

I haven't told what the mystery was.

Peer Editing

Problems such as the one Jill had with her ending can often be solved with peer editing. In peer editing you share your narrative with one or more classmates. Another person can sometimes see ways to improve a piece of writing that the writer overlooked.

By using peer-editing guidelines such as those on page 121, a peer editor can identify the strengths and weaknesses of a story. For example, he or she can note whether an introduction captures the reader's attention and moves the reader quickly into the story. A peer editor can also point out any places in the plot that are confusing or that need further development.

Read the peer editor's comments below. These helped Jill work out the problem with her ending and make changes that added interest and excitement to her story.

Peer Editor: I like the word *raspy*. I can almost hear her voice, but I can't tell how you feel. Can you add more detail?

Jill's Change: *As I stood up to peek in Mrs. Hayes's window, my foot got tangled in a bush. I fell backwards and yelled, "Help!"*

Peer Editor: The part where Mrs. Hayes comes out could be more exciting. What did she say that solved the mystery? Maybe it would help to use dialogue. I still don't know who she was talking to.

Jill's Change: *Mrs. Hayes rushed out. "What are you doing in my bushes?" she shouted. "You scared me to death! There I was, quietly repairing my antique dolls, when I heard screaming. I nearly cracked one doll's arm off. Get on home with you!"*

Peer Editor: I read the last sentence, but I still don't have the feeling that the story is over. Can you tell more about how you felt?

Jill's Change: *Discovering that Mrs. Hayes carried old dolls in her mysterious package did not make my cuts and bruises feel any better. I think I will leave detective work to the professionals.*

Read the final copy of Jill's story on page 123.

The guidelines below can help you or a peer editor evaluate, revise, and improve your narrative writing.

Revision and Peer-Editing Checklist

1. Can readers clearly picture the characters and setting?
2. Will the plot hold a reader's interest?
3. Does the story have an introduction, a body, and a conclusion?
4. Do the events in the story follow chronological order?
5. Would adding description and dialogue make the story seem more real to the reader?
6. Does the story include powerful verbs, precise nouns, and descriptive adjectives and adverbs?

Proofreading Your Narrative

You have worked hard to make your story interesting. Now you want to make certain that it contains no errors. Before you make your final copy, proofread your writing carefully, using the proofreading symbols on page 54. Look for any mistakes you may have made in grammar, capitalization, punctuation, and spelling. Refer to the rules in the punctuation chapter as you check dialogue. Ask another person to read your writing. Sometimes someone else can see errors you may have missed.

The sign painter needed to proofread *before* presenting.

Writing Activities Revising a Narrative

A On your paper, copy the following conversation from a story. Add the punctuation that is needed.

> I think I would like to be an astronaut someday, Beth told her best friend, Simone. Why an astronaut, Simone asked. Beth said it would be fun to visit other planets. I'm interested in science and space. I'd be a good astronaut. Simone smiled and said, You probably would.

B Writing in Process Exchange narratives with a classmate. Use the Revision and Peer-Editing Checklist on page 121 to make suggestions for improvement. Then consider your classmate's suggestions and revise your own story.

8
Presenting Your Narrative

Focus Make a final copy of your story and present it.

Here is Jill's final copy.

Monday's Mystery

Student Model

I always thought there was something mysterious about Mrs. Hayes. Maybe it was the long black cape she wore. Every Monday she came home on the four o'clock bus. She carried a big brown box wrapped tightly with string. I had to know what was in that package.

Mrs. Hayes lived in the house next door. It was an old white house with peeling paint. Its shutters creaked whenever the wind blew. Tall, scraggly bushes grew beneath each window. Last Monday, I hid under those bushes. I was determined to discover what was in the mysterious package.

Inside, Mrs. Hayes was talking. I could hear her raspy voice as she croaked, "And how are you, my little ones?" Who could she be talking to? Mrs. Hayes lived alone!

As I stood up to peek in Mrs. Hayes's window, my foot got tangled in a bush. I tumbled backwards and yelled, "Help!"

Mrs. Hayes rushed out. "What are you doing in my bushes?" she shouted. "You scared me to death! There I was, quietly repairing my antique dolls, when I heard screaming. I nearly cracked one doll's arm off. Get on home with you!"

Discovering that Mrs. Hayes carried old dolls in her mysterious package did not make my cuts and bruises feel any better. I think I will leave detective work to the professionals.

Writing Activity Sharing a Final Copy

Writing in Process Proofread your story. Add a title. Make a final copy and decide how to share the story with your class.

Speaking and Listening

A play is a story that is written to be acted out before an audience. A play, like a narrative, contains characters, a setting, and a plot. However, in a play, the story is told through the actions and dialogue of the characters. The audience learns what happens from what the characters do or say.

The playwright, or author, often includes special directions to help the actors. These are called **stage directions**. Stage directions are never read out loud. Instead, they tell the actor how to say a line or how to move on stage. For example, stage directions may tell an actor to pause at a certain point to show the audience that the character is uncertain.

Hearing-impaired teens presenting *The Wizard of Oz* at the Texas School for the Deaf in Austin.

Members of the audience participate in a play, too. They must listen carefully, so that they can understand the relationships between characters and actions. They must think about what is going to happen next. An audience must be quiet in order to listen. Talking during a performance is a distraction to others in the audience and to the actors.

Activity

Work with a group of classmates to choose a short scene from a play that can be presented to the class. Choose a play from your literature book, or one your teacher suggests. Decide who will play each character. Practice reading the characters' parts in your group. Create simple costumes and scenery if you wish. When you are ready, present the scene.

Creative Writing

A Choose one of the pictures below. Create a story, using that picture as your idea starter. Use the writing process that you have learned in this chapter as you write your narrative.

B Write dialogue for one of the following situations. Capitalize and punctuate dialogue correctly.

1. One slice of pizza speaks to another as hungry teen-agers approach the table.
2. Imagine that you have a Siamese cat. What would your cat tell your sister's new puppy?
3. Imagine that you can talk to any famous person from the present or the past. Write the conversation.

Crossroads

English and Science

Scientific knowledge and narrative writing can blend to form a special kind of fiction that is called **science fiction**. Some knowledge of science is necessary to write science fiction. In fact, many authors of science fiction are both scientists and writers. They have accurate knowledge about science today. They use this information to write about a world in which scientific possibilities have become scientific fact. For this reason, science fiction is often set in the future.

Because science fiction has such a strong base in real scientific fact, it often comes true. Many years ago some science fiction authors wrote about things that exist in our world today. Jules Verne wrote about an atomic-powered submarine. Arthur C. Clarke described communication satellites and space stations.

Activity

Choose one of the scientific inventions from the following list, or find one of your own. Use an encyclopedia or other reference source to learn about the invention. Take some notes on what you learn. Then, imagine how this invention or its use might change in the future. Now, write a narrative that uses the information you found and the ideas your imagination has supplied. Follow the steps you have learned in this chapter to write an exciting science-fiction narrative.

laser beams   robotics
antibiotics   computers and artificial intelligence

Application and Review

A Using Time Order Correctly sequence these story events.

After a long time, the boy surfaced on the other side of the swimming pool.

Pedro stood poised on the high dive as he studied the water beneath him.

He spouted water as he let the air out of his lungs.

The watching crowd applauded and cheered wildly.

His dark figure lifted off the platform, shot downward, and sliced through the water.

B Punctuating Dialogue Rewrite the following dialogue. Insert the correct capitalization and punctuation. Remember to begin a new paragraph each time the speaker changes.

I'm going downstream and try the hole by the bank. I think Big Old Sam is just waiting for my lure Kyle said. You're kidding, Faye replied. You mean you believe what those guys told us about Old Sam? Sure I do answered Kyle. They've been fishing this stream for years he pointed out. Haven't you ever heard of teasing asked Faye. I think they were really putting us on. But you go ahead and try. I will insisted Kyle. I'll even share Old Sam with you at dinner he boasted.

C Using Time Words and Phrases Copy the paragraph below. Fill in each blank with a suitable time word or phrase from page 115, or use others that you think of.

_____ , just when school gets out, the Posts fly to their cabin in Canada. They buy their tickets _____. _____ before they leave, they pack. _____ on the day of the flight, they leave for the airport. Their plane takes off and their adventure _____ begins.

8
Writing to Explain

Zzzzzzzzzzzt!

Neon lights. You see them in the barbershop window and above the door of the shoe repair shop. Now there is even a museum filled with neon sculptures like the one pictured on the right.

How can gas, trapped in a glass tube and zapped with electricity, produce such beautiful, glowing colors? How are the tubes shaped into letters, words, and limitless designs?

You may never have to explain neon lights, but you will often need to explain how other things work or how to do something. This chapter will help you learn to write clear explanations that will "enlighten" your readers.

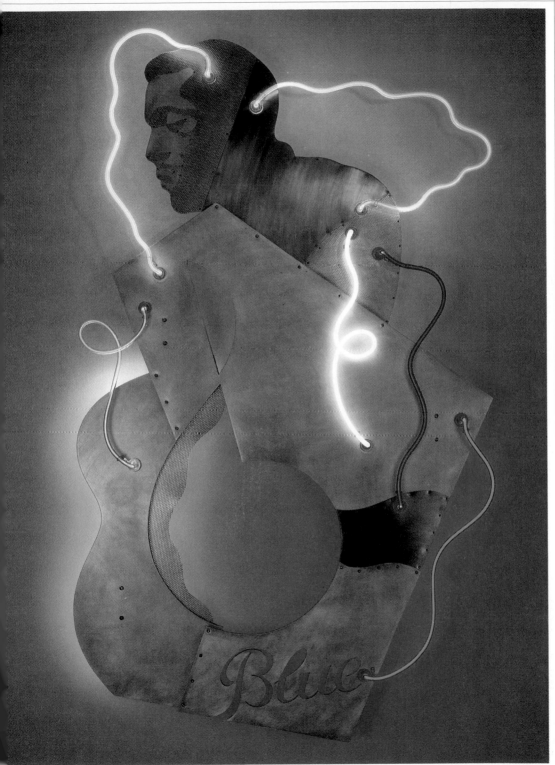

The Ghost of John Coltrane, Lili Lakich, 1985.

1
Thinking About Writing that Explains

Focus Writing that *explains* tells how to do something, how something works, or how something happens.

When people want to know more about their world, they often begin by asking *how*. *How* does a car engine work? *How* are railroad tunnels built? *How* can you fix a leaky faucet?

Pretend that your teacher asked everyone in the class to write a report explaining how to do a science project. How would you write your explanation?

Read and Think Rosa wrote these directions telling how to make rain using common household materials. Look for the steps she used to explain the process. Notice their order.

Student Model

When cold air and humid clouds meet, the cold air changes the humidity into rain. To make a model showing how this happens, first fill a kettle with water. Heat the water. In the meantime, fill a long-handled metal saucepan with ice. Then, place a short glass mug or cup under the spout of the kettle. Hold the pan of ice five inches above the steaming spout. "Rain" from the steam will begin to collect on the bottom of the pan. Soon, rain will begin to drop into the mug or cup.

Think and Discuss Read the following questions. Think about how to answer them. Discuss your ideas with your classmates.

1. Are all the steps included in Rosa's explanation?
2. In what order are the steps for making rain presented?
3. What might happen if the order of the steps were changed?
4. What might happen if Rosa left out some steps?

Read and Think Rosa's paragraph tells how to do something. The paragraphs below explain how something works.

Professional Model The alarm sounds at the fire department headquarters in Phoenix, Arizona. A member of the staff rushes over to the computer terminal and punches some figures on its keyboard. Within a few seconds, symbols and words appear on the video screen. The peculiar images pinpoint the location of the burning building by showing the streets that surround it.

Next, the information on the fire is relayed to the computer terminals in all the fire stations in Phoenix. This fire happens to be in an area that Company No. 7 is responsible for. At Company No. 7's station house, an official locates the fire on a wall map and gets a printout from the computer. The officer in charge speeds with a firefighting crew to the blaze, armed with the printout of information about the burning building.

From "The Science of Fighting Fires" by James A. Baggett

Think and Discuss Read the following questions. Then reread the paragraphs above and answer the questions. Discuss your ideas.

1. Do you now understand how firefighters respond to a fire?
2. Describe the order of the steps telling how firefighters respond to a fire.
3. Is each step stated clearly and simply?

Follow Up You have read and thought about two explanations that tell *how*. Each explanation uses clear, simple steps to explain how to do something or how something happens or works. In the next three pages you will read a longer example of a process explanation. Then you will learn how to write your own explanation that tells *how*.

Explanation in Literature

from *Flying to the Moon and Other Strange Places*

Michael Collins

In 1969 Michael Collins made history. With Buzz Aldrin and Neil Armstrong, he rocketed the first spacecraft to the surface of the moon. Getting dressed for such a flight was a complex process. In the following excerpt, Collins describes how it was done for an earlier journey.

First step

Detailed description of sensors

Getting dressed for a space flight takes a long time. First, medical sensors have to be attached to your body. These are thin disks about the size of a quarter which are stuck on your chest with a special kind of glue and then covered by adhesive tape. There are four of them and they are connected by wires to little electronic boxes in pockets around your waist, from which one cord goes out through your pressure suit and hooks up to the spacecraft. These sensors tell the doctors on the ground about your heart. The information from the four sensors can be shown on a television screen in the form of a line that jumps upward every time your heart beats. From this, the doctors can tell not only whether you are dead or alive but whether you are resting or working hard, or whether there is something wrong with your heart. It's called an electrocardiogram. Doctors, like scientists, love to give long names to things. If your chest is hairy, it takes even longer to get the electrocardiograph all hooked up, because first someone has to shave little bare patches for the medical sensors.

Signal word introduces second step

After the sensors are all attached, you put on long white cotton underwear and then crawl into your pressure suit, which is not an easy thing to do. You put your feet in first,

Details in chronological order

through a zipper in the back of the suit, and then bend over double. Ducking your head, you put your arms through the same zipper opening, and out through the arms of the suit. Then your head pops up through the neck ring. If you have managed to push your arms and legs as far as they can go, then you will be able to stand up, just barely, and

Transition to another step

get someone to zip the back closed. By this time, you have begun to sweat, so you are hooked up through

Signal word indicates final step of process

two hoses to an air-conditioning unit. Then you are ready to put on gloves and helmet, which are locked into place by metal rings that fit together. As soon as this happens, you are practically isolated from the rest of the world. You can hear only what is piped in over the radio; you can breathe only 100 percent oxygen, and it is usually odorless; you can't feel much through the gloves. The only sense which is unimpaired is sight. You can see the world fine, even if, locked up inside your pressure suit, you really don't feel you are part of it.

On the afternoon of July 18, 1966, John Young and I had gone through all this bother of suiting up and we were ready to go fly Gemini 10. The reason for launching late in the day was that the old Agena, which had been in orbit for four months, would not

Second three-step process explains approach to and entry of spacecraft

pass overhead until then, and we wanted to launch when we were precisely underneath it, so it would be easier to catch. We rode out to the launch pad in a small van, and then took an elevator up the side of the gantry to the spacecraft, which was perched up on the nose of the Titan rocket. The elevator was not much more than a wire cage, and as it slowly ascended, I could see the beautiful blue Atlantic Ocean just a stone's throw away. It was quite a contrast, to see a huge pile of complicated machinery on one side and nothing but blue water on the other. Then it was time to crawl aboard our Gemini, feet first, with people shoving us down far enough in our seats so that our heads would clear the hatches.

Michael Collins.

Once the hatches were closed and locked, John and I were in our own little world, far away from the blue ocean, and our friends and families. We were lying on our backs, with our feet up in the air, and in a few minutes we would be lying on our right sides, one hundred miles up, and going 18,000 miles per hour. I'm not sure I quite believed that, but I didn't have long to wait to find out, because now the voice on the radio was counting backward from ten.

Trying Out Explanatory Writing After reading Collins's account, write your own explanation of a process. Give a step-by-step account of the preparations you made for a trip or for some special day in your life.

2
Prewriting: Planning an Explanation

Focus Before you write, decide exactly what you want to explain. Then list all the steps and information needed to explain your topic.

Choosing a Topic

Sometimes the topic for an explanation is chosen for you. A friend sees you swimming. She asks you how to do the sidestroke. Your teacher assigns you to write a report on how a thermometer works.

At other times, you can select your own topic. Your choice may be something you already know well. If your hobby is rock collecting, you might explain how crystals are formed. You can also select a topic you want to learn more about. You might want to find out how a solar eclipse occurs.

Gathering Information

Once you have a topic, make some notes about what you want to cover in your explanation. What do you already know about your topic? What do you need to research?

If you know your topic well, the information in your notes will come from your own knowledge. If your topic is one you want to learn more about, you will have to get your information from outside sources. There are many outside sources for information. You might read magazines, newspapers, books, or an encyclopedia article. You might also talk to someone who is an expert on your topic. For more ideas about getting information from outside sources, see Chapter 14, Library and Research Skills.

Listing Important Steps

As you write notes about your topic, make sure to list all the steps in the process you are explaining. State each step simply and clearly. As you do, pretend you are writing for someone who knows nothing about your topic. Make sure that you have included every step in a logical order. Otherwise, your reader will be confused.

If you are telling how to do something, instructions for gathering necessary materials should be included in the list of important steps. These materials should include tools, ingredients, and any other supplies that may be necessary.

Writing Activities Preparing to Write

A Complete each of the following activities. They will give you ideas for writing topics. Keep these ideas in your writing folder.

1. Read several articles in a newspaper or magazine. Cut out any articles that explain how to do or make something. Look in the food, sports, and home life sections.
2. Complete the following sentence in ten different ways. "I wish I knew how _____ works."
3. Imagine that you have been asked to teach a class of kindergartners a simple skill. List five skills that you might teach this class.

A boomerang.

B Writing in Process Select a process that you would like to explain. You may choose your own topic, a topic from Activity A, or one listed in the Writer's Handbook, pages 548–549. You might also refer to Starting Points, pages 31–39. Then begin gathering information, making notes as you go. Write down all the steps in the process. If you are explaining how to do something, include any necessary materials.

3
Prewriting:
Organizing Information

Focus Use *chronological order* to arrange the steps in an explanation that tells *how*.

When you take swimming lessons, you first learn how to float and how to control your breathing. If you did not master these skills first, you would certainly have trouble later. The order in which you learn swimming skills is important.

Order is also important when you explain a process. To help the reader understand your explanation, arrange the steps in chronological, or time, order. **Chronological order** is the order in which the steps happen.

Arranging Your Details

To arrange your details, look at your notes. Write a 1 beside the step that happens first. Put a 2 beside the second step. Continue until all your steps are numbered. Your finished list is your **writing plan**.

If you are explaining how to do something, your first step should include instructions to gather the necessary materials. Your last step should state the final product or result.

After you have listed and numbered all the steps, check your work. Have you left out any steps? If so, add them. Are any steps in the wrong order? Make any necessary corrections.

A Sample Writing Plan

Damon did a project for geography class on the volcanoes of Hawaii. His writing plan on the next page tells how to make a model volcano. Notice how he numbered his steps. Notice, also, his thoughts as he looked over his notes.

4   Put baking soda in cup.

I should say what size cup.

                                6-ounce
1   Materials needed: paper cup, modeling clay,
                                    ^

                4 tablespoons baking soda,

                                                    I forgot to say which way the cup goes.

                ½ cup vinegar, newspaper

2   Cover table with newspapers.
                                right side up
3   Form clay around sides of cup to look like a mountain.
                                    ^

5   Add vinegar to baking soda in cup.

Writing Activities Arranging Details

A Imagine you want to explain how a balloonist flies a hot-air balloon. The notes you have made are listed below. Number your details in a step-by-step order.

> To take off, the balloonist lights the propane burner under the nylon bag. This heats the air in the balloon. Because hot air rises, the balloon will go up.

> To land, the balloonist turns down the burner to cool the air, or opens the vent in the top of the balloon to let out some hot air.

> Two people may get into the basket.

> A hot-air balloon is made up of a large nylon bag, or balloon, attached to a basket and a propane burner under the balloon.

> To make the balloon go higher, the balloonist turns up the heat in the burner.

B Writing in Process Look at the list of steps you wrote for Activity B on page 136 for your paragraph telling *how*. Make a writing plan. Number your details in chronological order. Add any missing details. Take out any unnecessary details.

4

Drafting Your Explanation

Focus Now that you have a writing plan, use it as a guide for drafting your explanation.

A good writing plan is the skeleton of your final paragraph or composition. Use your writing plan as the outline of your first draft. As you work on this draft, continue thinking about your topic. Try to make each step clear. Make sure each step flows smoothly from the step before it.

You may make changes at this point in the writing process. However, do not be concerned if your draft is not perfect at this time. Later, when you revise, you will have a chance to make your explanation even better and to correct any errors you may have made.

A Sample Draft

Damon used his writing plan to write a draft of his explanation telling how to make a model volcano. Notice his thoughts as he wrote.

You can make a model volcano in your own kitchen!

First, you'll need to get some newspapers, a 6-ounce paper cup, some modeling clay, 4 tablespoons baking soda, and ½ cup vinegar. Cover the table with 4 *layers of* newspaper. Put the cup, right side up, on the table.

> I should be more specific.

Form the clay around the *sides of the* cup. Next, put the baking soda in the cup. Add ¼ cup vinegar. *You can add another ¼ cup vinegar if you want to.*

> The clay must touch the sides of the cup.

> I'd better tell them how to keep the volcano going.

As he wrote, Damon thought about his explanation. He added two details and another step. Damon will make more changes as he continues the writing process.

Signal Your Steps

Certain words and phrases "signal" a new step. For example, Damon used *first* and *next* to signal steps in his draft. Here are some common signal words that you can use to help your reader understand the steps in your explanation.

Signal Words

first	last	now	until	the next step
second	finally	when	during	at the same
next	then	while	after that	time

Grammar in Action Adverbs tell *how, when, where,* or *to what extent* an action is done. Carefully chosen adverbs can help you explain more precisely the steps in your process. In the following example, note how the adverbs supply important information about the procedure.

Sand the arms, the seat, and the back of the chair *thoroughly* until the surfaces feel very smooth.

Next you can apply the stain. Move your brush *vertically,* following the grain of the wood. Apply the stain as *evenly* as you can. *Carefully* wipe off the excess stain with a rag.

Finally, finish the chair with a glossy varnish. You might also apply a coat of protective wax.

Writing Activities Drafting Your Explanation

A Rewrite the following sample draft. As you do, add two or three signal words to help a reader follow the steps more easily.

If you can't sink a toy boat in the bathtub, how does a craft as big as a submarine stay under water? The secret is in its special storage tanks. The submarine takes water into these tanks. Water pushes the air out of the storage tanks. Because water is heavier than air, the submarine sinks. When the crew wants to surface, air is blown into the tanks, forcing the water out. The submarine rises to the surface.

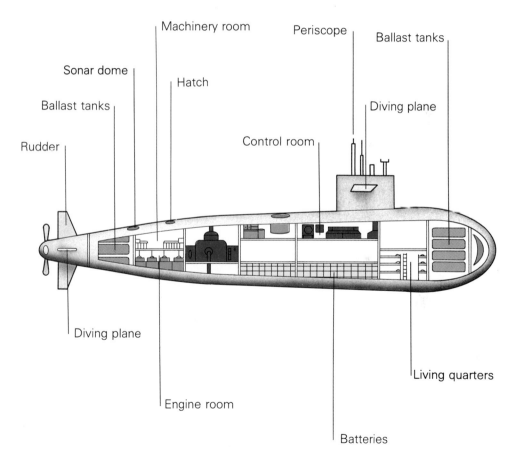

B Writing in Process Write a first draft of your explanation. Follow your writing plan from Activity B on page 138, adding to or rearranging your ideas if necessary. Remember to use signal words to help your reader follow the steps more easily.

Revising Your Explanation

Focus Check to make sure your explanation is simple, clear, and complete as you revise your first draft.

Writing that tells *how* must be well organized and easy to follow. Otherwise, the reader will become confused.

A good way to test your explanation is to have a peer editor read it. See if he or she can follow your directions or understand your explanation. If your peer editor becomes confused, mark your draft at that point. Go back later and rework that part. Also be prepared to peer edit a classmate's paper.

As you revise or peer edit, think about the questions below. They will help you produce a clear, precise explanation.

Revision and Peer-Editing Checklist

1. Are all the required materials and any other necessary information included?
2. Are all the steps of the process listed?
3. Are the steps stated simply and clearly?
4. Are the steps in the right order?
5. Have signal words been used to make the steps easy to follow?

A Sample Revision

Damon tested his explanation on a friend. At the end, Damon's surprised friend had a few questions.

> "What should people expect when they mix vinegar and baking soda? You never really say."
> "How quickly should you pour the vinegar into the cup?"
> "Why would you add more vinegar later?"

Because Damon did not want any of his other readers to be surprised, he thought about his friend's questions. Then, he revised his paragraph. Notice his thoughts as he worked.

You can make a model volcano *erupt* in your own kitchen!

I need to say what the volcano will do.

First, you'll need to get some newspapers, a 6-ounce

paper cup, some modeling clay, 4 tablespoons baking

soda, and ½ cup vinegar. Cover the table with 4 layers

of newspaper. Put the cup, right side up, on the table.

so it looks like a mountain

I should say how fast to pour.

Form the clay around the sides of the cup. Next, put the

Quickly *and watch the eruption.*

baking soda in the cup. Add ¼ cup vinegar. You can

I'd better say what happens here.

add another ¼ cup vinegar if you want to *make another eruption.*

Proofreading Your Explanation

Before you make a final copy of your explanation, proof-read it carefully. Look for mistakes in grammar, capitalization, punctuation, and spelling. Use the proofreading symbols you learned in Chapter 3, page 54, to mark corrections on your paper.

When Damon proofread his paragraph, he remembered that numbers under 100 are not written as figures. Instead, they are written out. So he changed his paragraph like this.

You'll need to get some newspapers, a *six* 6-ounce paper

cup, some modeling clay, *four* 4 tablespoons baking

one-half soda, and ½ cup vinegar.

Cover the table with *four* 4 layers of newspaper.

Writing Activities Revising an Explanation

A As your teacher directs, help a classmate revise his or her explanation. Read the rough draft. Try to follow the steps in your mind. Also keep in mind the questions in the box on page 142. Make at least two suggestions to the writer for improving the draft based on any questions you had as you read.

B Writing in Process Use the questions on page 142 to revise your explanation. Also, consider the suggestions of a friend or classmate who has read your draft. Finally, proofread your explanation. Make any necessary corrections.

6
Publishing and Presenting the Final Copy

Focus Choose an interesting title for your paper. Then make a clean, final copy. Share your writing with others.

Your final copy should show off your best work. Make sure it is clean and neat. Choose a title that names the topic being explained.

Here is Damon's final copy. Notice how he added the ideas from his friend.

Kitchen Volcanoes

Student Model

You can make a model volcano erupt in your own kitchen! First, you'll need to get some newspapers, a six-ounce paper cup, some modeling clay, four tablespoons baking soda, and one-half cup vinegar. Cover the table with four layers of newspaper. Put the cup, right side up, on the table. Form the clay around the sides of the cup so it looks like a mountain. Next, put the baking soda in the cup. Quickly add one-fourth cup vinegar and watch the eruption. You can add another one-fourth cup vinegar if you want to make another eruption.

Writing Activity Presenting the Final Copy

Writing in Process Think of an interesting title for your work. Then make a neat, clean, final copy. Check your final copy for any errors. Make any necessary corrections neatly. Finally, turn to pages 56–57 and choose a method of sharing your writing with your classmates. You might create class booklets or bulletin boards. You might even sponsor a contest.

Speaking and Listening

Tour guides give explanations every day. A tour guide in a printing plant might explain how the pages for a book are printed and how color pictures are processed. A guide in an automobile factory might explain how a car or small truck is assembled. A guide in a bakery might explain how giant mixers knead dozens of loaves of bread in a single batch.

These guides use the same methods you learned to explain *how*. First, they think about the process they are going to explain. Next, the guides gather details about the process and then put them in a logical order. Finally, they may make some note cards to help them practice the talk they will give during the tour.

Activity

Imagine that you have volunteered to take a group of younger students on a tour of a museum. You may choose to give a tour and presentation about how something happened, such as how dinosaurs became extinct. You may choose to explain how something is made, such as how fossils are formed. Your third choice is to explain how to do something. For example, you may explain how to identify certain varieties of birds or snakes. Choose the topic for your explanation. List the steps in the process. Put these steps in logical order. Finally, put your presentation on note cards. When you have finished writing, practice your presentation out loud. Ask your friends or family for suggestions about how to make your presentation better.

Remember to end your tour by asking if there are any questions. You may also wish to use posters or other visual aids to add interest to your presentation.

Creative Writing

A Pretend your cousin who lives in a different state visited you last summer. He taught you how to do the Green Frog, the latest dance at his school. It is so fantastic that you decide to teach the Green Frog to your friends. Write an explanation telling how this new dance step is done. For fun, ask your classmates to see if they can follow your instructions.

B Imagine that you are a reporter who has just been assigned to cover an exciting discovery that may help feed the world's populations. In addition to the already-known unusual substances that can serve as food, such as seaweed, acorns, and the fiber inside cattails, a new discovery has been made. Your news article will tell what the new discovery is, where it is found, how it is prepared, and what nutrition it offers.

C You have always wanted a Bingle Box. Before your parents will let you have one, they want to know more about it. Write a paragraph explaining what a Bingle Box is and how it works.

English and Computer Studies

In this chapter, you learned to explain how to do something and how something works. When you program a computer, you have to explain *how* to the computer.

The directions you give a computer are called a **program**. Sometimes the computer programmers make a map of the program as they write it. This map is called a **flow chart**. The flow chart might show how the computer will do a math function or where the computer makes decisions about the next step in the program.

Look at the flow chart below. It explains how to blow your nose. Notice that this flow chart has a *start* position and an *end* position. It also has *yes* and *no* options for each step. All steps finally lead to the end step, "Blow nose."

How to Blow Your Nose

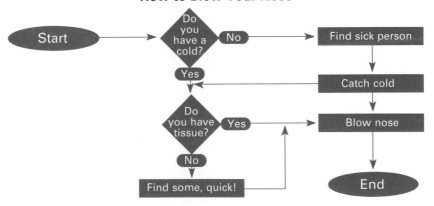

Activity

Choose any simple process such as combing your hair, brushing your teeth, or making a sandwich. Then make a humorous flow chart showing how to do this task. Use the flow chart above to guide you.

Application and Review

A Organizing an Explanation Look at the following notes telling how to make eight tacos. Copy the notes on your paper. Number them in the correct order.

> Put cooked hamburger in taco shells.
>
> Eat and enjoy.
>
> Ingredients needed: frying pan, one pound of hamburger, one large onion, salt and pepper, eight hard taco shells, two medium tomatoes, one small head of lettuce, six ounces of cheddar cheese, one bottle of taco sauce.
>
> Top hamburger with chopped tomatoes, shredded lettuce, and shredded cheese.
>
> Fry hamburger with onion, salt and pepper; drain grease.
>
> Top lettuce, tomatoes, and cheese with taco sauce.

B Finding Signal Words Read the following paragraph and answer the questions at the end.

> A rocket is launched in one direction by pushing in the opposite direction. First, fuel is burned inside the rocket. The burning fuel then produces hot gas inside the rocket. At the same time, the heat makes those gases swell. Soon, the gases grow to the point where they need to escape. The only place the gases can escape is through an opening in the back of the rocket. Finally, the gases force their way out, pushing against the earth. This pressure forces the rocket into the air.

1. What are the steps in this process?
2. Make a list of the signal words used in this paragraph.
3. What order is used in this paragraph?

9
Writing to Persuade

Not long ago baby harp seals like the one in the picture on the right were hunted and killed for their prized fur. It was used to make sleek, expensive fur coats. People opposed to the slaughter of baby harp seals used facts and opinions to convince others that the annual hunt should be stopped. Their efforts were successful. Large-scale hunting of baby harp seals is now illegal.

When you have a strong opinion about a particular topic, you may try to convince or persuade others to agree with you. To help you do the best job possible, use the persuasive techniques that you will learn in this chapter.

1
Thinking About Persuasion

Focus In persuasive writing you state an opinion and give reasons or arguments to support that opinion.

Suppose you want to form a new club at school. You must convince your principal that the club would be a good idea. You decide to write the principal a letter. You want to persuade him or her to support you. What would you write?

Read and Think The following paragraph is part of a letter that Janet wrote to her principal. As you read, look for the arguments that Janet used to support her opinion.

Student Model

I think we should have a club for left-handed people. We lefties could use the support, because being left-handed isn't easy. First of all, many school supplies like scissors are made for right-handers. Even some school desks are designed only for people who write with their right hands. It's also harder for a lefty to learn how to do some things from a right-handed teacher. Once, during an arts and crafts unit, my teacher tried to teach me to knit. It was hopeless! Being left-handed even caused me a problem at the school picnic. My job was to serve punch. I quickly found I was in trouble! The spout was on the wrong side for me. The ladle was made for right-handed pouring.

Think and Discuss Read the following questions. Discuss your answers to the questions with your classmates.

1. Which sentence tells Janet's opinion?
2. What main arguments does Janet give to support her opinion?
3. What examples does Janet use to support her arguments?

Read and Think In this paragraph, the writer is telling why Dr. Martin Luther King, Jr., deserved to have a holiday created for him. Look for her reasons.

Writing Model

Dr. Martin Luther King led a life worth celebrating. He believed that all people are equal, and have the right to equal opportunities no matter what color skin they have. Through his work, the country saw that black people were not being treated equally and were ready to work to change that. For example, blacks, especially in the South, used to be banned from many schools, restaurants, and stores. In some places, they were kept from voting. Dr. King showed people that they could protest this discrimination in a peaceful way. He led boycotts and marches, gave speeches, and inspired people across the nation.

By Melissa Kim

Think and Discuss Think about these questions. Discuss them with your classmates.

1. What is the topic sentence of the paragraph?
2. What reasons are used to support the topic sentence?
3. What examples does the writer give to support her opinion?

Follow Up In both sample paragraphs, the opinion is stated directly and supported with clear arguments. In a longer piece of writing, such as the excerpt that follows, the writer's opinion may not be stated in one sentence. Instead, you will have to **infer,** or come to an understanding of, the writer's opinion from the arguments she presents.

Persuasion in Literature

from *Our Fragile Earth*

Elizabeth S. Helfman

In this excerpt from Our Fragile Earth, *Elizabeth Helfman presents facts and examples to support her opinions. In doing so, she attempts to persuade her readers that saving the environment is still possible.*

Summarizing
the problem

*A*cres and acres of green land in this country, some of it good farmland, have been covered with cement and asphalt. This includes all the city streets, the hard surfaces of city playgrounds, the vast city and suburban parking lots, the airports, and the thousands of miles of roads. . . .

Opinion
inferred

Highways between big cities often offer the traveler a seemingly endless view of ugly billboards and junk-yards. We produce so much rubbish in this country, so many junked cars. Our refuse is being spread across the landscape and dumped into lakes, rivers, and the ocean.

Extended
example

Next time you see a junkyard, or a picture of one, try to imagine what that place was like before. Per-haps this junkyard is on the shore of a river—they often are. Factories upstream dump refuse into it. The water in the river moves sluggishly in a mass of oily frothy slime. It smells bad. Once this water ran clear between banks of ferns and grass and bushes. Fish swam there. Frogs hid beneath the banks. Thousands of small insects moved about in the water and under the stones in the streambed. Deer and other animals came to drink. Very little of this happens any more in the river beside the junkyard.

We must have roads. We must dispose of old cars and garbage and all the rubbish produced by our prosperous society. We cannot altogether avoid the wear and tear on the land that results from its use by increasing numbers of people. But must we spread ugliness across the land? There are people who say we must not.

First argument

Individuals can help. More than 74 billion cans and bottles are thrown away each year in the United States. You can reduce this number if you will buy soft drinks in bottles that can be returned instead of being thrown away. And then return them. If your town or city has a recycling program, collect glass jars and bottles and aluminum cans and turn them in.

Example

Newspapers, too. (Save trees!) Randy Shaw, an Arizona college student, borrowed his father's car and collected 80,000 aluminum beverage cans from highways and dumps. He got ten cents a pound for them and they were recycled.

Second argument

Of course, groups can do still more, but after all, they are made up of individuals. The City Council in Bowie, Maryland, was the first local government to ban throwaway beer and soft-drink containers.

Example

Ecology Action, Incorporated, in Baltimore, collects old bottles and paper and exchanges them for trading stamps.

People in Columbia County, New York, rounded up 12,000 junked cars. A crushing machine mashed the cars and they were trucked away. The metal in old cars can be melted and used again. The Rotary Club of Borger, Texas, puts on a campaign each year to clear away trash along the highways. All over the country groups like these are doing what they can to clean up the landscape.

Third
argument

Useful as this is, the job as a whole is too big for local groups. It will take millions of dollars to clean up all the junkyards and plant trees and bushes and grass there instead. Millions more to save green space in cities. People can tell the officials in their local and state governments, and in the federal government, too, that they want the environment cleaned up and taken care of even though it does cost money.

People do care. Thousands were asked, in a survey, whether they thought beauty was important, on the highways, in the cities, everywhere. Almost all of them said emphatically yes. People do not want ugliness in their surroundings. Too often, however, they are given no choice.

Opinion
stated

Perhaps, if people care enough, our country can still be America the beautiful, "from sea to shining sea."

And perhaps more people will discover that they, too are a part of the great community of things that live upon the earth and draw their sustenance from it.

Trying Out Persuasive Writing You have read some examples of persuasive writing. Now try it yourself. Think about something in the world that you would like to change. Then write a paragraph about it. Since this is a short piece of writing, you need to state your opinion quickly and clearly— probably in the first sentence. Then give at least three reasons that you think would persuade a reader to feel the same way.

2
Prewriting: Recognizing Facts and Opinions

Focus A *fact* can be proved true. An *opinion* cannot be proved, but it can be supported with reasons or arguments.

You encounter facts and opinions in all persuasive writing. It is important to recognize the difference between facts and opinions so that you can use both effectively when you try to persuade readers through your writing.

Recognizing Facts and Opinions

A **fact** is an idea that can be proved true. These are facts.

Two stars in the Big Dipper point to the North Star.
An astronaut first walked on the moon July 20, 1969.

An **opinion** is a statement that tells how a person feels about something. It cannot be proved true. It cannot be checked in a reference book. These are opinions.

Owning a pet is a good idea.
Collecting old comic books is an interesting hobby.

There are several ways to prove facts. One way to prove a fact is by personal observation. For example, at night you can look at the Big Dipper in the sky. You can prove by observation that the first example is true.

The second way to prove a fact is to use a reliable source. The source may be a person or a reference work. For example, you could ask your history teacher when an astronaut first walked on the moon. You could also check the date in an encyclopedia, a written source.

Supporting an Opinion

An opinion cannot be proved true. However, one opinion may be stronger than another. A sound opinion is supported with convincing evidence.

Try to go beyond your feelings about an issue. The best reasons or arguments are factual. A reason that only gives another opinion is not really a reason at all. For example, your friend Burt says, "I think the best instrument to play is the trumpet. It sounds better than the other instruments." Burt's reason, that the trumpet "sounds better," is just another opinion. It is not good support.

You can find evidence to support opinions through reading and research. You may also find evidence in your experiences or from talking with others. Try to find several strong arguments that will support your opinion.

Writing Activities *Finding and Supporting Opinions*

A With some friends, look through a newspaper or magazine for topics such as preventing pollution, protecting wildlife or national parks, and providing health care, homes, and jobs for people without them. Talk about what you read. What opinions do your friends have? What reasons do they give for their opinions? Write down five of their opinions. Do you agree or disagree with them?

B Writing in Process Find a topic you feel strongly about. For ideas, look over the topics from Activity A or those in the Writer's Handbook on pages 548–549. You might also check your journal, and look at Starting Points, pages 31–39. Next, begin your prewriting notes. Think of good reasons to support your opinion. Be sure your reasons are not just other opinions. Write down all your ideas.

3

Prewriting: Developing and Organizing

Focus As you gather your arguments, add supporting details. Then organize your information.

Adding Supporting Details

You should have three or four good reasons or arguments to support your opinion. Back up these arguments with details in the form of examples, stories, facts, or statistics.

Look again at Janet's letter on page 152. She gave several reasons to explain why being left-handed is difficult. For example, she stated that it is harder for a lefty to learn how to do some things from a right-handed teacher. She supported this with an example—her teacher trying to teach her to knit. Janet also used an anecdote, or brief story, to develop a reason. After you have listed your main arguments in your prewriting notes, add supporting details.

Organizing Reasons and Supporting Details

Study your notes. Identify your main arguments and mark them. Place each supporting detail under the argument that it helps to develop. Next, choose the order you will use to present your arguments. Putting the strongest and most important argument last will leave it fresh in your reader's mind. To decide which argument is the most important, think about your audience. Which one of your arguments will most strongly impress your audience? That argument should be your most important. You might wish to use a writing plan to help organize your information.

Writing Plan for Persuasion

Opinion: (State your opinion in a topic sentence. Begin or end your persuasive paper with your opinion.)

Argument or Reason #1:
 Details—examples, stories, facts, or statistics
Argument or Reason #2:
 Details
Argument or Reason #3: (Save your strongest reason for last.)
 Details

Peter heard a TV report on what Americans do with their pennies. Finding the report interesting, he went to the library and found two articles on pennies. He decided to write his paper on why pennies should no longer be minted. Peter's early prewriting notes are shown below. He starred his most important argument.

Opinion: Pennies should no longer be minted.

Arguments:
 2 — People throw pennies away.
 People just collect them, don't use them.
 ✮ 3 The government should not spend money
   making pennies; it should spend money
   on more important things.
 | Pennies are worth almost nothing—
   what can you buy for a penny?

This is my most important argument. I should add a fact.

These are really part of the same argument—pennies are a nuisance.

Writing Activity Finding and Organizing Reasons

Writing in Process Develop a writing plan for the topic you chose in Activity B of Part 2, page 158. Identify main reasons and supporting details and decide on the order in which you want to present them. Remember to put your most important reason last.

4
Drafting

Focus Put your ideas into sentence and paragraph form. Use your prewriting notes as a guide.

When you have finished your writing plan, you are ready to write your rough draft. Use your plan as a guide.

Write a strong opinion Begin your draft with a sentence stating your opinion. Avoid phrases such as "In my opinion . . ." or "I believe . . ." or "I think. . . ." State your opinion simply and clearly.

Develop your draft Follow your opinion statement with arguments from your writing plan. Explain each argument simply and clearly and support it with details. End your composition with your most important argument.

Look at this cartoon. Do you think Snoopy supported his opinion well?

Use signal words Signal words can "signal" a new idea, help your sentences flow together smoothly, and show how one idea is tied to another. On the next page are some signal words that are often used in writing about opinions. Use these words or others like them as you draft and revise.

Peter used his prewriting notes to develop the draft shown below. Notice his thoughts as he worked on his draft.

I don't need this.

~~I think~~ pennies are not important any more. Pennies are practically worthless. These days there is nothing you can buy for a penny. *In fact, pennies have so little value, that people won't even pick them up off the street.*

I need more support here.

Pennies are a nuisance. Each year the government mints tons of pennies and each year many of them disappear from circulation. Why? No one wants a pocket or purse full of pennies. Some people even throw their pennies away. *Finally, making pennies wastes money.*

I want to state this argument simply and strongly.

Our government ~~should stop wasting its money~~ *spends ninety million dollars a year* ~~making pennies.~~ ~~Why spend all this money on~~ *on something few people* ~~something that no one~~ wants or uses. There are better ways to spend this money. Making pennies doesn't make sense. We don't need them anymore.

Grammar in Action In persuasive writing you often use an indefinite pronoun as the subject of a sentence. An indefinite pronoun is a pronoun such as *everybody* or *someone*. Indefinite pronouns do not refer to a specific person or thing. When you use an indefinite pronoun as a subject, be sure that the verb agrees.

The following indefinite pronouns take a singular verb: *either, each, everyone, anyone, neither, one, everybody, nobody*.

> Everyone *is* interested in saving money.
> No one *wants* a pocket full of pennies.
> Each of us *is* responsible for forming an opinion.

A few indefinite pronouns take a plural verb: *both, many, few, several*.

> Many of the pennies *disappear* from circulation.
> Few of the people *pick* up pennies off the street.

For more information on indefinite pronouns see page 412.

Writing Activity Drafting

Writing in Process Use your writing plan to make a first draft of your persuasive paper. Begin your draft with a good topic sentence that states your opinion. State your supporting reasons simply and clearly. Use signal words to show the organization of your ideas.

5
Revising

Focus Review your draft. Make sure your arguments or reasons are presented clearly. Then carefully proofread what you have written.

Revising Your Paper

The revision stage is a time to look over what you have written and to make changes. Reading your paper aloud is one good way to catch errors that your eyes miss.

Another good way to improve your writing is to use a peer editor, especially with persuasive writing. When you try to persuade an audience, you want them to agree with your opinion or to act in a certain way. Because your peer editor may not share your strong feelings about a subject, he or she can see your work from a different point of view.

A peer editor can tell you whether your support is strong or weak, whether you back up your opinions with facts, and whether you keep on track throughout your paper. Consider your peer editor's comments carefully as you revise. They may help you to improve what you say and how you say it. Both you and your peer editor can use the following guidelines when you revise your work.

Revision and Peer-Editing Checklist

1. Is the opinion clearly stated in a topic sentence?
2. Does the topic have good support with strong reasons?
3. Do the supporting details develop those reasons? Are there enough examples, stories, facts, or statistics?
4. Is the most important reason mentioned last?
5. Would signal words make the ideas clearer?

Peer Editing

After reading Peter's draft, his peer editor said this.

Peer Editor: Your paper is interesting in the middle, but the beginning and end are dull.
Peter: *I agree. For the ending maybe I could use an expression that has the word* penny *in it.*
Peer Editor: What do you mean by "tons of pennies" and "many of them"? Can you be more specific?
Peter: *It wouldn't be hard to add those figures. That would make my second reason stronger.*

Peter made the following changes.

In the first place,
~~Pennies are not important any more.~~ Pennies are *almost* practically worthless. These days there is nothing you can buy for a penny. In fact, pennies have so little value, that people won't even pick them up off the sidewalk.

I could add signal words here.

Second,
Pennies are a nuisance. Each year *nine billion pennies* ~~the government mints tons of pennies~~ *are minted,* and each year *six billion* ~~many of them~~ disappear from circulation. Why? No one wants a pocket or purse full of pennies *, so the coins get tossed in a drawer or jar.* Some people even throw their pennies away!

People takes a plural verb.

I need a smoother transition.

Finally, making pennies wastes money. Our government spends ninty million dollars a year on something few people wants or uses. *Certainly,* There are better ways to spend this money. ~~Making pennies doesn't make sense.~~ *It's time to pitch the penny!* ~~We don't need them anymore.~~

Move to the beginning.

Proofreading for Errors

After you have completed your content changes, read through your writing again. This time, review it for errors in grammar, capitalization, punctuation, and spelling.

When you write a persuasive paper, you often use signal words and phrases at the beginning of sentences. These introductory words are usually followed by commas. Check carefully for the correct use of commas with signal words. Use the Guidelines for Proofreading on page 54 for further help. You may also wish to check the rules for capitalization and punctuation in the Writer's Handbook, pages 564–567.

Writing Activities Revising

A As your teacher directs, help a classmate revise his or her writing. Read the draft. Refer to the Revision and Peer-Editing Checklist on page 164. Write at least two ideas that the writer could use to improve his or her draft.

B Writing in Process Read your draft aloud. Think about changes you want to make. Consider the suggestions of your classmate, and follow the guidelines on page 164 to revise your writing. Carefully proofread your work for errors.

6
Making and Presenting a Final Copy

Focus Choose a good title for your persuasive paper. Make a final copy and decide how to present it.

Decide on a good title that briefly states the main idea of your paper. Make sure your final copy is clean and neat. Here is Peter's final copy.

Pitch the Penny

Student Model

Making pennies doesn't make sense. In the first place, pennies are practically worthless. These days there is almost nothing you can buy for a penny. In fact, pennies have so little value that people won't even pick them up off the sidewalk.

Second, pennies are a nuisance. Each year nine billion pennies are minted, and each year six billion pennies disappear from circulation. Why? No one wants a pocket or purse full of pennies, so the coins get tossed into a drawer or a jar. Some people even throw their pennies away!

Finally, making pennies wastes money. Our government spends ninety million dollars a year on something few people want or use. Certainly, there are better ways to spend this money. It's time to pitch the penny.

Writing Activity Making and Presenting a Final Copy

Writing in Process Choose a good title. Then make a clean, final copy of your paper. Proofread your final copy one last time for errors in copying. Choose a method from pages 56–57 and share your writing with your classmates.

Speaking and Listening

In a debate, two teams discuss one question or issue. For example, the statement "All students should study a foreign language," could be a debate topic. One team is "pro," or in agreement with the issue. The other team is "con," or not in agreement with the issue.

Each team has a set amount of time to present its opinion, reasons, and supporting details. The "pro" team goes first. Each team member presents a reason and some details. Then the "con" team presents its reasons. Finally, each team has a time for rebuttal, or a time to show weaknesses in what the other team has said. After the presentations and rebuttals, a judge decides which team has presented the stronger opinion. The more convincing team wins the debate.

If you are taking part in a debate, be well prepared. Have your reasons and evidence ready. Save your most important point until last. Speak slowly and clearly. Stress signal words like *first of all, secondly,* or *most importantly.*

If you are a judge, or part of the audience, listen with care to both teams. Take notes so you will remember what each person said. Then decide which team has presented the stronger reasons and should win the debate.

Activity

Your teacher will give you a topic and tell you whether you are part of the "pro" or "con" team. Prepare at least two reasons along with their supporting details to support your opinion. When you are not debating, listen carefully. Take notes so that you can decide fairly who won. Base your opinion on the strength of the supporting evidence.

Creative Writing

A Imagine that you are an important person in history. Next, select a current issue from your school, town, state, or nation. Decide how your important person would feel about this issue. Then write a letter, editorial, or some other form of persuasive writing. State your opinion and reasons as if you were this important person.

Here are some ideas for your explanation. How would Amelia Earhart feel about space travel? What would George Washington Carver think about today's farming practices? What would Abraham Lincoln think of today's television debates between presidential candidates?

George Washington Carver discovered more than three hundred uses for the peanut plant.

B Write a skit for two people. It should involve an opinion that needs good supporting reasons. For instance, have a driver explain to a police officer why he or she was speeding. Or, have a daughter explain to a parent why she should be allowed to have a slumber party. Your skit should present opinions, reasons, and supporting details. With a partner, perform your skit for the rest of the class.

English and Social Studies

Did you know that you are a consumer? A consumer is anyone who buys or uses products or services. A wise consumer thinks carefully about the products that are available. Then he or she forms an opinion about which product is best. To do this, a consumer must have facts about a product.

An advertisement for a product is one place you must look for facts about a product. Ads often begin with a statement of opinion such as "Spotless Soap is best." The ad then tells why this is true. Look closely at the statements in an ad that tell why you should buy the product. Are factual reasons given or are these statements just more opinions? A wise consumer makes decisions based on facts.

Look at this ad. What opinion is stated? What are the reasons for this opinion?

> The best way to start your day is with
> ### Natural Crunch Cereal.
> So great tasting you'll eat it for snacks, too. It's *good* for you. Has the nutlike taste of whole grain flakes. Enjoy the added flavor of dates, raisins, and nuts. Fortified with ten essential vitamins and minerals. All natural ingredients. Low in sugar.

Activity

Cut out some ads from magazines and newspapers. Paste each ad on a sheet of paper. Examine the ad. Underline or write the opinion stated by the ad. List the reasons that tell why you should buy the product. Beside each reason, tell if the statement is fact or opinion. Tell what opinion you have formed about the product.

Application and Review

A Organizing Ideas Below is a set of notes for a piece of writing. The notes have not yet been organized into an effective prewriting plan. Copy the notes on your paper. Mark each main reason with a star. Find the supporting details that can be used with each main reason. Then arrange the reasons and supporting details in the order in which you would present them. Remember to state your most important reason last. Rewrite the notes to show your organized writing plan.

Opinion: Molly is the best choice for class president.
           Has experience
           Is well liked
           Was the fifth-grade vice-president
           Wants to raise money with a school car wash
           Voted most popular girl in class
           Has good plans

B Recognizing Opinions and Reasons Read the following paragraph. Then answer the questions.

> A dog is a child's best friend and teacher. In the first place, caring for a dog teaches a child about responsibility. A dog's owner must exercise, feed, and groom the pet. Secondly, a pet dog can be a watchdog. For example, the dog could protect its owner's family from strangers and burglars. Finally, a dog can be a child's best friend. A dog will always listen to problems and play any game.

1. What is the writer's opinion?
2. What reasons does the writer give to support his or her opinion?
3. What details support each reason?

10
Writing a Report

Brontosaurus, stegosaurus, tyrannosaurus rex.

Are you interested in dinosaurs, what they were like, what happened to them? What other subjects fascinate you?

You can learn about dinosaurs or any other subject when you write a report. In this chapter you will choose a subject, gather information about it, and then organize, write, and present a report.

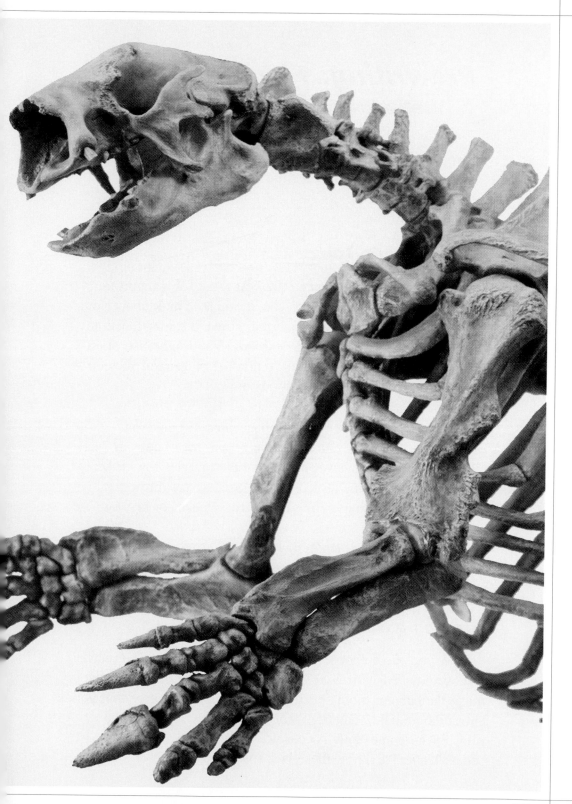

1

Prewriting: Finding a Topic

Focus Think about a general subject that interests you. Then narrow it to a specific topic that can be covered completely in a short report.

How to Find a Topic

Think about your interests The best topic for a report is often the subject that interests you the most. Think about your interests. Read through your journal. Have you mentioned any subjects that you might like to explore? You might also brainstorm with a friend to come up with a list of general subjects that would be fun to learn more about.

Visit the library Look through magazines or books on subjects that interest you. Check such reference books as encyclopedias, almanacs, and special dictionaries for further suggestions. You may also discover ideas as you browse through an interesting exhibit at an art, science, or history museum.

Look again at Chapter 2, pages 18–30, at Starting Points, pages 31–39, and at page 549 in the Writer's Handbook for more ways to think of writing topics.

Limiting a Subject

Now you must choose one of the general subjects you have discovered, and narrow or limit it. That means that you must make the subject more specific. For example, imagine that you chose the general subject *soccer*. Will you write about the rules of the game, how soccer was invented, or a famous soccer player? Each of these is a specific topic.

There are several methods you can use to limit a subject. You can read about it in reference and nonfiction books. You can ask *who, what, when, where, why,* and *how* questions about it. You can also use the table of contents and index in nonfiction and reference books. Both parts of a book could show you how other writers have broken down the subject.

Let's look at how one writer, Tony, limited his subject. Tony was interested in learning more about the American pioneers who settled in the West. He looked in the table of contents in a book about pioneers and jotted down these items.

Duties of a wagon master
Hardships on Oregon Trail
How pioneer children traveled west
Role of scouts
What happened to Native Americans
Why pioneers went west

Tony decided he wanted to learn more about the lives of the children on a wagon train.

Writing Activities Finding a Topic

A Limit two of the topics below so that each could be covered in a short report of about five paragraphs.

EXAMPLE   General topic—Medicine
Narrowed topic—How Penicillin Was Discovered

1. Aztecs
2. Mummies
3. Jungle cats
4. Labor Day
5. Swamps
6. Laser beams

B Writing in Process Make a list of five or more general topics for a report. Use the methods for finding topics suggested in this lesson. Choose one topic. Narrow it so that it can be covered thoroughly in a short report. You might look at the topics on page 549 in the Writer's Handbook.

2

Prewriting: Gathering Information

Focus   Gather information to develop your topic.

To find information, check the card catalog in the library and list the books on your topic. Use the *Readers' Guide to Periodical Literature* to find magazine articles. You can also read articles in encyclopedias and other reference books.

Taking Notes

As you read, write down facts in your own words on 3″ × 5″ note cards. If you quote an author exactly, use quotation marks.

At the top of each card, write the title of the book or article where the information came from, and list page numbers. Note the following publication facts on a separate sheet of paper:

Books—author, title, city of publication, name of publisher, and year of publication.

Magazines—author, title of article, name and date of magazine, and page numbers.

Encyclopedias—title of article, name of encyclopedia, year of edition.

Here is an encyclopedia entry that Tony used. Notice how he reworded the material on his note card on the next page.

As long as the pioneers of the 1840's kept moving west-ward, the Plains Indians allowed them to pass through their hunting grounds. Some tribes guided the early pioneers, or helped them at difficult river crossings.The Indians even supplied some wagon trains with vegetables and buffalo meat in exchange for tobacco, whiskey, or pieces of iron.

From *The World Book Encyclopedia*

The World Book Encyclopedia,

Title ———— *"Pioneer Life in America,"* page 441 ———— Page

Some Indians helped early pioneers by guiding them, assisting them at rough river crossings, or trading with them.

Information

Writing Activities Taking Notes

A Read this article. Write three note cards based on the article. Put the notes in your own words.

> **Mitchell, Arthur (1934–   ),** was the first black American to dance with a major classical ballet company. He performed with the New York City Ballet from 1955 to 1970.
>
> Mitchell was born in New York City and attended the School of American Ballet. In 1955, he joined the New York City Ballet. . . .
>
> While with the New York City Ballet, Mitchell began to teach ballet to underprivileged children. In 1969, he formed the Dance Theatre of Harlem, a professional ballet company and dance school in the city's chief black community. Mitchell directs the company, teaches in the school, and composes dances. As a *choreographer* (composer of dances), Mitchell created such works as *Holberg Suite* (1970), *Rhythmetron* (1972), and *Manifestations* (1976).
>
> By Dianne L. Woodruff, from *The World Book Encyclopedia*

B Writing in Process Look through books, magazines, or encyclopedias that have information on your topic. On 3″ × 5″ note cards, write down any information that will help you develop your topic. On a sheet of paper, make a list of publication facts for each source. Save your notes and paper.

3
Prewriting: Organizing Notes

Focus The information that develops your report topic must be organized logically.

You have done the reading for your report and taken notes. Now you are ready to organize your information.

Creating Idea Groups

Read through your notes. Most of your information is probably about two or three main ideas. List these main ideas. Then organize your notes by grouping each note card with the main idea it develops.

For example, if you were writing a report about the start of the American Revolution, your notes might tell about three main ideas: the Continental Congress, the Boston Tea Party, and the Battle of Lexington. You would put all cards about the Continental Congress in one pile. Cards about the Boston Tea

Paul Revere riding to warn the colonists before the Battle of Lexington.

Party would go in another stack. Information about the Battle of Lexington would go in a third pile. Each of these idea groups could then become a paragraph in your report.

When you sort through your notes, leave out any that are not related to one of the main ideas. If you do not have enough notes on an idea, do more reading. You can add or take out information at any point in the writing process.

After Tony put his cards into idea groups, he read through them again. Then he wrote a topic sentence that summarized the information in each group of cards. These sentences will give Tony a good start when he begins drafting his report.

1. The children spent most of each day walking.
2. The children had many chores to do each day.
3. At the end of the day, the children could enjoy themselves.

Writing Activities Organizing Notes

A Look at the following notes. They are for a report on the neon tetra, a tropical fish. Imagine that each fact is on a note card. Organize the notes into two groups of related ideas. Then write a summary topic sentence for each group.

1. Tetras breathe by pumping water past their gills.
2. The fish's shape has evolved over millions of years.
3. Water is pumped past the gills by the movement of the mouth.
4. The folds of the gills exchange oxygen for carbon dioxide waste.
5. A tetra's shape allows for top speed and agility.
6. Long and narrow, the tetra can cruise at speeds between three to six times its body length per second.

B Writing in Process Look at the note cards you wrote for Activity B on page 177. Divide the cards into groups of related ideas. Then write a sentence that summarizes the information in each group of cards.

4
Prewriting: Making an Outline

Focus Use an *outline* to arrange your ideas in logical order.

You are now ready to make a writing plan for your report. Usually, the plan is made in the form of an outline. An outline shows how each different part of a report works together to develop the topic.

Arranging Main Ideas

First, arrange the main idea groups in logical order. Each group of notes becomes a major division, or part, of the outline. The main idea of each group becomes the heading of the part. Number each heading with a Roman numeral followed by a period.

Arranging Facts

The important facts on your note cards become the subheadings for each main idea. To create your subheadings, summarize each card in a word, phrase, or sentence. Then list each subheading under its main idea, and label it with a capital letter and period. Indent the subheadings.

Do not use just one subtopic under a main idea. If the main idea cannot be separated into at least two ideas, it should not be separated at all.

An outline should have a title that tells what the outline is about. You might want to use the title of your outline as the title of your report.

After you have finished your outline, look it over carefully. Does anything look out of place? Can the order be improved? Make any changes that you think necessary.

Detail, *Children Collecting Logs,* R. Favelle, 1864.

Here is Tony's outline for his report.

The Youngest Pioneers

    I. Walked most of the day
        A. Walked 12–15 miles a day
        B. Rode in the wagons on the hottest afternoons
    II. Did many chores each day
        A. Searched for prairie dog holes
        B. Gathered "buffalo chips"
        C. Studied school lessons
        D. Learned how to hook rugs, make quilts, preserve
           meat in salt
   III. Free to enjoy themselves at the end of the day
        A. Played games like tag and hide-and-seek
        B. Sang around campfire

For other ways of organizing ideas, see pages 551–553 in the Writer's Handbook.

Writing Activity The Outline

Writing in Process Write an outline for your report. Use your list of main ideas and your note cards. Use correct form, and remember to give your outline a good title.

Drafting the Introduction

> ***Focus*** There are three parts to a written report: the *introduction, body,* and *conclusion.*

A report has the same three main parts that any composition has. The **introduction** tells what the report is about. It is usually one paragraph. The **body** may have several paragraphs. These paragraphs explain the main idea of the report. The **conclusion** is a paragraph that summarizes the report.

Use your outline to guide you as you write your draft. It lists the ideas you want to include. It also shows the best order for presenting them. Refer to your note cards as well. They may contain some details not included in the outline.

Writing the Introduction

The introduction of a report should tell the reader what the report is about and catch the reader's interest.

An introduction needs to do more than simply state the main idea of your report. Facts or examples will make your introduction more interesting. You may choose to begin with an anecdote, a brief story that illustrates your topic. You may use a good question to get your reader's attention, or a quotation that you found during your research.

Look at Tony's first draft of his introduction.

> Many children traveled west during pioneer days. They made this journey in a covered wagon. They traveled a long way.

Although this short paragraph tells the main idea of the report, it does not catch the reader's interest. It also does not provide much information about the subject.

Now read Tony's revised introduction. Notice how he added strong details and specific words to create interest.

Student Model

During the 1800's, thousands of children traveled west in long wagon trains. The trains moved slowly over the grassy plains. They crossed burning deserts and the cold, rugged mountains of the Oregon Trail. The children did their chores, studied

their lessons, and played games. In many ways, their days were just like they would have been at home. This time, though, "home" was a wagon moving across 2,000 miles of unknown and often dangerous land.

Writing Activities The Introduction

A Read the following introductions. Decide which one is good and which is poor. Explain the reasons for your choices. Rewrite the weak introduction to make it better.

1. Long ago, some people believed that gods lived among the stars. Others thought the stars held magical powers. Still others tried to predict the future by watching the changes in the sky. Today we know that stars are actually burning balls of gas.
2. Earthquakes under the ocean cause tidal waves. Tidal waves are gigantic and travel fast. They are interesting.

B Writing in Process Write the introductory paragraph of your report. Make sure that it includes your main idea and offers information that will catch the reader's interest.

6
Drafting the Body of a Report

Focus The *body* of a report presents information that develops the topic.

The body of a report presents most of the information about the subject. Each main divison in the outline becomes a paragraph in the body of the report. The subtopics are the supporting facts. Each paragraph might also include some additional facts that are on your note cards but are not included on your outline.

Writing Body Paragraphs

As you write, remember that you can constantly rework your ideas. You might realize that the order you used in your outline could be improved. You might find new information or you might think of better ways to present the ideas you already have. Include any of these changes as you draft. Just be sure that the report still flows smoothly and that it still develops only one topic.

Using Signal Words

When writing paragraphs that give facts, you must let your reader know when an important idea is coming up. You must also show how your ideas fit together.

Use signal words to help make your ideas clear. **Signal words** such as *first*, *next*, or *finally* show that an important point follows. Phrases like *in addition* or *for example* can signal interesting details. Use signal words within a paragraph, or to link two paragraphs together.

For more information about using signal words, see page 140 in Chapter 8 and page 162 in Chapter 9.

Analyzing Body Paragraphs

Here is Tony's draft of the body of his report. Tony followed his outline, but he also included some additional details.

The children spent most of the day walking alongside the wagons. Only on the hottest desert afternoons did many ride in the shelter of the jolting wagons. Every day except Sunday the wagons covered—and the children walked—twelve to fifteen miles. The only ones who did not walk were groups of older children. They herded the "cow column," the milk cows and spare horses and oxen that followed the wagon train. These children spent most of the long journey on horseback.

The children had work to do. They searched for prairie dog holes and alerted the hunters in the train to their locations. One of their most important jobs was gathering "buffalo chips." The children also studied their school lessons. In addition, they learned skills such as how to hook rugs, make quilts, and preserve meat in salt.

When the wagons finally pulled up at the end of a long day and the supper dishes were done, the children were free to have some fun. They could then get together with the children from other wagons to play games like tag and hide-and-seek. They could join the singing around the campfires and listen to the adults share their dreams of a new life in Oregon. Bedtime came early for those on a wagon train. Everyone had to be up before dawn to begin a new day.

Writing Activity The Body

Writing in Process Write the body of your report. Follow your outline, making any improvements that occur to you. Be sure each paragraph has a strong topic sentence. Include details from your note cards. Use signal words to make ideas flow smoothly.

7
Ending Your Report

Focus Write a clear *conclusion* for your report. Give credit to the sources you used for your information.

Writing the Conclusion

The last paragraph of your report is very important. It ties together all the ideas you have presented in the introduction and body paragraphs. The last paragraph also provides a clear, definite finish for the report.

The ending paragraph is often a summary of the main ideas. Yet it should not just repeat an earlier part of the report. Such an ending would bore the reader. A successful conclusion needs to be bright and fresh, so that the reader is left with a strong impression. However, you should make sure that no new ideas are introduced. Read Tony's first ending for his report.

Student Model

> The children on a wagon train did ordinary things, like you and I. But they also did some out-of-the-ordinary things. Which was more fun—riding in a wagon train or on an airplane?

This is a weak concluding paragraph. It does not pull together or summarize the ideas of the report. Instead, it tries to compare a wagon train to a new topic—an airplane.

Tony's revised conclusion is much stronger.

Student Model

> The children on a wagon train did the ordinary things that all children do. They worked, played, studied, ate, and slept. However, some of their experiences were difficult and far from ordinary. They suffered from hard wagon seats, tired feet, and fierce heat. They also faced long stretches of boredom as they traveled west. These children were true pioneers, just like their parents.

Giving Credit

Your final step in drafting a report is showing where you got your information. You must credit your sources.

Look at the list of sources you compiled in Activity B on page 177. Put the list in alphabetical order, using the authors' last names. If an author is not given, use the title of the book or article.

Here is Tony's list of sources. He included this list at the end of his report.

Student Model

My information was taken from these sources.

Bartel, Pauline. "Wagons on the Oregon Trail." Cobblestone Dec. 1981: 16–17.

Horn, Huston. The Pioneers. New York: Time-Life Books, 1974.

Lavender, David. Westward Vision: The Story of the Oregon Trail. New York: McGraw Hill, 1963.

"Pioneer Life in America." The World Book Encyclopedia. 1988 ed.

Notice that Tony underlined the titles of books and magazines. He put quotation marks around the titles of articles in magazines and encyclopedias. Follow this example when you credit your sources. Look at pages 508 and 536 for more information on how to capitalize and punctuate titles.

Writing Activity The Conclusion

Writing in Process Write the last paragraph of your report. Make sure that it ties your ideas together and shows the reader that the report is finished. Finally, list the sources you used for your report. Use the examples in this lesson as a guide.

8

Revising and Presenting

Focus Carefully revise, proofread, and share your report.

When writing a report, you must present facts clearly and accurately. The guidelines below can help you revise your paper.

Revision and Peer-Editing Checklist

1. Does the introduction state the topic of the report? Is the introduction interesting?
2. Is the body of the report informative?
3. Are the ideas presented in logical order?
4. Is each main idea in a separate paragraph? Is each idea developed thoroughly?
5. Does the conclusion summarize the main ideas of the report? Does it show that the report is finished?
6. Is the writing lively and clear?

This revised paragraph is from Tony's report on page 185.

They milked cows, fetched buckets of water from the creeks, and gathered wild fruits and berries.

I'd better give some examples.

The children had work to do.ₐThey searched for prairie dog holes and alerted the hunters

Who?

the children's

in the train to their locations. One of their

I should explain what this is.

These were the disks of dried buffalo dung that were burned for cooking and warmth.

most important jobs was gathering "buffalo chips."ₐ

They used books that had been packed into the wagons.

The children also studied their school lessons.ₐ

How did they study?

I can give more examples.

In addition, they learned skills such as how to hook rugs, make quilts, ~~and~~ preserve meat in salt,ₐ

start a fire from flint, and use an ax.

Proofreading

After you revise your report, you must proofread it carefully. Pay special attention to proper names and unusual or technical words. Check the accuracy of dates, figures, and other facts. Finally, check your spelling, punctuation, capitalization, and grammar.

Making a Final Copy

When you have revised your report, give it a good title. Then make a clean, final copy. Check to make sure that your handwriting is easy to read. Also, make sure you left margins and indented each paragraph. If you planned to use pictures or graphs as part of your report, add them to your final copy. Proofread your work, especially your list of sources, one last time. Neatly make any necessary changes.

Presenting

After you have finished, decide how to share your report. You might present similar reports in small groups. For example, you might ask your librarian to display groups of science, history, and sports reports. Add pictures or other items to make the display more interesting. For example, the "Sports Week" display might include sporting equipment, books about sports, and your reports.

Writing Activity Revising and Presenting a Report

Writing in Process Revise your report, using the guidelines given on page 188. Carefully proofread your report. Then make a clean, final copy. Include a good title. Put the list of sources at the end. Brainstorm with your classmates to find ways to publish or present your report. You may use the suggestions in the previous paragraph or think of other ideas.

Speaking and Listening

The news reports you see on television are much like the reports you have learned to write. Each news story begins with a lead. Like the topic sentence in a report, the lead states the topic of the news story and catches the listeners' attention.

The lead is followed by facts. These facts tell the *who, what, when, where, why,* and *how* of the story. The report usually ends with a summary statement.

Carefully watch a television news program. Notice that the reporters look directly into the camera. In this way, they have eye contact with their television audience. They know their copy, or report, well. They seldom glance at their copy.

Activity

With your class, prepare a news show. First, form several groups. Each group will be responsible for preparing a story about something interesting that has happened in your school in the past month.

Once your group has decided on a story, gather information. You may wish to interview people who are part of your story. Then write the story. Be sure to write a lead that will catch the audience's attention. Then add facts that develop your lead. These facts should tell the *who, what, when, where, why,* and *how* of your story. End with a summary statement. Now, choose one person in your group to be the on-camera reporter.

Practice the entire program with the on-camera reporters. Your classmates can be the audience. If you are on camera, remember to look directly at the audience, speak clearly, sit straight, and keep your hands still. Look at your written story only when necessary. After you have practiced, "broadcast" your news reports to another class.

Creative Writing

A Imagine that you are an inventor. You have invented a fantastic new product such as the one pictured below. Write a report about your product.

First, make a list of details. Include facts about what the item looks like, what it does, and what it is made of. Then organize your notes into an outline. Finally, draft your report. Remember to revise and proofread your report.

Put your garbage in the biodegradable projectile, place the projectile in the tube of the *Garbage Shoot,* and close the door. Pull back the plunger, then let go, and *shoot* your garbage to the disposal area.

B Imagine that you are a British redcoat spy in the American Revolution. Your assignment is to penetrate General Washington's lines. You are to bring back information about the number of Revolutionary soldiers and how well trained they are. You are to report on supplies, ammunition, and troop morale.

Write a short report on your findings. Be sure to include all of the requested information.

Crossroads

English and Reading

People often read fiction and nonfiction books just for enjoyment. When you find a good book, share your discovery with your friends. Tell them about it, or write a book report.

Once in a while, you will read a book you do not enjoy. In that case, you should tell what you did not like about the book. Then people who read your book review can decide for themselves whether they might like it anyway.

Book reports can be long or short. They may include many details or few. All book reports, however, must include the information listed below.

1. The title of the book
2. The author of the book
3. The topic of the book and if it is fiction or nonfiction
4. Reasons why you like or dislike the book

When you report on a fiction book, tell when and where the story takes place, a little about the people or animals in the story, and at least one problem they face. Don't tell everything.

When you report on a nonfiction book, tell about the subject covered in the book. You might tell a few especially interesting or unusual facts that you learned.

Give good reasons why you like or dislike the book. Whoever reads this report will be interested in your opinion.

Activity

Write a book report about a book you have read recently. Be sure to include the information every book report needs. Correct your mistakes and make a clean copy. Share your report with your class.

Application and Review

A Using Note Cards Make a note card for this information. Your topic is "Achievements of the Maya." You only need to record information related to your topic.

> [The] Maya were an American Indian people who developed a magnificent civilization in Central America and south Mexico. The Maya civilization reached its period of greatest development about A.D. 250 and continued to flourish for more than 600 years. The Maya produced remarkable architecture, painting, pottery, and sculpture. They made outstanding advancements in astronomy and mathematics and developed an accurate yearly calendar. They were one of the first peoples in the Western Hemisphere to develop an advanced form of writing.
>
> From *The World Book Encyclopedia*

B Organizing Notes into Idea Groups Look at these notes for a report on the ostrich. Imagine that each note is on a separate note card. Organize the notes into four groups of related ideas. Divide your paper into four columns. Label the columns *Looks, Behavior, Diet,* and *Offspring*. Write each fact in the correct column.

Has large feathers, or plumes, once popular for decorating hats

Does not bury its head in the sand

Eats plant food—leaves, seeds, fruit

Can run very fast—40 to 60 miles per hour

Eggs weigh about three pounds each

Does not fly—uses wings only for turning or braking

Protects itself by running away or kicking

Adult bird weighs up to 200 pounds

Babies are the size of full-grown chickens

Resources and Skills

In this painting, the artist Henri Rousseau has used color and shape to bring the scene of a tropical storm to life. A writer uses words in the same way. A rich vocabulary and research skills help a writer produce works as striking as this painting.

11

How Language Grows

What do the words *skyscraper* and *tepee* have in common? You may answer that both are names of structures, but they also have something else in common. Both words first came into the English language less than 200 years ago.

New words are added to English in several ways. The words *sky* and *scrape* were combined to make *skyscraper*. The word *tepee* was borrowed from the Dakota Indian language.

In this chapter you will learn how new words enter English. You will see that many words are borrowed and other words are made by clipping, combining, and blending existing words. You will also learn how some words come from the names of people and places or from initials.

1
Borrowed Words

Focus Many words in English have been borrowed from other languages.

Throughout its history, the English language has taken many words from other languages. Even today, English is still borrowing words. The chart below shows some words English has borrowed. You will see that the spelling and meaning of a word may change slightly when it comes into English. However, the original meaning and the English definition are usually very close.

English Word	Original Language	Original Word	Original Meaning
bonanza	Spanish	bonanza	fair weather, prosperity
pecan	Algonquian	pakan	hard-shelled nut
bouquet	French	bouquet	bunch of flowers
barbecue	Caribbean Indian	barbacoa	frame of sticks
bureau	French	bureau	writing desk
okra	African	okra	okra plant
chop suey	Chinese	tsa-sui	mixed bits
cookie	Dutch	koekje	little cake
drama	Greek	drama	a play
chipmunk	Algonquian	chipmunk	type of squirrel
ranch	Spanish	rancho	large farm
robot	Czechoslovakian	robota	forced labor
crime	French	crimen	verdict, offense
waffle	Dutch	wafel	a crisp batter cake
pretzel	German	brezel	biscuit baked in the form of crossed arms

Exercises *Identifying the Origin of Words*

A Use the dictionary to find out from what language each of the words below is borrowed. Write the correct abbreviation.

Fr.   = French   Du. = Dutch
Sp.   = Spanish   G.   = German
Algon. = Algonquian (Native American)

1. kindergarten
2. wigwam
3. sombrero
4. margarine
5. chaise lounge
6. moccasin
7. ersatz
8. snoop
9. snorkel
10. patio

B Sometimes a borrowed word does not come directly into English from another language. Use a dictionary to find out about the words *chowder* and *alligator*. In your own words, tell how these words came into English and how they got their meanings.

2
Clipped Words, Compounds, and Blends

Focus Some new words can be made by changing the forms of words that already exist.

Words that are already a part of our language are often changed to make new words. Sometimes words are shortened. The shortened word then becomes a new word in the language. New words can also be made by putting two or more words together.

Words Made by Clipping

When a long word is used a great deal, it is often given a shortened form. For example, people say *fan* for *fanatic* or *vet* for *veterinarian*. Shortening a long word is called **clipping**. Look at the examples of clipped words below. Do you know the long form of each?

burger	gas	champ
lunch	bike	drape

Putting Words Together

Compound Words Sometimes two or more words are put together to make a new word. The new word is called a **compound word**. English has many compound words. New ones are being made all the time. Some compound words you may be familiar with are *bookkeeper, football, teen-age, downtown,* and *input*.

Blended Words Sometimes when two words are put together to make a new word, some of the letters are dropped. The new word is then called a **blend**. You may know some blends. The word *smog* is a blend of *smoke* and *fog*. *Paratroops* is a blend of *parachute* and *troops*.

Exercises Finding Clipped Words, Compounds, and Blends

A Study the following words. Write the clipped form for each.

1. omnibus
2. laboratory
3. taximeter cabriolet
4. advertisement
5. gymnasium
6. influenza
7. telephone
8. periwig
9. mathematics
10. promenade
11. submarine
12. dormitory

B Write whether each word below is a compound or a blend. Write the two words from which each blend is made. If you need help, look up the words in a dictionary.

1. carryout
2. motel
3. cloudburst
4. drugstore
5. turtleneck
6. skyscraper
7. chortle
8. bellhop
9. bedspread
10. telethon
11. motorcade
12. brunch

3
Words Made from Names and Initials

Focus New words come into our language from the names of people and places. Initials can also be put together to make a new word.

Some words come into our language from the names of people and places. Other words are made from the first letters, or the first few letters, of a group of words.

Words from Names of People

Read how one person's name became part of our language.

The Earl of Sandwich lived about 200 years ago. He loved to gamble. He did not even want to leave the gambling room for meals. Therefore, he asked for a more portable kind of meal, something he could eat as he played. His snack became known as a *sandwich*.

Here are some other examples of common words that came from the names of people.

boycott (Charles Boycott)   pasteurize (Louis Pasteur)
teddy bear (President Teddy Roosevelt)

Words from Names of Places

Words can also come from names of places.

In 490 B.C., the Greeks won a war against the Persians at the battle of Marathon. One of the Greeks ran twenty-six miles to bring the news of victory from Marathon to Athens. Today the word *marathon* usually means a twenty-six-mile race.

Here are other words that came from the names of places.

> hamburger (Hamburg, Germany)
> Tabasco sauce (Tabasco, Mexico)
> cashmere (Kashmir, India)

Words from Initials

Sometimes the initials of a group of words are put together to make a new word. These words are called **acronyms**. An acronym is often a simpler way to say something. For example, it is easier to say *NASA* than to say *National Aeronautics and Space Administration*. Acronyms are always pronounced as words, not said as initials. Here are some common acronyms.

> AWOL (absent without leave)
> NOW (National Organization for Women)
> ZIP (Zoning Improvement Plan)

Exercises Discovering the Origin of Words

A Look up each of the following words in the dictionary. Find out what name or place each came from. Write the name on your paper.

1. Braille	5. cardigan	9. tangerine
2. macadam	6. tuxedo	10. magnolia
3. calico	7. chesterfield	11. sousaphone
4. guillotine	8. pompadour	12. macadamia nut

B Look at the following list of names. Write down the well-known acronym for each.

1. Wide Area Telecommunications Service
2. Cooperative for American Relief Everywhere
3. North Atlantic Treaty Organization
4. Radio Detecting and Ranging
5. Strategic Arms Limitation Talks

Crossroads

English and Social Studies

You have studied the cultures of many countries in your social studies class. Word study will also tell you about a people's culture.

You have learned that many of the words in English were borrowed from other languages. Usually, the borrowed words show the areas for which a certain culture was known or admired. For example, many of the words used in music—*largo, andante, violin, soprano*—were borrowed from the Italian language.

Activity

Study the lists of borrowed words below. Look up any unfamiliar words in a dictionary. Briefly write what you can tell about each culture from the words English borrowed from each language. For what knowledge or abilities were the people known or admired?

Native American	Spanish	French	German and Dutch
hickory	bronco	sauté	sauerkraut
sequoia	corral	boil	pumpernickel
kayak	lariat	au gratin	delicatessen
Minneapolis	rodeo	court	coleslaw
Mississippi	stampede	witness	sleigh
skunk	mustang	baron	Santa Claus

Application and Review

A Studying How Our Language Grows Here are five ways that words are added to the English language.

1. By borrowing
2. By making a word from initials
3. By using the name of a person or place
4. By using part of another word
5. By putting two words together

Decide how each of the following words came into our language. Write each word on your paper. After each word, write the number of the way that the word was added. Use your dictionary for help.

1. earthworm
2. ambulance
3. BASIC
4. sunrise
5. diesel
6. poinsettia
7. gas
8. SCUBA
9. saxophone
10. salami
11. jerseys
12. UNICEF
13. spacewalk
14. coyote
15. mike
16. petite
17. boutique
18. lacrosse
19. deb
20. paisley

B Words Around You Use a dictionary to find the origin of each word below. Write the name or place and the language from which the word originated.

1. Thursday
2. cologne
3. August
4. silhouette
5. maverick

12

Building Your Vocabulary

Did you recognize the bicycle gears in the picture above before you looked at the picture on the right? Could you easily identify the gears when you saw them in *context*—that is, within the whole picture?

Words have a context too. A word's context is its surrounding words and sentences. When you are reading, you can use context clues to figure out the meanings of some unfamiliar words.

In this chapter you will learn to use context clues to discover the meanings of new words. You will also learn to examine word parts to unlock the meanings of unfamiliar words.

1
Using Context Clues

Focus You can use *context clues* to unlock the meaning of an unfamiliar word in a sentence. A context clue may define, restate, or give an example of an unfamiliar word.

Definition and Restatement

A writer may define an unfamiliar word or restate it in a different way. Read these examples.

> Lindsay bought an *aspidistra*, which is a type of lily with stiff, glossy leaves. (definition)
>
> I just want a *morsel*, a tiny piece, of your delicious banana bread. (restatement)

Example

An example in a sentence may also help to explain an unfamiliar word. Read this sentence.

> *Crustaceans*, such as crabs and lobsters, are plentiful in these waters. (example)

The context tells you that crabs and lobsters are examples of a class of creatures called *crustaceans*. This helps explain the meaning of *crustaceans*.

Sometimes the unfamiliar word itself is the example. Then you can use the general term to decide what the word means.

> Woodworking tools, like the *lathe* and saw, should be a part of every workshop.

The context tells you that a *lathe* is a type of woodworking tool found in a workshop.

Certain key words and punctuation marks signal that a writer is giving a context clue.

Key Words Signaling Definition or Restatement

| also known as | that is | or |
| in other words | which is | also called |

Punctuation Marks Signaling Definition or Restatement
dashes, commas, and parentheses

Key Words Signaling an Example

| and other | for example | like |
| especially | for instance | such as |

Exercises *Mastering Context Clues*

A Use the context clues in each sentence to write a definition for the word in italics. Check your definition in a dictionary.

1. The *joey,* or baby kangaroo, lives in its mother's pouch.
2. Some seasonings have a strong flavor, especially *curry*.
3. The magician's cape was *magenta* (purplish red).
4. The cages held *quetzals* and other tropical birds.
5. Cindy likes Greek desserts—*baklava,* for example.
6. Melody is *ambidextrous;* that is, she can use both hands with equal ease.
7. *Pit vipers,* such as rattlesnakes, are poisonous.
8. A vaccine against *pertussis,* also known as whooping cough, is given to infants.
9. The report contained many *visual aids,* such as graphs and charts.
10. Some insects, *locusts* for example, appear in cycles.

B Look up the following words in a dictionary. Use each word in a sentence that contains a context clue to explain the meaning of the word.

1. rebus 2. marmoset 3. awl 4. brocade 5. herbivorous

2
Using Word Parts: Base Words

Focus A word part can be added to the beginning or end of a base word to form a new word.

Many words are made up of several parts. Often, there is a **base word,** or main word. One or more word parts may be added to the beginning or end of the base word. Sometimes, you can unlock the meaning of an unfamiliar word by studying the parts.

When a word part is added to a base word, a new word is formed. For example, the word part *dis-* is added to the beginning of the base word *agree* to form *disagree*. Adding the word part *-ment* to the end of the base word *agree* makes the word *agreement*.

What base word is in these three words?

thoughtless   rethought   unthoughtful

Just as builders start with the foundation of a building and add on to it, you can add on to a base word.

The base word is *thought*. The word part *-less* was added to make *thoughtless*. The word part *re-* was added to make *rethought*. Two word parts, *un-* and *-ful*, were added to make *unthoughtful*. What is the base word in each of these two sets of words? Notice that the base word may change slightly when a word part is added.

preshrink   shrinkable   unshrinkable
imaginary   imaginative   unimaginative

Exercises Building on Base Words

A Read the following list of words. Find and write each base word on a sheet of paper.

1. senseless
2. mouthful
3. unreadable
4. preview
5. restatement
6. misfit
7. thunderous
8. incomplete
9. kicker
10. nonprofit
11. happiness
12. successful
13. unlucky
14. helper
15. redo
16. prewrite
17. inhuman
18. penniless
19. spoonful
20. colorless

B Add a word part to the beginning or the end of each of the following base words. If you wish, add word parts to both places. Write the new words you have made on your paper. Tell what each new word means.

1. flaw
2. move
3. heat
4. speak
5. wonder
6. lock
7. worth
8. paint
9. spell
10. joy
11. equip
12. care

3
Using Word Parts: Prefixes

Focus A *prefix* is added to the beginning of a word.

When you add a prefix to a base word, you create a new word with a different meaning. By knowing the meanings of common prefixes, you can often understand new words.

Prefix	Base Word	New Word
non-	+ stop	nonstop

The prefix *non-* always means "not." Therefore, *nonstop* means "to go on without stopping." Here are other prefixes.

im-, in-	These prefixes mean "not." *Impossible* means "not possible." *Inaccurate* means "not accurate."
mis-	The prefix *mis-* means "wrong." *Mislead* means "to show the wrong way." You give the wrong information when you *misinform* someone.
pre-	This prefix means "before." To *preheat* an oven means "to heat an oven before using it."
re-	This prefix has two meanings. It may mean "back." To *recall* means "to call something or someone back." *Re-* may also mean "again." To *recopy* means "to copy again."
un-	This prefix sometimes means "not." *Unwashed* means "not washed." *Un-* may also mean "the reverse of." *Unlock* means the reverse of lock, or "to open or release."

When you look at a new word, see if it has a prefix and a base word. Remember that not all beginning letters that look like prefixes are prefixes. For example, the letters *un* are not a prefix in the word *under,* nor are the letters *mis* in *missile.* That is because neither *der* nor *sile* are base words.

Remember that the spelling of the base word never changes when a prefix is added to it.

Exercises *Adding Prefixes to Base Words*

A Answer these questions.

1. If a *mature* plant is fully grown, what is an *immature* plant?
2. If an *essential* ingredient in a recipe is necessary, what is a *nonessential* ingredient?
3. Write today's *date*. What is a time or event that *predates* today?
4. If a goal is *attainable*, it can be reached. What is an *unattainable* goal?
5. If you *dye* fabric, you color it. What do you do when you *redye* it?

B Here are lists of prefixes and base words. Build as many new words as you can by matching prefixes and base words. Not all of the base words and prefixes will go together. Check your new words in the dictionary. Tell what each new word means.

Base Words	Prefixes
spell	im-
view	re-
perfect	in-
correct	mis-
turn	pre-
washed	non-
stop	un-

4
Using Word Parts: Suffixes

Focus A *suffix* is added at the end of a base word.

When you add a suffix to a base word, you create a new word. The new word has a different meaning than the base word. By knowing the definitions of common suffixes, you can often understand the meanings of new words.

Base Word	Suffix	New Word
hazard	+ -ous	hazardous
glory	+ -ous	glorious
joy	+ -ous	joyous

The suffix *-ous* means "full of" or "having." A *hazardous* trip is full of hazards or dangers. A *glorious* celebration is one that is full of glory. A *joyous* event is full of joy. Here are some other common suffixes.

-able, -ible	These suffixes have two meanings. They can mean "can be." A *washable* sweater can be washed. *Digestible* food can be digested. The suffixes can also mean "having this feature." For example, a *valuable* necklace has value.
-er, -or	These suffixes mean "a person or thing that does something." A *baker* bakes and a *demonstrator* demonstrates. The suffix *-er* may also mean "more." *Stronger* means "more strong."
-ful	This suffix has two meanings. One is "full of." A *fistful* of pennies means "a fist that

> is full of pennies." The suffix *-ful* can also mean "having." A *peaceful* country has peace.
>
> **-less** The suffix *-less* means "without." *Speechless* means "without speech."

Sometimes the spelling of a base word changes when a suffix is added. Look at these examples.

> value + -able = valuable   fat + -er = fatter

Review the spelling rules for adding suffixes on pages 570–573. When in doubt about a suffix, refer to a dictionary.

Exercises Adding Suffixes to Base Words

A Copy these words. After each word, write the base word and the suffix that was added. Remember that sometimes the spelling of the base word has been changed. Then write the meaning of each word.

> EXAMPLE   driver = drive + -er; one who drives

1. beautiful
2. courageous
3. merciless
4. worrier
5. director

6. spineless
7. stressful
8. dangerous
9. sensible
10. laughable

B Answer these questions.

1. If *indicate* means "to point out," what is an *indicator*?
2. If *spite* means "a feeling of anger or annoyance toward someone," what is a *spiteful* person?
3. If *rest* is "peace or ease," what does *restless* mean?
4. If a *cavern* is "a cave," what does *cavernous* mean?
5. If *flame* means "the blaze of a fire," what does *flammable* mean?

Application and Review

A **Using Context Clues** Number a sheet of paper from 1 to 15. Use context clues to write a definition for each word in italics. Use a dictionary to check your definitions.

1. The *cobbler* who mended these shoes always does excellent work.
2. The photographer put the camera on a *tripod*, a three-legged stand.
3. The homes of the Pueblo Indians are made of *adobe*, or sun-dried brick.
4. The *cyclamen*—a plant of the primrose family—made a lovely centerpiece.
5. The *plantain*, unlike other bananas, is eaten as a cooked vegetable.
6. Cheryl has such *zeal*, or enthusiasm, for ballet that she practices willingly.
7. *Nocturnal* animals like owls, raccoons, and bats sleep during the day.
8. You can grow *basil* and other herbs in pots on a window sill.
9. The *pterodactyl*, a prehistoric reptile, looked like an enormous ugly bird.
10. The knight was on a *quest*, or search, for dragons.
11. Those drops make the pupils of your eyes *dilate*, or become larger.
12. The *centaur* and other imaginary creatures appear frequently in Greek and Roman myths.
13. The *petrel*, a truly seagoing bird, will die if only fresh water is available to drink.
14. The pirates searched the cave without finding the *cache*—hiding place—of the treasure.
15. I am often confused by *homophones*, or words that sound the same.

B Finding Base Words Copy each of the following words on a sheet of paper. Write the base word after each word.

1. gracious
2. rebid
3. unwashable
4. beautiful
5. immeasurable
6. sailor
7. nonsmoker
8. effortless
9. reusable
10. previewer
11. misprint
12. indefinite

C Finding Meaning from Word Parts Answer the following questions.

1. If a *significant* fact is important, what is an *insignificant* fact?
2. If a *ferrous* metal contains iron, does a *nonferrous* metal contain iron?
3. If *daunt* means "to discourage," what is a *dauntless* person?
4. If a *peer* is an "equal," what does *peerless* mean?
5. Do *preflight* instructions help a pilot to take off or to land?
6. If a *shorn* sheep has no wool left, what does an *unshorn* sheep look like?
7. If a *mobile* fixture can be moved, can an *immobile* fixture be moved?
8. To *trespass* is to go onto another's property without permission. What is a *trespasser*?
9. If *immerse* means "to plunge into a liquid," what can you do with an *immersible* coffee pot?
10. If *stenography* is the skill of writing in shorthand, what is a *stenographer*?
11. When do announcers make *pregame* comments, before or after the game starts?
12. If *locate* means "to put in a place," what does *relocate* mean?

13
Speaking and Listening Skills

The race is on! Coming into the stretch, it's the little red tricycle by four lengths of an air hose!

Have you ever been part of anything as wild and wacky as an underwater tricycle race? When you are asked to give a talk for your classmates, do you wish that you had done something as unusual as this?

Even if you haven't pedaled across the bottom of a swimming pool, you *do* have interesting or useful things to tell others. Maybe you have cared for an animal, taken a trip, or won an award. Any of these topics—and many others that only you know about—can be organized into a talk that others will want to hear. This chapter will show you how to share information with others and how to enjoy the experiences and information that others share with you.

1
Preparing a Talk

> **Focus** To prepare a talk, use the process of writing. Then prepare note cards and practice your talk.

Writing is only one way to communicate ideas. Speaking is another form of communication. On many occasions you may be asked to prepare a short speech, or talk. In Chapter 3, you learned about the stages in the process of writing.

Most of these steps can be used to prepare a talk. To begin, choose a topic and purpose, gather ideas, and organize your material. You will not write your talk word for word, however. Instead, you will make note cards and practice presenting your talk out loud.

Using Note Cards

Your talk will be more effective if you do not read it word for word. Note cards can help you remember ideas and keep you on the subject. Use 3″ × 5″ note cards. They are easy to hold, and each one can be set aside after it is used. Write only enough information to jog your memory—a fact or two on each card. Study this example of a note card. Notice that it is in outline form.

II. Setting of American musicals
   A. *The Music Man* —small town Iowa
   B. *South Pacific* —tropical island
   C. *West Side Story* —New York City

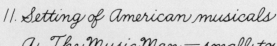

Practicing Your Talk

After you have prepared your talk, it is a good idea to practice it out loud. This will make you more comfortable with the material when you give your talk. Here are some practice guidelines.

Guidelines for Practicing a Talk

1. **Read and reread your notes.** Know your material.
2. **Practice giving your talk in front of a mirror.** Remember to stand straight, use appropriate gestures, and look directly at the audience.
3. **Practice your talk out loud.** If possible, record yourself on a tape recorder. Try to speak clearly and be careful not to hurry through your material. Stress important points.
4. **Give your talk in front of family members or friends.** They may have useful suggestions for you.
5. **Practice until you feel relaxed and confident.**

You will learn more about delivering your talk in part 2 of this chapter.

Exercises Preparing and Practicing a Talk

A Prepare a short talk on something interesting that you have seen. It could be an unusual animal, a "talking" cash register, a robot, a tornado, or any other unusual thing or event. Follow the process of writing to prepare your talk. Write notes on 3″ × 5″ note cards. These notes should remind you of what you want to say.

B Practice in a group of four or five students. Comment on each talk presented in your group. Give at least two helpful suggestions for each talk. The Guidelines for Delivering a Talk, which are presented in part 2, may give you additional help.

2
Presenting a Talk

Focus How you present a talk is as important as what you say in the talk.

Your report may be interesting and well prepared. However, you must present it in an appealing way or you will not reach your listeners. You need to think about your voice, your posture, your eye contact, and your gestures. Here are some suggestions to help you put across your ideas.

Guidelines for Delivering a Talk

1. **Be aware of your posture.** Stand tall and still, but not stiffly. Taking a deep breath will help you relax.
2. **Look at your listeners.** Make each person in the audience feel that you are talking directly to him or her. This is called eye contact.
3. **Use your hands and face in a meaningful way.** You can send your message with gestures as well as with words. If you are talking about something sad, do not smile. On the other hand, do not look glum if you are presenting a funny talk. Do not make distracting hand motions.
4. **Use your voice effectively.** Speak clearly and at a comfortable rate for you and your listeners. Be sure to speak loudly enough to be heard. On the next page, you will learn more about using your voice.
5. **Use visual aids.** If they help make your talk clearer, include maps, charts, and pictures. Be sure they are large enough to be seen by everyone.

Using Your Voice Effectively

You know that **volume,** the power of your voice, is important. To make the most of your talk, you must also pay attention to the **rate** at which you speak. If you speak too slowly, the audience may become bored. If you speak too quickly, the audience may not understand you.

Articulation is the way sounds are joined to form separate words. Always speak clearly and distinctly. A dictionary will help you with the standard American pronunciation of words. People in various parts of the country may pronounce words in different ways. These differences are called **dialects.**

To get your meaning across, you must phrase your ideas correctly. **Phrasing** is putting together words into meaningful groups. This often requires **stressing,** or emphasizing, different words. Look at the following sentences. Then say them out loud. Who is the great swimmer in each sentence?

> The boy says his sister is a great swimmer.
> "The boy," says his sister, "is a great swimmer."

You can see how phrasing affects the meaning of these sentences. Be aware of how you phrase sentences when you give a talk.

Exercises Delivering a Talk

A Show the difference in meaning as you say these pairs of sentences.

> "You hope," she said, "too much."
> You hope she said too much.

> Ms. Sanders, our teacher, was late.
> Ms. Sanders, our teacher was late.

B Present the talk you planned and practiced in part 1. Follow the guidelines presented in this lesson.

3
Becoming a Good Listener

Focus A good listener overcomes communication barriers and develops good listening skills.

A communication barrier is something that interferes with the messages between the speaker and the listener. Some barriers are created by listeners. For example, a listener might daydream or might refuse to accept new ideas. Other barriers are created by speakers. For example, a speaker might present confusing ideas or make distracting gestures.

This chart lists some communication barriers. It also tells how good listeners deal with these barriers.

Barriers to Communication

Barrier	Overcoming the Barrier
Distractions	Good listeners pay attention. They tune out distractions and concentrate on what the speaker is saying.
Information overload	Good listeners sort information. They remember main ideas and devote less effort to remembering details.
Lazy listening	Good listeners work hard to get the most out of what they hear. They pay attention even when what they hear does not seem especially important.
Hasty conclusions	Good listeners are careful not to jump to conclusions. They make thoughtful judgments at the end of a presentation.
Narrow thinking	Good listeners are open to new ideas.

Critical Listening

A **fact** is a statement about something that has really happened or is true. It can be proved. An **opinion** is one person's idea about something or someone. Opinions cannot be proved.

Every speaker uses facts and opinions. A good listener must separate them. Watch out especially for overgeneralization.

A **generalization** is a statement of fact based on details. For example, imagine that fifteen out of twenty students in your class say that the Ferris wheel is their favorite ride. You could generalize that *most* of the class likes the Ferris wheel best. An **overgeneralization** is a statement that is too broad to be true. If you said that the favorite ride of *all* students is the Ferris wheel, that would be an overgeneralization. To spot overgeneralizations, listen for words such as *everyone, always, never, every, nobody, everybody, all the time,* and *no one.*

Exercises Using Listening Skills

A In pairs, act out the following situations. Discuss the communication barriers that you notice between the characters.

1. A student comes home from school two hours late and meets a parent at the door.
2. A brother and sister both believe it is the other's turn to do the dishes.
3. One student has lost another student's book. The second student did not even know the first had borrowed the book.

B With a partner, make up a commercial to sell a product. Present your commercial for the class. The class should do the following:

1. Point out facts that were presented in the commercial.
2. Identify opinions.
3. Identify any generalizations and overgeneralizations.

4

Listening to and Judging Talks

Focus There are two parts to every talk: the *content* and the *presentation*. Use listening skills to evaluate fairly both parts of the talk.

Listening is a skill just as speaking is a skill. A good listener gets much more out of a talk than does a lazy listener. Follow these guidelines for listening to talks.

Guidelines for Listening to a Talk

1. **Be sure you can see and hear the speaker.**
2. **Look directly at the speaker.** Show that you are interested.
3. **Listen closely to the speaker's opening statements.** They will give you an idea of what the speaker is going to talk about.
4. **Listen for the main ideas.** Important ideas often follow signal words such as *first, next, finally, therefore, however,* and *for example*. Also look for ideas that are repeated or stressed.
5. **Listen to the speaker's final statements.** They may highlight or summarize the main points.

When your classmates give talks, you may be asked to evaluate their presentations. Being a good listener will allow you to make fair and helpful comments. Learning what to listen for in someone else's talk will also help you plan your own presentation.

Follow the guidelines on the next page when you evaluate a talk.

Guidelines for Evaluating a Talk

Content

1. **What was the topic of the talk?** Did the speaker make the topic clear and easy to understand?
2. **Was there enough information?**
3. **Did the information appear to be correct and to the point?**
4. **Was the information well organized?** Was the talk clear and easy to follow?

Presentation

1. **Did the speaker look directly at the audience?** Did he or she make eye contact with every part of the audience?
2. **Did the speaker look relaxed, yet stand tall?**
3. **Was the speaker easy to hear and understand?** Did he or she speak slowly and clearly?
4. **Were the speaker's gestures helpful and natural?**

Exercise Listening to and Evaluating a Talk

Listen to someone give a talk. It may be a coach giving a pregame pep talk, or a newscaster on a television news program. Evaluate the talk by answering the questions in the Guidelines for Evaluating a Talk. How might the talk have been improved?

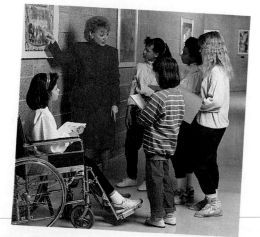

5
Conversations and Discussions

Focus Conversations and discussions are good ways to share ideas. You can learn how to prepare for a good conversation and discussion.

You have conversations and discussions every day, both in and out of school. You talk on the phone, answer questions, and share stories with friends and family. Most **conversations** are unplanned and unstructured.

You also have more formal, planned **discussions**. You can have a discussion to plan an event, solve a problem, or discuss a school subject. For example, a group of students might set a time for a meeting to plan a hallway mural or to decide the rules of a contest.

In both conversations and discussions, participants must be polite and respect other speakers. They must be ready to suggest ideas and solutions. In other words, to take part in any exchange of ideas, you must listen and think as well as speak.

Follow these guidelines when you take part in a discussion. Most points also apply to a conversation.

Taking Part in a Discussion

1. **Prepare for the discussion.** Gather information that others may not know about the topic.
2. **Listen carefully.** Respond to other participants. You may either support what is said or disagree.
3. **Add ideas.** Offer positive suggestions.
4. **Ask questions for these specific reasons:**
   a. to clarify a point;
   b. to get more information;
   c. to move the discussion forward.
5. **Be polite.** Respect and accept ideas that are different from yours. When you disagree with a point, do not interrupt. Wait your turn and then explain why.
6. **Pay attention to the reactions of your listeners.**

Leading a Discussion

One person in a discussion group acts as the leader, or chairperson. He or she makes sure that the discussion is orderly. The leader keeps the participants on the subject and sees that everyone has a chance to contribute ideas.

Duties of a Discussion Leader

1. **State the problem or ask another participant to do so.**
2. **Draw participants into the discussion through questions.** Make sure everyone takes turns talking. If a speaker strays from the subject, gently remind the group of the issue being discussed.
3. **Ask questions to clarify points.**
4. **Sum up what has been discussed or decided.**

Exercises Talking in Groups

A Imagine that your student council wants to organize a faculty baseball game to raise money for new bleachers. Read the following comments by a discussion leader. Which of these comments seem out of place? Which show the qualities of a good discussion leader? Be prepared to discuss your answers in class.

1. We are trying to decide if a faculty baseball game to raise money for new bleachers is a good idea. Are there any comments?
2. Can't you talk about anything except the Detroit Tigers? Let's get back to *our* game.
3. Alex, we haven't heard from you. How would you organize the ticket sales?
4. That's an interesting idea, Sandy. What do you mean by winner's circle?
5. Did you see the football game last night?

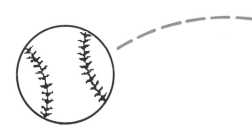

B Choose a partner. Act out a solution for each of the following problems.

1. One person has been talking for several minutes.
2. One person has listened carefully but has not talked.
3. You and another person speak at the same time.
4. Someone makes a statement you know to be incorrect.
5. Someone begins to change the topic before the original topic has been completed.

6
Critical Listening

Focus A speaker communicates in many ways. Learn to recognize and interpret a speaker's *nonverbal messages, motive, point of view,* and *bias*.

You are always sending messages, even when you do not speak. These **nonverbal messages** include body movements such as smiles, frowns, yawns, straight posture, and fidgeting.

Most communication is a mixture of verbal and nonverbal signals. A good speaker makes sure that his or her verbal and nonverbal signals are the same. A careful listener will notice if nonverbal signals do not match what is being said and think about what such differences mean.

Good listeners also focus on the aims of a speaker. **Motive** is a person's reason for saying something. A speaker may want to inform, persuade, or contribute a new idea.

Point of view, including a person's likes and dislikes, may also affect the speaker's message. For example, two members of the school board discuss the purchase of new equipment for the football team. One enjoys football; the other does not. Each person's point of view will affect the decision.

Bias occurs when a person feels so strongly about an issue that he or she ignores important facts. The speaker presents only one side of the issue.

Exercise Using Critical Listening Skills

Pretend you are a reporter for your local newspaper. If possible, attend a PTA or school board meeting, or listen to a discussion on television. Write a brief report, giving the speakers' motives, points of view, and any bias you can detect. What kind of body language did the speaker use?

7
Evaluating Group Discussions

Focus A good discussion depends on the skill of the participants and the leader.

Students at McDowell School are not using the school library often enough. The student council discusses the problem. Present are Wendy, Salina, Matt, Lisa, Paul, and Fred. You learned about the guidelines for discussion in part 5. Keep those guidelines in mind as you read this discussion.

Wendy Mrs. Garcia, the librarian, would like ideas about ways she can encourage library use. Any suggestions?

Salina I think that the library should be open later. Now, kids have to go to the public library where . . .

Matt Ha! Who wants to hang around after school?

Salina Not you, that's for sure!

Wendy Matt, Salina, we all have different ideas about ways to spend after-school time. Let's get back on the track. Salina has a good idea—lengthening library hours. Paul, have you come up with any ideas?

Paul Many students don't know their way around the school library. Could Mrs. Garcia arrange for small groups to visit the library?

Lisa Mrs. Garcia might be willing, but what about the teachers? Would they let students leave their classes?

Matt Nah, teachers never let students out.

Wendy Lisa, I think that's a good question. I'll ask Mr. Rehage today. We have to stop now. We do have two good ideas here: lengthening the library's hours and arranging library tours. Tomorrow, let's talk about some new books for the library's collection.

Exercise Evaluating a Discussion

Look over the guidelines for discussion in part 5. Number your paper from 1 to 8. Then answer the following questions about the sample discussion.

1. How does Wendy get the discussion off to a good start?
2. Which three comments do not follow the guidelines? Explain your answer.
3. Why is Salina's first comment important?
4. How could Wendy encourage Fred to participate?
5. Which participant most needs to improve his or her discussion skills? Why?
6. Which participant keeps the discussion moving?
7. How does Wendy end the discussion?
8. How should Wendy open the next discussion of this same subject?

Crossroads

English and Health

You have just learned a very valuable skill—how to take part in and lead a group discussion. You will be able to use this skill both in and out of school.

Health is a topic that comes up in many classes. It is discussed in science, in gym, and in health class itself. It is a frequent topic of newspaper and magazine articles.

There are two areas of health that are often discussed: physical health and mental or emotional health. Physical health discussions may focus on topics such as illness, eating right, and exercise. Emotional health topics may include feeling good about yourself, your role as a family member, or how you relate to friends.

Support groups are often formed to help people deal with emotional health concerns. Everyone in the group takes part. Group members tell how they have handled a situation. They also listen to the experiences of others. By sharing ideas, the members support and help each other.

Activity

Meet with three or four other students. Choose a discussion leader. Discuss what kinds of support groups might be formed in your school. Also discuss the following questions.

1. What are some of the special needs of the students?
2. What topics are of special concern?
3. What would be the best way to start a support group?
4. What teacher or administrator might help organize and sponsor a support group?
5. What would be the best time and place to meet?
6. What might be accomplished by forming a group?

Application and Review

A Giving Talks and Participating in Group Discussions
Read the following statements. Number your paper from 1 to 10. If the statement is correct, write *True* on your paper. If it is incorrect, write *False*. Be ready to explain what is wrong with the statement.

1. Prepare a talk by using the steps in the writing process.
2. When you prepare a talk, you should use note cards with your entire speech written out.
3. State all of your information in the same tone of voice when you give a talk.
4. When you give a talk, you should look at your notes the entire time so you do not forget anything.
5. When giving a talk, use natural gestures and expressions.
6. A good listener should try to pick out the main ideas.
7. You should judge the content and presentation.
8. You should not gather extra information before a group discussion. This will give you an unfair advantage.
9. When you disagree with someone in a group discussion, keep your opinion to yourself.
10. The leader of a discussion should always keep the discussion on the topic.

B Giving a Talk Choose one of the following topics. Prepare, practice, and present a one- to two-minute talk on this topic. Use the guidelines in this chapter to help you with each step.

1. Something new at school
2. A hobby
3. Your pet
4. Something funny that happened to you
5. An important game that you participated in

14

Library and Research Skills

Surprises, excitement, adventure—you may not expect to find these in a library. But the library can be an exciting place when you know how to find the often surprising information tucked away on its shelves.

This chapter will show you how to uncover the many surprises in the library. You will learn how to find fiction and nonfiction books, to use the Dewey Decimal System and the card catalog, and to use the encyclopedia and other reference sources. You will also learn how to take notes, to plan and conduct a research interview, and to use graphic aids.

Detail, untitled illustration, John Martin, 1981.

1
The Classification of Books

Focus There are two kinds of books, *fiction* and *nonfiction*.

Libraries can have thousands of books. Finding a particular book among so many may seem to be an impossible task. However, the job is not difficult when you learn how books are arranged in the library. Basically, books are divided into two groups: **fiction** and **nonfiction**.

Fiction

Fiction books are stories that were made up by a writer. Since fiction comes from the author's imagination, it is not necessarily true. The writer of a fiction book may base a story on some real events or experiences, but then invent certain elements to make a good story. All fiction books are grouped together in the library.

Fiction books are arranged on shelves alphabetically according to the author's last name. For example, books by an author whose last name is Adams are placed before books by an author named Byars. Books by Byars are placed before those by Cleary.

If someone has written more than one book, all of those books are placed together on the shelf. They are then arranged alphabetically by the first word in the title. Words like *a, an,* or *the* are not considered in arranging titles alphabetically.

Nonfiction

Nonfiction books are about real people and events. They report facts or ideas. For example, a book about dinosaurs and a book about the history of fashion are nonfiction. These books are classified and arranged according to their subjects. These subjects are grouped together in larger categories.

There are several classification systems for nonfiction. One is the **Library of Congress System,** used by most university libraries. The other classification system is the **Dewey Decimal System,** used by most school and public libraries. You will learn more about the Dewey Decimal System in part 2.

Exercises Fiction and Nonfiction

A Arrange these authors and fiction titles in the order in which they should appear on the shelves of a library.

1. Snyder, Zilpha *Eyes in the Fishbowl*
2. Sherburne, Zoa *Jennifer*
3. Speare, Elizabeth *The Witch of Blackbird Pond*
4. Snyder, Zilpha *The Velvet Room*
5. Klein, Norma *Mom, the Wolf Man, and Me*
6. Kjelgaard, Jim *Outlaw Red*
7. Gault, William *The Last Lap*
8. Kjelgaard, Jim *Big Red*
9. Snyder, Zilpha *Below the Root*
10. Speare, Elizabeth *The Bronze Bow*

B Number your paper from 1 to 5. Write *Fiction* or *Nonfiction* to identify each title.

1. *The History of China*
2. *The Mystery of the Summer House*
3. *The Future of Robotics*
4. *Bicycle Repairs: A How-To Book*
5. *Adventure in the Hidden Cave*

The Dewey Decimal System

Focus The *Dewey Decimal System* classifies all nonfiction books into ten major categories. A specific identification number, a *call number,* is assigned to every nonfiction book.

The **Dewey Decimal System** classifies all nonfiction books into ten categories. Most school and public libraries arrange their nonfiction books according to this identification system.

Each of the categories in the Dewey Decimal System is assigned a number, counting by hundreds. For example, the numbers 600-699 are assigned to Useful Arts. This category includes cookbooks, garden books, and books about cars. The chart on the next page shows what kinds of books are found in each of the ten categories.

In the Dewey Decimal System, a specific identification number is assigned to every nonfiction book. This number, known as the **call number,** is like the address of the book. It tells exactly where each book in the library can be found on the shelves. The call number of each nonfiction book is printed on its back, or spine. For example, the book *The Log of a Cowboy* has the call number 808.3. Each nonfiction book is arranged in numerical order on a shelf in the library according to its call number.

Double Readings,
Buzz Spector,
1987.

The Dewey Decimal System

000–099	**General Works**	(encyclopedias, handbooks)
100–199	**Philosophy**	(conduct, ethics, psychology)
200–299	**Religion**	(the Bible, mythology, theology)
300–399	**Social Science**	(statistics, economics, law, education, government, folklore, legend)
400–499	**Language**	(languages, grammar, dictionaries)
500–599	**Science**	(mathematics, chemistry, biology, physics)
600–699	**Useful Arts**	(medicine, farming, cooking, sewing, radio, nursing, engineering, television, business, gardening, cars)
700–799	**Fine Arts**	(music, painting, acting, photography, games, sports)
800–899	**Literature**	(poetry, plays, essays)
900–999	**History**	(biography, travel, geography)

A special section in the nonfiction area contains biographies. A **biography** is the true story of a person's life written by another person. An **autobiography** is the true life story written by the person himself or herself. A **collective biography** contains the life stories of more than one person. The 920 call number is reserved for collective biographies. A call number beginning with 92 or the letter B may be used for individual biographies and autobiographies.

Most libraries keep fiction books that contain several short stories in a special section. These books are usually marked *SC,* for "Story Collection."

Exercises Using the Dewey Decimal System

A Number your paper from 1 to 10. Assign the correct Dewey Decimal category number to each of these books.

1. *The Rainbow Book of Nature* by Donald Peattie
2. *America in Legend* by Richard M. Dorson
3. *Ecology* by Peter Farb
4. *Illustrated Motor Cars of the World* by Piet Olyslager
5. *Making Mosaics* by Edmond Arvois
6. *Compton's Encyclopedia*
7. *The World of Ballet* by Anne Geraghty
8. *Ancient China* by John Hay
9. *Poetry Handbook* by Babette Deutsch
10. *The Story of Language* by Mario Pei

B Each book below belongs in one of the special categories of biography, autobiography, collective biography, or short story collections. Read the title of each book carefully. Decide on the right category. Copy each title and author. Then write the correct category for each book.

1. *Georgia O'Keeffe: The "Wilderness and Wonder" of Her World* by Beverly Gherman
2. *O. Henry's Best Stories* edited by Lou P. Bunce
3. *Women Who Changed History* by Mary L. Davis
4. *If You Could See What I Hear* by Tom Sullivan (with Derek Gill)
5. *Martin Luther King: The Peaceful Warrior* by Ed Clayton
6. *Stories Boys Like* compiled by Franklin M. Reck
7. *My Animals and Me* by Nan Hayden Agle
8. *Baseball's Greatest Pitchers* by Milton J. Shapiro
9. *The Youngest General: A Story of Lafayette* by Fruma Gottschalk
10. *Evel Knievel and Other Daredevils* by Joe Scalzo

3
Using the Card Catalog

Focus Use the *card catalog* to locate a library book.

Most libraries have thousands of books. However, you can easily locate a specific book by using the card catalog.

The Card Catalog

The **card catalog** is a cabinet of small drawers filled with cards printed with information about every book in the library. The cards are arranged alphabetically according to the top line of each card. In the upper left-hand corner of each card in the catalog is the **call number** of the book listed on the card. This call number makes it easier to find the book.

On the outside of each drawer, there is a label that tells which letters of the alphabet are contained in that drawer. Inside each drawer there are **guide cards** that have tabs extending above the regular book cards. The tabs may have letters of the alphabet, complete words, or general subject headings printed on them. The guide cards separate the drawer of cards into small groups.

More and more libraries today have computerized card catalogs. Computer catalogs can provide a list of books available on a certain subject or show whether the library has a book by a particular author or title. Some computer catalogs will even tell if a book has been checked out.

Types of Catalog Cards

There are usually three cards for the same book in the card catalog: the **author card,** the **title card,** and the **subject card.** All three cards give you the same information about the book, but in a slightly different order. They provide the title, the author, the publisher, the date of publication, the number of pages, a notation about illustrations, and the call number.

An author card has the name of the author on the top line. A title card has the title on the top line. A subject card has the general subject on the top line. The author, title, and subject cards for one book have the same call number in the upper left corner. Books of fiction do not have call numbers and are usually arranged alphabetically by their authors' last names.

Look carefully at the following examples of card catalog cards for the book *Wildlife in America* by Peter Mathiessen.

The Author Card

When you know the author of a book, use the card catalog to look up the author's name. All the cards for one author will be filed alphabetically by the first word in the title.

591.97   **Mathiessen, Peter.**
Mat   Wildlife in America. Illus. with photos.
          N.Y., Viking, © 1987

The Title Card

When you know the title of a book, but not its author, look for the title card. Title cards are filed alphabetically by the first word. *A, an,* and *the* do not count as first words.

591.97   **Wildlife in America.**
Mat   Mathiessen, Peter
          Wildlife in America. Illus. with photos.
          N.Y., Viking, © 1987

The Subject Card

If you have a general topic in mind but do not know any book titles or authors, use the subject cards. For example, if you were writing a report on wildlife, you would look in the card catalog under the subject heading *wildlife*. The subject on every subject card is frequently in capital letters.

591.97 **WILDLIFE—CONSERVATION**
Mat   Mathiessen, Peter.
        Wildlife in America. Illus. with photos.
        N.Y., Viking, © 1987

Some cards, called **cross-reference cards,** refer you to other subject headings related to the one on the card. Cross-references are listed after the words *See* or *See also*.

Exercises Using the Card Catalog

A What subject cards might give you information about the following topics? Think of several subjects for each topic.

1. How to study for a test
2. Famous women swimmers
3. Rules of chess
4. History of the airplane
5. How to grow a vegetable garden

B Use the card catalog to find the title, author, and call number of a book on three of the following subjects.

1. skiing
2. detective stories
3. dinosaurs
4. poems by Robert Frost
5. Pablo Picasso
6. Harriet Tubman
7. The Alamo
8. U.S. Presidents
9. UFO's
10. math games

4
Using the Encyclopedia

Focus Because it contains general articles on many subjects, an *encyclopedia* can be a valuable reference tool.

When you need the answer to almost any question, go to the reference section of your library. The books in this section are usually marked with an *R* above the call number. In the reference section, you will find one of the most frequently used reference tools, the encyclopedia.

An **encyclopedia** is a reference book that contains general articles on many subjects. Most encyclopedias are made up of several volumes, covering a wide variety of subjects. Sometimes a whole set of encyclopedias is about one subject, such as art or biography. There are some special encyclopedias that consist of one volume on a single subject, such as baseball, mythology, ships, or careers.

Encyclopedias are easy to use. Information is arranged in the volumes alphabetically by subject. Articles about people are usually alphabetized by the last name. Other articles are organized by the key word in the subject.

Volumes are usually numbered to keep them in order. On the spine of each volume are letters or words to tell you which part of the alphabet is included in that volume.

At the top of each page of the encyclopedia are guide words. They help you find the page that will have the article you need.

The Encyclopedia Index

Every set of encyclopedias has an index. The index may be a separate volume, or it may be part of the last volume. The index will direct you to every volume and page that contains information on your topic.

For example, if you were doing a report on the rotary engine, you might look in *The World Book* index. The sample index entry below directs you to three articles appearing in volumes *W, A,* and *G.* The index also tells you what page to look at in each of these volumes.

Rot [plant disease] **R:447**
  Alfalfa (Pests and Diseases) **A:330**
Rota [island, Pacific] **R:447**
Rotary bottom [tool]
  Plow *picture on* **P:511**
Rotary Club [organization]
  Rotary International **R:447**
Rotary-cut method [industrial process]
  Veneer **R:238**
Rotary drilling
  Petroleum (Methods of Drilling) **P:300**
    with picture

Rotary engine
  Wankel Engine **W:20** *with pictures*
  Automobile (The Gasoline Shortage)
    A:930–932
  Gasoline Engine *picture on* **G:64**

Rotary International [organization] **R:447**
  with picture
Rotary motion [physics]
  Machine *diagram on* **M:11**
Rotary pendulum
  Pendulum (Other Pendulums) **P:212**
Rotary plow
  Plow (Other Types of Bottoms) **P:512**

Rothschild, Guy de [German banker] **R:448**
Rothschild, House of [European history]
  Rothschild **R:448**
Rothschild, James Mayer [German banker]
  Rothschild, Mayer Amschel **R:448**
Rothschild, Karl Mayer [German banker]
  Rothschild, Mayer Amschel **R:448**
Rothschild, Lionel [British political leader]
  R:448
Rothschild, Mayer Amschel [German
  banker] **R:448**
Rothschild, Nathan Mayer [1777–1836.
  German banker] **R:448**
Rothschild, Nathan Mayer [1840–1915.
  British political leader]
  Rothschild, Lionel **R:448**
Rothschild, Salomon Mayer [German
  banker]
  Rothschild, Mayer Amschel **R:448**
Rotifer [microorganism] **R:448** *with pictures*
  Microscope *picture on* **M:425**
Rotogravure [printing]
  Intaglio **I:241**
  Printing (Printing by Gravure) **P:705**;
    (Gravure Presses) **P:705** *with picture*

The Encyclopedia Article

Each encyclopedia entry includes a written article on the topic. If the topic is long, the article will be divided into parts, usually indicated by subheads in boldface type. By examining the subheads, you can quickly tell what is covered.

In addition to the written text, an article may contain photographs, charts, or other illustrations. An entry may also include cross-references, which refer the reader to related articles in the encyclopedia. Some encyclopedias also list additional references at the end of an article.

Exercises Using an Encyclopedia

A Here are five topics. Choose an encyclopedia. Write its name on your paper. For each topic, write the key word that you would look up in the encyclopedia. Find the article on that topic. Write the letter or number of the volume and the page number of the article.

1. The talents of Benjamin Franklin
2. Beverly Sills's career in the opera
3. Where active volcanoes can be found
4. The description of a Neanderthal man
5. The economy of Thailand

B Look up one of these topics in an encyclopedia index. List four articles on that topic. Give the titles of the articles, their volumes, and their pages.

1. Mummies   3. Soccer   5. Dentistry
2. Porpoise   4. Fashion   6. Music

C Look up one of the following topics in an encyclopedia. List the cross-references that appear at the end of the article.

1. Hercules   3. Pepper
2. Extrasensory perception   4. Amazon River

5
Using Other Resources

Focus The *reference section* has special books and materials that provide facts and information on countless topics.

When you need specific information about a topic, go to the reference section of your library. There you will find valuable sources of current information. The **reference section** has special books and materials that provide facts and information on countless topics. You have already learned about the encyclopedia. Here are some other common reference works.

Dictionaries

There are two types of dictionaries: abridged and unabridged. **Abridged** dictionaries contain fewer words and less detailed definitions than unabridged dictionaries. An **unabridged** dictionary, such as *Webster's Third New International Dictionary,* is the most complete collection of English words available. This edition has over 450,000 words.

A reference section may also contain dictionaries on specific topics. For example, there is a dictionary of Indian tribes of North America and another on American history.

The Atlas

An **atlas** is a book of maps. To use an atlas, you refer to an index. The index gives you the page number of the map you want. It also gives the exact location of cities and towns on a map. In addition, the index of an atlas provides the populations of cities, states, and countries. Many atlases also include points of interest, such as national, state, and provincial parks. In addition, atlases frequently list time zones and mileage charts.

Hurricane Gilbert
SEPT. 15 1988
9 AM EDT

TEXAS

MEXICO

Texas Herald

Hurricane Gilbert
Storms Ashore

Magazines and Newspapers

Most libraries have current magazines and newspapers from all over the country. Libraries also save back issues of their magazines for future reference. These are often bound into book form. They are valuable sources of information. To find an article on a specific topic, refer to the *Readers' Guide to Periodical Literature*. Ask a librarian to help you use the *Readers' Guide*.

Almanacs and Yearbooks

Almanacs and **yearbooks** are collections of current facts and statistics. For example, you can find out who won last year's World Series or who the current senators from the state of California are. To find information in an almanac, use the index. Almanacs are printed yearly. Use the most recent almanac for the most accurate information.

Vertical File

A **vertical file** is a file cabinet filled with newspaper and magazine clippings, and pamphlets. They are filed in folders alphabetically according to topic. A vertical file can often provide current information that is difficult to find elsewhere.

Exercises *Using Reference Materials*

A Choose a foreign country that interests you. Then go to the reference section of the library to find the answers to the questions that are listed below. Write down the title of the source that you used for each answer.

1. Who is the current head or ruler of the country? What is the population? (Use an almanac or yearbook.)
2. Draw or trace a map of the country. (Use an atlas.)
3. Label the major bodies of water, mountain ranges, and large cities on the map you traced. (Use an atlas.)
4. What are the major exports of the country? (Use an encyclopedia.)
5. What are the major imports of the country? (Use an encyclopedia.)

B Go to the reference section of your library. Number your paper from 1 to 10. Write the answers to the following questions. Also, write down the title of the reference work where you found the answer. You may use dictionaries, atlases, magazines, newspapers, almanacs, yearbooks, encyclopedias, and the vertical file.

1. What are five fire hazards that can be found around the house?
2. What is the population of Santa Fe, New Mexico?
3. What is the official language of Sri Lanka?
4. What three seas touch the shores of Turkey?
5. Draw the flag of Italy.
6. Who is the current governor of Kentucky?
7. What is the longest suspension bridge in North America?
8. What river forms the southern border of Texas?
9. Where was the first large-scale nuclear test site in the United States?
10. Who is the current women's world record holder in the mile run?

6
Taking Notes

Focus When you do research, take notes. Taking notes as you read helps you to remember facts and ideas.

You will often use the library to research a topic for a report. When you are gathering information for a report or composition, always take notes. Your notes will help you remember facts and ideas accurately.

Write notes on 3″ × 5″ note cards. On each card, write only one piece of information. That way you can organize your notes easily. Include the source on each card.

Note cards for books should include the title, the author, and the page number where you found the information. For magazines, include the name and date of the magazine, the title and page number of the article, and the author's name, if given. For encyclopedias, give the name of the encyclopedia, the volume number, and the title and page number of the article.

When you take notes, do not copy the author's words exactly. Paraphrase the material instead. To **paraphrase,** read the information carefully and write it in your own words. If you do copy an author's words exactly, you must enclose them in quotation marks.

At the top of the next page, you will see how a student paraphrased this excerpt from an encyclopedia.

For centuries, musicians played *acoustical* guitars, which produce sound from the vibration of the strings. During the 1900's, *electric* guitars became popular. An electric guitar has an electromagnetic device that picks up the sound of the strings and sends it through an amplifier. An electric guitar can produce a greater range of sounds than an acoustical guitar.

By Winston Irving Tan, from *The World Book Encyclopedia*

Encyclopedia

> *The World Book Encyclopedia, Volume 8* — **Volume**
>
> **Title** — "Guitar," pp. 418-419 — **Pages**
>
> Electric guitars have become popular in the 1900's. — **Information**

Exercises Taking Notes on a Subject

A Read this article from *The World Book Encyclopedia*, Volume 14, page 643. Write three note cards based on the article. Put the notes in your own words.

> **OAKLEY, ANNIE** (1860–1926), an American marks-woman, starred in Buffalo Bill's Wild West Show for 17 years. She was popular throughout the United States and Europe. She was an expert shot with a pistol, rifle, or shotgun. Once, with a .22 rifle, she shot 4,772 glass balls out of 5,000 tossed in the air on a single day. At 90 feet (27 meters), she could hit a playing card with the thin edge toward her, and puncture a card five or six times while it fell to the ground. Since then, free tickets with holes punched in them have been called "Annie Oakleys."
>
> Annie Oakley was born Phoebe Anne Oakley Mozee on Aug. 13, 1860, in a log cabin in Patterson Township, Ohio. She began shooting at the age of 9. After her father died, she supported the family by shooting small game. Only 5 feet (152 centimeters) tall, she was called "Little Sure Shot." Annie Oakley joined Buffalo Bill's Wild West Show in 1885 (SEE BUFFALO BILL). By Howard R. Lamar

B Choose any wild animal. Then look up the article on that animal in an encyclopedia. Read the article to find out how the animal survives in the wilderness. Make five note cards to help you remember the facts. Remember to paraphrase when you take notes.

7

The Interview

Focus Sometimes an expert is the best source of information on a topic. *Interview* an expert to gather information.

When you are writing a report, you may need first-hand information on your topic. In this case, your best source may be an expert. For example, if you were doing a report on a career as a paramedic, you could interview a paramedic to get first-hand information about the job.

There are two steps to completing an interview: preparation and the interview itself. Follow these guidelines to prepare for and conduct an interview.

Guidelines for Planning an Interview

1. **Contact the expert and politely request an interview.** Give your name and the reason you would like the interview. Arrange a time and place to meet.
2. **Learn about the expert's background.** Then you will have some idea what information he or she can share.
3. **Know something about the topic.** It is important to have some basic knowledge about the subject. Then you will be able to ask good questions.
4. **Make a list of questions to ask the expert.** Make sure your questions require more than *yes* or *no* answers. Give the expert a chance to talk freely about the topic.
5. **Decide how to record the interview.** Using a tape recorder is one way to be certain you are accurate. If you use a tape recorder, make sure it works before you begin the interview. In any case, have enough paper and pencils to take notes.

Guidelines for Conducting an Interview

1. **Be prompt.** Have ready your questions, your note paper, and your pen.
2. **Listen carefully.** Take notes.
3. **Ask questions.** If you do not understand what the expert is saying, ask him or her to clarify. Ask the person to repeat if you do not have time to write down all the information you need.
4. **Review your notes.** See if the expert answered your questions completely. If not, ask for a further explanation.
5. **Thank the expert for the interview.** Also send a thank-you letter. You will learn more about writing thank-you letters in Chapter 17.

Exercises Conducting Interviews

A Read the following list of topics. Then name a type of expert you could interview for information on each one.

1. How to set up an aquarium
2. Kinds of fossils
3. How to write a children's book
4. How to open a bank account
5. The value of solar energy
6. Starting a vegetable garden
7. Eating nutritious foods
8. How to "tune-up" a bicycle
9. Blood types
10. How to train for a triathlon
11. First aid
12. Identifying constellations

Trilobite fossil.

B Choose one of the topics from Exercise A. Make a list of questions that you would ask the expert in an interview.

8
Getting Information from Graphic Aids

Focus *Graphic aids* include photographs, illustrations, diagrams, maps, charts and tables, and graphs.

Some information is easier to understand if you can see it in pictures. Graphic aids allow you to see factual information.

Photographs and **illustrations** put ideas into picture form. Always read captions that appear with photographs and illustrations.

Diagrams identify the parts of an object. They tell how each part is related to other parts. Read all labels on diagrams.

Maps are drawings of areas of land and bodies of water. There are different kinds of maps. Some maps show the boundaries of countries and locations of cities. Others show geographical features like mountain ranges or deserts. Always read the legend on a map. The legend explains the symbols used on the map.

Charts and **tables** present groups of facts. Part of the information is usually in number form. Charts are often

Illustration	Diagram	Map
	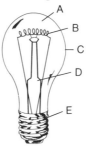	

Queen Angelfish
Holocanthus ciliaris
12 to 18 inches long
(30 to 46 centimeters)

Incandescent Bulb
A. inert gas filling; **B.** coiled tungsten wire filament; **C.** glass envelope; **D.** glass support; **E.** metal base

Dismal Swamp

 City
Swamp

arranged in columns. Always read the title and the column headings in a chart.

A **graph** is a special kind of chart. It shows how one fact is related to another. When you study a graph, read the title. Also read the key to any symbols used in the graph. Next, read what is printed inside and next to the graph. Finally, read the caption, if there is one.

Chart

Activity	Calories per hour
reading, writing, eating, watching T.V.	80 to 100
walking moderately fast, making a bed	170 to 240
swimming, running, dancing, bicycling	350 and more

Graph

World Area Occupied by Continents

- Asia 29.8%
- Antarctica 8.9%
- Africa 20.5%
- Australia 5.2%
- Europe 7.0%
- N. America 16.4%
- S. America 12.1%

Exercise Using Graphic Aids

Answer the following questions by referring to the graphic aids shown.

1. How long is a Queen Angelfish?
2. What is the scientific name for a Queen Angelfish?
3. What is inside an incandescent bulb?
4. What type of wire is used in the filament of an incandescent bulb?
5. In what two states is Dismal Swamp located?
6. What body of water is south of Dismal Swamp?
7. How many calories per hour does a person burn while reading a book?
8. Which activity will burn more calories, walking fast or bicycling?
9. Which continent is the largest?
10. What percentage of world area is occupied by Australia?

Crossroads

English and Art

There are many types of artists. You are probably familiar with painters, photographers, and sculptors. One special kind of artist is a graphic artist. Graphic artists prepare newspaper and magazine illustrations, posters, and pamphlets. Graphic artists also create illustrations, maps, and charts for encyclopedias and textbooks. They create advertising logos and design the packaging for the items you buy in the department store and the supermarket.

Activity

Pretend that you are a graphic artist for a textbook company. Your assignment is to draw diagrams for a science book. Use the following information to draw a diagram of either a spider web or a tornado. Label the parts of your diagram.

A A spider web is often spun between two branches. First, the web is anchored in several spots on each branch by short *foundation lines*. The foundation lines are then connected and a rough outer circle is made. Lines called *spokes*, or *radials*, extend from the outer circle to the *center*, or *hub*, of the web. The web is completed by *spiral* lines that circle around and around the web from the outer circle to the hub.

B The funnel-shaped tornado is easy to recognize. The top of a tornado is a dark, heavy mass of swirling clouds, dirt, and debris. It is called the *cumulonimbus*. Extending down toward the ground is the *vertical updraft*. The air is swirling so rapidly here that large objects can be pulled high into the air. Finally, making contact with the earth, is the *tornado funnel*.

Application and Review

A Using the Library Write the correct category for each of these nonfiction books. You may refer to the Dewey Decimal list on page 241.

1. *The New World of Amateur Radio* by Nancy Warren Ferrell
2. *The Sierra Nevada* by Roderick Peattie
3. *Complete Guide to Running* by Jim Alford
4. *The New Roget's Thesaurus in Dictionary Form*
5. *Plants for Kids to Grow Indoors* by Adele Millard

B Using Reference Works Look at these sources of information. Then read each question or statement. Number your paper from 1 to 7. Next to each number, write down the reference source or sources you might use to find information.

the card catalog	the vertical file	an atlas
the almanac or yearbook	an encyclopedia	

1. What is the population of Austin, Texas?
2. Name a recent book about lasers.
3. Who is the mayor of Denver, Colorado?
4. What were some of the causes of the Civil War?
5. Where would you find pamphlets on bicycle safety?
6. How does a Wankel engine work?
7. Where is the island of Madagascar?

C Using Graphic Aids Study the following illustration. Then write two note cards based on the information given.

Twig

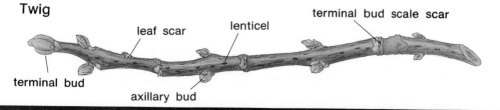

terminal bud scale scar

leaf scar

lenticel

terminal bud

axillary bud

15

Using the Dictionary and Thesaurus

Have you ever done something that required careful, precise work such as putting together a complex model or creating an intricate design like the one pictured above? What special tools did you use as you worked?

The carving above, called *scrimshaw*, was first done by Native American whale hunters. Working on a small piece of whalebone or whale ivory, the scrimshaw artist carefully carved each line using a variety of specialized tools.

As a writer you must be as precise as a scrimshaw carver. You must choose words carefully, and you must learn to use the writer's tools—a dictionary and a thesaurus. These tools will help you find specific words that express your precise meaning.

1
Locating the Word You Need

Focus The words in a dictionary are always arranged in alphabetical order.

It is easy to use a dictionary because the words are always arranged in alphabetical order. This helps you quickly locate the information you need.

Using Alphabetical Order

The words listed on a dictionary page are called **entry words**. The entry words are usually listed in two columns in alphabetical order. The first words in a dictionary begin with *a*. The last ones begin with *z*.

Two words may begin with the same letter. When that happens, they are alphabetized by the second letter. *Pinto* comes before *punt* because *i* comes before *u*. Many words have the same first and second letters. Then the words are alphabetized by the third letter. For example, *dormouse* comes before *double* because *r* comes before *u*. This process can continue to the fourth and fifth letters and even beyond.

Here are some groups of words that are arranged in alphabetical order.

1	2	3	4
amateur	sacred	channel	interchange
bridge	scallop	check	interfere
corner	seal	cheese	intermediate
nighthawk	shadow	chickadee	intern
shiver	silence	chimney	international
unicorn	slash	chowder	interoffice
visor	somber	church	interruption
X-ray	strange	churn	intersection

Exercises Using Alphabetical Order

A Below are three columns of words in alphabetical order. Insert the additional words in the correct place in each column. Then rewrite the new columns.

1	**2**	**3**
magic	plateau	skycap
magnify	platypus	skydiver
mockingbird	pleats	skylight
mosquito	plenty	skywrite

Additional Words

1. Merlin, math, mustang, moss, meteor
2. plastic, plywood, pledge, plunge, platform
3. skylark, skyrocket, skyward, skywalk, skyline

B Create your own mini-dictionary of words you learn in science. Collect about ten terms. List them in alphabetical order. Use a dictionary and give a short definition for each term. Here are a few to get you started.

albumen	The white of an egg
biology	The study of living things
cell	The simplest unit in the structure of living matter

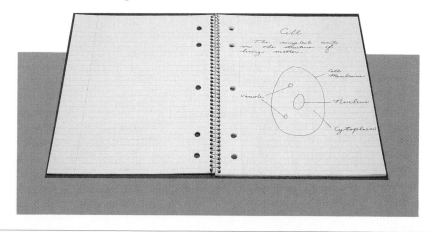

2
Using Guide Words

Focus *Guide words* tell the first and last entry words on a dictionary page. Guide words are printed in heavy black type at the top of the page.

Look at the sample dictionary page on page 265. Look at the two words printed in heavy black print at the top of each column. These words are called guide words. **Guide words** help you quickly locate the correct page with the entry word and information you need.

The guide word on the left tells you the first entry word on the page. The guide word on the right tells you the last entry word on the page. The guide words on page 265 are *pliers* and *plumate*. Now look at the word entries on that page. The word *pliers* is the first entry on the page. The word *plumate* is the last entry on that page. All of the other entry words fall between *pliers* and *plumate*.

Dictionaries can straighten out a jumble of words like this.

Premiere, Stuart Davis, 1957.

pli·ers (plī′ərz) *n.pl.* [< PLY¹] small pincers for gripping small objects, bending wire, etc.

plight¹ (plīt) *n.* [< Anglo-Fr. *plit,* for OFr. *pleit,* a fold] a condition or state of affairs; esp., an awkward, sad, or dangerous situation [the *plight* of the men trapped in the mine]

plight² (plīt) *vt.* [OE. *plihtan,* to pledge < *pliht,* danger] to pledge or promise, or bind by a pledge —**plight one's troth** to make a promise of marriage

Plim·soll mark (or **line**) (plim′səl, -säl, -sôl) [after S. *Plimsoll* (1824–98), Eng. statesman] a line or set of lines on the outside of merchant ships, showing the water level to which they may legally be loaded

☆**plink** (pliŋk) *n.* [echoic] a light, sharp, ringing or clinking sound —*vt., vi.* **1.** to make such sounds on (a piano, banjo, etc.) **2.** to shoot at (tin cans, etc.)

plinth (plinth) *n.* [< L. < Gr. *plinthos,* a brick, tile] **1.** the square block at the base of a column, pedestal, etc. **2.** the base on which a statue rests

Plin·y (plin′ē) **1.** (L. name *Gaius Plinius Secundus*) 23–79 A.D.; Rom. naturalist & writer: called *the Elder* **2.** (L. name *Gaius Plinius Caecilius Secundus*) 62?–113? A.D.; Rom. writer & statesman: called *the Younger:* nephew of *Pliny the Elder*

Pli·o·cene (plī′ə sēn′) *adj.* [< Gr. *pleōn,* more + *kainos,* new] designating or of the last epoch of the Tertiary Period in the Cenozoic Era —**the Pliocene** the Pliocene Epoch or its rocks: see GEOLOGIC TIME CHART

☆**Pli·o·film** (plī′ə film′) [< PLIABLE + FILM] *a trademark for* a sheeting of rubber hydrochloride used for raincoats, as a covering for packages, etc.

plis·sé, plis·se (pli sā′) *n.* [< Fr. < pp. of *plisser,* to pleat] **1.** a crinkled finish given to cotton, nylon, etc. with a caustic soda solution **2.** a fabric with this finish

plod (pläd) *vi.* **plod′ded, plod′ding** [prob. echoic] **1.** to walk or move heavily and with effort; trudge [the old horse *plodded* along the street] **2.** to work steadily and monotonously; drudge [to *plod* away at one's work] —*n.* **1.** the act of plodding **2.** the sound of a heavy step —**plod′der** *n.* —**plod′ding·ly** *adv.*

-ploid (ploid) [< Gr. *-ploos,* -fold + -OID] *a combining form* meaning of or being a (specified) multiple of the basic (haploid) number of chromosomes characteristic of a group of related organisms [diploid]

plonk (pläŋk, pluŋk) *n., vt., vi., n. same as* PLUNK

plop (pläp) *vt., vi.* **plopped, plop′ping** [echoic] **1.** to drop with a sound like that of something flat falling into water **2.** to drop heavily —*n.* the act of plopping or the sound made by this —*adv.* with a plop

plo·sive (plō′siv) *adj.* [< (EX)PLOSIVE] *Phonet.* produced by stopping and then suddenly releasing the breath, as the sounds of *k, p,* and *t* when used at the beginning of words —*n.* a plosive sound

plot (plät) *n.* [OE., a piece of land] **1.** a small area of ground [a garden *plot*] **2.** a chart or diagram, as of a building or estate **3.** a secret, usually evil, scheme **4.** the plan of action of a play, novel, etc. —*v.* **plot′ted, plot′ting 1.** *a)* to draw a plan of (a ship's course, etc.) *b)* to mark the position or course of on a map **2.** to make secret plans [to *plot* a robbery] **3.** to plan the action of (a story, etc.) **4.** *a)* to determine the location of (a point) on a graph by means of coordinates *b)* to represent (an equation) by joining points on a graph to form a curve **5.** to plan together secretly; scheme [to *plot* against the king] —**plot′less** *adj.* —**plot′less·ness** *n.* —**plot′ter** *n.*

SYN.—**plot** is used of a secret, usually evil, project or scheme the details of which have been carefully worked out [a *plot* to keep him from getting his inheritance]; **intrigue,** implying more complicated scheming, suggests hidden, underhanded dealing often of an illegal nature [the *intrigues* of the royal court]; **machination** emphasizes trickery and slyness in forming plots intended to harm someone [the *machinations* of the villain]; **conspiracy** suggests a plot in which a number of people plan and act together secretly for an unlawful or harmful purpose [a *conspiracy* to seize the throne]; **cabal** suggests a small group of persons involved in a political intrigue

plough (plou) *n., vt., vi. chiefly Brit. sp. of* PLOW

A　　B　　C
PLIERS
(A, slip joint; B, needle nose; C, arc joint)

plov·er (pluv′ər, plō′vər) *n., pl.* **plov′ers, plov′er:** see PLURAL, II, D, I [< OFr., ult. < L. *pluvia,* rain] a shore bird with a short tail, long, pointed wings, and a short beak

plow (plou) *n.* [ME. *ploh* < Late OE.] **1.** a farm implement used to cut and turn up the soil ☆**2.** anything like this; specif., a SNOW-PLOW —*vt.* **1.** to cut and turn up (soil) with a plow **2.** to make furrows in with or as with a plow **3.** to make as if by plowing [he *plowed* his way through the crowd] **4.** to cut a way through (water) —*vi.* **1.** to use a plow in tilling the soil **2.** to cut a way (*through* water, etc.) **3.** to go forward with effort; plod **4.** to begin work vigorously (with *into*) **5.** to strike against forcefully (with *into*) —**plow back** to reinvest (profits) in the same business enterprise —**plow up 1.** to remove with a plow **2.** to till (soil) thoroughly —**plow′a·ble** *adj.* —**plow′er** *n.*

PLOVER
(to 11 in. high)

plow·boy (plou′boi′) *n.* **1.** formerly, a boy who led a team of horses drawing a plow **2.** a country boy

plow·man (plou′mən) *n., pl.* **-men 1.** a man who guides a plow **2.** a farm worker

plow·share (-sher′) *n.* the share, or cutting blade, of a moldboard plow

ploy (ploi) *n.* [? < (EM)PLOY] an action or maneuver intended to outwit or confuse another person in order to get the better of him

pluck (pluk) *vt.* [OE. *pluccian:* for IE. base see PILE²] **1.** to pull off or out; pick [to *pluck* an apple from a tree] **2.** to drag or snatch [he *plucked* a burning stick from the fire] **3.** to pull feathers or hair from [to *pluck* a chicken, *pluck* eyebrows] **4.** to pull at (the strings of a musical instrument) and release quickly to sound tones [Slang] **5.** to rob or swindle —*vi.* **1.** to pull; tug; snatch (often with *at*) [he *plucked* at his long mustache] **2.** to pluck a musical instrument —*n.* **1.** a pulling; tug **2.** courage to meet danger or difficulty; fortitude —**pluck up** to stir up one's (courage); take heart —**pluck′er** *n.*

pluck·y (pluk′ē) *adj.* **pluck′i·er, pluck′i·est** brave, spirited; determined —see SYN. at BRAVE —**pluck′i·ly** *adv.* —**pluck′i·ness** *n.*

plug (plug) *n.* [MDu. *plugge*] **1.** an object used to stop up a hole, drain, etc. **2.** *a)* a cake of pressed tobacco *b)* a piece of chewing tobacco **3.** a device, as with prongs that stick out, for fitting into an electric outlet, etc. to make electrical contact **4.** *same as: a)* SPARK PLUG *b)* FIREPLUG **5.** [Colloq.] a defective or obsoworn article ☆**6.** [Slang] an old, worn-out horse ☆**7.** [Colloq.] a boost, advertisement, etc., esp. one slipped into the entertainment part of a radio or TV program, a magazine article, etc. —*vt.* **plugged, plug′ging 1.** to stop up (a hole, etc.) with a plug (often with *up*) **2.** to insert (something) as a plug [he *plugged* the putty in the hole] ☆**3.** [Colloq.] *a)* to promote (a song) by frequent performance ☆*b)* to promote with a plug (*n.* 7) **4.** [Slang] to shoot a bullet into —*vi.* [Colloq.] to work or study hard and steadily; plod —**plug in** to connect (an electrical device) with an outlet, etc. by inserting a plug in a socket or jack —**plug′ger** *n.*

☆**plug hat** [Old Slang] a man's high silk hat

☆**plug·o·la** (plug′ō lə) *n.* [PLUG, *n.* 7 + (PAY)OLA] [Slang] the paying of a bribe, or a bribe paid, for the dishonest promotion of something or someone on radio or TV

☆**plug-ug·ly** (-ug′lē) *n., pl.* **-lies** [Old Slang] a ruffian or gangster

plum (plum) *n.* [OE. *plume*] **1.** *a)* any of various small trees bearing a smooth-skinned fruit with a flattened stone *b)* the fruit eaten as food **2.** a raisin, when used in pudding or cake [plum pudding] **3.** the dark bluish-red or reddish-purple color of some plums **4.** something excellent or desirable [the new contract is a rich *plum* for the company]

plum·age (plōō′mij) *n.* [MFr. < L. *pluma,* a feather] a bird's feathers

plu·mate (-māt, -mit) *adj.* [< L. *pluma,* a feather] *Zool.* resembling a feather, esp. in structure

fat, āpe, cär; ten, ēven; is, bīte; gō, hôrn, tōōl, lŏŏk; oil, out; up, fʉr; get; joy; yet; chin; she; thin, then; zh, leisure; ŋ, ring; ə for *a* in *ago, e* in *agent, i* in *sanity, o* in *comply, u* in *focus;* ' as in *able* (ā′b'l); Fr. bàl; ë, Fr. coeur; ö, Fr. feu; Fr. mon; ô, Fr. coq; ü, Fr. duc; r, Fr. cri; H, G. ich; kh, G. doch; ‡foreign; ☆ Americanism; < derived from. See inside front cover.

Exercises Using Guide Words

A Number your paper from 1 to 10. In the list below are ten sets of guide words. After each set of guide words is another word. Decide whether you would find that word on a page before the guide words, on the page with the guide words, or on a page after the guide words. Write *Before, With,* or *After* beside each number on your paper. Look at this example.

Guide Words		**Other Word**
obtain	ocean	occupant

Since the word *occupant* comes between *obtain* and *ocean* in the alphabet, you would find *occupant* on the page with the guide words *obtain* and *ocean*. *With* is the correct answer.

Guide Words		**Other Word**
1. rap	rat	rant
2. steep	step	stereo
3. enlist	enter	enough
4. jubilee	jukebox	judge
5. nip	noble	nobleman
6. cafeteria	calcium	cafe
7. diffuse	dilemma	diminish
8. grew	gripe	grief
9. preservative	presume	present
10. self-reliant	Seminole	spinet

B Remember that the purpose of guide words is to help you find words more quickly. Find the following words in a dictionary. Copy the guide words from the page where you find each word.

1. ladybug
2. kiwi
3. pheasant
4. goat
5. iguana

6. millipede
7. falcon
8. sailfish
9. trawler
10. gazelle

11. narwhal
12. lamprey
13. snake
14. bat
15. cricket

Kiwi.

3

The Parts of a Dictionary Entry

Focus The information a dictionary gives about a word is called the *entry*. The entry may contain several parts.

You can learn a great deal about a word from reading the entry. Look at the information in an entry for the word *plot*.

plot (plät) *n.* [OE., a piece of land] **1.** a small area of ground *[a garden plot]* **2.** a chart or diagram, as of a building or estate. **3.** a secret, usually evil, scheme **4.** the plan of action of a play, novel, etc.—***vt.* plot'ted, plot'ting 1.** *a)* to draw a plan of (a ship's course, etc.) *b)* to mark the position or course of on a map **2.** to make secret plans for *[to plot a robbery]* **3.** to plan the action of (a story, etc.) **4.** *a)* to determine the location of (a point) on a graph by means of coordinates *b)* to represent (an equation) by joining points on a graph to form a curve —***vi.*** to plan together secretly; scheme *[to plot against the king]*—**plot'less *adj.*** —**plot'less · ness** *n.*—**plot'ter** *n.*

Entry Word

The first part of an entry is the entry word. In most dictionaries, it is divided into syllables by a space or a centered dot. For example, the word *pliers* would be printed like this: **pli·ers**.

Pronunciation

The next part of an entry is the pronunciation. In most dictionaries, the pronunciation is printed in parentheses. When you pronounce a two-syllable word, one syllable gets a stronger emphasis than the other. The emphasis is shown in a dictionary by using accent marks (′).

pli·ers (plī′ərz)　　**plum·age** (plo̅o̅′mij)

Notice that in some pronunciations, the words are respelled. This kind of spelling is a way of showing the sounds in the word. In the word *plot,* the letter *o* has the short *o* sound as in the words *hot* and *top*. The dictionary shows this sound as *ä*. At the bottom of the right-hand pages of most dictionaries there is a **pronunciation key**. This explains the sound of each letter in the respellings.

Part of Speech

After the pronunciation, the dictionary gives the part of speech. Most dictionaries use these abbreviations.

n. = noun	**adv.** = adverb
v. = verb	**prep.** = preposition
adj. = adjective	**conj.** = conjunction
pro. = pronoun	**interj.** = interjection

Some words may be used as more than one part of speech. Each part of speech is followed by the appropriate definition. The word *plot* is defined as a noun **(n.)**, then as a verb **(v.)**.

Word Origin

Next comes the origin of the word. This tells what language first used the word and what the word originally meant. **OE.** in the entry for *plot* on page 267 stands for Old English. The dictionary contains a list of the abbreviations used and tells what each one means.

Definition

The definition is an explanation of the meaning of a word. Many words have more than one meaning. Each definition is numbered. A definition may be followed by an example of the way a word is used, shown in brackets.

Synonyms

A list of synonyms is found in some dictionaries. The list is usually found at the end of an entry. It can help you choose words that will make your writing more precise.

> **SYN.—plot** is used of a secret, usually evil, project or scheme the details of which have been carefully worked out *[a plot* to keep her from getting her inheritance]; **intrigue,** implying more complicated scheming, suggests hidden, underhanded dealing often of an illegal nature *[the intrigues* of the royal court]; **machination** emphasizes trickery and slyness in forming plots intended to harm someone *[the machinations* of the villain]; **conspiracy** suggests a plot in which a number of people plan and act together secretly for an unlawful or harmful purpose *[a conspiracy* to seize the throne]; **cabal** suggests a small group of persons involved in a political intrigue

Exercises Using the Dictionary Entry

A Use the sample dictionary page on page 265 to answer the following questions.

1. From what language did the word *plissé* come? What does the word mean?
2. Divide the word *plumate* into syllables.
3. Write a synonym for *plot* that means "a group of people working together secretly."
4. What parts of speech can the word *plod* be?
5. What do the words *plough* and *plow* have in common?
6. Who was Pliny the Elder?
7. Which entry word is plural?
8. Which word has the same meaning as *plunk*?

B Use your dictionary to learn how each of the following words is pronounced. Be prepared to pronounce each one in class. Then write a definition for each word and its part of speech.

    xenon   psyche   gnu   err   pneumatic

4

Multiple Meanings

Focus A dictionary may list several meanings for an entry word.

Information about the meanings of a word makes up the largest part of a dictionary entry. Many English words have more than one meaning, such as the word *dip*, used in the cartoon on this page. When you look up a word, you have to choose a meaning that matches how the word is being used.

Look up the word *go* in your dictionary. How many definitions are given for it? The Student Edition of *Webster's New World Dictionary of the American Language* gives forty definitions for this one word!

Look at the definitions for the word *dip* on page 271. Notice that each definition is numbered. Notice also that for some of the definitions there is a sentence or phrase given as an example. These examples show how the word is used for a particular definition. Sometimes these examples are as much help to you as the definitions themselves.

In each of the following sentences, the word *dip* has a different meaning. Can you find the definition on page 271 that matches each use?

My parents had my baby shoes *dipped* in bronze.
The plane *dipped* suddenly during the flight.
Dad loves butterscotch *dip* on ice cream.

Exercise Using the Multiple Meanings of a Word

Use the following dictionary entry for the word *dip*. Write the definition that fits the use of the word *dip* in each sentence at the bottom of the page. Choose from the first seven definitions and the last ten definitions in the entry.

dip (dip) *vt.* **dipped, dip'ping** [OE. *dyppan:* for IE. base see DEEP] **1.** to put into liquid for a moment and then quickly take out **2.** to dye in this way **3.** to baptize by immersion **4.** to bathe and clean (sheep or hogs) in disinfectant **5.** to make (a candle) by putting a wick repeatedly in melted tallow or wax **6.** to take out as by scooping up with a container, the hand, etc. **7.** to lower and immediately raise again [*dip* the flag in salute] —*vi.* **1.** to go down as into a liquid and quickly come up again **2.** to sink or seem to sink suddenly [the sun *dips* into the ocean] **3.** to undergo a slight decline [sales *dipped* in May] **4.** to slope downward, as a road **5.** to lower a container, the hand, etc. into liquid, a receptacle, etc., esp. in order to take something out: often used as a figure of speech [to *dip* into one's savings] **6.** to read or study casually or superficially (with *into*) [to *dip* into a book] **7.** *Aeron.* to drop suddenly before climbing —*n.* **1.** a dipping or being dipped **2.** *a)* a brief plunge into a liquid *b)* a brief swim **3.** a liquid into which something is dipped, as for dyeing **4.** whatever is removed by dipping **5.** a candle made by dipping **6.** *a)* a downward slope or inclination or a deviation *b)* the amount of this **7.** a slight hollow **8.** a short downward plunge, as of an airplane **9.** *a)* a sweet liquid sauce for desserts ☆*b)* a thick, creamy sauce into which one dips crackers or other appetizers **10.** [Slang] a pickpocket

1. The color guard *dipped* the flag as they passed us.
2. Our scout troop *dipped* candles by hand.
3. The two ranch hands *dipped* the ewes before the lambs.
4. The frozen yogurt cone was covered with delicious raspberry *dip*.
5. The traveler *dipped* out three ladles of water from the well.
6. There is a slight *dip* in the road at the crossing.
7. Our kite *dipped* sharply and snagged in a tree.
8. Mom's dill *dip* is great on vegetables.
9. We took a *dip* in the ocean before dinner.
10. A *dip* can snatch your wallet without your knowing it.

5
Using a Thesaurus

> **Focus** A *thesaurus* is a book of synonyms and antonyms. *Synonyms* are words with similar meanings. *Antonyms* are words with opposite meanings.

Writers find that the thesaurus is a helpful reference book. It lists commonly used words and some synonyms and antonyms for these words. A thesaurus can help a writer find lively and specific words to replace words that are dull or general.

Some thesauruses are arranged alphabetically. Others have an index you must use to locate a word. The index contains a listing of all the words and synonyms in the thesaurus and the location of each word. For example, if you look up the word *tiny* in a thesaurus index, you will see that you can find that word in the entries for *little* and *small*.

Read this sentence.

The chef cooked the muffins.

Cook is a very general word that means to "to prepare food." If a writer wished to replace *cook* with a more specific verb, the thesaurus would be helpful. Read this sample thesaurus entry for the word *cook*.

> *V.* **cook,** boil, coddle, parboil, steam, precook, poach, scald; heat, warm, prepare, fix *(colloq.)*; broil, sizzle, barbecue, grill, fry, frizzle, brown, braise, griddle, roast, rotisserie, sauté, pan-fry, sear, stew, simmer, fricassee, bake, escallop, pressure-cook, autoclave.
> *Adj.* **cooked,** boiled, etc. (see *Verbs*); well-cooked, well-done; overcooked, overdone; undercooked, underdone, rare; uncooked, raw; underbaked, half-baked, doughy.
> [*pert. to cooking*] culinary.
> See also **CONTAINER, FIRE, FOOD, HEAT.**

Try substituting *bake* for *cook*.

The chef baked the muffins.

The word *baked* tells exactly how the muffins were cooked. *Baked* is more specific than *cooked*.

Choose synonyms carefully when you use a thesaurus. Synonyms are similar in meaning, but they are not exactly the same. Sometimes a synonym will not fit the situation. Check a dictionary to see if *poached* is used correctly in this sentence.

The chef *poached* the steak.

Poach means to cook in a simmering liquid such as water. *Poach* does mean "to cook," but it would not be a good choice in this sentence because steak is not cooked in liquid.

When you see a thesaurus, be careful to look up the correct part of speech. For example, *cooked* was used as a verb in the sample sentence. Look again at the sample thesaurus entry. *Cooked* can also be an adjective. Choose the synonym that is the same part of speech as the word it replaces.

Note that there is a thesaurus in this book on pages 574–588. It is arranged a bit differently than the ones described. It provides extra help for student writers. The introduction on pages 574–575 will tell you how to use this special thesaurus.

Exercise Using a Thesaurus

Look up each word in italics in the special thesaurus on pages 574–588. Rewrite the sentences using suitable synonyms.

1. Mr. Barclay *asked* about job openings at the new computer factory.
2. Jenny *broke* her glasses playing touch football.
3. The candidate *ended* his speech with a reminder to vote.
4. Julie *saw* a cave deep in the woods.
5. A *group* of birds was attracted by the birdfeeders.

English and Sports

Sports such as football and soccer burst with action and excitement. That is why sports reporters and writers look for verbs that will keep their writing especially active. For example, a reporter would not write, "The Celtics defeated the Hawks with a score of 90 to 49." Instead, the line might read, "The Celtics destroyed the Hawks with a score of 90—49."

Often, you will want to write about or tell about an exciting game you saw. Always imagine that you, too, are a reporter. Look for words that will re-create the game for others.

Activity

Use a dictionary and a thesaurus to rewrite the following article. Replace commonplace words with active, lively words. Take special care with verbs. Make the reader see what is happening.

Rockets Beat Lions

The Rockets won their second game this season. They beat the Lions 24–8 Tuesday on the home court.

Rich Rupeg led the offense with twelve points. Rich made four baskets in four tries in the first half. Jon Greeb helped the offense by making five points.

In the second half, the Lions fought back. Kurt Wolf ran down the court and made a spectacular shot. Berg, Herbeth, and Beck all scored, too.

The effort was too late. The Rockets scored and held the lead. The crowd cheered as the winning basket lit up the scoreboard.

Application and Review

A Using Guide Words Below are the guide words for ten dictionary pages. Number your paper from 1 to 10. Beside each number, write a word that you would find on the dictionary page having those guide words.

1. anther   antidote
2. drill   drop
3. fisher   fix
4. immune   impel
5. matted   maximum

6. one   ooze
7. prize   procession
8. rondo   rose
9. stir   stock
10. vanilla   various

B The Multiple Meanings of a Word Read the sentences below. Each of the italicized words is used in an unusual way. Use your dictionary to find the meanings.

1. My mother allowed me to get a *hunch* of pineapple.
2. Men and women have not worn *ruffs* since the seventeenth century.
3. Aaron is Lauren's *spark*.
4. He tried to *cow* us by telling a scary story.
5. The movie cameraman *panned* the crowd.
6. Because the ship was always *listing*, many of the passengers were sick.
7. In the attic was an old *fell* rug.
8. John used a *spinner* to catch that large bass.
9. Lynn's piano teacher told Lynn to count out each *rest*.
10. In the spring Frank bought a *flat* of tomatoes.

C Using the Thesaurus Look in the thesaurus on pages 574–588 to find a synonym for each of the following words. Select three synonyms for each word. Using the words correctly, write a sentence with each synonym.

1. quiet   2. bad   3. walk   4. terrific   5. important

16
Study and Test-Taking Skills

You have planned and practiced your part in a skit. You have studied and memorized your script. Now it is time to leave the script behind. You know you will do well because you have mastered your material. Good study and test-taking skills will give you the same kind of confidence when you are doing class assignments or taking tests.

In this chapter you will learn to manage class assignments, to skim and scan, and to use the SQ3R study method. You will learn how to use the parts of a book and how to memorize. Finally, you will learn how to prepare for and take tests and how to master different types of test questions.

1
Managing Assignments

> ***Focus*** To complete an assignment, you must first understand it. Then plan your time to finish it at home.

To complete projects successfully, develop a plan. Follow the steps below to develop a plan for managing assignments.

Understand the Assignment

To complete any assignment successfully, you must first understand exactly what you are expected to do. You must be able to answer four key questions.

1. **What type of assignment is it?** Must you draw a diagram, answer questions, or write a composition?
2. **What should the final product be?** Should it be a report, a skit, answered questions, or a completed worksheet?
3. **What materials are needed?** Do you need textbooks, a notebook, tools, or art supplies? Will you need to visit the library or some other resource center to gather material or further information?
4. **When is the assignment due?** Is the work due the next day? Is it due next week? Can you complete it in stages?

Record the Assignment

Once you understand the assignment, write it in a special section of your notebook or in a separate assignment notebook. Record these details.

1. The subject or class
2. The exact assignment, including special instructions
3. The date the assignment is given
4. The date the assignment is due

Set Goals

In order to complete an assignment by its due date, you must learn to plan your study time wisely. The first step in planning is learning how to manage both long- and short-term assignments.

A **short-term assignment** can be completed in one study session. Reading a poem, working several math problems, and reading a social studies assignment are short-term projects.

Long-term assignments require several days or weeks to complete. They must be broken into smaller tasks, each of which can be completed in one session. Writing a computer program or a three-page paper on a poet are long-term projects.

Make a Study Plan

A study plan is a tool for planning your study time. It is especially helpful to have a study plan for long-term projects.

To make a study plan, draw seven columns on a large piece of paper, one for each day of the week. First, put on the chart activities that have already been planned. Sports practices and recreation activities should be included. Daily homework and household chores should also be listed.

Next, take the long-term project and divide it into smaller, manageable parts.

The study plan below was made by a student who had one week to complete a science project. Notice how this long-term assignment was broken down into several manageable tasks.

Monday	Tuesday	Wednesday	Thursday	Friday	Saturday	Sunday
After school go to library for books. Take notes	Piano Lesson 3:30	Practice piano 4:30-5:30 4:00 Dentist			Clean porch J.J.'s party 1:00-4:00	Dinner at Grandma's Make final copy
Homework- 6:30-7:30	Take notes	Organize notes	First draft	Help decorate for J.J.'s party	Revise first draft	Homework 6:30-7:30

Exercises Managing Assignments

A Imagine that your teacher has given you the following assignments. Read each assignment carefully. Then divide your paper into four columns: *Subject, Assignment, Date Given,* and *Date Due.* The *Assignment* column should be wider than the others. Write the information for each assignment as you would record it in an assignment notebook.

1. "Here is a worksheet that will test your skill at multiplying fractions. The worksheet gives directions for making invisible ink. It lists how much of each ingredient you need. Next to the list, write the amount of each ingredient you need to make half the basic recipe. Then list the amount of each ingredient needed for one and a half times the recipe. Today is Wednesday. Have the worksheet finished by Friday."

2. "Today you studied the importance of colorful, precise verbs. For homework, look for lively verbs in newspaper headlines. Copy each headline and underline the verb. You should find at least ten examples. This assignment is due tomorrow."

Flying Saucer Descends at State Fair: Aliens Crave Lemonade

Bulls Lasso Cowboys

Gymnast Vaults Through Roof

Midgets Trounce Giants

B Make a one-week study plan that includes the completion of a long-term project. Choose a long-term project that has been assigned in one of your classes, or pretend that you have been assigned a particular long-term project. Your study plan should include your daily chores, homework, and any other planned activities. Then break down the long-term project into smaller tasks, and assign them specific time slots. Your study plan should be similar to the model plan on page 279.

2
Skimming and Scanning

Focus *Skimming* and *scanning* are important reading and study skills.

Usually you read books and assignments word for word. Sometimes, however, you need to read quickly to find certain types of information. **Skimming** and **scanning** are two types of reading that help you gather information quickly.

Skimming

Skimming is one type of fast reading. Use skimming to get a general idea of what a book, chapter, or article is about. To skim, let your eyes travel quickly down the page. Do not try to read every word. When you skim, pay special attention to the following items.

titles	key words	pictures and captions
headings	topic sentences	charts and graphs

Scanning

Scanning is also a type of fast reading. It is used to find specific information. To scan, quickly glance down the page. Keep reading in this way until you notice key words and phrases that show you are near the information you need. Then slow down and read more carefully.

To understand the importance of scanning, imagine how difficult it would be to find a number in the phone book if you had to read every name! Suppose you had to find out the year in which Abraham Lincoln became a lawyer. How long would it take to find the information if you had to read an entire encyclopedia article? Scanning would help you complete both tasks quickly.

Exercises Practicing Skimming and Scanning

A Skim the article below in Exercise B. What is it about?

B Scan the article. Write the answers to these questions.

1. What is a thermostat?
2. Where does Freon go after it leaves the compressor?
3. Is Freon a gas or a liquid at the end of the cooling cycle?

Freon and the Cooling Process

The cooling process of a refrigerator takes place in a cycle.

Stage 1—The cooling cycle begins when the **thermostat,** the temperature regulator, signals that the refrigerator is too warm. The signal starts the pump, which pushes a coolant, liquid **Freon,** at a high pressure through a small hole in a long tube.

Stage 2—After the liquid has passed through the small hole into the **evaporator coils,** it is no longer under pressure. Therefore, the Freon evaporates and becomes a gas. As it evaporates, the Freon absorbs heat from the refrigerator.

Stage 3—Next, the Freon travels to the **compressor,** which forces the Freon under pressure into the **condenser coils**. In these coils, the Freon changes back into a liquid and releases heat into the air outside the refrigerator. The cooling cycle is now complete.

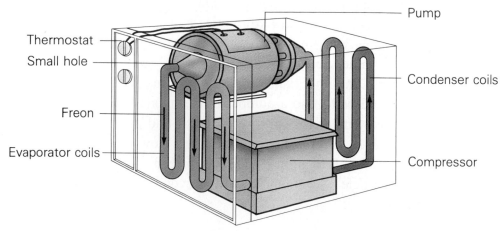

Thermostat

Small hole

Freon

Evaporator coils

Pump

Condenser coils

Compressor

3
Using the SQ3R Method

Focus Use the *SQ3R study method* to discover, understand, and remember important information.

For most of your assignments, you need to read and study written information. One way to help yourself learn the material is to use a study method called the **SQ3R method**. SQ3R stands for the five steps of the method: *Survey, Question, Read, Record,* and *Review*.

The SQ3R Study Method

Survey Quickly look over the material to get a general idea of the contents. Read the titles and subtitles. Look at any pictures, maps, tables, or graphs. Read the introduction or the first few paragraphs and the final paragraph.

Question Look at any study questions presented at the end of the material or given to you by your teacher. These questions will help you pick out information as you read.

Read Read the selection carefully. Identify the main ideas in each section. Look for answers to the study questions.

Record After reading, write the answers to the questions. Make brief notes to help you remember the answers and any other important ideas.

Review Read the questions again. Try to answer them without looking at your notes. If you can't, review the material to find the answers. Then study your notes so that you will be able to recall the information later.

The notes you take as you study should be in your own words. They should consist of key words and phrases that relate to main ideas. Notes need not be written in complete sentences, but they should be clear enough for you to understand later.

Keep your notes in a notebook with sections for each subject. Write the subject and the date at the top of each page of notes. Add other headings that will help you to locate your notes easily when you need to refer to them. These notes will provide you with a brief summary of everything you study. They can be used when you need to find information quickly or when you are reviewing for a test.

Exercise Using a Study Method

Read the article about roller skates, using the SQ3R method. Look at the review questions at the end of the article before you begin. They will help you study correctly. Answer the following questions when you have finished reading.

1. Where should you look for clues about the contents of the article? What clues do you find?
2. Take notes as you read each paragraph. What are the main ideas in the article?
3. Write the answers to the review questions on your paper.

Roller Skates

Joseph Merlin, a Belgian musician, invented the roller skate about 1760. James Plimpton, an American inventor, designed an improved roller skate in 1863. Plimpton's "rocking skate" enabled people to roller skate in a curve by simply leaning to one side. Skating in curves had previously been possible only on ice skates.

Most roller skates have two major parts, the *boot* and the *skate assembly*.

The Boot is made of leather. Boots worn for recreational and artistic skating have high tops and are

laced up the front to a point above the ankle. Speed skaters wear boots with low-cut tops. The boots of all roller skates should fit snugly and hug the heel firmly.

The Skate Assembly is a metal structure attached to the sole of the boot. The main parts of the assembly are the *plate,* two *truck assemblies,* the *toe stop,* and four wheels. The truck assemblies, which are mechanisms attached to the front and back of the plate, contain movable parts that enable skaters to turn corners. The toe stop is a device at the front of the skate that allows skaters to stop quickly and to perform maneuvers.

Two wheels are attached to axles at the front and two at the back of the skate. Early roller skate wheels were made of clay or wood. In the mid-1970's, roller skating was revolutionized by the introduction of wheels made of hard plastic called *polyurethane*. Such wheels are lighter and quieter than those made of clay or metal, and skaters can move faster on them. Polyurethane wheels also provide smoother, more comfortable skating.

Some people wear *clamp-on skates,* which are skate assemblies that they attach to their shoes.

From *The World Book Encyclopedia*

For Your Review

1. When was the first roller skate invented? One hundred years later, the design was improved. How?
2. What two parts make up most roller skates?
3. Why are polyurethane wheels superior to clay or metal wheels?

4

Using the Parts of a Book

Focus Use the parts of a book to find information quickly. In nonfiction books, the table of contents, the index, and the glossary are especially helpful.

Nonfiction books are useful when you are gathering information on a particular topic. However, there are many books on most topics. How can you find those that will be most useful to you? How can you quickly find information in the books you choose? There are three special parts of a book that can help you answer these questions: the **table of contents,** the **index,** and the **glossary**.

You will find a **table of contents** at the front of most nonfiction books. It lists the title of each chapter in the book and the page on which it begins. It may also list the main topics that each chapter discusses. Check to see whether the topic you are looking for is listed. Locate and study the table of contents in this book.

At the back of most nonfiction books, you will find an **index**. Every important topic that is discussed in the book is listed in alphabetical order in the index. Each topic is followed by the numbers of the pages on which it is discussed. Locate and study the index in this book.

The index is a good place to look for specific terms. Look for broader topics in the table of contents.

Another useful part of some nonfiction books is a **glossary**. A glossary lists difficult words in alphabetical order, and defines them according to the way they are used in the field discussed in that book. A glossary is especially handy in books that use many unfamiliar terms or familiar terms that are used in specialized ways. Frequently, difficult pronunciations are spelled out in a glossary.

Exercises Using Parts of the Book

A Look for each of these terms in the table of contents and the index of this book. Tell the part of the book that lists each term. Some terms can be found in both places. Some can be found in only one place.

1. suffixes
2. pronouns
3. card catalog
4. topic sentences
5. verbs
6. conjunctions
7. reference books
8. ZIP codes

B Look at the following table of contents. Then answer the questions below it.

Guide to Home Repair

1. Does this book give directions for building a go-cart?
2. In what chapter and part would you find information on a Phillips screwdriver?
3. What is a brad? Name two similar devices.
4. In what chapter and part would you find information on what type of stain to use on wood patio furniture?
5. Where would you find information on paint brushes?

5
Memorizing

Focus *Memorizing* is a skill that can be learned and improved with practice.

Memory makes it possible to learn information once, then recall and reuse it often. In school, you might memorize important dates in history, spelling words, or math formulas. At home, you might memorize a phone number or a recipe.

The first step in memorizing is to make sure you understand the material. If necessary, ask your teacher, a parent, or a friend to help you.

There are many ways to memorize. Try these methods to find which ones work best for you.

1. **Recite out loud.** If you read a list of words silently, you may remember several words. If you read the list out loud, you are likely to remember several more words. The sound of your own voice often helps you remember. Walking back and forth, or pacing, while reciting out loud may help you remember even better.

2. **Write the material.** Just as the sound of your voice can help you remember, the action of moving a pen or pencil on paper is a memory booster. Seeing what you have written also helps the material stay in your mind.

3. **Connect ideas.** It is easier to remember a list of facts if you can connect, or associate, them in some way. When you associate things, you think of some way they fit together. You might remember history dates by putting them in the order in which they happened. You might remember a list of vocabulary words by putting them in alphabetical order. A shopping list could be divided into categories: dairy products, fruits and vegetables, breads and cereals, and meat.

4. **Use memory games.** There are countless memory tricks and games that you may find helpful. Try visualizing what you want to remember. To visualize, close your eyes and picture the items you want to remember. Then, when you want to recall your list, visualize the same picture.

   Here is a popular game that uses letters rather than pictures to aid your memory. Take the first letter of each word you want to memorize. Then think of a phrase that uses each of those letters as a first letter of a word in the phrase. For example, the notes on the lines of a musical staff are *E, G, B, D,* and *F.* You might remember these notes on the lines of a staff by learning this phrase: "*Every Good Boy Does Fine.*"

5. **Repeat and review the material.** Repeat your list or memory game several times. Repeat it at different times of the day for several days until you can easily call it to mind.

Exercises Improving Memory Skills

A The following words name the parts of an octopus. Read the words out loud several times. Close your book. Then write as many words as you can remember.

trunk	skirt	eye
head	tentacles	siphon
suckers		

B Make a memory game that will help you remember the list of words in Exercise A. Can you write a sentence in which each word begins with the first letter of a word in the list? Write your sentence. Now can you recite the words in the list?

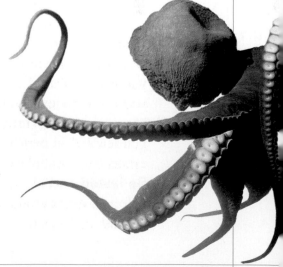

6

Preparing for and Taking Tests

> *Focus* Learning and using test-taking skills can help you improve your test results.

Knowing how to prepare for and take tests can improve your test scores. Use these guidelines to help you improve your test-taking skills.

Preparing for a Classroom Test

1. **Know what to study.** If you have questions about what the test will cover, ask your teacher before you begin to prepare. Focus your studying on the information the test will cover.
2. **Make a study plan.** Study on a daily basis. Do not wait until just before the test. Determine how much time you will need to prepare thoroughly for the test. Plan ahead for that time.
3. **Organize your study materials.** Keep a notebook. Organize lists of vocabulary and spelling words, completed assignments, and quizzes. These are your tools for review.
4. **Review.** Skim reading assignments and carefully reread class notes. Review the study questions and answers you wrote as you used the SQ3R study method. Complete and study any review guides or worksheets received in class.
5. **Memorize important facts.** Use the memorizing skills you learned in part 5 to remember important names, dates, events, or vocabulary terms. Have someone quiz you.
6. **Be rested and alert.** Plenty of sleep and good nutrition help you do your best. Now relax. You are ready to take the test.

Follow these guidelines for taking a test.

Taking a Classroom Test

1. **Skim the test.** Look at the length of the test and the types of questions. Plan your time accordingly.
2. **Read all directions before you begin.** Ask questions if you do not understand the directions. Follow directions exactly.
3. **Answer easy questions first.** Then go back to the longer or more difficult questions. Allow extra time for these.
4. **Review the test.** Look for missing answers, confusing answers, and messy handwriting. Make the necessary changes. Make sure all questions are answered.

Taking a Standardized Test

You have probably taken several standardized tests in the past few years. These tests compare your level of learning to that of other students. You cannot study for these tests. A good night's sleep before the test is the best preparation.

Most standardized tests measure the number of correct answers you write in a limited time period. If a question is very difficult and is taking too long, skip it and go to the next. If you finish the test early, return to the unanswered questions.

Follow directions carefully. Some standardized tests have sections on several subjects, such as reading comprehension, vocabulary, math, science, and social studies. Put your answers under the correct test heading on the answer sheet.

Exercise Preparing for and Taking a Test

Choose a test that you will be taking soon. Develop a study plan to prepare for this test. Use the guidelines on page 290 and the information on page 279 to write your plan. Prepare for this test by following your study plan. When you take the test, follow the guidelines at the top of this page.

7

Types of Test Questions

Focus There are many types of test questions. Know how to answer each kind.

Improve your test scores by learning how to master the different types of test questions.

1. **True-False** A true-false question is written as a statement. You must decide whether the statement is correct or incorrect. If *any part* of the statement is incorrect, the entire statement is false. Words such as *all, never, always,* and *none* are often found in false statements. Words such as *some, most, many,* and *usually* often signal true statements.

2. **Multiple Choice** A multiple choice question has three or more possible answers, usually identified with such small letters as *a, b, c.* Before answering, read all of the possible choices. Eliminate the incorrect choices. Then pick the best answer from those that remain. Pay special attention to choices such as *all of the above* and *none of the above.*

3. **Matching** In this exercise, you match numbered items in one column with lettered answers in another. You place the letter of the correct answer next to the question. In some cases, you will use a letter more than once.

4. **Fill-in-the-Blank** In this type of question, you add a missing word or words to a sentence. Sometimes you will be given a list of words to choose from. Remember to use proper capitalization and punctuation.

5. **Short Answer** Write your answer to this type of question in one or two sentences. Make sure sentences are complete. Use proper capitalization and punctuation.

6. **Essay** Most essay questions are answered in paragraph form. To organize your answer, follow a simple process of writing. Jot down ideas, organize the ideas in logical order, and write. Again, capitalize and punctuate correctly.

7. **Questions for Standardized Tests** Standardized tests are used to compare the progress of students in specific areas, such as school districts or states. Most standardized tests are multiple choice. To take these tests, follow the guidelines you learned for taking multiple choice tests. Standardized tests, as well as some classroom tests, may use separate answer sheets. To mark the correct answer, you fill in small circles, ovals, or squares with your pencil. You must mark answers carefully, because these answer sheets are read by machines. Fill in circles completely. Erase stray marks that may otherwise be read as an answer.

Exercise Understanding Different Types of Test Questions

Look carefully at the statement below. Then write four test questions based on that statement. Write one of each type: true-false, multiple choice, fill-in-the-blank, and short answer.

The deepest spot in the Atlantic Ocean is near Puerto Rico. It is 30,246 feet deep—almost six miles.

Crossroads

English and Math

You are now familiar with many different study skills. One of the most useful is the SQ3R study method. It will help you learn and understand many types of new materials.

You can create similar study methods for specific areas. One area where a study method might be especially helpful is math. Try the five steps of this study method to solve a word problem in math.

Survey	Read the math problem or word problem.
Question	Ask yourself these questions. "What do I have to find out?" "What information am I given?" "What process should I use to solve the problem?"
Compute	Work the math problem.
Record	Write the answer.
Review	Check over your work. Make sure that your answer is correct.

Activity

Use a study method to solve this word problem.

Ed's delivery truck can carry 2,700 pounds of produce. Ed is delivering pumpkins to several supermarkets. Each pumpkin weighs an average of 5 pounds. Approximately how many pumpkins can Ed's truck carry in one load?

Application and Review

A Mastering Study Skills Write the answers to the following "test" questions on your own paper. Then tell what type of question the items in each part are.

Part 1 Write *True* or *False* for each statement.

1. Short-term assignments can be completed in a few weeks.
2. To complete an assignment correctly, you must first understand the directions.
3. A study plan should allow time for your regular chores and activities.

Part 2 For each question, write the letter of the correct answer.

1. Which of the following is part of the SQ3R study method? _____
   a. Record   b. Repeat   c. Rest
2. What should class notes not contain? _____
   a. your own words   c. long detailed explanations
   b. key words and phrases

Part 3 Match the word in column 1 with its definition in column 2. Write the correct letter next to each number.

_____ 1. index   a. list of titles and subheadings
_____ 2. glossary   b. alphabetical listing of topics
_____ 3. table of   c. alphabetical list of terms
          contents   and definitions

B Using Memory Skills Try to make up two memory tricks to complete the following assignment. Describe each memory device in a paragraph.

> **Assignment** Memorize the names of the seven continents of the world: Asia, Europe, Antarctica, North America, Africa, Australia, and South America.

17

Writing Letters and Filling Out Forms

You are having a wonderful time on your vacation, but you miss your best friend. You promised to write, but you haven't had time. Then something *big* happens. You know you can't wait until you get home to tell this story! You get your pen and begin.

Everybody likes to get letters, even when they're not about such an unusual experience as the one pictured above. A letter from a friend can mean a lot, especially on a lonely day.

You will write friendly letters, social notes, and business letters throughout your life. This chapter will show you how to write clear and interesting letters about everything from a whale's tail to ordering tickets through the mail.

1
Writing a Friendly Letter

Focus A friendly letter is a way to share news.

When you have something to say to a friend, you can write a friendly letter. Your letter should sound natural, as if you were speaking to the person. Write about things that interest you and your friend. Share stories and experiences. Ask questions. Talk about your feelings. Use vivid details and strong verbs to make your descriptions come alive.

Read the following friendly letter. Notice the form and purpose of each part of the letter.

Heading

1201 West Leonard Street
Pensacola, Florida 32501
October 5, 19___

Salutation

Dear Miguel,

Body

Today our class went to a wooded area for a science lesson. We had to find specimens of different leaves. When I found some poison ivy, I thought of you right away! Remember when we went on that hike at camp and the poison ivy found you? Boy, did you itch!

Have you been doing a lot of skateboarding? We formed a neighborhood skateboarding team. You have much better hills in Georgia, so I bet you're really good.

Closing Your friend,

Signature Jerry

The Parts of a Friendly Letter

A friendly letter has five parts. Each part has its own purpose and form.

Part	Form	Purpose
Heading	The **heading** is written in the upper right-hand corner.	The **heading** tells where you are and when you are writing. It has three lines: house number and street name city, state, ZIP code month, day, year
Salutation or Greeting	The **salutation,** or **greeting,** is written on the line below the heading and begins at the left margin.	The **salutation,** or **greeting,** is the way you say "hello" to your friend. It can be casual, such as *Dear Mary, Hi,* or *Greetings.*
Body	The **body** begins on the line below the salutation.	The **body** of a letter is for talking to your friend.
Closing	The **closing** should line up with the first line of the heading.	The **closing** is a simple way of saying "goodbye," such as *Love, Sincerely,* or *Your friend.*
Signature	After the closing, skip a line. Your **signature** should line up with the first word in the closing.	In a friendly letter, only your first name is needed unless you don't know the person well.

Using Correct Capitalization and Punctuation

Using correct capitalization and punctuation will make your letter much easier for your friend to read. Review these rules.

Heading
1. Capitalize all proper names.
2. Place a comma between the name of the city and state.
3. Put the ZIP code after the state. No comma is needed between the state and the ZIP code.
4. Place a comma between the day and the year.

Salutation
5. Capitalize the first word and any proper nouns in the salutation.
6. Use a comma after the salutation.

Closing
7. Capitalize only the first word of the closing.
8. Use a comma after the closing.

Exercises Writing Friendly Letters

A Copy the following parts of a letter. Use correct capitalization and punctuation. Write the information on separate lines where necessary. Then label each part correctly.

1. 336 old mill road phoenix arizona 85040 august 7 19____
2. dear lorna jill
3. 852 main street mount prospect illinois 60056 june 3 19____
4. missing you tiffany
5. dear aunt lynn and uncle tom
6. sincerely yours jeff rodriguez

B Practice your letter-writing skills by writing to a pen pal. Request a pen pal from a pen pal organization. Your teacher can give you the names and addresses. In your letter, tell your age and a little about yourself. You may even be assigned a pen pal in a foreign country. When you send your first letter, write neatly. English may be a foreign language to your pen pal.

2
Writing Social Notes

Focus A social note can be a thank-you note, an invitation, or a note of acceptance or regret.

Social notes are a form of courtesy that people appreciate. A social note can be a thank-you note, an invitation, or a note of acceptance or regret. These notes have the same form as a friendly letter except that they are much shorter. Generally, social notes use only the date in the heading.

Writing a Thank-You Note

Here are some occasions that call for thank-you notes.

1. When you have received a gift
2. When someone has done you a special favor
3. When you have spent the weekend at someone's house

A Sample Thank-You Note

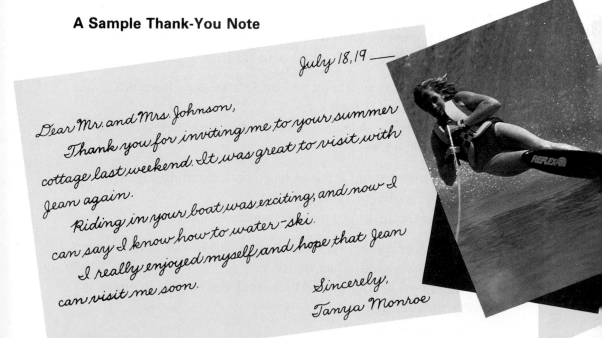

July 18, 19 —

Dear Mr. and Mrs. Johnson,
Thank you for inviting me to your summer cottage last weekend. It was great to visit with Jean again.
Riding in your boat was exciting, and now I can say I know how to water-ski.
I really enjoyed myself and hope that Jean can visit me soon.

Sincerely,
Tanya Monroe

Writing an Invitation

Everyone enjoys receiving an invitation. You write an invitation to ask someone to a party or special event. An invitation should contain a complete heading and this information:

1. Type of activity
2. Purpose of activity
3. Where the activity will take place
4. The day, date, and time of the activity
5. How the person should reply

Notes of Acceptance or Regret

Many invitations contain the letters *R.S.V.P.* near the end. This is an abbreviation for a French phrase that means "please respond." Respond to an invitation as soon as possible. Use the same form you use for a thank-you note. For notes of acceptance or regret, thank the person for the invitation.

Exercise Writing Social Notes

Choose one situation from each group—*A*, *B*, and *C*. Write the appropriate form of social note for each situation.

A 1. A note to your aunt and uncle after they have taken you on a tour of their city
2. A note to your grandmother after you have spent the weekend with her

B 1. A note asking a friend to go on a camping trip with you and your family
2. A note inviting a new classmate to a party

C 1. A note telling your cousin you will not be able to spend the weekend at her house
2. A note telling a friend you will not be able to attend a skating party

3
Writing Business Letters

Focus You can get information or order a product by writing a business letter.

A business letter is written for a specific purpose. It is used to request information or order materials. A business letter is more formal than a friendly letter.

Parts of a Business Letter

1. **Heading** The heading of a business letter is the same as the heading for a friendly letter. The heading belongs in the upper right-hand corner of the page. It consists of your address, town, state, ZIP code, and the date on which you are writing.

2. **Inside Address** The inside address contains the name and address of the person or company to which you are writing. The inside address comes below the heading, but begins at the left margin.

3. **Salutation** The salutation of a business letter is more formal than that of a friendly letter. If you are writing to a specific person, use *Dear* followed by a person's name.

Dear Mr. Anderson: *Dear Ms. Garcia:*

If you do not know the name of the person to whom you are writing, use a general greeting such as the following.

Dear Sir or Madam:

The salutation begins two lines below the inside address at the left margin. The salutation of a business letter ends with a colon(:).

Study the following business letter. Notice how all the parts of the letter work together in a clear, well-organized manner.

A Business Letter

Heading
51 Bank Street
Stamford, Connecticut 06901
September 22, 19 ___

Inside Address

Tropical Shell Institute
Dept. BH-8
Box 21490
Fort Lauderdale, Florida 33335

Salutation

Dear Sir or Madam:

Body

In the August issue of _Better Homes_ and _Gardens_, I read your advertisement for your shell collection offer and catalog. I would like to order both of these items. Please send me the following order as soon as possible.

1 shell collection (150 shells)	$12.95
1 catalog	1.00
postage	3.00
total	$16.95

I am enclosing a money order for the amount of $16.95.

Closing Sincerely,

Signature Laurie Douvris
Laurie Douvris

4. **Body** The body of a business letter should be short and courteous. It should clearly state your subject.

The **letter of request** should tell what specific information you need as well as why and when you need that information.

An **order letter** should include the name of the product and the number of items you want. You should also tell where you saw the advertisement. Include the catalog number, size, color, and price. List postage and handling separately. Add up the total price of the order. Finally, tell what you are enclosing with the letter, such as a check, subscription form, order form, or money order.

A **letter of complaint** should politely state the nature of the problem and ask about how the problem might be corrected.

5. **Closing** The closing appears on the second line below the body. The closing should line up with the heading. The most common closings for a business letter are these.

Sincerely,   *Respectfully yours,*
Very truly yours,   *Yours truly,*

6. **Signature** Write your signature below the closing. Then print or type your name below the signature.

Exercise Writing Business Letters

Write a business letter in which you order or request one of these items.

1. You plan to visit California. Write to ABC Guest Relations, 4151 Prospect Avenue, Hollywood, California 90027. Ask for tickets to your favorite TV show on ABC. Include all necessary information.
2. Write for information on the programs and ways you or your classmates may help people in countries suffering from famine. Write to Group Programs 3-3-1, The UN Committee for UNICEF, 331 E. 38th St., New York, NY 10016.

4
Addressing an Envelope

Focus Your letter will reach its destination quickly if the envelope is addressed correctly.

Use the following checklist when addressing envelopes.

Guidelines for Addressing Envelopes

1. Make sure the envelope is the right size for the paper. Do not fold the paper more than three times.
2. Put your return address on the envelope in the upper left-hand corner.
3. Write the address almost halfway down the envelope. Indent the address about one-fourth to one-third of the way from the left edge.
4. Check the correctness of street numbers, apartment or suite numbers, and ZIP codes.
5. Use standard postal abbreviations for states. These are two-letter abbreviations, such as CA for California and MN for Minnesota.

Here is an example of a correctly addressed envelope.

Miss Faith Copeland
510 South Fulton Avenue
Mt. Vernon, NY 10550

         Miles Kimball
         2244 Bond Street
         Oshkosh, WI 54091

Envelopes for social notes are usually smaller in size. In this case, the return address may be put on the back of the envelope.

Ms. Alice Dodson
223 Sixth Avenue
San Francisco, CA 94118

Alan Campbell
280 Briar Road
Oak Park, MI
48237

Two-Letter State Abbreviations

The abbreviations listed here may be used in addresses.

Alabama	AL	Kentucky	KY	North Dakota	ND
Alaska	AK	Louisiana	LA	Ohio	OH
Arizona	AZ	Maine	ME	Oklahoma	OK
Arkansas	AR	Maryland	MD	Oregon	OR
California	CA	Massachusetts	MA	Pennsylvania	PA
Colorado	CO	Michigan	MI	Rhode Island	RI
Connecticut	CT	Minnesota	MN	South Carolina	SC
Delaware	DE	Mississippi	MS	South Dakota	SD
District of Columbia	DC	Missouri	MO	Tennessee	TN
Florida	FL	Montana	MT	Texas	TX
Georgia	GA	Nebraska	NE	Utah	UT
Hawaii	HI	Nevada	NV	Vermont	VT
Idaho	ID	New Hampshire	NH	Virginia	VA
Illinois	IL	New Jersey	NJ	Washington	WA
Indiana	IN	New Mexico	NM	West Virginia	WV
Iowa	IA	New York	NY	Wisconsin	WI
Kansas	KS	North Carolina	NC	Wyoming	WY

Exercise Addressing Envelopes

Draw two envelopes on your paper. Address the envelopes, using the addresses in the exercise on page 305. Use your home address as the return address.

5
Filling Out Forms

Focus Fill out forms neatly and accurately.

During your lifetime, you will probably fill out thousands of forms. When you register for school, you fill out information forms and medical forms. To get a library card, you must fill out a form. Every time you apply for a job, you will fill out an application form. Here are some guidelines.

Guidelines for Filling Out Forms

1. Read all of the instructions carefully before you begin to write. Before you begin, make sure you have the correct spellings for names and the correct addresses and telephone numbers. Then you will avoid errors.
2. Print the information requested. Printing is easier to read than handwriting. Read the instructions to see whether you should use pencil or pen.
3. Correct any errors neatly. If you are using pencil, erase the mistake carefully and write in the correction. If you are using ink, draw a single line through the error. Then write the correction neatly above it.
4. Proofread the form to make sure you have filled in all of the necessary information.

Sometimes when you are filling out forms, you will need special information. For example, when you fill out a school health form, you may need to write the name, address, and telephone number of your family doctor. Some forms require the name, address, and telephone number of a close relative that does not live with you. You may also need to know your mother's or father's business address and phone number. Try to have all the necessary information with you.

Exercises *Filling Out Forms*

A Copy this form on your paper. Then complete it correctly. Use your imagination to supply the information asked for.

VILLAGE OF DARIEN
☐ Dog
☐ Cat
Dog/Cat License Application
Expiring December 31st
19___

Please print in black ink.

Date _____ 19 _____

Name _____

Address _____

Phone _____

Name	Age	Male ☐
		Female ☐
Breed	Color	
Rabies Tag No.	Date Vaccinated	Vaccinated By

A rabies certificate or a copy thereof which has been issued within one year prior to date of issuance of license must accompany application. Fee $3.00 or $5.00 — Separate application for each dog/cat required.

Written Signature of Owner x _____

VILLAGE USE ONLY

Tag No. _____ Fee _____

B Look at the activities listed below. Choose one. Get the proper form and complete it correctly.

1. Complete an application for a social security card.
2. Fill out the forms for opening a savings account.
3. Apply for and obtain a library card at your local public library.
4. Complete the forms for bicycle registration.
5. Complete the forms for participation in a local park district or community center activity.

Crossroads

English and Social Studies

You can learn about foreign countries by writing to embassies or consular offices. The material you receive will help you gather information for reports, learn about a country in which a pen pal or relative lives, or learn about countries you might like to visit someday. Your letter-writing skills can help you learn about faraway countries.

Activity

Here are the addresses of embassies and consular offices for five countries. Choose one, or get the address of the consular office of another country that interests you. Then write a letter requesting information about the country you have chosen.

Review what should be included in a letter of request on page 305. After you have written the letter, address an envelope for it. Use the materials you receive to make a display about the country.

1. Canadian Consulate
   General
   Suite 1200
   310 S. Michigan
   Chicago, IL 60604
2. Korean Consulate General
   Suite 600
   500 N. Michigan Avenue
   Chicago, IL 60611
3. Indian Embassy
   2107 Massachusetts
   Avenue NW
   Washington, DC 20008
4. Australian Embassy
   1601 Massachusetts
   Avenue NW
   Washington, DC 20036
5. Irish Embassy
   2234 Massachusetts
   Avenue NW
   Washington, DC 20008

Application and Review

A Mastering Forms of Letters and Envelopes Number your paper from 1 to 10. Tell whether each statement is *True* or *False*. Rewrite the false statements so that they are correct.

1. A friendly letter should sound like a conversation.
2. A friendly letter must include an inside address.
3. The closing contains only your name.
4. Only respond to invitations that you cannot accept.
5. ZIP codes must always appear in addresses.
6. A letter of request is another name for an invitation.
7. The salutation often begins with "Dear."
8. A business letter is informal.

B Writing Letters and Addressing Envelopes Read the following invitation from Bruce Weinstein. Then write a note of acceptance or regret. Draw an envelope and address it properly, using your home address for the return address.

> 4402 Nancy Lane
> Phoenix, Arizona 85040
> October 17, 19 ___
>
> Dear Ellen,
>   You are invited to attend a Halloween party at my house on Saturday, October 31, at 7:30 P.M. This is going to be a costume party, so start thinking of something original.
>
>   Sincerely,
>   Bruce
>
> R.S.V.P.

Grammar, Usage, and Mechanics

T. H. Benton's paintings are easy to recognize. His special technique creates figures that seem to swirl across the canvas. However, before Benton could develop his own unique style, he had to study the basic rules of color and form. A writer must also begin with the basics. Mastering the rules of grammar, usage, and mechanics is the first step to clear, vibrant writing.

18
Understanding Sentences

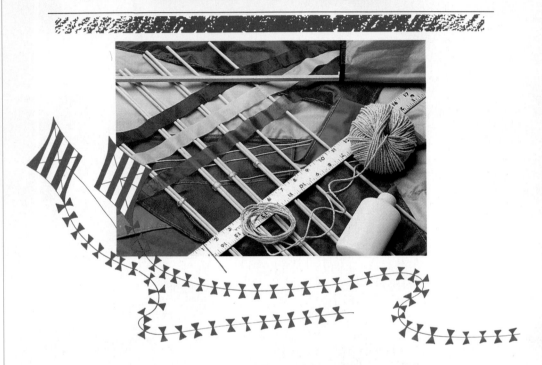

Imagine you are building a kite. What would happen if you forgot to attach part of the frame, or if you put the frame together incorrectly? Your kite probably would not fly!

Like a kite, a sentence must have all its parts, and they must be put together properly. If a part is missing, a sentence cannot do what it is supposed to do—express a complete thought.

In this chapter you will learn about the basic parts of a sentence and about the four kinds of sentences. In addition, you will learn to recognize and write complete sentences.

Paper kites in Santiago Sacatepéquez, Guatemala.

1
Sentences and Fragments

Focus A *sentence* is a group of words that expresses a complete thought.

Look at this group of words.

The Japanese children

This group of words, or phrase, is about Japanese children. It does not, however, tell what happens to the children, or what the children do. It is not a complete idea.

Now consider this phrase.

Enjoy sliding on the ice sculpture

This group of words tells you *what happens*. However, **it** does not tell *who* or *what* enjoys sliding. This phrase also presents only part of an idea. A group of words that does **not** express a complete idea is called a **fragment**.

A **sentence** expresses a complete thought. Every sentence must tell *whom* or *what* the sentence is about. It must also tell *what happens*. Read the following group of words. Since it expresses a complete thought, it is a sentence.

The Japanese children enjoy sliding on the ice sculpture.

Grammar in Action Make sure every sentence you write tells a complete thought. Do not leave your reader with only part of an idea.

Exercises Recognizing Complete Sentences

A Label each group of words *Sentence* or *Fragment*.

1. A pocket of my jeans.
2. Sold ten tickets.
3. Two trucks blocked the intersection.
4. The day before the race.
5. We visited Mount Rushmore.
6. Between the laundromat and the corner.
7. Carefully climbed out on the roof.
8. Louis was asleep.
9. A fountain in Lincoln Park.
10. Three pounds of hamburger.

B Correct each fragment by adding words that make it a complete sentence. Write the complete sentences on your paper.

1. On Friday
2. All the bus drivers
3. Came at six o'clock
4. In the deep, dark night the mountain lion
5. Got stuck in the revolving door
6. Galloped across the bridge
7. Exploded in midair
8. Cautiously tried the ice on the pond
9. Too much water
10. Under a log

C *Write Now* These fragments tell about a mystery bonus package that Terry ordered from a catalog. Use the list to write a brief paragraph about the arrival of the mystery package. Add words to make each fragment a complete sentence.

1. An unusual package
2. The top, bottom, and sides
3. The earsplitting noises
4. Used all his strength
5. Tore it open
6. Had such an odd shape

2

★ *Subjects and Predicates*

Focus The *subject* of a sentence tells *whom* or *what* the sentence is about. The *predicate* tells what the subject *does* or *is*.

Every sentence has two parts. The **subject** tells *whom* or *what* the sentence is about. The **predicate** tells what the subject *does* or *did*. The predicate can also tell what the subject *is* or *was*.

Look at the subjects and predicates in these sentences.

Subject	Predicate
A small monkey (what)	chatters noisily at us. (what the subject does)
Angie Wood (who)	is the best artist in the class. (what the subject is)
The conch shell (what)	was large and pink. (what the subject was)
The blue car (what)	shines brightly. (what the subject did)

Notice that every sentence can be divided into two parts. All the words in a sentence are part of either the subject or the predicate.

1963 Morgan.

Exercises Finding Subjects and Predicates

A Copy each sentence. Draw one line under the subject. Draw two lines under the predicate.

1. The red sports car raced on the flats.
2. Thanksgiving falls on November 28 this year.
3. Charlie Brown walked the first batter.
4. Ducklings followed their mother around the barnyard.
5. A robin built her nest in the pear tree.
6. Jay's cat eats June bugs and other beetles.
7. The second-string players watched from the bench.
8. We paddled through the rough water.
9. Lisa took her hiking boots on the camping trip.
10. The blackout lasted six hours.

B Label each group of words in italics *Subject* or *Predicate*. Write a new sentence by changing the words in italics.

1. *Trivia games* are very popular.
2. The Girl Scout troop *collected food for needy people*.
3. *Bert's family* visited Badlands National Park.
4. The art class *decorated the hallways for Halloween*.
5. *Eighteen different planes* performed at the air show.
6. *Montgomery and Lansing* are both state capitals.
7. The jugglers on stage *delighted the audience*.
8. Lovely green crystals *remained in the dish*.
9. *Hanukkah and Yom Kippur* are Jewish holidays.
10. Every snowflake *has six points*.

C *Write Now* Write a news story about a school science fair. Include the following groups of words in your story. Complete each fragment by adding a subject or a predicate.

walked among all the displays   crowded around
some plant and fungus exhibits   judges with notepads
made a lot of noise   blue ribbons

3
The Simple Predicate, or Verb

> **Focus** A *verb* is a word that tells about action, or that tells what someone or something *is*. A verb is the most important word in the complete predicate.

You know that a sentence can be divided into two main parts. We call the subject part the **complete subject**. The complete subject includes all of the words that tell *whom* or *what* the sentence is about.

The predicate part of the sentence is called the **complete predicate**. The complete predicate includes all of the words that tell what the subject *does* or *is*.

Read the following examples of complete subjects and complete predicates.

Complete Subject	Complete Predicate
The talented young archer	shot.
The talented young archer	shot an arrow.
The talented young archer	shot an arrow into a straw target.
The grizzly bear	hibernated.
The grizzly bear	hibernated in a cave.
The grizzly bear	hibernated in a cave all winter.

Look at each complete predicate above. What is the key word in each one? The most important word in the first three complete sentences is *shot*. The most important word in the last three sentences is *hibernated*.

The most important part of every complete predicate is the **verb**. It is sometimes called the **simple predicate**. In this book, however, we will call the simple predicate the **verb**.

Types of Verbs

There are two types of verbs. Some verbs tell about an action. These are **action verbs**.

> We *hurried* to the beach.
> Rachel and Shane *brought* their goggles.
> Tara *collected* shells.

Other types of verbs may tell that something *is* or they may link the subject with some other words that describe it. These are called **state-of-being verbs** or **linking verbs**.

> The party *is* over.
> The guests *seem* disappointed.

Here are some common state-of-being and linking verbs.

am	was	has been	seem	become
are	were	have been	look	feel
is	will be	had been	appear	taste

You will learn more about verbs in Chapter 20.

Exercises Understanding Verbs

A Number your paper from 1 to 10. Copy each sentence. Underline the complete predicate once. Draw a second line under the verb.

1. A pack of dogs runs loose in the Arizona ghost town.
2. Reggie performs daring stunts on his skateboard.
3. The first movies were silent.
4. In spring, northern farmers boil maple sap into syrup.
5. The bike marathon is an annual event.
6. The guide told our group about the state capitol.
7. One of my cousins writes for *Newsweek*.
8. The divers appeared happy after the competition.
9. Thomas Jefferson invented the calendar clock.
10. Esther's stories are unbelievable but true.

B Sometimes by adding information to a verb, you can state an idea more clearly. Rewrite the following sentences. Add information to each predicate. Look at the chart on page 320 for examples.

1. Queen Elizabeth I ruled England.
2. Water freezes.
3. Everyone seemed tired.
4. Ponce de Leon explored.
5. Padre Island and the Alamo are tourist attractions.
6. Dale found a dollar bill.
7. America purchased Alaska.
8. Three young acrobats performed.
9. The lightning storm caused static.
10. Charlie Chaplin and Mary Pickford were famous.

c *Write Now* Imagine that it is a beautiful day, and you are out walking. Suddenly, the sky turns dark, the wind howls, and you find yourself in the middle of a terrible storm. Write a short story that tells about the storm and what you do to find shelter. The storm may be a rainstorm, blizzard, hurricane, or tornado. To help tell your story, use strong action verbs in the predicates of your sentences.

4
The Simple Subject

Focus The *simple subject* is the most important part of the complete subject.

In a complete sentence, every verb has a subject.

Complete Subject	Verb
The train	departed.
The eight o'clock train	departed.
The eight o'clock train to the city	departed.
The clock	chimed.
The grandfather clock	chimed.
The grandfather clock in the front hall	chimed.

Look at each complete subject above. What is the key word in each one? The most important words in each group of subjects are *train* and *clock*.

The most important word in the complete subject is called the **simple subject** of the sentence. Another name for the simple subject is the **subject of the verb**.

To find the subject of the verb, first find the verb. Then ask *who?* or *what?* before the verb. The answer names the simple subject in the sentence. Look at these examples.

1. The crowd at the rock concert cheered loudly.
   Verb: *cheered*
   Who or what *cheered?*   *crowd*
   Crowd is the subject of *cheered*.

2. After dinner, my whole family watched television.
   Verb: *watched*
   Who or what *watched? family*
   Family is the subject of *watched*.

3. Penguins are graceful in the water.

    Verb: *are*

    Who or what *are? penguins*

    Penguins is the subject of *are*.

Exercises Finding the Verb and Its Subject

A Copy each sentence. Draw two lines under the verb. Draw one line under the subject of the verb.

1. The centaur quite suddenly disappeared into the forest.
2. Indians in the Southwest used adobe for their houses.
3. A large brown package appeared mysteriously on our front porch.
4. Hornets buzzed angrily under the window.
5. Karen's new watch keeps accurate time.
6. Ripe wheat waved in the breeze.
7. The monster in the fun house glowed green and gold in the dark.
8. The little people in *The Wizard of Oz* were Munchkins.
9. All three paintings hang in the Metropolitan Museum of Modern Art in New York.
10. The porcupine's eyes reflected the glow of the headlights.

B Number your paper from 1 to 10. Copy each sentence. Draw two lines under the complete predicate. Then draw one line under the complete subject. Finally, write the simple subject.

1. Very few books were written for children before 1700.
2. The earliest ones taught lessons about virtue and religion.
3. Later selections offered entertainment as well as instruction.
4. A French publisher sold *Cinderella* and *Bluebeard* in France almost three hundred years ago.

5. The Grimm brothers collected fairy tales from German peasants in the nineteenth century.
6. Hans Christian Andersen wrote more than one hundred delightful tales.
7. He earned fame in his native Denmark and many other countries.
8. An American author receives the Newbery Medal each year.
9. This award honors the best children's book of the year.
10. Children's books are now an important part of publishing.

c *Write Now* Write a short story about an African photo safari. Use each of these animals as the subject of one of the sentences in your story: zebra, warthog, and giraffe. Add other sentences to complete your story.

5
The Subject in Different Positions

Focus The subject does not always come at the beginning of a sentence.

The subject usually precedes the verb. Writers, however, change the order of a sentence to add variety to a paragraph.

> An owl perched on the highest branch.
> On the highest branch, an owl perched. (The subject is near the end of the sentence, but before the verb.)
> On the highest branch perched an owl. (The order of the subject and verb are reversed.)

To find the subject in sentences with unusual order, first find the verb. Then ask *who?* or *what?* before the verb.

> Who or what *perched?* An *owl* perched.
> *Owl* is the subject of the sentence.

Sentences Beginning with Here, There, and Where

In sentences beginning with the words *here, there,* or *where,* the subject always follows the verb.

> There is your paintbrush.   Who or what *is? paintbrush*
> *Paintbrush* is the subject of *is.*

Grammar in Action Putting the subject in a different place can make a sentence more interesting.

> The flooding river poured over the dam.
> Over the dam poured the flooding river.

Exercises Finding the Subject

A Number your paper from 1 to 10. Copy each sentence. Draw two lines under the verb. Draw one line under the subject of the verb.

1. There are bats in that cave!
2. Into the pool plunged the diver.
3. Just before the storm, the girls zipped the tent flaps.
4. Where is the key to your locker?
5. Quickly, without hesitation, Holmes solved the mystery.
6. There are many commercials on that television program.
7. Under the bridge, the swallow nested.
8. Slowly, Sandy understood.
9. Across the black sky flashed the lightning.
10. Two blocks past the stoplight, we turned left.

B Number your paper from 1 to 10. Rewrite each sentence so that the subject comes after the verb.

1. The cheers echoed through the crisp, autumn air.
2. Our new practice schedule for the concert band is here.
3. A tiny hummingbird fluttered near the feeder.
4. New replacement parts for the dirt bike are over there.
5. The threatening waves crashed onto the shore.
6. A mole tunneled beneath our lawn.
7. Her playful friend jumped into the deep, muddy puddle.
8. The waterfall roared in the distance.
9. The children's kites floated in the swirling wind.
10. The young, graceful dancer moved across the stage.

c *Write Now* Write a paragraph describing your favorite place to be by yourself. Change the order of some of your sentences so that the verb comes before the subject.

> EXAMPLE A large *plant* hangs in the corner.
> In the corner hangs a large *plant*.

6
Four Kinds of Sentences

> **Focus** There are four types of sentences: *declarative, interrogative, imperative,* and *exclamatory*.

People use four types of sentences to express different kinds of thoughts and emotions. Sentences can state facts, ask questions, make requests, and show strong feelings.

1. A **declarative** sentence tells or states something. End a declarative sentence with a period.

   The teratosaurus was a meat-eating dinosaur.

2. An **interrogative** sentence asks a question. Use a question mark after an interrogative sentence.

   Did your friends march in the
   St. Patrick's Day parade?

3. An **imperative** sentence makes a request or gives an order. Use a period at the end of most imperative sentences. If an imperative sentence shows strong feeling, you may end it with an exclamation point.

   Keep your eyes on the ball.
   Don't be late!

4. An **exclamatory** sentence expresses a strong feeling, such as surprise, shock, or excitement. End an exclamatory sentence with an exclamation point.

   Ted won first prize!
   What a beautiful sky!

Exercises *Identifying the Kinds of Sentences*

A Number your paper from 1 to 10. Copy each sentence and punctuate it correctly. Write *Declarative, Interrogative, Imperative,* or *Exclamatory* to show what type each sentence is.

1. Measure the length of the table
2. You're out
3. Birds' bones are hollow
4. Take a break
5. Do you have an eraser
6. What a scary feeling I got
7. Is the pressure in the tires too high
8. Ms. Minden's cat had a rabies shot
9. Does a chipmunk have a stripe down its back
10. Tell me all about your problem

B Tell whether each sentence is *Declarative, Interrogative, Imperative,* or *Exclamatory*. Rewrite each sentence, changing it to the type shown in parentheses. Punctuate correctly.

1. There is a hornets' nest under the porch. (interrogative)
2. Will you please turn off the hose? (imperative)
3. Is Jupiter the largest planet? (declarative)
4. Finish your project. (interrogative)
5. Was the ukulele first played in Portugal? (declarative)
6. Mark is a terrific skater. (exclamatory)
7. The ballerina wore toe shoes. (interrogative)
8. Is the half hitch an easy knot to tie? (declarative)
9. Wait for the next elevator. (interrogative)
10. We won! (interrogative)

c *Write Now* Imagine that you can journey into the past. What year will you travel to? What will your first reaction be? What will you say to the first person you meet? What questions will you ask? Write a paragraph about this trip. Use all four types of sentences in your paragraph. Punctuate correctly.

7
Finding Subjects in Different Types of Sentences

Focus The subject in interrogative and exclamatory sentences may be difficult to find. First, rearrange the word order. Then follow the usual steps. In imperative sentences, the subject *you* is understood.

You have learned that some sentences are not arranged in the usual subject-verb order. Interrogative, exclamatory, and imperative sentences may all have unusual organization.

To find the subject of an interrogative sentence, change it to a declarative sentence. Then find the verb and ask *who?* or *what?* before it.

Interrogative Sentence	Is she happy about the news?
Declarative Sentence	She is happy about the news.
	Who *is? She* is.
	She is the subject of the verb *is*.

To find the subject in an exclamatory sentence, change it to a declarative sentence. Then find the verb and ask *who?* or *what?* before it.

Exclamatory Sentence	Was that movie boring!
Declarative Sentence	That movie was boring.
	What *was? Movie* was.
	Movie is the subject of *was*.

An imperative sentence appears to have no subject.

Sit down.   Wait a minute.

In these sentences, *you* is understood to be the subject.

(You) Sit down.   (You) Wait a minute.

Exercises *Finding Subjects and Verbs*

A Copy these sentences. Draw two lines under each verb. Draw one line under the subject of the verb. Write the subject of imperative sentences in parentheses.

1. Is the story about the bank robber true?
2. Finish your game before supper.
3. Was that a bumpy, uncomfortable ride!
4. Give me your autograph, please.
5. Will you ever forget Ben's strange costume?
6. Are you hungry yet?
7. Turn left at the first stoplight in town.
8. Proceed with caution.
9. Is the prickly pear a cactus?
10. Does that snake have sharp fangs!

B Rewrite each sentence with the subject before the verb. Add *(You)* to imperative sentences. Punctuate your new sentences correctly. Underline the subject once and the verb twice.

> EXAMPLE   Have you ridden a roller coaster before?
>
> <u>You</u> <u>have ridden</u> a roller coaster before.

1. Did you hear about the Screaming Flyer at the theme park?
2. Listen to my news about this wild roller coaster.
3. Will you ever be scared!
4. First, think about falling straight through the air.
5. Then think about your poor, uneasy stomach.
6. Can you imagine the roar of the screaming passengers?
7. Get ready for an unforgettable, hair-raising adventure.
8. Is the thrill of your life worth the queasiness and screams?
9. Decide for yourself.
10. Will you be thrilled by your ride!

C *Write Now* Write a story or tale featuring nonhuman characters. Maybe they can even talk! Use all four types of sentences.

8
Compound Subjects

Focus A *compound subject* has two or more parts.

Notice that the subject in the sentence below has two parts.

Subject **Predicate**
Rosemary and *Alan*   watched the hockey game.

When a subject has two or more parts, it is called a **compound subject**. *Compound* means "having more than one part."

The word *and* is often used to join the parts of a subject, but the word *or* can also be used. The words *and* and *or* are conjunctions. A **conjunction** is used to join the two parts of the subject.

Sometimes a subject has three or more parts. Then, use commas to separate the parts. Place a conjunction before the last part. Look at this example.

The *trees,* the *bushes,* and the *flowers* need rain.

Grammar in Action Compound subjects can make your writing and speaking flow smoothly. Use them to combine sentences that repeat similar ideas.

Awkward   After school, Lana played a computer game.
After school, Marty played a computer game.

Better   After school, Lana and Marty played a computer game.

Exercises Compound Subjects

A Copy the following sentences. Draw two lines under each verb and one line under each part of the compound subject.

1. Emily, Charlotte, and Anne Brontë wrote novels.
2. The Knicks or the Celtics are in the play-offs.
3. Shirley, Della, and Pat are best friends.
4. The comma, semicolon, and period have special meanings in computer programming.
5. Radishes, carrots, and potatoes grow underground.
6. A stuffed dog or a bright mobile is a good baby gift.
7. Strawberries and cabbage are good sources of vitamin C.
8. Marisa and Juan tied for first place in the contest.
9. Cereal, milk, juice, and toast make a good breakfast.
10. The Mohawks and four other tribes joined forces as the powerful Five Nations.

B Copy the following sentences. Draw two lines under each verb and one line under each part of the compound subject.

1. Erik and I learned a lot from Todd's report on Morocco.
2. The Mediterranean Sea and the Atlantic Ocean border Morocco on the north and west.
3. Morocco and Spain are separated by the Strait of Gibraltar.
4. Farmlands, deserts, and mountains form the Moroccan landscape.
5. Arab and Berber are the two main groups of people.
6. Casablanca or Tangier is the tourists' favorite city.
7. Mining and agriculture are the two main industries.
8. Rugs, pottery, and jewelry can be found in the markets.
9. Couscous or tabouli is eaten at many meals.
10. Soccer, basketball, and track are the most popular sports.

c *Write Now* Imagine that you are a store manager. Write an advertisement for your big year-end sale. Use compound subjects to name several specific items.

9
Compound Predicates

Focus A *compound predicate* has two or more parts.

Notice that the predicate in the sentence below has two parts.

Subject	Predicate
The horse	*took the lead* and *won the race*.

When a predicate has two or more parts, it is called a **compound predicate**. When a predicate has three or more parts, use commas to separate the parts. Place the conjunction before the last part. Read this sentence.

Meg *went home, ate a snack,* and *started her homework.*

Grammar in Action Use compound predicates to make your writing and speaking flow smoothly. Use them to combine sentences with similar ideas.

Our class played lacrosse.
Our class won.
Our class played lacrosse and won.

Exercises Finding Compound Predicates

A Copy the following sentences. Draw one line under the subject of each sentence. Then draw two lines under each part of the compound predicate. Be sure to copy the commas.

EXAMPLE William Clark explored with Meriwether Lewis and served as governor of the Missouri Territory.

1. Elizabeth left the muffins in the oven and burned them.
2. Ice covered the streets and caused numerous accidents.

3. Lydia's family went to the Grand Canyon, rode burros down the trail, and spent the night at the bottom.
4. The Angels scored four runs in the first inning and stayed ahead during the rest of the game.
5. Frederick Douglass escaped from slavery and became a speaker for antislavery groups.
6. Our class rented a bus and visited the Natural History Museum.
7. King Kong broke loose in New York City, climbed the World Trade Center, and fought off fighter planes.
8. Stephen Foster taught himself to play the piano at age six and published his first song at age sixteen.
9. Tracy saved her allowance and bought a new camera.
10. Hector came to bat, ignored three wide pitches, and smashed the fourth one into the stands.

B Rewrite the following paragraph. Use compound subjects and compound predicates to make this paragraph less choppy.

Everyone pitched in to plan a surprise farewell party for Mrs. Dawson. Janet painted a banner. Sue painted a banner. Kay painted a banner. Three boys collected money. The same three boys bought a present. Scott ordered a big cake. Scott bought other refreshments, too. I brought a camera. I hid behind the door. I hoped to get a good picture. When Mrs. Dawson walked into the dark room, we flicked on the lights. We threw confetti. We yelled "Surprise!" That was one of the few times our teacher was speechless.

c _Write Now_ Zany Zeke is a zookeeper at the San Diego Zoo. Zeke is going on vacation. Before he leaves, he must tell his assistant, Wanda, how to care for the animals. Write Zany Zeke's instructions. Include several compound predicates and compound subjects in your paragraph.

Linking Grammar & Writing

A *Wonderkid Magazine* asked you to interview an important scientist. You chose Dr. Robert Jarvik, who designed the first artificial heart for humans.

Write the interview and include some of the questions you asked and the answers you received. Your interview should contain all four types of sentences.

Dr. Robert Jarvik.

B You are opening a pet shop in town. To help shoppers make selections when they come into your shop, you need to make some signs. Write one sentence for each sign. The complete subject of each sentence should fully identify the animal. The compound predicate should tell two things the animal does.

> EXAMPLE   This colorful parrot sits on a perch and mimics voices.

C Using Compound Subjects and Verbs in Health Mrs. Verde's sixth-grade health class was surprised to learn that some snack foods can be healthful sources of energy. To put their knowledge to use, the class prepared a "snack feast." Write a brief paragraph that tells about some of the food combinations the students might have created for snacks. Use some compound subjects such as *peanuts and raisins* or *bran muffins and wheat bread*. Use some compound predicates such as *popped some corn and seasoned it* or *cut and stuffed pita pockets*.

Additional Practice

Part 1 Sentences and Fragments Label each group of words *Sentence* or *Fragment*. Then correct each fragment by adding words to make it a sentence.

1. Napoleon ruled France.
2. The capital of the state.
3. My favorite comic strip in the Sunday papers.
4. Charles Dickens wrote *A Tale of Two Cities*.
5. Was the first President of the United States.
6. In 1988 many temperature records were broken by the intense summer heat.
7. Down the Mississippi River to thc Gulf of Mexico.
8. The wind whistled.
9. I want to learn about computers.
10. Walked four miles during a blinding snowstorm in late February.

Part 2 Subjects and Predicates Label each group of words in italics *Subject* or *Predicate*.

11. Some redwood trees *are more than 300 feet tall*.
12. *Officials from twelve nations* attended the conference this year.
13. *Mesa Verde National Park* is located in Colorado.
14. Lacrosse *was first played by Native Americans*.
15. *One of the endangered species* is the condor.
16. More than one billion people *live in China*.
17. *The Great Depression* began in 1929.
18. The first woman to fly across the Atlantic Ocean *was Amelia Earhart*.
19. International Falls, Minnesota, *calls itself "The Nation's Icebox."*
20. *Hawaiians* celebrate King Kamehameha I Day on June 11.

Part 3 Simple Predicates Write the simple predicate in each sentence.

21. John Adams was the second President of the United States of America.
22. Dinosaurs ruled the land for about 140 million years.
23. The sun rose at 6:30 this morning.
24. Athletes compete in the summer and winter Olympic games every four years.
25. A decathlon contains ten track and field events, such as the one-hundred-meter dash and the long jump.
26. Harvey Kennedy invented the shoelace.
27. Texas became a state on December 29, 1845.
28. Flying buttresses supported two sides of the ancient church.
29. That company makes steel for the auto industry.
30. Ms. Martinez has been a teacher in this school for fifteen years.

Part 4 Simple Subjects Write the following sentences on your paper. Draw two lines under the complete predicate. Then draw one line under the complete subject. Finally, write the simple subject.

31. Heavy traffic jammed the Holland Tunnel.
32. Colorful sailboats dotted the glassy lake.
33. The hedge behind our garage was full of flowers.
34. Mr. Parker's class studied simple engines.
35. The dinosaur skeletons at the natural history museum were very interesting.
36. The crispy lettuce in that salad tasted fresh.
37. The blacksmith pounded the horseshoes on an anvil.
38. A rusty blue truck pulled into our driveway.
39. A metronome kept the beat for the pianist.
40. Pink and white dogwood trees lined the streets.

Part 5 Finding the Subject Rewrite each sentence so that the subject comes after the verb.

41. Six lions jumped through hoops.
42. The waves crashed onto the shore.
43. The birds darted across the treetops.
44. The uniforms for the soccer team are here.
45. The basketball fell out of bounds.
46. The five little brown foxes darted into their cozy underground den.
47. Juliette Low's house is there.
48. My picture hangs above our mantle.
49. The herds of majestic buffalo grazed on the wide open plains.
50. Your cab is here.

Part 6 Four Kinds of Sentences On your paper write the correct end mark for each sentence. Then label each sentence *Declarative, Imperative, Interrogative,* or *Exclamatory.*

51. Do you think the Cardinals will make the National League play-offs
52. The luge is a type of sled
53. Read the first two chapters of *Island of the Blue Dolphins*
54. Listen to the magnificent jazz saxophone solo in this new song
55. Who holds the record for hitting the most home runs during a lifetime career
56. Watch out
57. An armadillo crossed the road
58. How angry the sky looks
59. The unicorn is a mythical beast
60. Please deliver these stacks of newspapers to the recycling center on the corner

Part 7 Finding Subjects and Verbs Rewrite each sentence to make the subject come before the verb. Add *(You)* to imperative sentences. Be sure to punctuate your sentences correctly. Then underline the subject once and the verb twice.

> EXAMPLE   Is Karen the youngest in her family?
>
> <u>Karen</u> <u>is</u> the youngest in her family.

61. Were you really the winner?
62. Am I too early for the show?
63. Give your collie a bath.
64. Was today's orange sunset beautiful!
65. Are Tony's tennis shoes new?
66. Take your time with this job.
67. Was that cave dark and spooky!
68. Were the athletes tired after the game?
69. Shovel the snow before lunch.
70. Were they excited by their unexpected victory!

Parts 8 and 9 Compound Subjects and Predicates Each of the following sentences contains either a compound subject or a compound predicate. Copy the sentences. Then draw one line under the parts of the compound subjects. Draw two lines under the parts of the compound predicates.

71. Kangaroos and koalas are both marsupials.
72. Portland, Corvallis, and Eugene are cities in Oregon.
72. In the group she plays piano and sings.
74. I cleaned up my room, washed the dishes, and fed the dog.
75. Soup or salad is served with the meal.
76. We visited Yellowstone National Park and saw Old Faithful.
77. The same person wrote the movie and directed it.
78. The lute and mandolin were popular Renaissance musical instruments.
79. Delia turned down the stereo and answered the phone.
80. The phonograph and the stock ticker were invented by Thomas Edison.

Application and Review

Lesson Review

A Recognizing Complete Sentences Number your paper from 1 to 10. Label each group of words *Sentence* or *Fragment*. Then complete each fragment to make it a sentence.

1. Swooped from the sky.
2. Peanut butter and jelly.
3. Many airlines fly to Los Angeles.
4. Quickly chose players for their teams.
5. The lights of Broadway.
6. Won a prize in the broad jump.
7. We already mailed the contest entry blank.
8. The satellite monitored the weather.
9. Hovered just above the ground.
10. The Colorado River flows through Arizona.

B Finding Complete Subjects and Predicates Copy these sentences. Draw one line under the complete subject of each sentence. Draw two lines under the complete predicate.

1. Campaign workers hung posters of both candidates all over downtown.
2. The seaplane revved up its motors.
3. A six-foot snowdrift covered our driveway.
4. South Africa has many diamond mines.
5. Our coach put the fourth relief pitcher on the mound in the ninth inning.
6. A huge brown eagle glided over the mountain top.
7. The book from Japan shows pearl divers.
8. Many old apple trees by the barn were toppled in the storm.
9. The woolly mammoth became extinct in prehistoric times.
10. A heavy fog hid the old lighthouse.

C Finding the Verb Number your paper from 1 to 10. Write the verb in each sentence.

1. Sequoya invented the first Indian alphabet.
2. All the guests brought birthday presents.
3. Saturn was the Roman god of agriculture.
4. Clothing styles change every season.
5. Mrs. Figueroa runs a grocery store on South Homecrest Avenue.
6. The rug had a mysterious lump in it.
7. Jennifer pitched three scoreless innings.
8. Roger Bannister, an English medical student, ran the first four-minute mile.
9. The empty car slowly coasted down the hill toward the lake.
10. The huge whale surfaced from the ocean like a great gray volcano.

D Finding the Verb and Its Subject Number your paper from 1 to 10. Copy each sentence. Draw two lines under the verb. Draw one line under the subject of the verb.

1. Rain leaked through the roof and down the walls.
2. Eric usually takes his flippers to the lake.
3. The first official United States flag had only thirteen stars.
4. The weary joggers circled the cinder track again and again.
5. The foal stood on long wobbly legs.
6. Sunspots are cooler than the other parts of the sun's surface.
7. The high iron gate swung silently on giant hinges.
8. Rob water-skis barefoot.
9. Nearly out of breath, Sara dashed across the finish line to take first place.
10. A light on the instrument panel blinked on and off.

Chapter Review

A Recognizing Types of Sentences Write *Fragment* if the group of words is an incomplete sentence. If the group of words is a complete sentence, write the punctuation mark that the sentence needs. Finally, write *Declarative, Interrogative, Imperative,* or *Exclamatory* to tell what kind of sentence it is.

1. Is it difficult to learn a foreign language
2. What a frightful movie that was
3. Understood all the directions
4. When was Alaska purchased from Russia
5. Cricket is a sport played with a ball and bat
6. Choose a partner for the relay
7. Dashed around the track at school
8. Louisiana is nicknamed the Pelican State
9. Use an almanac to find the answers
10. Waited anxiously for spring to come

B Finding the Subject and Verb Copy the following sentences. Underline the subject once and the verb twice. In sentences with compound subjects or compound verbs, be sure to underline each subject and verb. If the subject is not given, write it in parentheses.

1. The statues in the museum were marble.
2. Where are the charcoal and paints?
3. What talented skaters Kim and Dana are!
4. Try this delicious coconut bread.
5. Anthony knew the story of *The Nutcracker* ballet.
6. Across the field trotted the ponies.
7. The receiver caught the pass, tumbled into the end zone, and scored a touchdown.
8. Lock the door and give the key to me.
9. Chipmunks and squirrels live in wooded areas.
10. How foggy it was by the pond!

19
Understanding Nouns

Microscopic cross section of a pine tree stem.

Do you remember looking at the stars on a clear, dark night? How many stars could you name? Have you ever peered through a microscope and discovered the world that exists in a single drop of water? Do you know the names of any of these tiny particles? Can you imagine finding names for all the parts that make up all the things in the universe?

The words we use to name things, people, and places are called *nouns*. In this chapter you will learn to recognize the different kinds of nouns. More importantly, you will learn to use nouns correctly and precisely so that you can describe your world just as you see it.

1
What Are Nouns?

Focus A *noun* names a person, place, thing, or idea.

There are many names that tell who you are. You may be an athlete, a musician, and a friend. These different names for you are nouns. Nouns are used to name persons, places, things, or ideas.

Many nouns name things that can be seen. Some examples are *secretary, village,* and *octopus*. Some nouns name things that can neither be seen nor touched. These include nouns such as *freedom, hope, shyness,* and *weakness*.

Here are some other examples of nouns.

Persons	Places	Things	Ideas
astronaut	desert	dinosaur	friendliness
dancer	ocean	robot	faith
Juanita	London	Eiffel Tower	intelligence
Paul	Africa	*Mayflower*	joy

Grammar in Action Choose the noun that names exactly what you mean. Do not say *boat* if you mean *canoe*. Do not write *fruit* if you mean *apple*.

Exercises *Identifying Nouns*

A Number your paper from 1 to 10. Find the nouns in the sentences below and list them on your paper.

1. Texas is the second largest state.
2. Did Mario have the courage to enter the haunted house?
3. The tip of my ski is stuck under the log.
4. Mrs. Holmes kept her promise to the boys.
5. Crocodiles are found in many rivers in Africa.
6. An alert lifeguard sat on the platform at the beach.
7. Some cities have problems with pollution.
8. My older sister moved to Maine because of her job.
9. Aaron watched three porpoises jump out of the water.
10. What skills did Kelly learn in gymnastics?

B List the nouns in each sentence. After each noun, tell whether it refers to a person, place, thing, or idea.

1. Alaska and Hawaii are not on the mainland.
2. The cheese on this pizza tastes funny.
3. There was excitement among the actors before the play.
4. A foil is a sword with a button on the point.
5. Mike and Brian have a strong friendship.
6. Sally was in Frontierland, looking at the old covered wagons.
7. People from Brazil speak Portuguese.
8. Beethoven is a famous composer.
9. The colonists wanted their freedom from England.
10. Mr. Martinez won't take any nonsense.

c *Write Now* A student from Australia will be visiting your school for one day. You have offered to take your visitor on a tour of your neighborhood. Think about the most interesting people, places, and things to point out. Make a list of those people, places, and things. Then write a paragraph explaining what your tour will include.

2
Common and Proper Nouns

Focus A *common noun* is a general name for a person, place, thing, or idea. A *proper noun* names a particular person, place, thing, or idea.

When you call yourself a student, you are giving yourself a name that you share with all the boys and girls in your class. This name is common to a whole group of people. Many other nouns are also common to whole groups of people, places, or things. Some examples are *country, town, book,* or *animal.* These are called **common nouns**.

Some nouns name particular persons, places, or things. Names like *José Canseco, Houston,* and *Washington Monument* are called **proper nouns**. Proper nouns are always capitalized. Look at these examples of common nouns and proper nouns.

Common Nouns	Proper Nouns
children	Jane Banks, Michael Banks
park	Grand Canyon National Park
road	Jefferson Road
town	Richmond
continent	Asia
artist	Grandma Moses
building	Sears Tower
river	Colorado River

Grammar in Action Use proper nouns to make your writing and speaking more specific.

General The girl went to the store.
Specific Marilyn went to Savemore Foods.

Exercises Finding Common and Proper Nouns

A Divide a piece of paper into two columns. Label one column *Common Nouns* and one column *Proper Nouns*. Write each noun in the correct column. Be sure to capitalize proper nouns.

1. maria
2. lake ontario
3. cowboy
4. martin luther king, jr.
5. elmwood middle school
6. harbor
7. actor
8. canyon
9. parrot
10. rocky mountains

B The following is a list of common nouns. Write a proper noun for each one.

      EXAMPLE island—Oahu

1. author
2. tribe
3. war
4. woman
5. president
6. car
7. actor
8. country
9. holiday
10. magazine

C *Write Now* You have just returned from a month-long trip. On this trip, you visited several cities and states. Think about the souvenirs you collected from each place that you visited. Make a list of those souvenirs. Write a paragraph describing the souvenirs and telling where each was collected. Underline all the common nouns once and the proper nouns twice in your paragraph.

3
Singular and Plural Nouns

Focus A *singular noun* names one person, place, thing, or idea. A *plural noun* names more than one person, place, thing, or idea.

Some nouns name just one person, place, thing, or idea. *Girl*, for example, names one person. It is a **singular noun**. Other nouns name more than one person. They are **plural nouns**. *Girls* is a plural noun.

Here are seven rules for forming the plurals of nouns.

1. To form the plurals of most nouns, just add *-s*.
   computer<u>s</u>   street<u>s</u>   hamburger<u>s</u>   player<u>s</u>
2. When the singular noun ends in *s*, *sh*, *ch*, *x*, or *z*, add *-es*.
   glass<u>es</u>   bush<u>es</u>   crutch<u>es</u>   tax<u>es</u>   waltz<u>es</u>
3. When the singular noun ends in *o*, add *-s*.
   radio<u>s</u>   taco<u>s</u>   piano<u>s</u>   Eskimo<u>s</u>

Exceptions: For the following nouns ending in *o,* add *-es.*

echo<u>es</u>   hero<u>es</u>   potato<u>es</u>   tomato<u>es</u>

4. When the singular noun ends in *y* with a consonant before it, change the *y* to *i* and add *-es.*

army—arm<u>ies</u>   company—compan<u>ies</u>

5. For most nouns ending in *f* or *fe,* add *-s.* For some nouns ending in *f* or *fe,* however, change the *f* to *v* and add *-es* or *-s.*

chief—chief<u>s</u>	elf—el<u>ves</u>	loaf—loa<u>ves</u>
roof—roof<u>s</u>	self—sel<u>ves</u>	calf—cal<u>ves</u>
belief—belief<u>s</u>	life—li<u>ves</u>	knife—kni<u>ves</u>
cuff—cuff<u>s</u>	leaf—lea<u>ves</u>	wolf—wol<u>ves</u>
safe—safe<u>s</u>	half—hal<u>ves</u>	shelf—shel<u>ves</u>

6. In some cases, the plural noun is exactly the same as the singular noun.

salmon   bass   scissors   news

7. Some nouns form their plurals in special ways.

ox—oxen   woman—women   goose—geese

Grammar in Action Always check a dictionary when you are unsure about how to form the plural of a word. If the plural form is not listed in the dictionary, just add an *-s* to the singular.

Exercises Forming Plurals

A Number your paper from 1 to 10. Write the plural form for each noun below.

1. monkey
2. cliff
3. ax
4. piano
5. deer

6. child
7. alley
8. life
9. candy
10. halo

B Proofreading Copy the following paragraph. Correct any misspelled noun plurals that you find.

> Eskimoes call themselfs Inuit, meaning "the people." Their familys consist of the husband, wife, childs, and married sons with their wifes and childes. Eskimoos live in the Arctic. They spend most of their lifes surrounded by snow and ice. In the winter the temperaturies can reach ninety degrese below zero. Using knifies made from bone, some Eskimoes cut blocks of snow to build snowhouse. In summer the top layer of the tundra thaws, creating pondes and marshs. In the past, the Inuit lived on the meat from whales, seales, fish, musk oxes, and deers. They used the skin from the deeres to make their garmentes and tentes. In summer they added rootes, stems, and berrys to their diet.

c *Write Now* You have just won a fifteen-minute shopping spree at your local department store. Think about your shopping spree and write a list of the items you would select. Write a paragraph describing the items.

4
Nouns That Show Possession

Focus A *possessive noun* shows who or what owns something.

Everyone owns things, from clothes, to toys, to pets. When you wish to say that someone owns something, you use the **possessive form** of the noun.

> The bill requires the *governor's* signature.
> (The possessive form of *governor* is *governor's*.)
> Ed borrowed *Becky's* skateboard.
> (The possessive form of *Becky* is *Becky's*.)

Making Singular Nouns Show Possession

To form the possessive of a singular noun, add an apostrophe and an -*s*.

Singular Noun	Possessive Form
grandfather	grandfather's
Mrs. Wills	Mrs. Wills's

Making Plural Nouns Show Possession

There are two rules to remember for forming the possessive of a plural noun.

1. If the plural noun ends in *s*, simply add an apostrophe to the end of the word.

Plural Noun	Possessive Form
pirates	pirates'
cats	cats'
owners	owners'

2. If the plural noun does not end in *s*, add an apostrophe and an *-s*.

Plural Noun	Possessive Form
children	children's
mice	mice's
women	women's

Grammar in Action Be careful to use punctuation correctly when you form possessives. Notice how changing the place of the apostrophe can change the meaning. The *student's pencils* means the pencils belong to one student. The *students' pencils* means the pencils belong to two or more students.

Exercises Writing Possessives

A Rewrite the following sentences. Use the possessive form for each word in italics.

1. A youth who lived seven hundred years ago was one of *history* greatest travelers.
2. It was Marco Polo who described *Kublai Khan* empire, China.
3. *Marco Polo* diary told of all the wondrous sights he saw.

4. Polo reported seeing coconuts the size of a *man* head.
5. He noted that the *coconuts* insides were white and delicious.
6. The *explorer* description of a crocodile was amazing.
7. He told of a serpent ten paces long and said that this *reptile* jaws were wide enough to swallow a man.
8. In addition, some of the *cities* features amazed Marco.
9. Underground drainage systems showed the Chinese *engineers* talents.
10. Gold-covered carvings demonstrated the native *artists* abilities.

Marco Polo kneeling behind his father as they arrive at the court of Kublai Khan, detail of an illuminated manuscript.

B Write the possessive form of each of the following nouns. Then write another noun after each possessive form to show what the first noun might possess.

EXAMPLE   Thomas Edison
Thomas Edison's invention

1. the mechanic
2. the secretaries
3. Louise
4. the children
5. Albert Jones
6. your neighbors
7. a monkey
8. some steel workers
9. an automobile
10. an ostrich

c *Write Now* Several friends are spending the summer at Camp Wonderlake. One night raccoons open the campers' lockers and spill the contents all over the cabin floor. Make a list matching the spilled belongings to the owners. Write a brief paragraph describing what items belong to whom.

Linking Grammar & Writing

A Did you ever wonder how the streets in your neighborhood got their names? Streets are often named for important people, places, and things. Cherokee Road, Sacramento Avenue, and Lake Street are three examples.

Imagine that the mayor has written you a letter asking you to name five new streets in your town. Answer the mayor's letter. In your reply, suggest five street names and give the reasons for your choices.

B Using Nouns in Science All plants and animals can be grouped or classified. The classification becomes more specific as the group is narrowed down. The animal kingdom may first be divided into groups: vertebrates (animals with backbones) and invertebrates (animals without backbones). Vertebrates can then be broken down into eight classes. One class is Mammalia, or Mammals. This class can further be divided into eighteen orders.

Use an encyclopedia to find the names of the orders in the Class Mammalia. Then choose three orders and find at least two species for each one.

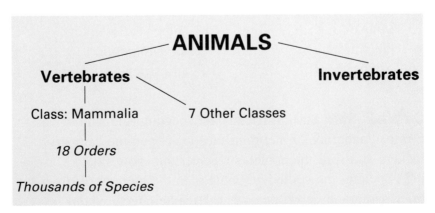

Additional Practice

Part 1 What Are Nouns? List the nouns in each sentence. After each noun, tell whether it refers to a person, place, thing, or idea.

1. The Colosseum is located in Rome.
2. The candidate for mayor asked for our trust.
3. Bill Cosby was born in Philadelphia.
4. Molly Ringwald starred in the movie.
5. The political leaders want to promote friendship among the nations of the world.
6. The Girl Scouts hiked along the trail through the mountains.
7. When do flowers bloom in the desert?
8. The coach expects leadership from the quarterback.
9. Many farmers in Iowa plant soybeans and corn.
10. Laurie said the award was a great honor.

Part 2 Common and Proper Nouns Copy these sentences. Capitalize each proper noun. Underline the common nouns once and the proper nouns twice.

11. The city of stockholm is in sweden.
12. Our neighbors visited yosemite national park on their vacation.
13. The atlanta hawks play in the national basketball association.
14. My cousin michiko and several friends go to college in north carolina.
15. The tallest player on the team is ralph.
16. Agatha christie has written exciting mysteries.
17. Has the class learned the names of the countries in africa?
18. What is the capital of your state?
19. Does the library have any more books by ann petry?
20. Denise plays the bassoon in the band.

Part 3 Singular and Plural Nouns Change each noun in italics to the plural form. Write the nouns on your paper.

21. The mail *carrier* delivered the *box*.
22. The *fly* were killed by the spray.
23. The *woman* cut the *sandwich* in *half*.
24. In some *country,* even adults believe in *elf*.
25. There are *goose* hiding under the *bush* in the *marsh*.
26. The *potato* and *tomato* ripened in the *garden*.
27. The *child* played on the *beach*.
28. The *man* displayed the *radio* on the *shelf*.
29. The paper uses *computer* to print the *news*.
30. The *dairy* in the *city* suffered *loss*.
31. Tara sharpened the *knife* before she cut the *loaf* of bread and the *cheese*.
32. *Wolf* howled in the cold, clear, night.
33. The *cuff* on your pants are dragging in the mud.
34. *Eskimo* spend most of their *life* surrounded by ice and snow.
35. The *bell* of the *church* ring at noon.

Part 4 Possessive Nouns Change each noun in italics to the possessive form. Write the nouns on your paper.

36. The trainer took the *runner* pulse.
37. We could see the *raccoons* tracks.
38. The new *girl* hair was long and curly.
39. Follow your *mother* advice.
40. A parade honored the *astronauts* homecoming.
41. Is that the *manager* phone number?
42. The *sailors* yellow slickers protected them from the salty ocean spray.
43. The *actress* smile looked real.
44. My *dogs* ears perked up.
45. *Tess* butterfly collection has at least two dozen different varieties.

Application and Review

Lesson Review

A Finding the Nouns Number your paper from 1 to 10. Write the nouns in each sentence below.

1. The corn was stored in the silo.
2. My sister Tanya invited her classmates to a picnic in the park.
3. Robin Hood led the fight against the Sheriff of Nottingham.
4. Directions are on the back of the package.
5. The eagle is a symbol of freedom in America.
6. Barbara brought the class some fresh peaches from Georgia.
7. Spring is my favorite season.
8. This thermometer is for the oven.
9. The librarian found the book about Tibet on the top shelf.
10. Coaches help athletes improve teamwork.

B Finding Common Nouns and Proper Nouns Copy these sentences. Capitalize each proper noun. Underline the common nouns once and the proper nouns twice.

1. A French explorer named cadillac founded detroit.
2. Memorial day is a national holiday.
3. My cousin ellen can change that tire.
4. Vicker's theater was showing a double feature.
5. When the volcano krakatoa erupted, the sound was heard in bankok, 3,000 miles away.
6. My family visited carlsbad caverns.
7. Morning glory pool in yellowstone national park looks like a blue morning glory.
8. John bought this syrup in vermont.

9. Payless drugstore was running a fantastic special on all wraparound sunglasses.
10. Death valley in california receives less than three inches of rain yearly.

C Forming Plurals Write the plural form of each noun.

1. dish
2. ox
3. deer
4. buzz
5. loaf
6. goose
7. box
8. ratio
9. lady
10. series

11. buoy
12. sheep
13. lobby
14. day
15. dwarf
16. wheelchair
17. dress
18. valley
19. roof
20. echo

D Writing the Possessive Form Write the correct possessive form of each word in italics.

1. *Darcy* math book was on the coffee table under the newspaper.
2. My *uncle* rustic fishing cabin is in the northern part of New Jersey.
3. Sue bandaged her *dogs* paws.
4. The *ladies* coats are in the closet and on the bed in the next room.
5. Three *dentists* offices are on Shirley Street.
6. A big white-cheeked Canada goose was in the *magician* black top hat.
7. Can you find your *puppy* leash?
8. My *grandmother* store is closed in July.
9. The *boys* appetites were huge.
10. *People* opinions vary.

Chapter Review

A Finding Common and Proper Nouns Label two columns *Common Nouns* and *Proper Nouns*. Write each noun from the paragraph in its proper column. Capitalize the proper nouns. If the same noun appears more than one time, you need to write it only once.

> The story of paul bunyan is a famous tale that began in the united states. People all over america have told stories of a giant lumberjack who could perform great deeds. paul's strength and abilities were amazing! He could drive stumps into the ground with his bare fists. He could squeeze water out of boulders. paul dug the mississippi river and cleared the states of iowa and kansas for the farmers. With a blue ox named babe, paul cleared western pastures so cattle could graze. The adventures of paul bunyan are still enjoyed by americans.

B Writing Singular, Plural, and Possessive Nouns Make four columns on your paper. Label them *Singular Noun, Plural Noun, Singular Possessive,* and *Plural Possessive.* Write each of the ten nouns listed below in the correct column. Then complete the chart by writing the three other forms of each noun in their proper columns.

EXAMPLE

Singular Noun	Plural Noun	Singular Possessive	Plural Possessive
astronaut	astronauts	astronaut's	astronauts'

1. guards'
2. lizards
3. hero
4. burro's
5. ghosts'
6. children
7. ponies
8. snakes'
9. firefighter
10. turtle

20
Understanding Verbs

The rider <u>clutches</u> the reins, <u>lurches</u> back in the saddle, and desperately <u>fights</u> to keep his balance. As the horse <u>plunges</u> down the hill, rocks and pebbles <u>scatter</u> from its hooves.

The underlined words in these sentences are verbs you might use to describe the action-filled picture on the right. The picture above has no action. What verbs can you use to describe it? You might say that the land *is* quiet and peaceful or that it *looks* lonely and deserted.

In this chapter you will learn about the kinds of verbs, about direct objects, and about verb tenses. You will also learn to use verbs correctly and to choose strong, descriptive verbs in your writing.

The Cowboy, Frederic Remington, 1902.

1
Kinds of Verbs

Focus *Verbs* are words that tell about action or state that something *is*.

You use two kinds of verbs when you speak or write. These are **action verbs** and **state-of-being** or **linking verbs**.

Action Verbs

Some verbs tell about action you can see.

> Pablo Picasso *mixed* colors carefully.
> He *applied* paint to the pottery.
> Artists often *paint* on canvas also.

Other verbs tell about action you cannot see. That is, there is no physical movement.

> Artists usually *plan* their work in advance.
> Painters often *think* up new ideas.
> Many people *wish* for artistic talent.

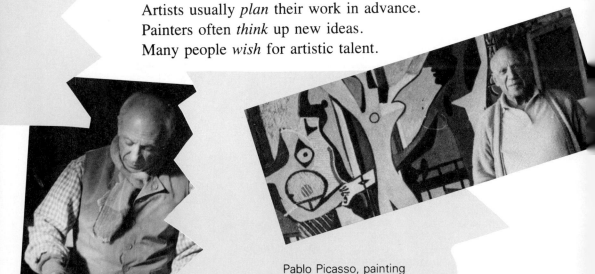

Pablo Picasso, painting
a plate and standing
before one of his
paintings.

State-of-Being or Linking Verbs

Some verbs do not show action. They tell that something is or they link the subject with a word or words in the predicate. Such verbs are called state-of-being verbs or linking verbs. Since state-of-being verbs and linking verbs are very similar, we will refer to them both as linking verbs from this point on. These are the most common linking verbs.

am	are	were	being
is	was	be	been

Look at the linking verbs in the following sentences.

Picasso's final products *were* dramatic.
This one *is* now in a gallery of a museum.
Other paintings by Picasso *are* near it.

Other familiar linking verbs include these.

look	appear	become
feel	sound	remain
taste	smell	seem

Seated Pierrot, Pablo Picasso, 1918.

Picasso's paintings *seem* full of life.
This one *looks* interesting.
Most artists *feel* proud of their creations.

Grammar in Action Strong action verbs add interest and life to your writing. Choose the most descriptive verbs you can find.

Fireworks *exploded* in the black sky.
The grizzly *snatched* a trout from the cold stream.

Exercises Finding Action Verbs and Linking Verbs

A Number your paper from 1 to 10. Write the verb in each sentence.

1. Good morning. I am your swimming instructor.
2. The yearling seems skittish.
3. Colorful ceramic pots lined the tables.
4. Put the potatoes on the grill first, then the meat.
5. The rand is a unit of money in South Africa.
6. Garth slid into home plate.
7. The burning hickory smells wonderful.
8. The vendors displayed their vegetables daily.
9. The puzzle answers are on the next page.
10. Delores bowled a strike.

B Number your paper from 1 to 10. Write the verb in each sentence. Then tell what kind of verb it is. Write *Action* or *Linking*.

1. The rabbit's big, velvety ears twitched.
2. This costume looks old.
3. Judy loves cheese on her hamburgers.
4. Listen to the crickets in the basement.
5. Your directions seemed very clear.
6. Suddenly, Sean's dark eyes flashed.
7. I know the name of our senator.
8. The first woman candidate for President was Victoria C. Woodhull.
9. The kingfisher swallowed a frog and two fish.
10. Richard's bike accident happened last June.

C *Write Now* Imagine that you have just been chosen to direct a movie starring your favorite actor or actress. Write a paragraph that records the action as the filming begins. Then underline all the verbs in your paragraph.

2
Main Verbs and Helping Verbs

Focus A verb may be a single word or a group of words.

You know that many verbs are single words. Read these sentences.

> Eric *rides* a moped.   Melita *played* her cello.

Often, however, a verb is made up of two or more words.

> Eric *is riding* a moped.

> Melita *was playing* her cello.

> Eric *has been riding* a moped.

> Melita *might have played* her cello.

When there are two or more words in the verb, the last word is the main verb. Other words are helping verbs.

Helping Verbs	Main Verbs	Verb
is	riding	is riding
has been	riding	has been riding
was	playing	was playing
might have	played	might have played

Forms of the verbs *be, have,* and *do* are the most commonly used helping verbs.

> **be**—be, am, is, are, was, were
> **have**—have, has, had
> **do**—do, does, did

Forms of *be, have,* and *do* can also be used as main verbs.

Used as Helping Verb	Used as Main Verb
Bob *is* going.	Bob *is* the pitcher.
Sally *has* finished.	Sally *has* a cold.

Several other helping verbs can be used with main verbs.

be	must	will	should
being	can	would	may
been	could	shall	might

Separated Parts of the Verb

The main verb and its helping verbs are not always together. They may be separated by other parts of the sentence.

The batter *was* not *watching* the signals.
Andrea *has* never *missed* a band practice.
Did the kindergartners *make* popcorn today?
Frankenstein *could*n't *control* his monster.

Notice that *not* and the ending *n't* in the contraction are not verbs. Also notice that in questions, one or more words often come between the helping verb and the main verb.

Exercises Finding Main Verbs and Helping Verbs

A Number your paper from 1 to 10. Make two columns. Head the first column *Helping Verbs*. Head the second *Main Verb*. Write the verbs for each of these sentences in the correct column.

1. The red wolf is becoming extinct.
2. The arm of an orangutan may be over three feet long.
3. The Bears were beating the Vikings, 7–0.
4. You should have eaten a nutritious breakfast.
5. Some words can be pronounced two ways.
6. Will Momoko bring her skateboard?
7. Have you ever written a poem?
8. Curt could have joined the hockey team.
9. Computers are already performing many useful and important tasks.
10. The President cannot be elected more than twice.

B Write the following sentences. Add one or two helping verbs to each sentence. Choose from the lists on pages 369–370.

1. I _____ not expecting your phone call.
2. The old chestnut tree _____ hit by lightning.
3. Where _____ we find a book about marine life?
4. You _____ seen the flames from there.
5. This contest entry _____ be too late.
6. The beach ball _____ completely collapsed.
7. Skip _____ never had the measles.
8. That bottle _____ floated here from Greenland.
9. We _____ already packed the picnic basket.
10. The team _____ not been defeated.

C *Write Now* Write one paragraph describing a funny incident you may have seen or heard about. Include several strong verbs that will help your reader picture the action you are describing. Underline the verbs in your paragraph.

3
Direct Objects of Verbs

Focus The *direct object* is the noun or pronoun that receives the action of the verb.

In some sentences, the subject and verb alone express a complete thought.

Subject	Verb
The audience	applauded.
Marilyn	coughed.
Everyone	laughed.

Other sentences, however, are not complete until a word or words are added after the verb.

> Paul polished the *trophy*.
> Lucia dropped her *magazine*.

The noun or pronoun that completes the action of the verb is the **direct object** of the verb. *Trophy* tells what Paul polished. *Magazine* tells what Lucia dropped. *Trophy* and *magazine* are direct objects.

To find the direct object in a sentence, first find the verb. Then ask *whom?* or *what?* after the verb. The word that answers *whom?* or *what?* is the direct object. If you cannot answer the questions *whom?* or *what?* there is no direct object.

> Christy likes salamanders.
> Christy likes *what? salamanders*
> The direct object is *salamanders*.

> Julio exercises in the morning.
> Julio exercises *whom?* Julio exercises *what?*
> You cannot answer the questions *whom?* or *what?* There is no direct object.

Exercises Understanding Direct Objects

A Copy the following sentences. Draw one line under the verb. Draw two lines under the direct object.

1. The scuba diver found a shipwreck.
2. Two shepherds sheared the ewes.
3. The pilot steered his craft onto the airfield.
4. Eun Lee stenciled the letters on the sign.
5. The children have built a huge sculpture.
6. The Bureau of the Mint manufactures all coins.
7. Kathy will repair the brakes on her bike.
8. Delores likes yogurt with cinnamon and honey.
9. The United States exports grains to the Far East.
10. A kangaroo carries her young in a pouch.

B Write the direct object from each sentence. If a sentence does not have a direct object, write *None*.

(1) Nine-year-old Maria de Sautuola wandered into a cave in Northern Spain. (2) Nearby, her father dug artifacts. (3) Suddenly, he heard screams. (4) He dropped his pick and rushed to Maria. (5) Lantern light revealed many primitive pictures. (6) Animals decorated the cave's ceiling. (7) In lifelike poses, they pawed the ground. (8) Maria had made an important discovery. (9) Experts estimated the age of the paintings from 15,000 to 10,000 B.C. (10) The Altimira caves produced perhaps the finest prehistoric art.

c *Write Now* Write a story about a weird scientist. Use direct objects to complete some of your verbs.

4
Linking Verbs

Focus A *linking verb* connects, or links, the subject with a word in the predicate that describes or renames the subject.

Linking verbs connect a word in the predicate with the subject. The word in the predicate says something about the subject.

Carrie *is* tall.   Mountain lakes *are* cold.

Linking verbs connect *Carrie* with *tall* and *lakes* with *cold*. The words *tall* and *cold* tell about the subject. They are linked to the subject in each sentence by the linking verbs *is* and *are*.

The words *am, is, are, was, were, be, been,* and *become* are often used as linking verbs. The words *seem, look, appear, smell, taste, feel,* and *sound* can also be linking verbs.

The words that follow linking verbs and tell something about the subject can be adjectives, nouns, or pronouns. They are called **predicate words** because they are in the predicate.

I *feel* ill. (*Ill* is an adjective.)

These pickles *taste* sour. (*Sour* is an adjective.)

A goat *became* our team mascot. (*Mascot* is a noun.)

My best friend *is* she. (*She* is a pronoun.)

Do not confuse nouns or pronouns following linking verbs with direct objects of verbs. In the examples just given, you can see that *she* and *mascot* tell something about the subject of each sentence. They do not receive the action of the verbs and are not direct objects. To identify a linking verb, decide whether the noun following the verb tells something about the subject of the sentence. If it does, the verb is a linking verb.

Exercises Mastering Linking Verbs

A Number your paper from 1 to 10. Write the linking verb in each sentence. Watch for helping and compound verbs.

1. The origin of the Polynesians remains a mystery.
2. They were not Asian and they were not South American.
3. Historians feel certain about these facts.
4. The Polynesians have always been excellent navigators.
5. Their dugout canoes look strange, but they are efficient.
6. Navigating by a sense of touch may seem unusual.
7. Yet, the Polynesians became masters of the Pacific.
8. Today, they are residents on almost every Pacific island.
9. However, the Polynesians remain a single culture.
10. Their languages sound similar; their people look alike.

Polynesian tiki god.

B Draw three columns on your paper. Label them *Subject*, *Linking Verb*, and *Predicate Word*. Find these three parts in each sentence. Write them in the proper columns.

1. A young kangaroo is a joey.
2. That clown's hat looks ridiculous.
3. By now, those tadpoles have become frogs.
4. The stew smells delicious.
5. Bullfighters seem brave.
6. Rachael's story sounds unbelievable.
7. The dungeon looks scary.
8. Under water, straight lines appear wavy.
9. Long John Silver is a character in *Treasure Island*.
10. The cast felt nervous during the rehearsal.

C *Write Now* Did you know that there is a book titled *Who's Who in America?* It contains information about well-known people. Write a "Who's Who in Our School" paragraph. Name important people and their positions. Tell what each person does and what he or she is like. You might include the principal, secretary, and librarian.

5
Verb Tenses

Focus Different forms of a verb are used to show time. These forms are called the *tenses* of a verb.

Verbs do more than tell of an action or a state of being. They also tell about time. By changing their forms, verbs tell whether the action or state of being is past, present, or future.

The **present tense** tells about an action or a state of being happening now.

> I *work* at school.   I *am* a student.   I *can study*.

The **past tense** tells about an action or state of being that was completed in the past.

> I *worked* all last summer.   I *was* a library aide.

The **future tense** tells about an action or a state of being happening in the future.

> I *will work* at the pool next year.   I *will be* a lifeguard.

Notice that verb tense changes are made in three ways.

1. By a change in ending: *look, looked*
2. By a change in spelling: *know, knew*
3. By a change in helping verbs: *did work, will work*

Forming the Present Tense

When the subject is plural, use the basic form of the verb. The basic form of the verb has no endings or changes. Use the basic form of the verb with the pronouns *I* and *you*. Add *-s* or *-es* to the basic form when the subject is singular.

> We *ride*.   They *ride*.   I *ride*.   You *ride*.   He *rides*.

Forming the Past Tense

Form the past tense of most verbs by adding *-ed* to the present tense. Verbs that form the past tense by adding *-ed* to the basic form of the verb are called **regular verbs**.

> laugh   laugh*ed*   tackle   tackl*ed*

Other verbs, called **irregular verbs,** change their spelling to show the past tense.

> do   *did*   think   *thought*

There is also another way that you can show a change in tense. You can use a helping verb with the main verb.

> smile   *had smiled*   ran   *had run*

Forming the Future Tense

Form the future tense by using the helping verbs *will* or *shall* with the present tense.

> write   *will write*   sing   *shall sing*

Grammar in Action   When you write, keep your verbs in the same tense. Do not switch from past to present or present to past.

Incorrect   I *paddled* the kayak. I *steer* it and *miss* a rock.
Correct   I *paddled* the kayak. I *steered* it and *missed* a rock.

Exercises Using Verb Tenses

A Write the verb in each of the following sentences. Then write the tense of the verb. Write *Past, Present,* or *Future.*

1. Kohinoor means "the mountain of light" in Persian.
2. The Kohinoor diamond sparkled through the destruction of two empires.
3. Emperor Mohammed Mogul once owned the stone.
4. His empire fell to the Shah of Persia.
5. The new owner, the Shah, soon died in a palace revolt.
6. Two legends surround the gem.
7. First, its owner will someday rule the world.
8. Second, a man can never wear the stone.
9. Will the legends come true?
10. At present, the diamond glitters over the head of the Queen of England.

B Write the form of the verb asked for in each sentence.

1. I (future of *read*) all of the Hardy Boys mysteries.
2. The lawyer (past of *argue*) her case.
3. Blake (present of *roast*) chestnuts in the fireplace.
4. Tyrone (past of *carve*) a duck decoy.
5. The airplane (future of *land*) in a few minutes.
6. Gypsy moths (past of *devour*) countless trees.
7. Evan and Teresa (past of *pick*) raspberries.
8. A cricket game (present of *confuse*) most Americans.
9. Sponges (present of *live*) in the deep seas.
10. The track team (future of *run*) in a meet tomorrow.

C *Write Now* You are a bicycle racer. You have just finished the second lap of a race and your teammate has now taken over. She is reaching the halfway mark. In a brief paragraph, tell how your team has done so far, how your teammate is doing, and what you think the outcome of the race will be. Underline the action verbs you use.

6
The Principal Parts of Verbs

Focus All verb tenses are made from the three *principal parts* of a verb: present, past, and past participle.

You have seen that every verb has many different forms. All of these different forms of a verb are made from just three parts. For this reason, the three parts of any verb are called its **principal parts**.

Look at the principal parts of the verbs below.

Present	Past	Past Participle
call	called	(have) called
climb	climbed	(have) climbed
hurry	hurried	(have) hurried
look	looked	(have) looked
paste	pasted	(have) pasted
stop	stopped	(have) stopped
talk	talked	(have) talked
walk	walked	(have) walked

The **present** part of the verb is its present tense. Add *-s* to form the singular. The present part used with *will* or *shall* forms the future tense.

The **past** part of the verb is its past tense.

The **past participle** is always used with a helping verb such as *have*. Look at these other examples.

is called	was being called
has called	shall be called
have called	has been called
had called	will have called
was called	should have been called
were called	

Notice that with regular verbs, the past participle is the same as the past form. This is not always true of irregular verbs. You will learn more about the principal parts of irregular verbs in part 7.

Exercises Mastering the Principal Parts of Verbs

A Divide your paper into three columns. Label one column *Present*, one column *Past*, and the third column *Past Participle*. Write each of the following words in the *Present* column. Then write the past and past participle forms in the proper columns. Use one or more helping verbs with the past participle.

1. print
2. decorate
3. paste
4. carry
5. use

6. help
7. confuse
8. list
9. cover
10. like

B Number your paper from 1 to 10. Write the form of each verb asked for in parentheses. Then use each verb you write in a sentence. You may use one or more helping verbs with the past participle.

1. introduce (present)
2. protect (past)
3. wobble (present)
4. add (past participle)
5. trade (past)

6. sound (past participle)
7. develop (past)
8. need (past participle)
9. improve (past)
10. organize (present)

C *Write Now* Reporter Ace Cunningham arrives on the scene. The assignment—to solve the mystery and break the story! The clues—shattered glass, a grinning tabby cat, and a *very* soggy carpet. Ace solves the mystery. Write Ace's story. Use *have, has,* or *had* with some of the verbs in the story.

7

Irregular Verbs

Focus Some verbs form the past tense in special ways. These verbs are called *irregular verbs.*

You have learned that the past form of a regular verb is made by adding *-ed* to the present form.

move   mov*ed*   block   block*ed*   tip   tipp*ed*

Some verbs, however, have special past forms. These verbs are **irregular verbs**. Here are some examples.

sing   *sang*   give   *gave*   go   *went*

Sometimes, the past participle of an irregular verb is the same as the past form.

brought   *(have) brought*   taught   *(have) taught*

Many irregular verbs have special past participle forms.

rode   *(have) ridden*   flew   *(have) flown*

Remember these rules whenever you use irregular verbs.

1. **The past form is used alone without a helping verb.**
   The camel *drank* the entire bucket of water.
2. **The past participle must always be used with a helping verb.**
   The camel *had drunk* the entire bucket of water.

On page 382 there is a list of the principal parts of the most common irregular verbs. Study this list. Refer to it whenever you are unsure about the proper form of an irregular verb. In addition, the dictionary also lists the principal parts of irregular verbs under the present form.

Principal Parts of Common Irregular Verbs

Present	Past	Past Participle
begin	began	(have) begun
break	broke	(have) broken
bring	brought	(have) brought
choose	chose	(have) chosen
come	came	(have) come
do	did	(have) done
drink	drank	(have) drunk
eat	ate	(have) eaten
fall	fell	(have) fallen
fly	flew	(have) flown
freeze	froze	(have) frozen
give	gave	(have) given
go	went	(have) gone
grow	grew	(have) grown
know	knew	(have) known
lay	laid	(have) laid
lie	lay	(have) lain
ride	rode	(have) ridden
rise	rose	(have) risen
run	ran	(have) run
say	said	(have) said
see	saw	(have) seen
sing	sang	(have) sung
sit	sat	(have) sat
speak	spoke	(have) spoken
steal	stole	(have) stolen
swim	swam	(have) swum
take	took	(have) taken
teach	taught	(have) taught
wear	wore	(have) worn
write	wrote	(have) written

Exercises Using Irregular Verbs

A Proofreading Rewrite the following paragraph. Correct any errors in the use of irregular verbs.

In 1925 Gertrude Ederle begun her career as a professional swimmer. She gived lessons and exhibitions to earn money. In 1926, at age nineteen, she swum the English Channel. Her time breaked all previous records. The feat taked fourteen hours and thirty-nine minutes. Other swimmers had nearly freezed in the cold water. Gertrude, however, weared a heavy coat of grease for warmth. Reporters had flew in from all over the world for the event. Some rided next to her in rowboats. In their articles, the reporters writed not only about this victory, but also about Gertrude's earlier Olympic medals.

B Number your paper from 1 to 10. Write the correct form of the verb in parentheses for each sentence.

1. Ricky Henderson (past of *steal*) second base.
2. Puffs of smoke (past of *rise*) from the chimney.
3. The ice on the skating pond is (past participle of *freeze*).
4. The clues have (past participle of *fall*) into place.
5. The Kahn family (past of *go*) to Jeckyl Island.
6. My sisters have (past participle of *eat*) all the pizza.
7. Becky has (past participle of *run*) in marathons.
8. Nobody (past of *know*) where the treasure was.
9. The chickens had (past participle of *lay*) many eggs.
10. Dr. Hirasawa (past of *speak*) to our team about safety in sports.

Gertrude Ederle

C *Write Now* Imagine that you entered a time machine and noticed two red buttons marked *Plymouth Rock*, A.D. *1620*, and *The Moon*, A.D. *1969*. You pushed one and instantly moved back in time. Write a paragraph about what you saw and did. Use the past and past participle forms of verbs.

8
Confusing Pairs of Verbs

Focus Several pairs of verbs are often confused. These include *can* and *may, let* and *leave,* and *lie* and *lay*.

Look at the correct way to use these confusing verbs.

Can and **May**
1. *Can* means "to be able."
2. *May* means "to allow" or "to permit."

    Melissa *can* run the fastest.
    You *may* go to the concert.

Let and **Leave**
1. *Let* means "to allow" or "to permit."
2. *Leave* means "to depart" or "to let stay or be."
Principal Parts   let, let, let
                  leave, left, left

    Let me see your scrapbook.
    What time do you *leave* for school?
    Leave the dog in the yard.

Lie and **Lay**
1. *Lie* means "to rest" or "recline."
2. *Lay* means "to put or place something."
Principal Parts   lie, lay, lain
                  lay, laid, laid

    My cat often *lies* on the windowsill.
    Lay paper on the floor before you paint.

Lay also means to produce eggs: A hen *lays* eggs.

Exercises Using Verbs Correctly

A Write the correct verb from the parentheses.

1. You're (lying, laying) on my towel.
2. (May, Can) Marcia and Fred really read that fast?
3. Certainly Jean (may, can) leave her bike in our garage.
4. (Let, Leave) the needle of the compass settle.
5. I often (lie, lay) on the couch when I read.
6. (May, Can) we take Trudy to the boat races tomorrow?
7. Cindy always (lets, leaves) her coat on the sofa.
8. Bricklayers (lie, lay) bricks with a trowel.
9. The bus (lets, leaves) from Fountain Square hourly.
10. (May, Can) you carry all those packages?

B Number your paper from 1 to 10. If a verb is incorrect, write the correct form. If the verb is correct, write *Correct*.

1. May I see your slides?
2. The fishing net leaves all the minnows through.
3. The lions laid still in the heat.
4. Don't lay your coat on the chair.
5. Can Chris and I go out in the canoe?
6. Let your wet umbrella on the porch.
7. The terrier lays on the front steps all afternoon.
8. Can you read the bottom line without glasses?
9. Don't ever lie plastic dishes on the hot stove.
10. "Please leave me stay up late," begged Karen.

c *Write Now* You often baby-sit for your three-year-old neighbor, "Miserable" Mervin Malone, but you are unable to sit this Saturday. Mrs. Malone has asked you to write brief notes for Mervin's new sitter. Using the words below, write some of the important things the sitter will need to know.

can	lie	leave
may	lay	let

9

Other Confusing Verb Pairs

Focus Other verb pairs that are often confused are these: *teach* and *learn, rise* and *raise,* and *sit* and *set.*

Here are more verb pairs that are often confused.

Teach and **Learn**
1. *Teach* means "to show how" or "to explain."
2. *Learn* means "to understand" or "to gain knowledge."
Principal Parts   teach, taught, taught
                   learn, learned, learned

Now I will *teach* you to play chess.
The kindergartners will *learn* to tie laces.

Rise and **Raise**
1. *Rise* means "to move upward" or "to get up."
2. *Raise* means "to move something upward" or "to lift."
Principal Parts   rise, rose, risen
                   raise, raised, raised

If we *rise* early enough, we can watch the sunrise.
Raise your hand and ask Mr. Kelly your question.

Sit and **Set**
1. *Sit* means "to be in a seat" or "to rest."
2. *Set* means "to put or place something."
Principal Parts   sit, sat, sat
                   set, set, set

The captain *sits* in the cockpit.
Set the casserole on the table.

Exercises Using the Right Verb

A Number your paper from 1 to 10. Choose the correct verb form from those in the parentheses. Write it on your paper.

1. (Teach, Learn) me how to make popcorn please.
2. After the long hike, I wanted to (sit, set) and relax.
3. Kathy should (rise, raise) and take her place on stage.
4. The hockey stick was (sitting, setting) where I left it.
5. Ron will (teach, learn) me the basic swimming strokes.
6. He was (teaching, learning) us to eat with chopsticks.
7. (Teach, Learn) Jessica and me how to throw a lasso.
8. Can Mr. Scot (rise, raise) the sail himself?
9. Did Jill (rise, raise) the flag this morning?
10. (Sit, Set) still while I take your picture.

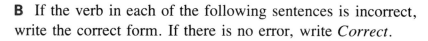

B If the verb in each of the following sentences is incorrect, write the correct form. If there is no error, write *Correct*.

1. Training programs rise guide dogs to help blind people.
2. Such programs learn the dogs special and valuable skills.
3. First, a family raises a dog for about a year.
4. The family sits typical goals for basic obedience.
5. Then, an intense course learns the dog specialized skills.
6. A guide dog even learns when to disobey commands.
7. For example, a dog teaches when not to cross a busy street.
8. In such cases, it will set still and refuse to move rather than endanger its owner.
9. Time is also sit aside for dog and owner to work together.
10. A well-trained guide dog will raise to almost any occasion.

c *Write Now* You spent a month at Camp Thunderbolt. Using the ideas below, write three entries in your camp diary.

Day 1—Describe waking in the morning. Use *rise* and *raise*.
Day 2—Describe some camp activities. Use *teach* and *learn*.
Day 3—Describe the preparations for a cookout. Use *sit* and *set*.

Linking Grammar & Writing

A Imagine that the World's Best Stuntperson Contest was held in your town. Use a variety of action verbs to write a paragraph describing what each of the three finalists did. Tell who won and explain why he or she was the best.

B You and your friends are in the cave at Haggar Hill. You are trying to convince your friends not to be afraid because the cave is not haunted. Then you discover you are wrong. It is haunted! Write a story about your adventure.

First, explain why you agreed to go into the cave. Then, describe what you are seeing and doing in the cave at this time. Finally, tell how you will feel when you get out. Remember to use the appropriate tenses for your verbs.

C Using Verbs in History Choose one of the following "firsts" in history. Read about it in an encyclopedia. Then write a brief paragraph in your own words. Tell about this famous first in history. Write your story in the past tense. Then write it in the present tense. Notice how the story comes alive when you give a present tense account.

1. Gold is discovered in California.
2. Sir Edmund Hillary climbs Mt. Everest.
3. Orville and Wilbur Wright fly the first airplane.

The Wright Brothers' first flight, Kitty Hawk, North Carolina, December 17, 1903.

Additional Practice

Part 1 Kinds of Verbs Write the verb in each of the following sentences.

1. The city of Manila is in the Philippines.
2. The sleek, graceful dolphin swam alongside the fishing boat.
3. Hector's chili tastes too spicy.
4. The capital of Brazil is Brasilia.
5. Nadia Comaneci achieved seven perfect scores in the 1976 Olympics.
6. Tina attended a performance of the Joffrey Ballet yesterday evening.
7. Argentina has a population of about thirty million people.
8. Bats usually fly at night.
9. Mr. Schultz travels internationally for his job.
10. I am a member of the computer club.

Part 2 Main and Helping Verbs Copy each sentence. Then underline each helping verb once and each main verb twice.

11. The President will sign the bill.
12. The raccoons have been eating our supplies.
13. The *Pieta* was sculpted by Michaelangelo.
14. Hawaii did not become a state until 1959.
15. Mercury is located nearer to the sun than any of the other planets.
16. Was Oscar Arias Sanchez awarded the Nobel Peace Prize in 1987?
17. You shouldn't have listened to your sister.
18. President Lincoln was elected in 1860.
19. That injury might have ended Josie's career.
20. Did Steffi Graf win the French Open singles tennis tournament?

Part 3 Direct Objects Copy each sentence. Then underline the verb once and the direct object twice.

21. The author Virginia Hamilton wrote *The House of Dies Drear*.
22. The Jordans grow wheat in the fields behind their barn.
23. The ancient Egyptian people built the gigantic stone pyramids.
24. Sheri was reading her poetry to the class when the bell rang.
25. My uncle raises orchids as a hobby.
26. The relay racer handed the baton to Pedro.
27. The earthquake damaged the new bridge.
28. Celia plays the piano beautifully.
29. The coach gave the sign to the batter.
30. The lawyer has presented the evidence to the members of the jury.

Part 4 Linking Verbs Write the linking verb in each of the following sentences. Then write a new sentence by changing the italicized word linked to the subject.

31. Her efforts were *successful*.
32. The stout man with a tiny black moustache is a very famous *actor*.
33. Vacations are always too *short*.
34. The police detective felt *uneasy* in the dark, deserted warehouse.
35. That down quilt seems very *cozy*.
36. Terika seems *tired* today.
37. Elizabeth and Michael's father is a talented and experienced *mechanic*.
38. Fred smelled the *pizza*.
39. Grace's costume looks *bizarre*.
40. Mopeds are efficient *vehicles*.

Part 5 Verb Tenses Write the form of the verb asked for in each of the following sentences.

41. Georgia O'Keeffe often (past of *paint*) scenes of the Southwest.
42. Sean's younger sister (future of *attend*) the University of Texas.
43. Wilbert (present of *play*) a battered silver tuba in the marching band.
44. Who (past of *discover*) the vaccine for polio?
45. The dinosaurs (past of *die*) out 65 million years ago, before humans ever lived.
46. The choir (future of *perform*) at the assembly.
47. The Jelineks' relatives (present of *live*) in Poland.
48. Tomorrow our group (future of *hike*) to the bottom of the isolated canyon.
49. Peter and Rich (past of *lift*) the refrigerator from the moving truck.
50. Laura (present of *play*) a dulcimer.

Part 6 Principal Parts of Verbs Write the verb in each of the following sentences. Then tell whether the verb is in the *present, past,* or *past participle* form.

51. How many people have climbed Mount Everest?
52. People call Chicago the "Windy City."
53. Kobe is one of the most important seaports in the country of Japan.
54. James Naismith invented the game of basketball.
55. Stalactites hang from the roof of the cave.
56. B. B. King calls his guitar Lucille.
57. The forest fire burned out of control for three days.
58. Frances Perkins was the secretary of labor for President Franklin D. Roosevelt.
59. Carrie has applied for a part time job.
60. The flat tire was repaired by the mechanic.

Part 7 Irregular Verbs Change the present form of the verb in parentheses to the past form. Write the verbs on your paper.

61. The band concert (begin) an hour ago.
62. Our hoe (break), so we can't plant the garden.
63. Sue (write) the sign using calligraphy.
64. Jack's beanstalk (grow) high into the clouds.
65. Seth (ride) his pony to the fiesta.
66. Carol (bring) helium balloons to the party.
67. Before breakfast, I (swim) ten laps.
68. On Christmas morning, all the churches in the village (ring) their bells.
69. The monarch butterflies (fly) all the way from Canada to Mexico.
70. Coach Baily (teach) me to play soccer.

Parts 8 and 9 Confusing Pairs of Verbs Choose the correct verb in parentheses in each sentence. Write it on your paper.

71. You should (let, leave) me help you pack your suitcase for our weekend trip.
72. Anne Sullivan Macy (learned, taught) Helen Keller to speak, read, and write.
73. Please do not (set, sit) on the newly painted roadside bench.
74. The stage hands (raised, rised) the curtain.
75. You (can, may) go to the movie if you finish your social studies homework.
76. Father (lies, lays) in the hammock to relax.
77. Manuel (can, may) jump higher than anyone else on the team.
78. Please do not (lie, lay) your jacket on the floor.
79. Just (sit, set) the groceries on the counter.
80. The weather forecaster said the temperature will (rise, raise) today.

Application and Review

Lesson Review

A Finding Action Verbs and Linking Verbs Make two columns on your paper. Head one column *Action Verbs* and the other *Linking Verbs*. Find the verb in each sentence and place it in the correct column.

1. The spider web was delicate and lacy.
2. Catherine considered the question carefully.
3. Were you at the bicycle shop this morning?
4. I am certain about the address.
5. The grandfather clock chimes every hour.
6. Brian knows about the battle of Saratoga.
7. Are you on the team?
8. The village slept under the stars.
9. Were the coyotes near the campsite last night?
10. Ivy clung to the crumbling chimney.

B Mastering Main Verbs and Helping Verbs Number your paper from 1 to 10. Make two columns. Head the first column *Helping Verbs*. Head the second *Main Verb*. Write the verbs for each of these sentences in the correct column.

1. Did you watch the eclipse of the moon?
2. A thermometer will be needed for the science experiment.
3. The sales clerk had quoted the wrong price for the down jacket.
4. I might have pushed the wrong button.
5. What else could we say?
6. That delegate may have voted against me.
7. The children were just pretending.
8. The fire could have destroyed the entire block.
9. The river has risen fifteen inches this spring.
10. Carol and Diane have been collecting seashells.

C Recognizing Direct Objects Number your paper from 1 to 10. Write the verb in each sentence. Then write the direct object of the verb.

1. Carrie delivers newspapers.
2. The kitten chased a slow, brown mole into a hole in the garden.
3. A snake can shed its skin.
4. The police have closed our street to traffic for the block party.
5. Spelunkers explore caves.
6. My aunt and uncle own a farm in Iowa.
7. I have been taking lessons in figure skating for three years.
8. Have you ever played rugby?
9. Joanna studied Portuguese for months before her trip to Brazil.
10. Pony Express riders changed horses every ten miles.

D Finding Linking Verbs Number your paper from 1 to 10. Make two columns. Head the first column *Linking Verbs*. Head the second column *Action Verbs*. Write the verbs for these sentences in the correct column.

1. The snail disappeared into its shell.
2. The trip seemed shorter on the way home from our victory match.
3. This surprise party for Marcella, Charlie, and Tony was my idea.
4. We remodeled our basement.
5. Ocean breezes always smell delightful.
6. The workers are building a new museum.
7. Yolanda collects shells of all kinds.
8. Hinduism is the major religion of India.
9. That noise in the attic sounds eerie.
10. Someone pulled the fire alarm.

E Recognizing Verb Tenses Number your paper from 1 to 10. Tell the tense of each verb in italics. Write *Present*, *Past*, or *Future*.

1. Al and Jim *waited* for their bus.
2. My dog *chases* cats and squirrels.
3. A plane *lands* at the international airport every twenty-eight seconds.
4. The artist accidentally *splattered* paint all over his canvas.
5. We *watch* the news on television every night right after supper.
6. Mark *will call* by ten o'clock.
7. The marketplace *buzzes* with busy shoppers.
8. The peacock *will fan* his tail feathers for his mate and everyone else to see.
9. I *looked* everywhere for my lost shoe.
10. Susan *will study* for an hour at the library.

F Recognizing Principal Parts Number your paper from 1 to 10. Write the verb in each sentence. Then tell whether the verb is in the *present*, *past*, or *past participle* form.

1. The carpenters have sanded all the desks.
2. The excited pitcher waved the championship trophy high over his head.
3. A monkey's tail curls tightly around a branch.
4. Anita had finished her painting.
5. Magnolia blossoms fall in the heavy rain.
6. The bristle worms feed on coral.
7. Four young sparrows begged for food.
8. That waterfall has poured over the cliff for hundreds of years.
9. Krista organized the scavenger hunt.
10. King Arthur called together the noble Knights of the Round Table.

G Using Irregular Verbs Number your paper from 1 to 10. On your paper, write the form of the verb asked for in parentheses.

1. The telephone (past of *ring*) loudly three times and abruptly stopped.
2. Charlie Brown always (present of *lose*) the game.
3. The actor has (past participle of *forget*) his lines.
4. The choir (future of *begin*) caroling at the hospital on Sunday mornings.
5. He (present of *know*) the answer to the riddle.
6. Miners have often (past participle of *dig*) here for gold.
7. Charlayne (past of *go*) to see the penguins.
8. Jenina (past of *catch*) a large salmon.
9. Alice (past of *shrink*) when she drank from the mysterious bottle.
10. Sitting Bull (past of *fight*) in the Battle of Little Bighorn.

H Choosing the Right Verb Number your paper from 1 to 10. Choose the right verb form from those in parentheses. Write it on your paper.

1. (Rise, Raise) the lid and insert the tape.
2. Don't (sit, set) that brush on the wet paint.
3. Who (teaches, learns) the players to punt?
4. The spray (rises, raises) high above the falls.
5. (Let, Leave) the huckleberries that aren't quite ripe yet for tomorrow.
6. Mark can (lie, lay) tile as fast as his father.
7. The panther (sits, sets) quietly in a tree until his prey appears.
8. (Let, Leave) me help you sand the cabinet.
9. Eric often (lies, lays) on the beach on sunny days.
10. Gary, (can, may) I please see your stamp collection?

Chapter Review

A Finding Verbs and Direct Objects Number your paper from 1 to 10. Write the verb in each sentence. Tell whether it is an action verb or a linking verb. Then write the direct object of each action verb.

1. The glass ornaments appear fragile.
2. The bird might have hurt its wing.
3. Grill the steaks for fifteen minutes.
4. Martin is hanging his coat in his locker.
5. The cellar smelled musty.
6. Sara spiked the volleyball over the net.
7. Mexico and Canada are both neighbors of the United States.
8. Black-and-white cows contentedly chewed their cuds among the daisies.
9. The Pacific may be the deepest ocean.
10. Ernie could never have ridden that wild horse.

B Using Verbs Correctly Number your paper from 1 to 10. Choose the correct verb from the parentheses. Write it on your paper.

1. (Can, May) I borrow your tennis racket?
2. Ling will (teach, learn) me about Chinese food.
3. The bat (lies, lays) near the dugout.
4. The peanuts (been, have been) on the counter since dinner yesterday.
5. Carman had (ran, run) his remote control car.
6. The baby has (drank, drunk) all her pineapple juice.
7. The audience (sang, sung) along with the group of performers on stage.
8. Beth really (done, did) a double back flip!
9. Sandra, please (lie, lay) that carpet on the floor.
10. I (rise, raise) the shades every morning.

Cumulative Review

A Finding Subjects and Verbs in Sentences Copy the
sentences below. Underline the subject once and the verb
twice. There may be compound subjects or verbs. If the
subject is understood, write *You* in parentheses.

1. The mountaineers leave tomorrow for Tibet.
2. Merlin was King Arthur's wise magician.
3. For eye surgery, the laser is sometimes used.
4. The volcano erupted spectacularly.
5. How did the prisoners escape from the Cyclops?
6. The graduating cadets cheered and flung their caps high.
7. Canoe that river at your own risk.
8. Gold, silver, and lead are mined in Arizona.
9. There was a parade for the returning astronauts.
10. In 1814, Francis Scott Key wrote "The Star-Spangled
    Banner."

B Finding Nouns Copy these sentences. Capitalize each
proper noun. Underline the common nouns once and the
proper nouns twice.

1. In tennessee the tourists visited graceland, the home
   of elvis presley.
2. Our team rode on elephants at busch gardens in florida.
3. The netherlands is also called holland.
4. Aunt tess once panned for gold in alaska.
5. The giant statues on easter island are still a mystery.
6. The gymnast from russia cried as she received the medal.
7. Nathan hale was a teacher in east haddam, connecticut.
8. Uncle bob said that truth is often stranger than fiction.
9. At the party for celebrities, michael jackson and
   sylvester stallone talked briefly.
10. Most americans say that blue is their favorite color.

C Finding Verbs Write the form of the verb asked for in each sentence. Tell whether it is an action verb or a linking verb.

1. Janet Evans (past of *win*) three gold medals in the Seoul Olympics.
2. The Tennessee River has (past participle of *be*) a great source of hydroelectricity.
3. Last night I (past of *see*) Mars in the eastern sky.
4. The Hawaiian word *aloha* (present of *mean*) "welcome," "good-by," "love," and "friendship."
5. A short novel (present of *be*) a novella.
6. Professor Kahane (past of *find*) an interesting dinosaur bone in Eastern Montana.
7. Cassius (past of *look*) lean and hungry.
8. Elena (future of *give*) a carnation to her boyfriend.
9. There (present of *be*) four hundred pet cemeteries in the United States.
10. Soon the runners (future of *approach*) the halfway point.

D Combined Review Make three columns and label them *Subject, Verb*, and *Direct Object*. Write each subject and verb from these sentences in the proper column. Subjects and verbs may be compound. If there is a direct object, write it also.

1. A robin has almost three thousand feathers.
2. *Park* is the most common name for a street in America.
3. Most snakes would rather avoid humans.
4. The climbers trained for their assault on Mt. Blanc.
5. Florence Griffith-Joyner broke several world track records.
6. From our plane, the Continental Divide resembled a giant's backbone.
7. The visitor approached the bulldog cautiously.
8. Sasha revised and then typed her report on Pakistan.
9. An elephant may live a long life—over sixty years.
10. Will Ralph and Rhonda return from Reno?

21
Understanding Pronouns

Have you ever bumped into a store mannequin and excused yourself? When you looked more closely, of course, you realized that the mannequin was a stand-in, doing a job that would be awkward for a real person.

Words can have stand-ins too. In speaking and writing you can use pronouns to replace nouns. This chapter will show you how to use pronouns correctly. With these "stand-in" words at your command, your writing will be smooth and precise.

1
Pronouns and Antecedents

Focus A *pronoun* is a word used in place of a noun.

Read these sentences.

> Gina tuned *Gina's* guitar before *Gina* played the *guitar*.
> Gina tuned *her* guitar before *she* played *it*.

The second sentence is less awkward than the first because some nouns have been replaced with pronouns. *Her, she,* and *it* are pronouns. **Pronouns** take their meaning from the words they replace. *Her* and *she* refer to *Gina*. *It* refers to *guitar*.

The word a pronoun stands for is the **antecedent** of the pronoun. In the examples above, *Gina* is the antecedent of both the pronouns *her* and *she. Guitar* is the antecedent of *it*.

Two nouns may also serve as the antecedent of a pronoun.

> *Gina* and *Ray* played a duet when *they* performed.
> (*Gina* and *Ray* are both antecedents of *they*.)

Note that when a pronoun refers to the person speaking, there may not be a stated antecedent.

> *I* found the performance very entertaining.

Usually, the antecedent appears before the pronoun it stands for in a sentence. However, sometimes a pronoun and its antecedent may appear in separate sentences.

> The *musicians* entered. *They* began to practice.
> (*Musicians* is the antecedent for *they*.)

Sometimes the antecedent of a pronoun is another pronoun.

> Did *you* bring *your* music?
> (*You* is the antecedent of the pronoun *your*.)

Pronouns can be either singular or plural. Pronouns may be used to refer to yourself, to someone you are addressing, or to other persons, places, or things.

Singular Pronouns			
Person Speaking	I	my, mine	me
Person Spoken To	you	your, yours	you
Other Persons, Places,	he	his	him
and Things	she	her, hers	her
	it	its	it

Plural Pronouns			
Person Speaking	we	our, ours	us
Person Spoken To	you	your, yours	you
Other Persons, Places,	they	their, theirs	them
and Things			

Pronoun and Antecedent Agreement

Use a singular pronoun with a singular antecedent. Use a plural pronoun with a plural antecedent. This is called making the pronoun **agree** with its antecedent in number.

> *The music* (singular) began. *It* (singular) was lovely.
> *People* (plural) applauded. *They* (plural) were pleased.

Exercises Recognizing Pronouns

A Write each pronoun in the following sentences. After the pronoun, write its antecedent if one is given.

1. Donna promised she would loan me her snorkel.
2. I watched the swan preen its snowy feathers.
3. We couldn't wait to tell them about our bulldozer ride.

4. Will you find Jesse's marbles and return them to him?
5. We watched the army helicopters approach their landing pads.
6. Have you ever seen a snake shed its skin?
7. I opened the box and quickly closed it.
8. He coaxed the chickens out of their coop.
9. Jo and Ted will help us fire our pottery in their kiln.
10. Did Mr. Wong ask you to help him move his computer?

B List the pronouns in each sentence of the following story. One sentence has no pronouns. Beside each pronoun, write its antecedent if one is given.

(1) Cory went to the post office to mail his letter. (2) He hoped it would arrive on time. (3) He had entered contests many times before. (4) Unfortunately, he had never won any of them. (5) The contest rules said to write a paragraph titled "Why I Want to Go to Washington, D.C." (6) He could send only one contest entry. (7) First prize was a trip to the capital of the United States. (8) Cory hoped very much to win it. (9) At the post office, other people hurried to mail their letters. (10) Cory watched them and wondered if they were entering the contest, too.

c *Write Now* You saw an exciting magic show. The featured performers were Zena Zodiac, Waldo the Wonderful, and the comedy team of Porke and Beanes. In a paragraph, describe each performer and his or her act. Include at least five pronouns in your paragraph.

2
Using Subject Pronouns

> **Focus** The *subject pronouns* are *I, you, he, she, it, we,* and *they*. Use them as subjects of sentences and after state-of-being or linking verbs.

Use only subject pronouns as the subject of a verb.

Look at these sentences.

> Nicole saw the ball coming.
> *She* snatched it from the air.

In the first sentence, *Nicole* is the subject. In the second sentence, *She* is the subject. Only the pronouns *I, you, he, she, it, we,* or *they* can be used as the subject of a verb. For example, you would never say, "*Her* snatched it from the air."

You probably have no trouble choosing the correct pronoun when it appears by itself in the subject. Sometimes, however, one or more pronouns appear in a compound subject. Read this sentence.

> Jeff and (he, him) grilled fish over the campfire.

The pronoun appears in the subject part of this sentence. Therefore, you use the subject pronoun *he*. If you are unsure about what pronoun to use, try dividing the compound subject into two parts. Then try each part individually as the subject.

> *Jeff* grilled fish over the campfire.
> *He* grilled fish over the campfire.

Put the parts together, using the same pronoun you used when it was alone in a sentence.

> Jeff and *he* grilled fish over the campfire.

3
MILES

4
MILES

Follow the same steps to choose pronouns for the following example sentence.

(She, Her) and (I, me) hiked four miles.

She hiked four miles. *I* hiked four miles.

She and *I* hiked four miles.

Sometimes a pronoun is followed by a noun in the subject of a sentence. To know which pronoun is correct, use the steps listed above.

(We, Us) girls swam across the lake.

We swam across the lake.

The girls swam across the lake.

We girls swam across the lake.

Use subject pronouns after linking verbs.

2
MILES

Look at these sentences.

He was the highest scorer. The highest scorer was *he*.

Both sentences mean the same thing. The pronoun following *was* can be made the subject without changing the meaning of the sentence. Any pronoun that follows a linking verb can be made the subject of the sentence without changing the meaning of the sentence. Therefore, only a subject pronoun can be used after a linking verb.

Grammar in Action   Subject pronouns are often used as linking words to connect the ideas in two sentences.

EXAMPLE   My hiking boots are lightweight and sturdy.

They help prevent injuries.

1
MILE

Exercises *Identifying Subject Pronouns*

A Write the correct pronoun from each parentheses.

1. (They, Them) sent us a bill for the plumbing.
2. (Him, He) and (I, me) both ran to answer the phone.
3. The fastest swimmers were Dwight and (she, her).
4. When did (he, him) last see the missing red shirt?
5. (Her, She) and Juanita both love your monster stories.
6. Hurry! (Us, We) are late for their Halloween party!
7. (Them, They) always laugh at our jokes.
8. (Us, We) neighbors often have a cookout on July 4.
9. Seth and (me, I) peered through our telescopes.
10. The team captains are Amy and (he, him).

B Rewrite the second sentence after each number, using a pronoun to replace the repeated words.

(1) My family and I watched a travel film on Australia. My family and I saw a strange sight. (2) Near Scone, a fire burns in a mountain. The fire never goes out. (3) Explorers first thought the fire was a volcano. The explorers were wrong. (4) A scientist learned that the cause is a burning seam of coal. The scientist found the coal to be five hundred feet below ground. (5) The native aborigines fear the place. The natives think a god lives there. (6) The god is Turramulan. The god "speaks from smoke." (7) My sister wondered how the fire started. By the end of the film, my sister had the answer to her question. (8) Two theories were given. The theories suggest spontaneous combustion or lightning first started the fire.

C *Write Now* Write a paragraph about the members of your favorite music group and the instruments they play. Use subject pronouns, including a subject pronoun after a linking verb.

3
Using Object Pronouns

Focus The *object pronouns* are *me, you, him, her, it, us,* and *them.* Use them as the objects of verbs or prepositions.

Pronouns After Action Verbs

A noun does not change its form when it is used as the object of a verb. Pronouns, however, have special object forms.

The object pronouns are *me, you, him, her, it, us,* and *them. You* and *it* can be used as both subject and object pronouns. Look at the object pronoun used in this sentence.

> The lifeguard warned *us* about the jellyfish.

Pronouns are sometimes part of a compound object. If you are not sure which pronoun to use, try each part separately.

> Have you seen (he, him) or (she, her)?
> Have you seen *him*? Have you seen *her*?
> Have you seen *him* or *her*?

Pronouns After Prepositions

One kind of word always has a noun or pronoun after it and shows a relationship between that noun or pronoun and the rest of the sentence. This kind of word is called a **preposition**. The noun or pronoun that follows a preposition is called the **object of the preposition**. Object pronouns are used as objects of prepositions. Look at these sentences.

> We waited for *Zach* and *Ramona*. We waited for *them*.

You will learn more about prepositions in Chapter 24. To find a list of common prepositions, see page 462.

Exercises Mastering Object Pronouns

A Some sentences below have both object and subject pronouns. Write only the object pronouns from each sentence on your paper.

1. We left for the picnic and Carla followed behind us.
2. The last time I was at bat, the ball almost hit me.
3. Sasha played the mandolin for Yuri and them.
4. The ranger led the bird watchers and us to the nest.
5. The parrot's answer amused him.
6. Mom will bake the muffins if you will deliver them.
7. Magicians' tricks always amaze her.
8. We recognized him from the artist's sketch.
9. Call me when the grill is hot.
10. Liz ate the nuts while the monkeys chattered at her.

B Number your paper from 1 to 10. Write the correct pronoun from the parentheses in each sentence.

1. Engineers can program computers to talk to (we, us).
2. I can ask a computer something, and it will answer (I, me).
3. People must speak to (they, them) in a certain way.
4. Computers can fail; background noise confuses (them, they).
5. One computer can distinguish between Jason and (I, me).
6. The computer knows Jason's voice belongs to (he, him).
7. A computer amazed (we, us) by understanding 900 words.
8. Ann asked too much; the computer didn't answer (her, she).
9. Instead, it gave (she, her) a printed reply.
10. Computers help the blind by reading aloud to (they, them).

C *Write Now* A farmer finds a tiny safe in his field. In the metal box is a yellowed piece of paper titled "The Miser's Will." Write what the farmer reads in this unusual will. Include at least three object pronouns. Here is the first line to get you started. "To my cat, Pinky, I leave a silver bell for his collar. I leave *it* to *him* for his years of loyalty."

4
Possessive Pronouns

Focus *Possessive pronouns* show ownership.

Possessive pronouns are used to show ownership. The possessive pronouns are *my, mine, his, her, hers, its, our, ours, their, theirs, your,* and *yours*.

> *My* kite has a longer tail than *your* kite.
> *His* beagle and *her* hound chase squirrels.

In the first sentence, the pronouns *my* and *your* tell whom the kites belong to. *His* and *her* point to the owners of the dogs in the second sentence.

To make a noun show possession, you add an apostrophe and an *-s*. Pronouns, however, have special possessive forms. Possessive pronouns never use apostrophes.

Possessive pronouns may be confused with contractions that are spelled similarly. Look at the difference in these pairs.

Possessive Pronoun	The dog licked *its* paw.
Contraction	*It's* going to snow today. (It is)
Possessive Pronoun	*Their* costumes are in the wardrobe.
Contraction	*They're* moving to Nebraska. (They are)
Possessive Pronoun	*Your* film is being developed.
Contraction	*You're* next in line. (You are)

Exercises *Using Possessive Pronouns*

A Write the correct pronoun to replace the noun in parentheses.

1. Anna entered (Anna's) Irish setter in the dog show.
2. Dave thought that (Dave's) was the best carving.

3. The Plishkas painted (the Plishkas') rocking horse blue.
4. The male peacock is brightly colored and (the peacock's) mate is brown.
5. Sam hoped the winning name would be (Sam's).
6. Do you know the Reeds? This family crest is (the Reeds').
7. Sue looked at the watch and said it was not (Sue's).
8. The raccoon is washing (the raccoon's) food.
9. The players wore (the players') new uniforms.
10. Aunt Jan tasted (Aunt Jan's) freshly baked bread.

B Proofreading Rewrite the following paragraph correcting all errors in possessive pronouns.

Without water, your only going to live a few days. You're body needs water to turn food into energy. Certain life forms do not have you're problem. They're able to go long periods without water. Their bodies shrivel up and look dead. Add water and they regain they're shape. Their in a state of cryptobiosis. Its a word that means "hidden life." A life form's ability to "play dead" helps it's chances of survival during a drought. Cryptobiosis puzzles scientists.

c _Write Now_ At Camp Winona the evening activities are planned by the campers. In a paragraph, tell what item related to music, crafts, or games each of the campers brought. Tell how each camper entertained the group. Use possessive pronouns in your paragraph.

5
Indefinite Pronouns

Focus An *indefinite pronoun* is a pronoun that does not refer to a specific person or a specific thing.

Pronouns such as *someone* or *anybody* do not refer to any definite person or thing. These pronouns are called **indefinite pronouns**. Indefinite pronouns do not have clear antecedents because the persons or things they refer to are unknown. Most indefinite pronouns are singular.

Singular Indefinite Pronouns

another	anything	everybody	neither	one
anybody	each	everyone	nobody	somebody
anyone	either	everything	no one	someone

Use the singular possessive pronouns *his*, *her*, and *its* with singular indefinite pronouns.

> Someone left *her* barrette in the locker room.
> Neither brought *his* permission slip.
> Everyone should bring *his or her* sack lunch.

When the person referred to could be either male or female, *his or her* may be used. A few indefinite pronouns are plural.

Plural Indefinite Pronouns

both	many	few	several

Use the plural possessive pronoun *their* with plural indefinite pronouns. Refer to page 488 for information on making indefinite pronouns agree with verbs.

> Both gave *their* reasons.   Few left *their* seats.

Exercises Using Indefinite Pronouns

A Write the indefinite pronouns in the following sentences.

1. Both of the hermit crabs took up residence in snail shells.
2. Will everybody fit into the auditorium at the same time?
3. Anyone who enters the contest will have his or her picture in the newspaper.
4. On my block, no one has a garage.
5. In the stack of letters, only a few had ZIP codes and several had no stamps.
6. I don't know anything about computers.
7. You can plant begonias or hosta; either grows well in shade.
8. Everything on the table looked tempting.
9. Neither of the chairs can be used; each is broken.
10. That toothbrush is worn; buy another.

B Write the correct possessive pronoun given in parentheses.

1. Neither of the knights lost (his, their) courage in battle.
2. Anybody with (her, their) feet on the furniture is rude.
3. Everyone must complete (his or her, their) application now.
4. Both of the twins paid (her, their) money for the show.
5. Each of the processes has (its, their) drawbacks.
6. Several of the bikers passed (his or her, their) safety test.
7. One must develop (his or her, their) own study methods.
8. Can anyone loan me (her, their) sheet music?
9. Either the king or the minister will wave (his, their) banner to signal the start of the tournament.
10. The cast isn't ready; few know (his or her, their) lines.

C *Write Now* Imagine that each of your classmates is designing his or her own coat of arms. The coat of arms may truly represent a family, or it may represent the interests and accomplishments of each student. In a brief paragraph, describe some of your classmates' crests. Use indefinite pronouns to tell how they represented themselves.

Linking Grammar & Writing

A Choose a team sport and imagine you are the coach. Write a speech to motivate your team. Use several pronouns in your talk. Here is a line to get you started. "The game is *ours,* team. Now, go out there and show *them* what *you* can do."

B Imagine you are a movie director. Choose a book or short story you wish to make into a movie. Write a paragraph explaining what actor or actress you will cast to play the main character. Tell why you chose this person. Be sure to use both subject and object pronouns in your paragraph.

C Using Pronouns to Write About History

Choose a character from history and write a letter to this person. Begin by briefly introducing yourself and telling something about your family. Tell the historical character how the world is different now from when he or she lived. Include details that would interest this person. For example, Ben Franklin might like to know how we use electricity in today's world.

"So, then . . . Would that be 'us the people' or 'we the people'?"

Use several pronouns in your letter. Your letter may include some of the following phrases.

my name is	*it* has	*we* like
I live	*your* invention	how did *you*
in *our* town	*their* ideas	*she* began

Additional Practice

Part 1 Pronouns and Antecedents Write all the pronouns and each antecedent that is given.

1. I focused my camera on the peacock with its tail fanned.
2. The conductor raised his baton and signaled for us to play.
3. An oyster has three chambers in its heart.
4. Follow them if you want to find your way out of the maze.
5. The idea was his, but she actually wrote the card.
6. We lost our luggage, so Tom loaned me his clothes.
7. The climber picked his way up the ledge to find us.
8. I asked my uncle to drive us to the airport.
9. We helped Dave unsnag his fishing line from ours.
10. You can hook your computer up to my printer.

Part 2 Subject Pronouns Write the correct pronoun.

11. Lucinda and (me, I) want to try windsurfing.
12. (We, Us) Foresters will sing at the White House.
13. John Audubon and (he, him) were both naturalists.
14. Did Maria and (he, him) cook the turkey?
15. The last two to qualify were (he, him) and (I, me).
16. The Canadians and (we, us) share a common border.
17. Is (her, she) training for the Olympics?
18. For a year, (they, them) lived in Spain.
19. The new art teacher is (he, him).
20. (She, Her) and (I, me) are both weavers.

Part 3 Object Pronouns Write the correct pronoun.

21. Slowly, the bear lumbered toward (I, me).
22. The sultan ruled (them, they) long and wisely.
23. Do you believe Irma or (she, her)?
24. Ms. Lee complimented the class and (he, him).

25. Uncle Burt chased (we, us) out of the barn.
26. Don't tell (I, me) the answer. Let (I, me) guess.
27. Sharp stalactites hung all around (we, us).
28. The puppy curled up beside (him, he) and fell asleep.
29. This relay race depends on Francine and (her, she).
30. The skunk just ignored Toby and (they, them).

Part 4 Possessive Pronouns Write the correct pronoun from the parentheses in each sentence.

31. Did you say (you're, your) learning Morse code?
32. (It's, Its) a question of whose tale you like better.
33. Is this (you're, your) record or mine?
34. The swallow is about to build (it's, its) nest.
35. Wendy said (you're, your) hammer was broken.
36. I like (they're their) special cheese sauce.
37. (You're, Your) photos are on display at the art exhibit.
38. (They're, Their) lost oar washed up on shore.
39. The cricket makes a sound with (it's, its) legs.
40. (They're, Their) the new handlebars I bought.

Part 5 Indefinite Pronouns Write the correct pronoun from the parentheses in each sentence.

41. Several of the spices have lost (its, their) flavor.
42. Anybody who is late will have to pay (his, their) own way.
43. Each ewe can find (her, their) lambs in the flock.
44. One must make (his or her, their) own career choice.
45. Mysteries or westerns, both have (its, their) merits.
46. Would someone move (his or her, their) chair over here please?
47. Everyone told (his, their) version of the folk tale.
48. No one can get (his or her, their) form signed until Monday.
49. Neither wrote under (her, their) own name.
50. Did many want (him or her, their) books autographed?

Application and Review

Lesson Review

A Recognizing Pronouns Write all the pronouns in each sentence. Write the antecedent for each if there is one.

1. My aunt called us long distance from Alaska.
2. If your calculator works, use it.
3. Tell Kevin to invite Maggie when he sees her.
4. Mark's new shoes crunched his toes.
5. The Jacobs didn't fly their seaplane.
6. I saved my allowance, but Ian and Ted spent theirs.
7. Jon took our binoculars on his hike.
8. Throw your best slider and watch me hit it.
9. The Plains Indians pitched their teepees near water.
10. The peacock turned toward me and fanned its tail.

B Mastering Subject Pronouns Write the correct pronoun.

1. (He, Him) and (me, I) put decals on our new skateboards.
2. (We, Us) students voted for a picnic at the beach.
3. The marchers and (them, they) lined up at 8:30.
4. Davy, (her, she), and (I, me) rode in the helicopter.
5. The winner was (she, her).
6. When Val wore her mask, we did not know it was (her, she).
7. (He, him) came early and (us, we) weren't ready.
8. For the party, (we, us) girls made papier-mâché piñatas.
9. Did you know that the winning pitcher was (me, I)?
10. The lead actors are (they, them).

C Using Object Pronouns Write the correct pronoun.

1. Mrs. Nohr introduced (we, us) to the choir director.
2. Ramon wrestled (he, him) for the championship.
3. You've convinced (I, me) that I need a haircut.

4. Wash the berries and put (they, them) in a bowl.
5. Frank helped (he, him) build a model of a windmill.
6. The storm caught (we, us) by surprise.
7. Aunt Liz took (we, us) to see the musical *Cats*.
8. Please feed the baby and put (she, her) to bed.
9. Put the pages in order and number (them, they).
10. Jan would not take the ski lift; it frightened (she, her).

D Using Possessive Pronouns For each sentence, write the correct possessive pronoun to replace the word in parentheses.

1. Todd shook (Todd's) head in amazement.
2. This is Bob's notebook and (Bob's) compass.
3. Jan always gives away the punch line of (Jan's) jokes.
4. The river had shrunk to (the river's) original depth.
5. The comet seemed to lose (the comet's) tail as it fell.
6. The diseased oaks lost (the oaks') leaves before fall.
7. Evelyn gave (Evelyn's) report clearly.
8. The lion roared and shook (the lion's) shaggy mane.
9. Molly and I cleaned up (Molly's and my) room.
10. The balloon slipped (the balloon's) mooring.

E Using Indefinite Pronouns For each sentence, choose the correct possessive pronoun from those in parentheses.

1. Both of the candidates will make (her, their) speeches now.
2. One of the quiz shows offered a car as (its, their) prize.
3. Neither of the men recognized (his, their) own baby picture.
4. Many of the cast supplied (his or her, their) own props.
5. Few are willing to admit (his or her, their) own mistakes.
6. Anyone who wants to go should buy (her, their) ticket now.
7. Few attended, but many sent (his or her, their) best wishes.
8. Did someone ask for (his, their) money back?
9. Everyone who returns merchandise needs (his, their) receipt.
10. Either of the tax plans has (its, their) advantages.

Chapter Review

A Choosing the Correct Pronoun Number your paper from 1 to 10. Write the correct pronoun from the parentheses in each sentence.

1. Did Marnie or (they, them) show you the fossils they found in the old creek bed?
2. It was (he, him) in the Dracula costume.
3. The horse nibbled my hand when I fed (he, him) the carrot.
4. It was (her, she) and (them, they) who volunteered.
5. (We, Us) hikers made it to the top of the mountain!
6. The Kominskis and (we, us) vacation at the seashore every year.
7. The firefighter saved (them, they) and their pets.
8. Don't (I, me) have an appointment with the dentist this morning?
9. Surely you don't believe (she, her)!
10. If Ryan doesn't finish, Clark will help (he, him).

B Mastering Possessive Pronouns Number your paper from 1 to 10. Write the correct word from the parentheses in each sentence.

1. (It's, Its) raining more in July than it did in June.
2. (They're, Their) smoke alarm went off accidentally when they burned the toast.
3. Does the cat see (it's, its) reflection in the mirror?
4. (You're, Your) setting up the tent, aren't you?
5. The baby wren broke (it's, its) wing learning to fly.
6. (You're, Your) vote carried the motion.
7. (They're, Their) canoe is an aluminum twelve-footer.
8. (It's, Its) a twenty-minute ride from here to the amusement park.
9. (They're, Their) telling a story to the class.
10. Do Sharon and you write (you're, your) own poetry?

22

Understanding Adjectives

Splash on the color: red, green, blue, yellow! Paint it bright! Make it one-of-a-kind!

What special touch could *you* add to the painting on the right? How would you express your own personality and style?

Good writers and good painters have a lot in common. They both want their work to be unique and bright with personality. Painters can express themselves with color and shape. Writers make their ideas colorful and exciting with words called *adjectives*.

In this chapter you will learn how to use adjectives to add color and personality to your writing.

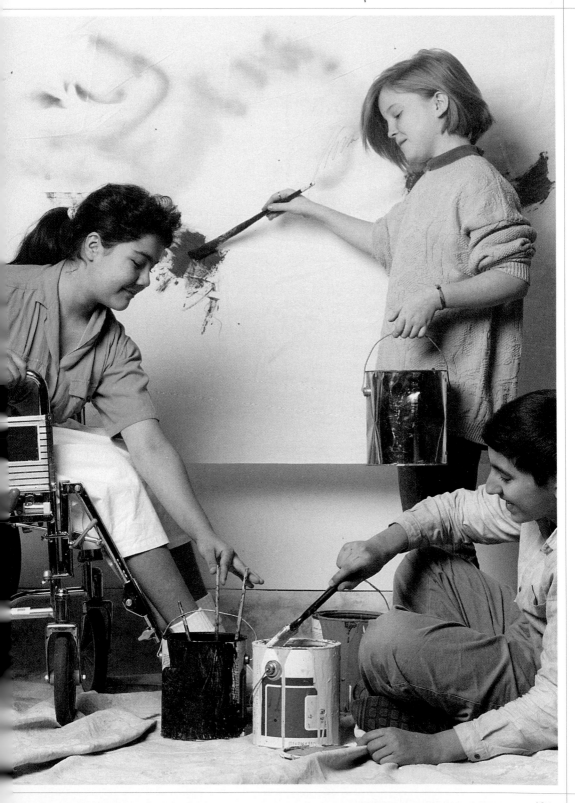

1
What Are Adjectives?

Focus An *adjective* is a word that modifies, or describes, a noun or pronoun.

Look at these sentences.

A giraffe roams the plains.
A graceful, spotted giraffe roams the hot African plains.

What words in the second sentence tell you more about the giraffe and the plains? *Graceful* and *spotted* describe *giraffe*. *Hot* and *African* tell about the *plains*. Each word adds more specific information to the sentence.

These words are **adjectives**. Adjectives describe, or modify, nouns and pronouns.

One or more adjectives may be used before the noun or pronoun being modified. Very often, when you use two or more adjectives together, you separate them with commas.

The *thick, hot, glowing* lava poured from the volcano.

Adjectives may also follow the word being modified.

I found Al, *tired* and *hungry,* at the end of the trail.

Proper Adjectives

Some adjectives, such as *African*, are made by adding endings to proper nouns. These are called **proper adjectives**. Always begin a proper adjective with a capital letter.

Australia + *-n* = Australian
Vietnam + *-ese* = Vietnamese

Other proper adjectives do not have special endings.

Hitchcock thriller   *Thanksgiving* dinner

Exercises *Identifying Adjectives*

A Number your paper from 1 to 10. Find the adjectives in each sentence. Write them on your paper.

1. Michael avoided the murky swamp.
2. The yellow and white daffodils are in bloom.
3. A timid kitten peeked out of the wicker basket.
4. A Newfoundland dog can pull heavy sleds.
5. The fisherman wore tall rubber boots in the stream.
6. I ordered Cantonese food at the Chinese restaurant.
7. José needs a new reed for the clarinet.
8. The poinsettia is a tropical American shrub.
9. The raccoon in the elm tree looks as if it is wearing a black, furry mask.
10. Tonya collects European and African coins.

B Number your paper from 1 to 10. Write an adjective for each blank in the following sentences.

1. Charlie Brown has a _____ dog named Snoopy.
2. Walking along the beach, I found a _____ starfish.
3. _____ sounds came from the attic.
4. _____ instructions came with this model kit.
5. The plate shattered when it hit the _____ floor.
6. You will need _____ eggs for that recipe.
7. _____ movies are the best!
8. I always write letters in _____ ink.
9. Lana spent the entire evening reading a _____ book.
10. In the telescope, Tim could see _____ stars.

C *Write Now* One day, Amy was sitting on a log watching a colony of ants. After a short time, one of the ants came over and started talking about itself and the colony. In a paragraph, describe Amy and the ant colony. Use adjectives to make your description lively and precise.

2
Kinds of Adjectives

Focus An *adjective* can tell *what kind, how many,* or *which one* about the word it modifies.

Every adjective has one of three functions. It may tell *what kind, how many,* or *which one.*

Some Adjectives Tell **What Kind**

Some adjectives describe by telling *what kind.*

Susan wore a *red* sweater and a *plaid* skirt.

Many adjectives that tell *what kind* are formed by adding an adjective ending to a noun.

rain*y*   danger*ous*   care*less*   color*ful*   comfor*table*

Some Adjectives Tell **How Many**

Some adjectives limit by telling *how many.*

Five boys ate *fifteen* hamburgers and *many* potatoes!

Some Adjectives Tell **Which One**

Adjectives point out specific nouns or pronouns by telling *which one* or *which ones.* Remember that possessive pronouns are used as adjectives.

Adjectives that tell *which one* or *how many* always come before the word they modify.

Your scissors are sharper than *these* scissors.

Grammar in Action   Adjectives that tell number, size, shape, color, and age often do not require commas.

Incorrect   I skipped the *small, gray* rock across the pond.
Correct   I skipped the *small gray* rock across the pond.

Exercises Using Adjectives

A Divide your paper into three columns. Label the columns *What Kind, How Many,* and *Which One.* Find all of the adjectives in each sentence and write them in the correct columns.

1. That bright light signaled to some people on shore.
2. Many people like this popular brand of fruity yogurt.
3. Those trucks have eighteen wheels.
4. That channel broadcasts several commercials hourly.
5. Is this English saddle for Sara?
6. These blue cards belong to your game.
7. Janet used her small wrench to fix my leaky faucet.
8. We ordered rye bread from that German bakery.
9. Each biker in the race carried spare parts.
10. Few people have traveled to all fifty states.

B Number your paper from 1 to 5. Supply the kind of adjective asked for in parentheses.

1. A(n) _____ howl made Rich shiver. (what kind)
2. The rally attracted _____ excited students. (how many)
3. All of the _____ darts belong to Belinda. (what kind)
4. Peculiar squeaky sounds came from _____ closet. (which one)
5. The campers quickly added twigs to their _____ campfire. (what kind)

C *Write Now* Describe one of the following unbelievable sights: the Loch Ness monster, a creature from outer space, or an underwater city. Use different types of adjectives.

3

Articles and Demonstrative Adjectives

Focus *A, an,* and *the* are special adjectives called *articles. This, that, these,* and *those* are *demonstrative adjectives.*

Articles

The words *a, an,* and *the* are **articles**. Because these words always modify nouns, they are also adjectives.

Use *a* before words beginning with consonant sounds.

  a moth   a kilt   a rose   a horse   a cup

Use *an* before words beginning with vowel sounds.

  an ant   an egg   an island   an ostrich   an uncle

Some words begin with a silent *h.* When you pronounce these words, you do not say the *h* sound. Instead, you begin the word with the vowel sound after the *h.* Therefore, you follow the rule given above and use *an.*

  an heiress   *an* hourglass   *an* honest answer

A and *an* are used with singular nouns. *The* may be used before either a singular or a plural noun.

Demonstrative Adjectives

This, that, these, and *those* are **demonstrative adjectives**. They point out specific things. Use *this* and *that* with singular nouns. Use *these* and *those* with plural nouns.

  This peach tastes sweeter than *that* one.
  These pens cost a quarter. *Those* pens cost a dollar.

Demonstrative adjectives are often paired with the nouns *kind* and *sort*. Both *kind* and *sort* are singular words. Therefore, we say *this kind* and *this sort*. We use *these* and *those* only with the plurals: *these kinds* or *those sorts*.

> *This kind* of book lets you pick your own ending.
> *Those sorts* of illnesses are caused by poor nutrition.

Adjectives or Pronouns?

Demonstrative words can be adjectives or pronouns. A demonstrative word is an adjective if it answers the question *which one?* about a noun. A demonstrative word is a pronoun if it takes the place of a noun. Look at these examples.

Adjective   *This* bug is a beetle. (*This* tells which bug.)
Pronoun   *This* is a beetle.

Adjective   *These* eggs are fresh. (*These* tells which eggs.)
Pronoun   *These* are fresh.

Adjective   I bought *that* poster. (*That* tells which poster.)
Pronoun   I bought *that*.

Adjective   We gathered *those* shells. (*Those* tells which shells.)
Pronoun   We gathered *those*.

Them is always a pronoun. It is never used as an adjective. It is always used as an object, never as the subject of a sentence.

Incorrect   *Them* model airplanes are mine.
Incorrect   *Them* are my model airplanes.
Correct   *Those* are my model airplanes. I built *them* myself.
              (*Them* is a pronoun. It replaces the noun *airplanes*.)

Grammar in Action   Use demonstrative adjectives to tell if an object you are pointing out is near or farther away.

> *Near:* this, these   *Far:* that, those

Exercises Using Demonstrative Adjectives and **Them**

A Number your paper from 1 to 10. Choose the correct word from the parentheses. Write it on your paper.

1. Do you see (those, them) light bulbs around us?
2. (They, Them) are not all alike.
3. (These, Those) common bulbs near us are incandescent.
4. Inside (them, these) bulbs, wires or filaments are heated.
5. (Them, Those) heated wires then produce light.
6. (That, Those) fluorescent bulb does not rely on wires.
7. Your school probably uses (this, these) fluorescent lights.
8. (They, Them) contain gas and mercury vapor.
9. Currents run through (these, them) tubes; light is produced.
10. (This, These) kind of colorful tube contains neon gas.

B Twelve nouns are listed below. Write six sentences, using two of the nouns in each sentence. Use an adjective in front of each noun. Add articles and demonstrative adjectives.

1. boat	4. rain	7. lighthouse	10. sea
2. sails	5. minnows	8. rocks	11. lightning
3. wind	6. fish	9. storm	12. thunder

C *Write Now* Your school is having a rummage sale to raise money for the United Way. The following items are on the sporting goods counter. Write five sentences using articles and demonstrative adjectives that explain the value and the price of the items.

1. Two baseball pennants (both are close to you)
2. One basketball
3. Two bowling balls (one is near and one is far away)

4

Predicate Adjectives

Focus A *predicate adjective* is an adjective that follows a linking verb. It describes the subject of the sentence.

When an adjective follows a linking verb, it is part of the predicate. Therefore, it is called a **predicate adjective**. A predicate adjective modifies the subject.

The crocodiles are hungry.

The rock climbers look tired.

A predicate adjective is different from the adjectives you have studied. Unlike most other adjectives, a predicate adjective comes after the word it modifies. It also is separated from the word it modifies by a linking verb.

Here are some common linking verbs that often come before predicate adjectives.

am	was	become	look	taste
are	were	feel	seem	sound
is	appear	grow	smell	remain

Exercises Predicate Adjectives

A Copy the following sentences. In each sentence, draw one line under the predicate adjective. Then draw two lines under the word or words it modifies. Remember that more than one predicate adjective can follow a verb.

1. Do frogs and toads look alike to you?
2. Both creatures are cold-blooded and amphibious.
3. They are well suited to life on both land and water.
4. Yet, the skin and shape of frogs and toads seem different.
5. Frogs feel smooth and slippery.

6. In contrast, toads appear dry and bumpy.
7. After the tadpole stage, frogs grow long and graceful.
8. Toads remain squat and pudgy.
9. People seem needlessly fearful about handling toads.
10. The rumor about toads and warts is untrue.

B Number your paper from 1 to 10. Write each sentence. Complete it with a predicate adjective. Then draw a line under the word it modifies.

1. The flight to Los Angeles will be _____ .
2. The early settlers became very _____ .
3. The hermit crab looks _____ .
4. That mystery book was _____ .
5. The week-old milk smells _____ .
6. Without water, the plants will become _____ .
7. Vincent's violin sounds _____ .
8. This apple tastes _____ .
9. The sandpaper feels _____ .
10. The pictures of our vacation were _____ .

C *Write Now* Imagine that you are a scout for a group of explorers. Because you travel ahead of the others, you are the first to reach the peak of a mountain. You are all alone. Describe the scene from the mountain peak. What do you see all around you? How do you feel? Use some linking verbs and predicate adjectives to write a paragraph about this experience.

5
Making Comparisons with Adjectives

Focus Use the *comparative form* of an adjective to compare two things. Use the *superlative form* of an adjective to compare three or more things.

A bear is big. A hippopotamus is big. An elephant is big.

All of these animals are big, but they are not the same size. You can show the differences in size by using special forms of adjectives.

Use the word *bigger* to compare two things. *Bigger* is the **comparative form** of *big*.

The hippopotamus is *bigger* than the bear.

Use *biggest* to compare three or more things. *Biggest* is the **superlative form** of *big*.

The elephant is the *biggest* of the three animals.

Follow these rules to make the comparative and superlative forms of adjectives.

1. **Use the comparative form to compare two things.** To make the comparative form of most short adjectives, add *-er*.

2. **Use the superlative form to compare three or more things.** To make the superlative form of most short adjectives, add *-est*.

Adjective	Comparative Form	Superlative Form
calm	calmer	calmest
big	bigger	biggest
cute	cuter	cutest
noisy	noisier	noisiest

Notice that when an adjective ends in a single consonant following a single vowel, such as *big,* you must double the final consonant before adding the ending. When the adjective ends in silent *e,* such as *cute,* drop the *e* before adding the ending. When the adjective ends in a *y* following a consonant, such as *noisy,* change the *y* to *i* before adding the ending.

Using More *and* Most

The comparative and superlative forms of some adjectives are not made by adding *-er* or *-est.* For longer adjectives, use the word *more* before the adjective to make the comparative form. Use the word *most* before the adjective to make the superlative form.

Adjective	Comparative Form	Superlative Form
difficult	more difficult	most difficult
noticeable	more noticeable	most noticeable
careful	more careful	most careful

Irregular Adjectives

The comparative and superlative forms of some adjectives are completely new words. Here are some of those forms.

Adjective	Comparative Form	Superlative Form
good	better	best
bad	worse	worst
little	less	least
much	more	most

Grammar in Action Never use the *-er* ending with the word *more.* Never use the *-est* ending with the word *most.*

Incorrect This pillow is *more softer* than that one.
Correct This pillow is *softer* than that one.

Exercises *Making Comparisons with Adjectives*

A Number your paper from 1 to 10. Choose the correct form of the adjective from the parentheses. Write it on your paper.

1. Claire is the (more careful, most careful) skier I know.
2. Tomorrow will be (colder, more colder) than today.
3. Of the two kickers, Bill scored (more, most) points.
4. Air pollution is (worse, worser) in large cities.
5. Everest is the (taller, tallest) mountain in the world.
6. Of all the contestants, Kelly is the (less, least) nervous.
7. *The Far Side* was the (funnier, funniest) of the three cartoons.
8. Cindy has the (newer, newest) guitar in our group.
9. Have you heard the (latest, most late) announcement?
10. My boots were (less muddy, least muddy) than yours.

B Write each sentence. Use the comparative or superlative form of the adjective in parentheses.

1. Without a doubt, diamonds are the (hard) of all gems.
2. They are also the (more) prized.
3. However, an emerald (large) than a diamond might cost more.
4. Rubies are (rare) than sapphires.
5. Therefore, rubies are (valuable) than sapphires.
6. How do you judge which is the (good) of two sapphires?
7. All of the world's (good) sapphires are a deep blue.
8. The (dark) opals of all are black and very expensive.
9. In contrast, the (white) of two pearls would cost more.
10. The (important) quality of all is for a gem to be flawless.

c *Write Now* Imagine that you write television commercials. You are going to show how great your product is by comparing it to another brand. Make up a product and give it a name. Then write an ad that will persuade audiences that your product is the best!

Linking Grammar & Writing

A Movie sets can be realistic and exciting. Think of an especially impressive scene from a movie you have seen recently. Write a paragraph about the scene. Use adjectives to describe all the people and objects. Use demonstrative adjectives to point out things that are near and things that are farther away.

B Explore a cookbook for ethnic foods or tell about eating at an ethnic restaurant, such as Japanese, Mexican, East Indian, Italian, French, Greek, or Scandinavian. Describe several items that are offered. Tell what you think is the best dish and what is the least appetizing. Finally, rate the cookbook or restaurant from one to four stars.

C Using Adjectives in Art Look at the painting below. Do you like it? Try to describe it to a friend. Use adjectives to describe such things as color, size, texture, shape, and design. Also, give reasons why you do or do not like it.

House In Landscape, Jean-Pierre.

Additional Practice

Parts 1 and 2 Recognizing Adjectives Make three columns on your paper. Label them *What Kind, How Many,* and *Which One*. Find all the adjectives in each sentence and write them in the correct columns. Do not include articles.

1. His noisy old car needed a new muffler.
2. Canada has ten provinces and two territories.
3. The frightened kitten scampered into a dark corner and whimpered softly.
4. This empty building used to be a busy factory, and it will soon be redesigned as fifteen condominiums.
5. The chestnut colt is kept in that stall.
6. Five members of our swimming team set records.
7. Several yellow warning signs marked the dangerous corner.
8. That movie was nominated for seven Oscars.
9. We bought these pastries at the French bakery.
10. Many young athletes dream of winning gold medals in the Olympics.

Part 3 Demonstrative Adjectives Choose the correct word from the parentheses in each sentence. Write it on your paper.

11. Bill needs (that, those) kind of car to finish his model train set.
12. (Them, Those) unusual flowers are snapdragons.
13. Do you like (this, these) kind of art?
14. (These, Them) girls with me are my cousins.
15. (Them, These) muffins have chopped walnuts.
16. Lois often buys (this, these) sorts of shoes.
17. (Them, These) are illustrations by Wanda Gág.
18. I think (this, these) kinds of crackers are the best.
19. (Them, They) are great photographs!
20. Can you see (those, them) geese flying south?

Part 4 Predicate Adjectives Copy the following sentences. In each sentence, draw one line under the predicate adjective. Then draw two lines under the word it modifies.

21. The weather is chilly in April.
22. Your directions to the park were helpful.
23. The key lime pie tastes tart.
24. I feel confident about the test.
25. The water in the pond looks stagnant.
26. Objects in the rearview mirror appear smaller than they actually are.
27. At dawn our house is peaceful.
28. The music on the radio sounded soothing.
29. The trail to the campground was steep.
30. Alberto was exhausted after the game.

Part 5 Making Comparisons Write each sentence. Use the comparative or superlative form of the adjective in parentheses.

31. This puppy is (frisky) than that one.
32. I tried all the flavors and this one tastes (good).
33. Eric's jokes were (original) than Ed's.
34. Tuesday was the (warm) day of the week.
35. This is the (salty) stew I have ever tasted.
36. Seventy was Sarah's (bad) bowling score.
37. These pillows are (fluffy) than those.
38. The subway train was (crowded) than the bus.
39. The cherries were the (tasty) of the three desserts at the open house.
40. That is the (wonderful) news I have heard all day!
41. Your embroidery design is (pretty) than mine is.
42. That was the (awful) movie I have ever seen.
43. Mr. Chambers thought Adam's paper was (good) than Stan's.
44. This is the (sweet) grapefruit in the entire bushel.
45. This novel is (interesting) than that one.

Application and Review

Lesson Review

A Using Adjectives Make three columns on your paper. Label the first column *What Kind,* the second column *How Many,* and the third column *Which One.* Number your paper from 1 to 10. Find all of the adjectives in each sentence and write them in the correct columns. Do not include articles.

1. That lake has a beautiful sandy beach.
2. There are nine planets in the solar system.
3. Those Canadian coins fell out of my back pocket.
4. For several miles, we drove in dense, soupy fog.
5. That heavy rain ended many months of drought.
6. The Russian players won three games of chess in the recent tournament.
7. These four months are named for Roman gods.
8. Strong west winds bent those willow trees.
9. Tonight, Kim killed twenty pesky mosquitoes.
10. That experimental model made many trial flights.

B Using Articles and Demonstrative Words Number your paper from 1 to 10. Choose the correct word from the parentheses. Write it on your paper.

1. Mr. Redlin gave the sketch pads back to (those, them) art students.
2. A figure with eight sides is (a, an) octagon.
3. Many people like (that, those) kind of music.
4. Mary Poppins always carried (a, an) umbrella.
5. (A, An) huge crowd turned out for the fireworks.
6. Joanne listened to (those, them) tapes all afternoon.
7. The governor's visit is (a, an) honor for our school.
8. I'll wash the windows. (Them, They) are streaked.

9. (That, Those) kinds of shoes are not for hiking.
10. I can eat (them, those) pieces of pizza.

C Mastering Predicate Adjectives Copy these sentences. In each sentence, draw one line under the predicate adjective. Then draw two lines under the word it modifies.

1. The custard is still warm.
2. The water in the mountain lake feels icy.
3. The doe appeared frightened.
4. The ambulance siren sounded shrill.
5. Burning leaves smell fragrant.
6. After the parade, the streets looked littered.
7. California oranges are sweet.
8. Courtney will look very tall on those stilts.
9. Cajun food is far too spicy for me.
10. The audience grew restless before intermission.

D Making Comparisons with Adjectives Number your paper from 1 to 10. Choose the correct form of the adjective from the parentheses. Write it on your paper.

1. Of the two sisters, Jean sings (better, best).
2. Elena is our (fastest, most fast) swimmer.
3. One path is (closer, more close) than the other.
4. Mr. Jensen is the (most honest, most honestest) person I know.
5. This is the (better, best) of the three shows.
6. My alarm clock has a (louder, more loud) buzzer than yours.
7. You should use a (lighter, more light) bowling ball than that one.
8. This magazine is (recenter, more recent) than that one.
9. Sean has the (baddest, worst) temper in the family.
10. Mandy bought the (freshest, most freshest) fish in the market.

Chapter Review

A Identifying Adjectives Number your paper from 1 to 10. After each number, write the adjectives that modify each italicized noun. After each adjective, write *What Kind, How Many,* or *Which One.* Do not include articles.

1. Your *whistle* makes a shrill *noise*.
2. Many *people* crowded into the tiny *elevator*.
3. The judges gave my *painting* a blue *ribbon*.
4. Ken studied in a peaceful *room*.
5. Eileen jogs two *miles* every *day*.
6. Judy has black wavy *hair*.
7. Put these thirteen *candles* on Frank's cake.
8. A manx is a tailless *cat*.
9. That *photographer* took several *pictures* of the new *mayor*.
10. Are those *girls* waiting to buy some *tickets*?

B Using Adjectives Correctly Number your paper from 1 to 10. Choose the correct adjective from the parentheses. Write it on your paper.

1. Our bus was (a, an) hour late yesterday afternoon.
2. Dennis bought (this, these) kind of gym shoes.
3. We rode on the (faster, fastest) of the two trains.
4. Is the United States postal system the (more reliable, most reliable) postal system in the world?
5. I ordered (this, these) kinds of foods at the international restaurant.
6. Nora and Molly used (them, those) computers to write their programs.
7. The domestic cat is the (gentlest, most gentle) of all.
8. Please put your ballots in (a, an) sealed envelope.
9. Mr. Scott prefers (that, those) kind of chili to (this, these) kind.
10. Of all stories, Glen thinks mysteries are (more exciting, most exciting).

23

Understanding Adverbs

If you <u>ever</u>, <u>ever</u>, <u>ever</u> meet a grizzly bear,
You must <u>never</u>, <u>never</u>, <u>never</u> ask him where
He is going,
Or what he is doing;
For if you <u>ever</u>, <u>ever</u>, dare
To stop a grizzly bear,
You will <u>never</u> meet another grizzly bear.

"Grizzly Bear" by Mary Austin

Chances are you'll *never* meet a grizzly bear, but if you *ever* do, keep this silly poem in mind. It's good advice!

Try reading the poem again, leaving out the underlined words. How does the meaning of the poem change? Is it still good advice?

The underlined words in the poem are adverbs. This chapter will show you how to use adverbs to make your writing precise and lively.

1
What Are Adverbs?

Focus An *adverb* modifies a verb, an adjective, or another adverb.

In Chapter 22, you learned how adjectives can help you add excitement and clarity to your language. Adverbs can also help you improve your language by making it more precise.

An **adjective** modifies a noun or pronoun.

An **adverb** modifies a verb, an adjective, or another adverb.

> Cats pounce *silently*. (*Silently* modifies the verb *pounce*.)
> Jon was *almost* late. (*Almost* modifies the adjective *late*.)
> Camille sings *very* well. (*Very* modifies the adverb *well*.)

An **adverb** tells *how, when, where,* or *to what extent* about the word it modifies.

> Liz ran *swiftly*. (*Swiftly* tells *how* Liz ran.)
> The Washington County Dog Show begins *tomorrow*.
> (*Tomorrow* tells *when* the show begins.)
> Three carpenters are working *upstairs*. (*Upstairs* tells
> *where* the carpenters are working.)
> My sand sculpture is *nearly* finished. (*Nearly* tells *to
> what extent* the sand sculpture is finished.)

An adverb that modifies an adjective or another adverb often comes before the word it modifies.

> *completely* clean   *very* slowly

Other common adverbs include such words as *there, now, never, almost,* and *too*.

An adverb that modifies a verb may be found in one of several positions.

> He smiled *often*.   He *often* smiled.   *Often*, he smiled.

Many common adverbs are formed by adding the ending *-ly* to adjectives.

careful—carefully   usual—usually   quiet—quietly

Grammar in Action Make your writing and speaking specific. Use adverbs to tell more about the time, place, and extent of the action.

Exercises Using Adverbs

A Number your paper from 1 to 12. Write each adverb and tell whether it answers *How, When, Where,* or *To What Extent.*

1. poorly
2. later
3. very
4. inside

5. almost
6. totally
7. sometimes
8. cautiously

9. too
10. recently
11. up
12. merrily

B Write each adverb and the word it modifies in the following sentences.

1. Roberto quit early today.
2. Marcy played the same song twice.
3. My two calico cats often play.
4. Vacation always ends too soon.
5. There are my missing keys.
6. Hummingbirds' wings move very rapidly.
7. The explosion happened quite suddenly.
8. Please step forward.
9. Nancy rode the train downtown.
10. The firefighters responded so quickly.

2

Making Comparisons with Adverbs

Focus Use the *comparative form* of an adverb when you compare two actions. Use the *superlative form* of an adverb when you compare three or more actions.

Since adverbs, like adjectives, are words that describe, they can be changed to the comparative or superlative form.

Use the **comparative form** when you compare two actions.

Lisa jumped *higher* than Anne.

Use the **superlative form** when you compare three or more actions.

Of the three students, Dan jumped the *highest*.

The comparative and superlative forms of adverbs are formed in three different ways.

1. **Some short adverbs add *-er* to form the comparative. They add *-est* to form the superlative.**

Adverb	Comparative	Superlative
late	later	latest
high	higher	highest
soon	sooner	soonest

2. **Most adverbs that end in *-ly* form the comparative with the word *more*. They form the superlative with *most*.**

Adverb	Comparative	Superlative
recently	more recently	most recently
brightly	more brightly	most brightly
cheerfully	more cheerfully	most cheerfully

3. **Some adverbs change completely to form the comparative and superlative.**

Adverb	Comparative	Superlative
well	better	best
badly	worse	worst
much	more	most
little	less	least

Exercises Using Adverbs to Compare

A Number your paper from 1 to 12. Make three columns. Label the columns *Adverb*, *Comparative*, and *Superlative*. Copy the words below in the first column. Write the comparative form of the adverb in the second column and the superlative form in the third.

1. often	5. well	9. much
2. sweetly	6. easily	10. early
3. carefully	7. gently	11. hard
4. late	8. bravely	12. little

B Write the correct form of the adverb in parentheses in the following sentences.

1. You must drive (carefully) on the detour than on the road.
2. Of all birds, I think the swan moves (gracefully).
3. Which flew (high), Rick's kite or Jeff's?
4. Of the three brothers, Rich was the (strong).
5. Shakespeare is probably the writer quoted (more) often.
6. The *q* may be the key I use (little) on my typewriter.
7. Violets grow (well) in partial shade than in full sun.
8. Which costs (little), the record or the tape?
9. Do you sleep (late) on Saturdays than on school days?
10. She performed (badly) the last time than she had the first.

c *Write Now* A wizard has just cast a spell. You and your best friend will be fish for the next twenty-four hours. You will be a shark and your friend will be a goldfish. Write a brief paragraph telling who has the better time and why. Use several adverbs in the comparative form in your paragraph. For example: As a shark, I can swim *faster*. However, the goldfish fits into a bowl *more easily* than I do.

3
Adjective or Adverb?

Focus An *adjective* describes a noun or pronoun.
An *adverb* modifies a verb, an adjective, or another
adverb.

Look at these lists of words.

Adjective	Adverb
playful	playfully
nice	nicely
slow	slowly
cautious	cautiously
easy	easily
cheerful	cheerfully
beautiful	beautifully

Adjectives and adverbs are both modifiers. Because adverbs
are often formed from adjectives, they look very much alike.
For these reasons, it is sometimes difficult to know when to
use each type of word.

To decide whether to use an adjective or an adverb in a
sentence, ask yourself what word is being modified.

Read this example.

Emanuel removed the sliver very (careful, carefully).

Which word is correct? In this case, the verb *removed* is
being modified. Therefore, choose the adverb *carefully*.

Now look at this sentence.

Snow Treasure is a (real, really) good book.

Which word did you choose? In this sentence, the adjective
good is being modified. Therefore, the adverb *really* is the
correct choice.

> **Remember these rules:**
> **Adjectives** tell *which one, what kind,* or *how many* about nouns and pronouns.
> **Adverbs** tell *how, when, where,* or *to what extent* about verbs, adjectives, and other adverbs.

Using Good *and* Well, Bad *and* Badly

Good and *well, bad* and *badly* are often confused.
Good and *bad* are adjectives. They tell *what kind.*

> Those peaches look *good.* (*Look* is used as a linking verb here. Therefore, *good* is a predicate adjective that modifies *peaches*).
> I feel *bad* about this. (*Feel* is a linking verb. *Bad* is a predicate adjective.)

The words *well* and *badly* are adverbs. Use them to modify verbs. *Well* and *badly* tell *how* something is done.

> Jon behaved *badly.* (*Badly* tells *how* Jon behaved.)
> Ellen dances *well.* (*Well* tells *how* Ellen dances.)

> *Grammar in Action* Here is an exception to the rule about using *good* and *well. Well* is an adjective when it describes a noun or pronoun and means "healthy."
>
> Thomas does not feel well.

Exercises Choosing the Correct Modifier

A Choose the correct modifier from the parentheses.

1. I performed (bad, badly) in the finals.
2. In training camp, the football players eat (good, well).
3. News broadcasters must speak (slow, slowly) and clearly.
4. The hot air balloon rose (silent, silently) into the sky.

5. The Doberman turned (sudden, suddenly) and growled.
6. The hawk screeched (shrill, shrilly) and snatched its prey.
7. Flan, a Mexican custard, is (real, really) delicious.
8. The child blushed (shy, shyly).
9. These plants grow (bad, badly) in dim light.
10. Do you feel (good, well) enough to play?

B Proofreading Copy the following paragraph and correct all the errors in usage of adjectives and adverbs.

Have you ever careful observed a carnivorous plant such as the Venus's-flytrap? These plants grow especially good in damp boggy areas. White blossoms rise bright from the flower's leaves. The shape of the flytrap's hinged leaves appears strangely. A fly buzzes unsuspecting over the flower stalk. To the fly, the red center of the leaves looks attractively. Tiny hairs on the leaves are extreme sensitive. Buzzing closer, the fly light touches a hair. The leaves of the flytrap instant clamp shut. The flytrap's digestive juices gradual set to work. Soon the fly does not feel too good.

C *Write Now* In old westerns, the good cowboys wore white hats, and the bad cowboys wore black hats. In movies about King Arthur and Sir Lancelot, good knights wore white armor and bad knights wore black armor.

Write a short story about cowboys or knights. Compare the good guys and the bad guys. Use both adjectives and adverbs.

4

Double Negatives

Focus Never use a *double negative* when you write or speak.

The word *not* is an adverb that often causes problems. It is a negative. A negative is a word that says "no."

You remember that many contractions end in *-n't*. The *-n't* ending is a shortened form of *not*. Therefore, contractions that use *-n't* are negatives. Look at this list of negatives.

was + not = wasn't	would + not = wouldn't
have + not = haven't	can + not = can't

Not all negatives are contractions. Look at these examples of negatives. They are easy to remember because most of them contain the word *no*.

no	no one	nothing	not
none	nobody	nowhere	never

When two negatives appear in one sentence, they result in a **double negative**. Avoid double negatives in both your writing and speaking.

Wrong   Marcia *didn't* have *nowhere* to sit.
Right   Marcia *didn't* have anywhere to sit.
Right   Marcia had *nowhere* to sit.

Exercises Mastering Negatives

A Number your paper from 1 to 10. Choose the correct word from the parentheses. Write it on your paper.

1. Gary can't think of (nobody, anybody) else to ask.
2. Don't you want (any, no) help?
3. After the tornado, not a tree stood (nowhere, anywhere).

4. Albert will not climb (any, no) ladder.
5. We aren't going (nowhere, anywhere) this summer.
6. I don't (never, ever) want to eat this again.
7. Don't go (anywhere, nowhere) near the poison oak.
8. I haven't heard (nothing, anything) about the accident.
9. We haven't (no more, any more) stamps for these letters.
10. Nina wouldn't like (no, any) macaroni.

B Each of the following sentences contains a double negative. Number your paper from 1 to 10. Write each sentence correctly. Some sentences may be corrected in more than one way.

1. In 1912 no ships weren't better built than the *Titanic*.
2. Everyone said there wasn't nothing that could sink the ship.
3. But the *Titanic* didn't never complete its only voyage.
4. On the night of April 14th, the crew sighted an iceberg, but there wasn't nothing they could do to avoid hitting it.
5. The *Titanic* didn't take no more than three hours to sink.
6. Many passengers couldn't find no way to escape the ship.
7. The lifeboats couldn't hold no more than half of the people.
8. Today ocean liners aren't never without strict safety rules and the help of the International Ice Patrol.
9. For years divers couldn't find the sunken *Titanic* nowhere.
10. In 1985 explorers finally found the sunken ship, but they haven't never disclosed its exact location.

CAPT. E. J. SMITH.

Linking Grammar & Writing

A Imagine that you are Maria's gym shoes. On her way home after track practice one night, you drop out of her gym bag. Before you can do anything about it, Maria is gone. You finally are reunited with Maria three days later. In diary form, write the story of your three-day struggle to find Maria. Use adverbs to tell *when, where,* and *how* the action takes place.

B Imagine that you are the principal of a school. Your basketball team is playing in the Holiday Tournament. Because this is a very special event, you have decided to give all the students in your school a "Guide for Tournament Dress and Sportsmanship." Write this announcement. Be sure to use negatives correctly.

C Using Adverbs in Health In health class, you learn how important it is to take care of yourself. Now, put that knowledge to work. In a paragraph, explain how to do one of the following: eat healthful meals, handle stress, take your pulse, exercise safely, take care of your teeth, or help a choking victim. You may refer to your health text or an encyclopedia to help you with this exercise. Use adverbs correctly.

Additional Practice

Part 1 What Are Adverbs? In each sentence, write each adverb and the word it modifies.

1. The Victorian house has been completely restored.
2. The manager walked slowly to the pitcher's mound.
3. Yesterday we saw a total eclipse of the sun.
4. The Grand Canyon is quite beautiful.
5. You will get a stomachache if you eat too quickly.
6. We rose extremely early to watch the sun rise.
7. Those coins are very rare.
8. Darren slept soundly under the stars.
9. The gas tank was nearly empty.
10. Sometimes I surprise myself.

Part 2 Making Comparisons In each sentence, write the correct form of each adverb in parentheses.

11. Theresa pitches (fast) than Sylvia.
12. Gayle skis (carefully) than Ken.
13. Of these two kinds of soup, I like pea soup (well).
14. The swift flies (rapidly) of all birds.
15. That stunt driver is driving (recklessly) than before.
16. Of the three light bulbs, the 150-watt burns (bright).
17. Chad is the (little) noisy person in the room.
18. I did (badly) than you on the test.
19. I like bran flakes (well) than oatmeal.
20. Of all the letters in the English language, *e* is used (much) often.
21. I will get home (soon) than my brother.
22. Which of the three movies did you see (recently)?
23. You climbed (high) than I did.
24. Of all the guests, we arrived at the party (late).
25. Amanda smiled (cheerfully) than Audrey in our class photo.

Part 3 Adjective or Adverb? In each sentence, write the correct modifier in parentheses. Then tell whether it is used as an *Adverb* or *Adjective*.

26. We were (real, really) fortunate to get the tickets to the concert.
27. The weather has been (good, well) all week.
28. The turtle waddled (slow, slowly) across the road.
29. Uncle Albert's car does not work (good, well) in hot weather.
30. (Sudden, Suddenly) the wind shifted.
31. Too much sun is (bad, badly) for the skin.
32. The chemist (quick, quickly) adjusted the formula for the new antibiotic.
33. The pier was damaged (bad, badly) by the storm.
34. The librarian spoke (quiet, quietly) to Rita.
35. Maurice thought the test was (easy, easily).

Part 4 Double Negatives In each sentence write the correct word in parentheses.

36. No one told Kiyo (nothing, anything) about the surprise party.
37. Alabama doesn't look (nothing, anything) like I thought it would.
38. That new store doesn't have (no, any) cassette tapes or compact discs.
39. I couldn't find (no one, anyone) who needed a babysitter for Saturday night.
40. Lisa doesn't (never, ever) watch television.
41. None of the vegetarians ate (any, no) hamburgers.
42. Nobody in our group could speak (any, no) French.
43. That trail doesn't lead (nowhere, anywhere).
44. My brother never puts (any, no) dirty dishes in the dishwasher.
45. Hiro hasn't (ever, never) seen a hockey game.

Application and Review

Lesson Review

A Finding Adverbs Number your paper from 1 to 10. Write each adverb and the word it modifies.

1. The elephant contentedly ate grass.
2. Come here quickly.
3. Wednesday, our art class will paint outside.
4. That old tomcat has fought too many battles.
5. Janelle rarely spoke in the library.
6. We had so many choices for lunch today.
7. Jim and Cora left the game first.
8. The race ended here.
9. Kevin has told that story very often.
10. The tiny green caterpillar curled into a ball.

B Using Adverbs Correctly Number your paper from 1 to 10. Choose the correct adverb from the parentheses. Write it on your paper.

1. Meg sings (more better, better) after she warms up.
2. Of the four sisters, which one looks (more, most) like her mother?
3. The wind blew (more hard, harder) as the storm approached.
4. Of all the goalies on the team, Jeremiah kicked the ball (farther, farthest).
5. In the forest, the fawn stood (more quietly, quieter) than the rabbit.
6. Sally likes bird watching (less, lesser) than Bill.
7. Of these two books, I like *Rascal* (better, best).
8. Does the robin or cardinal fly (higher, highest)?
9. Which costs (less, least), pizza or a hamburger?
10. I run (more fast, faster) in summer than in winter.

C Choosing the Right Word Write the correct modifier on your paper. Next, write the word it modifies. Then write *Adjective* or *Adverb* to show how the modifier is used.

EXAMPLE   The soloist sang very (soft, softly).
softly, sang, Adverb

1. The actors knew their parts (perfect, perfectly).
2. The goal line was drawn (uneven, unevenly).
3. That (sudden, suddenly) storm last night surprised and frightened us.
4. Was the baby sleeping (sound, soundly)?
5. In this fog, I cannot see (good, well).
6. The mountains that look so small are (real, really) gigantic.
7. The ocean seemed (calm, calmly).
8. The dragonfly hovered (silent, silently) above the rose bushes.
9. Mr. Steven's speech was very (good, well).
10. Red Hawk and his brothers work together (good, well) as a team.

D Using Negatives Correctly Number your paper from 1 to 10. Rewrite each of the sentences correctly. Some of the sentences may be corrected in more than one way.

1. Carter didn't need nothing from the grocery store.
2. I won't have no glue left when I finish this kite.
3. Wanda never went nowhere without her best friend.
4. Didn't you bring no present either?
5. None of us knew no one at the first troop meeting.
6. Walt is not never going camping again.
7. The sky diver doesn't have no spare parachute.
8. Due to the rain, there wasn't no one at the park.
9. Please don't use no more tape on the streamers.
10. Hal didn't have no balsa wood to carve a sailboat.

Chapter Review

A Identifying Adverbs Copy the following paragraph on your paper. Underline the ten adverbs. Then draw an arrow from each adverb to the word it modifies. Can you guess the name of this mystery animal?

> This animal has a large, flat head. Its eyes almost never move, but it can see farther than most animals. It has good ears and hears well. It flies silently and swoops down quickly to catch its food. This animal often hoots softly as it sits high on its perch.

B Using Adverbs Correctly Number your paper from 1 to 15. Each of the following sentences has an error in adverb usage. Rewrite each sentence so that it is correct.

1. Paul does back flips easier than Lauren does.
2. Of the three girls on the camping trip, Patty could see more clearly in the dim light.
3. Does the cat Garfield or his pal Odie trick Jon most often?
4. Manuel won't never agree with Erin.
5. The logger chopped near six cords of wood.
6. Tina never did none of her homework.
7. A gopher has real large cheek pouches.
8. Of the six chess players, Ricardo is less patient.
9. No one didn't want to ride in the old, rickety hay wagon.
10. The octopus silently wrapped its tentacles tight around its prey.
11. Fen-Ann hasn't never seen the Grand Canyon.
12. Ben ties his shoes looser than Greg does.
13. Faisal never missed none of his rehearsals.
14. Of the five flashlights, mine shines more brightly.
15. Mother's banana bread is real delicious.

Cumulative Review

A Using Pronouns Correctly Choose the correct pronoun from those in parentheses.

1. The telethon emcees were Jerry Lewis and (he, him).
2. Eric the Red and (he, him) explored areas of the North Atlantic.
3. Mom measured Bert and (I, me) for our band uniforms.
4. Each of the performances had (its, their) good and bad points.
5. Neither Gail nor Helen had (her, their) house keys, so we waited outside.
6. Radium was discovered by Marie Curie and (he, him).
7. Can anyone loan me (his or her, their) scissors?
8. The lost lamb bleated for (it's, its) mother.
9. (We, Us) spectators were drenched by the performing dolphins.
10. On vacation Cathy and (she, her) went clam digging.

B Using Adjectives Choose the correct adjective from those in parentheses.

1. (That, These) kind of penguin grows four feet tall and can weigh nearly one hundred pounds.
2. Chili peppers are (hotter, more hotter) than bell peppers.
3. (A, An) ostrich egg would make quite an omelet.
4. (These, Those) pennies are collectors' items; (these, those) coins over there are nearly worthless.
5. Both shirts are imperfect, but the flaw in this one is (more noticeable, most noticeable).
6. Some inland lakes are (saltier, saltiest) than the sea.
7. My fingers were (less, least) sticky than yours after pulling taffy.
8. This winter has been (colder, more cold) than last winter.

9. (That, Those) sorts of sailing ships have two masts.
10. I've tried all the flavors; this one is (better, best).

C Using Adverbs Rewrite the following sentences to correct the errors in adverb usage. If a sentence has no error, write *Correct.*

1. It is interesting to learn about people of other cultures who live different than we do.
2. Some early settlers near perished from hunger and cold.
3. Which live longest, elephants or turtles?
4. Is a pizza more nutritious than a hamburger?
5. It is real difficult to tell the twins apart.
6. Elliot never puts no laundry in the hamper.
7. Athletes train and exercise regularly to stay fit.
8. The movie wasn't nothing like the book.
9. An otter can move quicker in the water than on land.
10. Which sees better at night—a bat, an owl, or a nighthawk?

D Combined Review Choose the correct word or phrase from those in the parentheses.

1. Does everyone have (his or her, their) instrument tuned?
2. The forward recovered the rebound (quick, quickly).
3. Which travels (faster, fastest), sound or light?
4. These directions are (real, really) hard to follow.
5. (We, Us) pizza fans insist on thin crust.
6. Goose down is the (more durable, most durable) of all insulators.
7. (It's, its) (you're, your) coat in the lost and found.
8. (That, Those) breed of horses was used by the cowboys.
9. Coach Suarez feels (confident, confidently) about our winning.
10. Few were able to find (his, their) way in the dark.

24
Understanding Prepositions and Conjunctions

On the other side of the world, a runner leaps out of the starting blocks, as TV cameras zoom in for a close-up. Out in space, a satellite picks up the broadcast signal and within seconds the image is in your home.

A space satellite is one of the many links that connect us to other people, places, and ideas. In language, connections are made with conjunctions and prepositions. This chapter will show you how prepositions and conjunctions function in a sentence. You will also learn to identify words that can be used as more than one part of speech.

1

What Are Prepositions?

> **Focus** A *preposition* relates its object to some other word in the sentence. The noun or pronoun following the preposition is the *object of the preposition*.

Prepositions relate the words following them to the words before them. Read these sentences.

> The groceries are *in* the trunk.
> Four fire engines zoomed *past* our house.

In and *past* are prepositions. They show the relationship between the groceries and the trunk and between the fire engines and the house.

The noun or pronoun following a preposition is called the **object of the preposition**. In the sentences above, *trunk* and *house* are the objects of the prepositions.

You can change the relationship between words in a sentence by changing the preposition.

> The sheepdog walked *behind* Anthony.
> The sheepdog walked *around* Anthony.

Here is a list of words often used as prepositions.

about	before	down	of	to
above	behind	during	off	toward
across	below	for	on	under
after	beneath	from	onto	underneath
against	beside	in	out	until
along	between	inside	outside	up
among	beyond	into	over	upon
around	but (except)	like	past	with
at	by	near	through	without

Exercises Finding Prepositions

A Number your paper from 1 to 10. Write the preposition in each of the following sentences.

1. A tugboat pushed barges down the river.
2. There is gum stuck on my shoe.
3. The pinch hitter drove the ball deep into left field.
4. This portrait of George Washington is two hundred years old.
5. Louisa May Alcott wrote about her own times.
6. The kitten crawled onto the limb and mewed.
7. Mom's tire was sliced by some broken glass.
8. The Plains Indians depended greatly upon the buffalo.
9. Under the new rules, our team can't compete.
10. After dinner, we will sing carols.

B Number your paper from 1 to 10. Write the preposition in each of the sentences below. After the preposition, write the object that follows the preposition. Write *None* if there is no preposition.

1. B. J.'s hamster was running on a treadmill.
2. Cornelia heard a creaking noise in the hall.
3. Tommy and Michael played basketball yesterday.
4. Jeff opened his book to the index.
5. Who put the butter near the oven?
6. Don't swim beyond that sign.
7. Paul washed and waxed the van.
8. We found these coins under the bookcase.
9. Did Marge park her bike beside the fence?
10. The apples on this tree aren't ripe yet.

c *Write Now* Your science class is taking a field trip to visit a cave. Write a brief paragraph telling about your adventures with stalagmites, stalactites, and bats. Use prepositions to show relationships of people and objects in the cave.

2
Using Prepositional Phrases

Focus A *prepositional phrase* is a group of words that begins with a preposition and ends with its object.

Look at this picture. Think of two sentences that describe what is happening.

The team is listening
to the coach.
They are planning a strategy
for the game.

Your sentences probably contain phrases like the ones in italics. Look at the first italicized phrase. The phrase starts with a preposition. It ends with a noun, *coach,* that is the object of the preposition. The preposition, its object, and all the words that modify the object combine to form a **prepositional phrase**. If a preposition has a compound object, all the parts of the object are included in the prepositional phrase.

Weeds grew *in the lawn, the flower garden,* and *the vegetable garden.*

Grammar in Action Prepositional phrases are especially useful when you are describing or giving directions. They help you say exactly what you mean.

EXAMPLE Go down the street and around the corner to the building on the left.

Exercises *Finding Prepositional Phrases*

A Write all the prepositional phrases in these sentences.

> EXAMPLE   The yarn was stuck to the paper with glue.
> to the paper, with glue

1. The fish in that tank have fins with blue stripes.
2. Both of us heard the footsteps in the attic.
3. Draw a line under the word that begins with a vowel.
4. Maria waded along the beach for hours.
5. On Sundays, there is music in the gazebo at the park.
6. The acrobat fell into the net from the tightrope.
7. Mary Ann waited near the theater until four o'clock.
8. Alone in the room, Shawn listened to his stereo.
9. The house across the street has been empty for a month.
10. I hung a clock with a flower design above the door.

B Number your paper from 1 to 10. Use each of the prepositional phrases below in a sentence. Underline the object or objects in each prepositional phrase.

1. past Mars, Jupiter, and Saturn
2. for her cousin
3. from El Paso
4. along the bank of the river
5. in Stacy's play
6. after the hurricane
7. outside my window
8. on the menu
9. among the new members
10. near the airport

c *Write Now* To surprise your friend on his birthday, you hired a clown to deliver balloons and a singing telegram. The clown arrived at your front door by mistake. Give the clown directions to get across town to your friend's house.

3
Pronouns After Prepositions

Focus When a pronoun is used as the object of a preposition, its object form must be used.

Object forms of pronouns must be used as objects of prepositions. Here are the object forms.

    me   you   him   her   it   us   them

Notice the pronouns used as objects in these sentences.

Mary Kay took an umbrella with *her.*
Three swans were gliding toward *them.*

The object of a preposition may be compound.

Simple Object	**Compound Object**
Study with *her.*	Study with *Darren* and *her.*
Give that basket to *me.*	Give that basket to *him* and *me.*

If you are confused about which pronoun form to use, say the sentence with the pronoun alone following the preposition. Then say the complete sentence.

All the team members played but Reba and (we, us).
All the team members played but *us.*
All the team members played but Reba and *us.*

Exercises *Using Pronouns After Prepositions*

A Make two columns on your paper. Head one column *Preposition* and the other *Object*. For each sentence write the preposition and the pronoun used as its object.

1. The museum's dinosaur expert was talking to us.
2. With her as our guide, we toured the museum.

3. Behind her was a giant skeleton labeled "Tyrannosaurus."
4. We walked around it and gaped.
5. The teeth were six inches long—there were rows of them!
6. Near me was a fascinating display: "Stegosaurus Eggs."
7. Above us hung a pterodactyl, a huge flying reptile.
8. "How many of you have questions?" the expert asked.
9. "What happened to them?" I asked.
10. The expert explained that no one knows exactly what happened to them.

B Write the correct pronoun.

1. Joanna hit the baseball between (we, us).
2. A letter from (he, him) arrived Thursday afternoon.
3. The lava oozed toward the guide and (they, them).
4. My puppy trailed along behind (she, her) and me.
5. A hummingbird is hovering just above Ian and (he, him).
6. The article about Mrs. Bush and (they, them) appeared in today's paper.
7. Without John and (I, me) the race cannot start.
8. Is Lenny performing the stunt with Juan and (we, us) or with Jenny and (they, them)?
9. In the picture, Jill is standing next to Ana and (I, me).
10. The myna bird would talk only for Dad and (we, us).

c *Write Now* Write a paragraph about playing a board game with three friends. Tell who played and where each person sat. Include phrases that have pronouns as objects of prepositions.

4
More About Prepositions

Focus Some prepositions need special attention.

Several words that are used as prepositions also are used as adverbs. Some examples are *up, down, around, in,* and *out.*

We looked *up*. (adverb)
We looked *up* the chimney. (preposition)

The children ran *around*. (adverb)
The children ran *around* the track. (preposition)

Look at how a word is used to determine if it is an adverb or a preposition. If it is used alone, it is probably an adverb. If it begins a phrase, it is probably a preposition.

Using Between *and* Among

You may hear the prepositions *between* and *among* used as if there were no difference between them. You should know the difference between them so that you can use them correctly.

Use *between* when you speak of two persons, things, or groups. Use *among* to speak of three or more.

Choose *between* these two programs.
The next game is *between* the Jefferson team and us.

We will divide the jobs *among* Nancy, you, and me.
Honey bees darted *among* the jasmine blossoms.

Grammar in Action Avoid using a preposition when one is not necessary.

Incorrect Where is my pencil at?
Correct Where is my pencil?

Exercises Using Prepositions Correctly

A Number your paper from 1 to 10. Label each word in italics as an *Adverb* or a *Preposition*.

1. *Around* the world, people celebrate birthdays in many ways.
2. Do you blow *out* the candles on your cake?
3. That custom first became popular *in* Germany.
4. A Korean baby's first birthday may tell *about* the child's future.
5. The baby sits *at* a table covered with objects.
6. The first object the baby picks *up* foretells his or her future.
7. In China, long noodles are associated *with* long life.
8. For birthdays, people give bowls of long noodles *away*.
9. In England, guests dig *around* in a tub of sawdust for prizes.
10. Mexican children get prizes and candy *from* a piñata.

B Number your paper from 1 to 10. Write the correct word from the parentheses.

1. This is a secret (between, among) you and me.
2. Confetti was scattered (between, among) all the seats.
3. In our solar system, Saturn is (between, among) Jupiter and Uranus.
4. The prize money was divided (between, among) Mario, Seth, and Anna.
5. Loyalty was strong (between, among) the five friends.
6. The championship game was (between, among) the Dolphins and the Falcons.
7. I live (between, among) the Smiths and the Olsens.
8. (Between, Among) all the dishes on the menu, lasagna is my favorite.
9. Our car was difficult to find (between, among) all the others in the parking lot.
10. Is Elm Lane (between, among) Oak Way and Poplar Road?

What Are Conjunctions?

> **Focus** A *conjunction* is a word that connects words or groups of words.

A conjunction can be used to join sentence parts or whole sentences. The words *and, but,* and *or* are conjunctions. The conjunctions below are joining sentence parts.

> Glenna *and* her sister sped down the hill on saucer sleds. (*and* joins subjects)
>
> The forward took a jump shot *but* missed it. (*but* joins predicates)
>
> Buy raisin bread *or* muffins. (*or* joins direct objects)

You have learned that *compound* means "having more than one part." In the example sentences above, conjunctions are used to join compound sentence parts. Conjunctions may also join whole sentences that are closely related in meaning.

> The theater lights dimmed. The curtain went up.
>
> The theater lights dimmed, *and* the curtain went up.

Notice that a comma is used at the end of the first sentence, before the conjunction. Commas are not used to join sentence parts. Also, you may leave out the comma when the two sentences that you join are very short.

Exercises Using Conjunctions

A Write the *compound* construction in each sentence below. Underline the conjunction and tell whether the compound is a subject, predicate, or object.

1. Gary and his brother dug for clams this morning.
2. For breakfast, Lorraine likes eggs or oatmeal.

3. The wind shook the roof and rattled the door.
4. Glue the string and the toothpicks to the cardboard.
5. Astronomers study planets and stars.
6. Gerald takes piano lessons but doesn't practice.
7. The puppy yawned and shook himself.
8. Football and soccer are Lennie's favorite sports.
9. Trudy splashed Doug and me with her paint.
10. The snow and ice made the roads impassable.

B Combine each of the following pairs of sentences into one sentence. Join related sentence parts. Choose a conjunction and use commas where necessary. Leave out words in italics.

1. Susan Butcher is a dogsled racer. *She is* the winner of Alaska's famous Iditarod race.
2. The race goes for 1,158 miles. *It* takes over ten days.
3. Sled dogs must be strong. They could not survive.
4. Early in the race Butcher's sled got stuck in an icy creek. *The sled* broke in four places.
5. Her sled no longer steered properly. She continued.
6. Later she faced a brutal snowstorm. *There was* fierce wind.
7. Butcher could wait out the snowstorm. She could go on.
8. Two other opponents were close. They had to stop.
9. She trusted her dogs' abilities. Her dogs trusted her.

Susan Butcher and her lead dog Granite.

10. She drove all night long through the storm. *She* beat the next dogsled racer by fourteen hours.

c *Write Now* Write a short poem in which every other line begins with a conjunction.

6

Using Words as Different Parts of Speech

Focus Sometimes the same word may be used as several parts of speech. When a word is used as a certain part of speech, it follows the rules for that part of speech.

In part 4 of this chapter, you learned that the same word could be used as either a preposition or an adverb. You learned that you must figure out how the word is used in a sentence to determine what part of speech it is. Many words can be used as more than one part of speech. Look at this example for the word *book*.

As a noun
This is my English *book*.

As a verb
The travel agent *booked* a seat for us on the earliest flight to Houston.

The travel agent *will book* a seat for us on the earliest flight to Houston.

As an adjective
Trudy gave a *book* report in social studies class yesterday.

Remember the rules for each part of speech when using words in different ways. For example, when you use *book* as a noun, you form the plural by adding *-s: books*. When you use it as a verb, you form the past tense by adding *-ed: booked*. When you use *book* in the future tense, you add the helping verb *will*.

There is only one sure way to decide what part of speech a word in a sentence is. Read the sentence carefully and see how the word is used.

Exercises *Identifying the Part of Speech*

A Write what part of speech each word in italics is. The word may be a *Noun, Verb, Adjective, Adverb,* or *Preposition.*

1. How well can you predict the *weather*?
2. Generally, wind from the *north* is a good weather sign.
3. However, a *south* wind often brings rain or snow.
4. A red sky at sunrise can be a *warning* of coming rain.
5. A red sky in the evening *promises* good weather.
6. Prior to a storm, *everyday* sounds seem clearer and louder.
7. A tree with curling leaves is *warning* about a storm.
8. It is a bad *weather* sign when all the birds are perching.
9. If bees stay *inside* the hive, a storm is approaching.
10. If bees are *outside*, the next few hours will be nice.

B In each pair of sentences that follows, one word is used as two different parts of speech. Number your paper from 1 to 5. After each number, write *a.* and *b.* After each letter, write the word in italics and tell what part of speech it is.

1. a. The class president will *chair* the meeting. b. This *chair* is too hard.
2. a. A lyric soprano sings *high* notes. b. The team's fortunes have reached a new *high*.
3. a. My family moved to a new *house*. b. The school will *house* the visiting athletes.
4. a. Vince went *outside* for a walk. b. We saw several deer *outside* the cabin.
5. a. Ms. Taylor made a *pencil* sketch of the waterfall.
   b. I have to sharpen my *pencil*.

c *Write Now* Write two sentences for each word below. Use the word as the parts of speech shown in the parentheses.

1. well (Noun, Adverb)
2. walk (Noun, Verb)
3. cold (Adjective, Noun)
4. fly (Noun, Verb)

Linking Grammar & Writing

A Imagine that you are a comet traveling through space. Write a paragraph telling what you see as you zip past, between, and among other heavenly bodies in the solar system.

B You are on the committee to plan Field Day for the sixth grade. Your job is to design an obstacle course for the obstacle course relay. First, think of ten safe objects, such as tires, empty boxes, and hoops, to use as obstacles. Then write the directions for successfully completing the course.

C Using Prepositions and Conjunctions in Science Your science class was studying the systems of the human body. After a lecture on the circulatory system, you suddenly shrank and became a red blood cell. Write about your adventures as you carried oxygen through the body.

Additional Practice

Parts 1 and 2 Prepositions Write the prepositional phrase
in each sentence. Underline the preposition once and the
object of the preposition twice.

1. Mt. Rainier is located in Washington.
2. Pet rocks were a fad during the 1970's.
3. The Bartleys live in a neighboring county.
4. Gary has hockey practice after school.
5. Inside the laboratory, the experiment proceeded.
6. We camped near the lake yesterday.
7. The sun disappeared behind the clouds.
8. The snow fell throughout the night.
9. *Romeo and Juliet* was written by William Shakespeare.
10. Before the game, a ceremony was held.

Part 3 Pronouns After Prepositions Choose the correct
pronoun from the parentheses in each sentence.

11. The new office building on the corner was designed by
    (she, her).
12. The roof over Marcia and (they, them) started to leak.
13. The puppy scampered up to Leo and (I, me).
14. A flock of beautiful, wild geese flew across the gray sky
    above (we, us).
15. My advice to Norita and (him, he) was ignored.
16. The eerie howling of the wolves echoed around
    (they, them).
17. The winners will play against you and (she, her).
18. Five heavy, bulky packages for Felipe and (she, her) came
    today.
19. Big, fluffy snowflakes fell upon Ricardo and (me, I).
20. Did the first group of bicyclists race past Jamie and
    (they, them)?

Part 4 More About Prepositions Write the correct word from the parentheses in each sentence.

21. Spain is located (between, among) France and Portugal.
22. Gregory had the highest score (between, among) all the gymnasts.
23. Choose (between, among) the salad and the fruit.
24. (Between, Among) peas, carrots, and celery, I prefer peas.
25. The Golden Gate Bridge is a link (between, among) San Francisco and Marin County.

Part 5 Conjunctions Combine each pair of sentences with *and*, *but*, or *or*. Use commas where needed.

26. You can fly to Miami. You can take the bus.
27. The Confederate troops won many battles. The Union troops won the Civil War.
28. On Thursday night Joan studied. On Friday she went to a movie.
29. That sweater is beautiful. It is expensive.
30. The Cohens might move to Boston. They might stay here.

Part 6 Words as Different Parts of Speech Write *Noun*, *Verb*, *Adjective*, *Adverb*, or *Preposition* to identify the part of speech of each italicized word.

31. The judge set his gavel *down*.
32. The contact lens fell *down* the drain.
33. That *chair* is very uncomfortable.
34. As class president, Lisa *chaired* the meeting.
35. Police officers directed traffic *around* the accident.
36. Wildly, the top spun *around*.
37. The *pencil* sharpener is broken.
38. Make your corrections with red *pencil*.
39. The fans waited *outside* the stage door.
40. *Outside*, the weather had turned bitter cold.

Application and Review

Lesson Review

A Finding Prepositions Copy the following sentences. Underline the prepositions in each sentence.

1. A stunt man perched on the tall flagpole.
2. The lamp beside the couch is broken.
3. Are those flowers along that fence geraniums?
4. Jeanette's baby sister toddled toward her mother.
5. An army helicopter landed among the tall pines.
6. The popcorn with butter costs more.
7. Penguins plunged into the icy water.
8. Did you paint your poster with watercolors?

B Recognizing Prepositional Phrases Write the prepositional phrases and underline the object or objects in each.

1. A mole tunneled under our back lawn.
2. Before breakfast, the newspaper is delivered.
3. Richard paddled his canoe around the lake.
4. Christie searched beneath her bed for her sneakers.
5. The airplane disappeared behind the clouds.
6. Leave your boots on the mat outside the door.
7. We drove to the drive-in window at the restaurant.
8. On New Year's Eve, I stayed awake past midnight.

C Using Pronouns as Objects of Prepositions Choose the correct pronoun from the parentheses. Write it on your paper.

1. Dad adjusted the handlebars for (I, me).
2. That present is from Ella and (her, she).
3. Do you live near Tom and (he, him)?
4. Gino dedicated his poem to (we, us).
5. Sonia has been asking about (them, they).

D Choosing the Right Prepositions Number your paper from 1 to 5. Choose the correct preposition from the parentheses. Write it on your paper.

1. Spread the delicious banana filling (between, among) the two layers.
2. (Between, Among) the stories in the collection, "Rip Van Winkle" is my favorite.
3. Keep this information (between, among) you and me.
4. Was Greta (between, among) the new members?
5. Decide (between, among) the wool or orlon yarn.

E Using Conjunctions Rewrite the following sentences. Combine each pair with *and, but,* or *or.* Use commas where needed.

1. The letter on the chart may be an *E*. It may be an *F*.
2. I sprayed insect repellent on my arms. Mosquitoes bit me anyway.
3. Jarita has several assignments. They are all difficult.
4. You may have pudding for dessert. You may have an orange.
5. The car had engine trouble. We finally had to call a tow truck.
6. Rhea's arm is in a cast. She played baseball today.
7. The bread is delicious. The price is high.
8. You can wait in the car. You can come inside.

F Using Words as Different Parts of Speech Write two sentences for each word below. Use the word as each part of speech shown in parentheses.

1. paper (Noun, Adjective)
2. phone (Noun, Adjective)
3. jam (Noun, Verb)
4. print (Noun, Verb)
5. water (Noun, Adjective)

Chapter Review

A Identifying Prepositional Phrases Write the prepositional phrases in the following sentences.

1. Who moved into the brick house across the street?
2. Uncle Tex sent me a cowboy hat from Dallas.
3. Hail pounded against the classroom windows.
4. Mom put my bowling trophy on a shelf in the living room.
5. He hid the secret message beneath a large pile of mystery books.
6. Is Justine's kitten under the raspberry bush?
7. Divide the cost of the food among the four boys.
8. Please don't leave without me.
9. I like all fruit except pineapple.
10. The girl behind Alexis is from France.

B Using Conjunctions Rewrite each of the following pairs of sentences as one sentence. Choose a conjunction to join related ideas. Use commas where necessary. Leave out any words in italics.

1. Peas are legumes. Nuts *are legumes*.
2. I play hockey. *I do* not *play* basketball.
3. Last July, we swam in the pond. It's too cold now.
4. The book was long. *The book was* interesting.
5. I drew a map of our town. Saul labeled the streets.
6. Amanda sings well. *Amanda* dances *well*.
7. The pilots got on the plane. The passengers didn't board until later.
8. My new wool sweater is bulky. *It is* warm.
9. I looked everywhere for my lost library book. *I* never found it.
10. Have you ever seen a sugar beet? *Have you ever seen* sugar cane?

25
Mastering Subject–Verb Agreement

Tell me, O Octopus, I begs,
Is those things arms, or is they legs?
I marvel at thee, Octopus;
If I were thou, I'd call me Us.

"The Octopus" by Ogden Nash

"I begs"? . . . "is they legs"?

This poet's subjects and verbs are as tangled as an octopus's arms (or are they legs?)! While intentional errors in subject–verb agreement can be humorous, sentences are usually confusing when subjects and verbs don't work together. Until you are as famous as Ogden Nash, make sure that your subjects and verbs agree. Use singular verbs with singular subjects and plural verbs with plural subjects. This chapter will show you how to keep your subjects and verbs working together.

1
Subject and Verb Agreement

A singular noun stands for one person, place, thing, or idea.

woman   city   fox   joy

A plural noun stands for more than one person, place, thing, or idea.

women   cities   foxes   joys

Verbs also have singular and plural forms. In a sentence, the verb must **agree in number** with its subject. A subject and verb agree in number when they are both singular or both plural.

Singular	**Plural**
One *cloud floats* in the sky.	Many *clouds float* in the sky.
The *movie starts* soon.	The *movies start* soon.

The *s* at the end of verbs such as *floats* and *starts* shows that the verbs are used with singular nouns.

When the noun is plural, the *s* is dropped from the verb. The noun *clouds* is plural. Therefore *float* does not have an *s*. *Movies* is plural, so *start* does not end in *s*. *Float* and *start* are plural verbs.

Most singular verbs are formed by adding -*s*. However, there are some exceptions to this rule. To form singular verbs, follow the same spelling rules that you learned on pages 352–353 about forming the plurals of nouns. Read these examples.

Singular	**Plural**	**Singular**	**Plural**
watch*es*	watc*h*	hiss*es*	his*s*
hurr*ies*	hurr*y*	go*es*	g*o*

Exercises Making Subjects and Verbs Agree

A Label three columns *Subject, Verb,* and *Number*. For each sentence, write the subject and verb in the correct column. Then write *Singular* or *Plural* in the last column.

1. My sister studies at Tulane University.
2. The teacher keeps supplies in the metal cabinet.
3. Rico's airplane lands at Gate H.
4. Frogs hibernate in the mud.
5. Children play in the vacant lot on Fifth Street.
6. Wombats make affectionate pets.
7. Some students learn foreign languages in school.
8. Ivy covers the north side of the brick house.
9. Heavy rainstorms cause erosion.
10. My parrot says twenty different words.

B Choose the correct verb form in parentheses.

1. Snoring (result, results) from a blocked passage of air.
2. Experts (think, thinks) thirty million Americans snore.
3. Yearly, inventors (design, designs) anti-snoring devices.
4. Muzzles (keep, keeps) snorers' mouths from opening.
5. One device (prevent, prevents) sleepers from turning over.
6. Another device (strap, straps) the forearm to the chin.
7. One plan (remove, removes) salt from the snorer's diet.
8. Some people (try, tries) hypnotism to stop snoring.
9. Others (seek, seeks) surgery to enlarge nasal passages.
10. Earplugs (provide, provides) a solution for people sleeping in the same room.

C *Write Now* Write a paragraph in the present tense. Use three or more phrases from the list below as subjects in your sentences. Be sure the subjects and verbs agree.

| a haunted house | a hundred bats | a musty odor |
| a ghostly figure | thick spider webs | a creaky door |

2
Agreement with Special Verbs

Focus Some verbs have special forms. Follow the rules of agreement for these verbs.

Special Forms of Certain Verbs

A few verbs have special forms. Make sure to choose the verb form that matches your subject in number.

Is, Was, Are, Were The verb forms *is* and *was* are singular. The forms *are* and *were* are plural.

Singular Carlos *is* here. Carlos *was* here.
Plural The boxes *are* here. The boxes *were* here.

Has, Have The verb form *has* is singular. *Have* is plural.

Singular Pam *has* a plan.
Plural They *have* a plan.

Does, Do The verb form *does* is singular. *Do* is plural.

Singular Joe *does* the cooking.
Plural They *do* the cooking.

There Is, Where Is, Here Is

Many sentences begin with *There*, *Where*, or *Here*. These words are never subjects of sentences. To decide whether to use a singular or plural form of a verb in such a sentence, first find the subject by asking *who?* or *what?* before the verb.

There is the Big Dipper.

Who or *what* is? The Big Dipper is.
Big Dipper is the subject.
Big Dipper is singular. Use the singular verb *is*.

Exercises Using the Right Verb Form

A Number your paper from 1 to 10. Choose the correct form of the verb from the parentheses. Write it on your paper.

1. Two ski poles (was, were) standing in the drift.
2. This watch (has, have) a tiny battery inside.
3. Where (is, are) my new sweater?
4. (Doesn't, Don't) a rhea look like an ostrich?
5. Toni's knee (was, were) swollen.
6. Here (is, are) the oars for the canoe.
7. Native American war bonnets (was, were) made with long feather tails.
8. Where (does, do) these bike paths lead?
9. Tube worms (has, have) no stomach or mouth.
10. There (was, were) three coconuts on the palm tree.

B For each sentence, write the correct verb form. Use the present tense of the verb in parentheses.

1. There (be) strange tales about the Bermuda Triangle.
2. The Triangle (be) an area of the ocean near Florida.
3. Sometimes vessels (have) difficulty there.
4. In fact, there (be) reports of disappearances.
5. Often, wreckage (do) not even appear.
6. Where (have) these vessels gone?
7. Here (be) one explanation.
8. The vessels (be) thrown off course by violent storms or swift ocean currents.
9. (Have) any person thought of other reasons?
10. What (do) you think?

C *Write Now* After months of working with your invention, you have succeeded in communicating with life on a distant planet. Write a brief account of your conversation. Include information such as "Life here is . . . " or "Things there are . . . " or "Where is . . . . "

3
Special Agreement Problems

Focus Watch compound subjects and prepositional phrases when making subjects and verbs agree.

Compound Subjects

When two or more parts of a compound subject are joined by the conjunction *and,* use the plural form of the verb.

> The mayor and the police chief *were* in the parade.
> Speed skating and downhill skiing *are* Olympic sports.

When the parts are joined by *or, either-or,* or *neither-nor,* use the form of the verb that agrees with the nearer subject.

> Carol or Janet *is* singing.
> Either six pencils or one pen *costs* a quarter.
> Neither Matthew nor his brothers *are* coming.

Prepositional Phrases After the Subject

Be careful with prepositional phrases that come between the subject and the verb. Do not confuse the subject of the verb with the object of the preposition. Look at this sentence.

> The *gate* near the pines *makes* squeaky noises.
>
> The verb is *makes.* Who or what makes? *Gate*
> *Gate* is the subject of the sentence.
> *Gate* is singular, so you use the singular verb *makes.*
> *Near the pines* is a prepositional phrase. The verb agrees
>   with the subject, not with the prepositional phrase.

Grammar in Action Do not rely on what "sounds right" to make subjects and verbs agree. Follow the rules.

Exercises Choosing the Right Verb Form

A Make two columns on your paper. Label them *Subject* and *Verb*. Write the subject and verb for each sentence in the correct column.

1. Many new recruits for the Army are women.
2. The customer at the counter needs service.
3. The corn and buns for the picnic cost six dollars.
4. Radio and television inform people about the news.
5. Many students from Harper School audition today.
6. Skiers and snowmobilers wait for big snowfalls.
7. In autumn, smoke from burning leaves fills the air.
8. The road through the countryside is narrow.
9. Neither the clay nor the paint for your project is here.
10. Gina or Joan plays badminton every weekend.

B Proofreading Rewrite the following paragraph correcting any errors in subject–verb agreement.

Each year millions of tourists flock to Yellowstone National Park. Here, the earth's inner heat and minerals creates unbelievable effects. Lakes of colored mud bubbles furiously. Springs and geysers burst from cracks in the ground. Hot water jets and vapor sprays high into the air. Tiny plants of brilliant color fills steaming pools. Hot water in the center of the pools stay blue. Because the water is so hot in the center, neither yellow nor brown algae grow there. Near the edges of the pools sprouts tiny red mushrooms and thick moss. A boardwalk for spectators go right to the water's edge.

C *Write Now* Imagine that you find a strange coin. You turn it over three times, and a genie appears. You are granted three wishes. You may make two things disappear from the world and one thing appear. In a paragraph, explain your choices. Use several compound subjects.

4
Agreement with Pronouns

> **Focus** Follow special rules of agreement with the pronouns *I* and *you* and with indefinite pronouns.

I *and* You

The pronoun *I* stands for a single person. However, the only singular verb forms used with it are *am* and *was*.

> I *am* in my room.   I *was* here yesterday.

Otherwise, the plural form of the verb is always used.

> I *do* my work.   I *have* a cold.   I *throw* a good fastball.

Although *you* can be singular or plural, always use a plural verb with this pronoun.

> "You *were* late," the coach said to the player.
> "You *were* late," the coach said to the players.

Indefinite Pronouns

The indefinite pronouns below are singular. They use singular verbs.

> | either | each | everyone | anyone |
> |--------|------|----------|--------|
> | neither | one | everybody | nobody |

> Either *is* right.   Neither *was* famous.

In the sentences above, a singular verb follows a singular subject. When a prepositional phrase follows one of these pronouns, the verb must still agree with the pronoun subject.

> Either of the answers *is* right.
> Neither of the scientists *was* famous.

Exercises *Choosing the Correct Verb Form*

A Make three columns on your paper. Label the columns *Subject, Prepositional Phrase,* and *Verb.* Find these three parts in each sentence. Write them in the correct columns.

1. Nobody in our class swims a full pool length.
2. One of the propellers was bent.
3. Either of those skaters needs more practice.
4. Neither of the cats sleeps silently.
5. One of the bathroom faucets leaks.
6. Everyone on the scavenger hunt reads the clues.
7. Neither of the digital clocks tells perfect time.
8. Anyone from Montana understands blizzards.
9. Each of the displays is ready.
10. Nobody at the picnic wants a hammock.

B Choose the correct form of the verb for each sentence.

1. Everybody (has, have) a favorite food or snack.
2. Each of the world's countries (is, are) known for some food.
3. If you (is, are) French, you (has, have) probably eaten snails.
4. Someday, I (am, is, are) going to try frog legs.
5. Either of these French dishes (is, are) cooked in butter.
6. Neither (is, are) prepared without garlic.
7. Anyone from Greece (knows, know) about dried octopus.
8. One (cuts, cut) the octopus into chunks and then broils it.
9. (Have, has) you ever tasted sushi?
10. Everyone in Japan (eats, eat) this dish made from raw fish.

c *Write Now* Imagine that you are a bowling ball. Some friends have arrived at the alley to bowl. The least experienced bowler is heading for you. Write a paragraph about what happens next. Use at least three indefinite pronouns.

Linking Grammar & Writing

A Imagine that your pen pal from Italy is visiting. Take him or her on a tour of your town. In a paragraph, write what you would say to your pen pal. Begin some of your sentences with phrases such as "Here is . . ." or "There are . . . ."

B Combine one or two of the following noun phrases and verb phrases to make sentences. Use the sentences in a story. Add more sentences to complete the story. Make sure that subjects and verbs agree in number.

Noun Phrases
the cat and the kangaroo
a frog with three eyes
an eagle and a mouse
the jack-o'-lantern with the crooked smile
a family of raccoons

Verb Phrases
knock(s) loudly on the door
eat(s) spaghetti with a ruler and pliers
jump(s) onto my bed thinking it is a trampoline
hop(s) down to the basement in search of spider webs
race(s) out the door as the clock strikes 11:59

C Using Subject–Verb Agreement in Computer Studies
Write a paragraph on the function of parts of a computer. Use an encyclopedia or textbook if necessary. These computer terms can be the subjects of some sentences. Make sure that your subjects and verbs agree.

| disks | monitor | printer |
| function keys | disk drive | keyboard |

Additional Practice

Part 1 Subject and Verb Agreement Choose the correct verb in parentheses.

1. Keiko always (finishes, finish) basketball practice before dinner.
2. Brightly colored fireworks (flashes, flash) on Independence Day.
3. Spiders (spins, spin) silky webs.
4. That robot (moves, move) its arms and legs.
5. Lifeguards (learns, learn) to handle emergencies.
6. Big plows (clears, clear) our snowy and icy streets in winter.
7. That restaurant (serves, serve) unusual kinds of sandwiches.
8. Archaeologists (digs, dig) for artifacts.
9. The concert (starts, start) earlier than I thought.
10. Hugh (mows, mow) lawns every summer to earn extra spending money.

Part 2 Agreement with Special Verbs Choose the correct form of each verb in parentheses and write it on your paper.

11. Where (are, is) the science fiction books shelved in our school library?
12. Jerome (do, does) the dishes on Mondays.
13. Here (is, are) the album by the new group.
14. New York City (have, has) five boroughs.
15. Who (was, were) the first settlers of Virginia?
16. There (is, are) a chance of rain today.
17. That stray cat (don't, doesn't) have a home.
18. Pearl Buck (was, were) an American novelist.
19. Where (do, does) geese fly each fall?
20. The judges (has, have) posted the results.

Part 3 Agreement in Special Situations Choose the correct verb in each sentence and write it on your paper.

21. The scenic trail through the mountains (are, is) eight miles long.
22. The quarterback and the linemen (need, needs) more practice.
23. Sydney and Melbourne (is, are) cities in Australia.
24. Neither Carlene nor her sisters (sing, sings) in the choir.
25. The twins and Doris (is, are) learning calligraphy in art class this semester.
26. The villages along the river always (floods, flood) during storms.
27. Either Wade Boggs or Kirby Puckett (lead, leads) the league in hitting.
28. The cabinet members and the President (meet, meets) frequently.
29. The disks for the computer (is, are) missing.
30. Neither the teachers nor the principal (believe, believes) the school should be closed.

Part 4 Agreement with Pronouns Choose the correct verb in each sentence and write it on your paper.

31. When it snows hard, everyone (get, gets) to go home early.
32. You (was, were) the best performer in the recent piano recital.
33. Each of the states (have, has) its own government.
34. Neither (was, were) chosen for the lead part.
35. One of the tires (are, is) flat.
36. Either of the answers (are, is) correct.
37. Nobody (want, wants) to miss the new movie.
38. I (does, do) exercises daily.
39. Of all the pitchers, I (am, is, are) the youngest in the league this year.
40. Everyone in the tournament (win, wins) a prize.

Application and Review

Lesson Review

A Using the Right Verb Form Number your paper from 1 to 10. Choose the correct form of the verb from the parentheses. Write it on your paper.

1. Many horses (huddles, huddle) in the shade.
2. One large furnace (heats, heat) the entire apartment building.
3. Termites often (hides, hide) under old logs.
4. A tattered umbrella (stands, stand) in the closet.
5. Two secretaries (works, work) in our school office.
6. Police officers (protects, protect) our citizens and our community.
7. A kangaroo (carries, carry) its young in a pouch.
8. That pianist (plays, play) classical music and jazz.
9. Scary movies (gives, give) me goose bumps.
10. Calculators (adds, add) numbers quickly and accurately.

B Writing the Correct Verb Form Number your paper from 1 to 10. Write the correct form of the verb in parentheses.

1. (Was, Were) the three of you too hot?
2. How (does, do) Corrine get to school?
3. The equipment (has, have) been moved to the attic of the civic center.
4. My four pet fish (doesn't, don't) need a lot of attention or care.
5. Here (is, are) some larger pieces of fabric.
6. Our book order (is, are) in the mail.
7. Where (does, do) Mrs. Alvarez keep the stapler?
8. (Isn't, Aren't) there any tomatoes left?
9. There (has, have) been many warm days in October.
10. The muffins (was, were) toasted in the oven.

C Choosing the Right Verb Form Number your paper from 1 to 10. Choose the correct form of the verb for each sentence. Write it on your paper.

1. Dan and Joanie (takes, take) turns on the rope swing hanging from the tree.
2. The men in the corral (looks, look) scared.
3. Neither the apples nor the pears (tastes, taste) ripe.
4. Posters and mobiles (decorates, decorate) our room.
5. The monkeys in that cage (is, are) amusing.
6. Either Raymond or his brothers (collects, collect) newspaper money this week.
7. Balloons and streamers (hangs, hang) from the ceiling of the gym.
8. The antique glass figures in this display case (breaks, break) very easily.
9. Neither the scouts nor their leader (sees, see) the bear inside the cave.
10. The wheels on the hay wagon (needs, need) oil.

D Making Verbs Agree with Certain Pronouns Number your paper from 1 to 10. For each sentence, write the correct present form of the verb in parentheses.

1. Everyone usually (crowd) the stadium entrance before the game.
2. Each of the egg baskets (look) full.
3. Nobody on the camping trip (have) a compass.
4. I usually (come) home by four o'clock.
5. Nobody on the basketball team (practice) free throws every day.
6. You always (be) welcome at my house.
7. Neither of the crepes (be) blueberry.
8. You and I (be) going with Audrey.
9. Sometimes, one of the ferrets (get) loose.
10. Everyone in the theater (cry) during that movie.

Chapter Review

A Making Subjects and Verbs Agree Number your paper from 1 to 10. Choose the correct verb from the parentheses. Write it on your paper.

1. Either football or rugby (is, are) my favorite sport.
2. Steam from the geysers (fills, fill) the air.
3. Where (has, have) you been?
4. One of the film projectors (makes, make) clicking sounds when it is turned on.
5. There (was, were) five pigeons on our roof.
6. I (have, has) the answer to the puzzle.
7. You (draws, draw) the funniest cartoons.
8. The glass ornaments in this box (is, are) shattered.
9. Cindy or Lauren (takes, take) tap-dancing lessons.
10. Everybody (thinks, think) you (is, are) right.

B Choosing the Correct Verb Number your paper from 1 to 10. Write the correct present tense form of the verb in parentheses.

1. Our neighbors or my aunt (feed) our hamster when we're away.
2. The instructions for my tape recorder (seem) confusing.
3. Where (do) this maze begin?
4. Neither those stores nor that restaurant (open) on Sundays or Mondays.
5. "There (go) my allowance!" Sammy said.
6. The coins in Meghan's collection (be) valuable.
7. Near the White House (be) a famous monument, the Lincoln Memorial.
8. Either three small pizzas or one large pizza (serve) six people.
9. The dogs on our block (bark) every morning.
10. The musicians in the orchestra and the actors (have) a dress rehearsal tonight.

Cumulative Review

A Identifying Prepositional Phrases Write all of the prepositional phrases in these sentences. Underline each preposition once and the object of the preposition twice.

1. One thousand doves flew over the Olympic stadium.
2. The other planets in our solar system could all fit inside Jupiter.
3. For many countries, rice is the chief food.
4. Among other inventions, da Vinci made the first scissors.
5. Pablo parked near the plaza.
6. The animal with the largest brain for its size is the ant.
7. The Great Wall of China is visible from space.
8. My dad's platoon landed at Normandy Beach on D-Day.
9. In the Maracana Stadium a moat around the field protects the players from the enthusiastic spectators.
10. During class we read a story about polar explorers.

B Using Conjunctions Combine each pair of sentences with *and, but,* or *or*.

1. Rhode Island is the smallest state. Alaska is the biggest.
2. Johnny Weissmuller was a champion Olympic swimmer. He is better known for his portrayal of Tarzan.
3. My great grandfather grew up in the Wild West. He once met Buffalo Bill Cody.
4. To raise money, the sixth grade will have an auction. Perhaps they will wash cars.
5. *E* is the most frequently used letter. *Q* is the least used.
6. Some think that Florida is the southernmost state in the United States. Hawaii is farther south.
7. Make sure you smile at our dog Grumpy. He will growl.
8. Siberia makes up one-half of the Soviet Union's land area. Only one-eighth of the Soviet people live there.

9. Just shoot the ball. Pass it to Nora.
10. Gutenberg is known as the inventor of printing. Printed books existed in China five hundred years before he lived.

C Making Subjects and Verbs Agree Number your paper from 1 to 10. Choose the correct verb from those in parentheses. Write it on your paper.

1. Television (was, were) developed in the 1920's.
2. Neither Dubois nor the other challengers (was, were) able to defeat the great Rantini.
3. Here (is, are) the results of the Gallup poll.
4. Some queen termites (lives, live) for fifty years.
5. Every one of the astronauts (has, have) undergone many months of training.
6. Where (does, do) houseflies go in winter?
7. Several children's TV shows (is, are) based on toys.
8. Each of the soldiers (was, were) awarded the Bronze Star.
9. There (goes, go) Carl and the other sprinters.
10. The average person (laughs, laugh) fifteen times per day.

D Combined Review Rewrite the following paragraph on your paper. Correct any run-on sentences or errors in subject–verb agreement.

Siamese twins are physically joined at some part of their bodies they are commonly joined at the hip, chest, or head. This phenomenon happen once in about 50,000 births. An internal organ, such as the heart, are sometimes shared by the twins. The separation of Siamese twins have been performed successfully in a few cases. The term originate from the most famous Siamese twins—Eng and Chang. They were born in Siam, which is now Thailand in the 1800's, these brothers appeared in many traveling shows.

26
Capitalization

Above, you see pictures of cats—gray cats, black cats, striped cats, ginger cats. On the right you see a picture of *Cats*—the musical comedy. What a difference a capital letter can make!

In writing, you capitalize proper nouns—the names of specific people or things—to distinguish them from common nouns. Capitalization helps make your meaning clear. In this chapter you will learn rules for capitalizing proper nouns and adjectives; first words in sentences, in lines of poetry, and in lines in an outline; and words in titles.

1
Proper Nouns and Proper Adjectives

Focus Capitalize *proper nouns* and *proper adjectives*.

A **common noun** is a general name of a person, place, thing, or idea. A **proper noun** names a particular person, place, thing, or idea. A **proper adjective** is made from a proper noun. All proper nouns and adjectives are capitalized.

Common Noun	Proper Noun	Proper Adjective
queen	Elizabeth	Elizabethan
country	Mexico	Mexican

A proper noun can be made up of one or more words. Capitalize all important words in a proper noun.

New Year's Day   Ohio River   Peter the Great

Proper adjectives are often used with common nouns. Do not capitalize the common noun.

French dressing   Greek alphabet   Siamese cat

There are many kinds of proper nouns. The following rules will help you recognize words that need to be capitalized.

Capitalize the names of people and pets.

Begin every word in a name with a capital letter. An initial stands for a name. Write initials as capital letters. Put a period after an initial.

Rip Van Winkle   A. J. Foyt   Muggins

Often, a word for a family relation is used as the name of a particular person, or as part of the name. *Mom* and *Grandpa Lewis* are two examples. Capitalize a word used in this way.

Capitalize a title used with a person's name.

A **title** is a term of respect used in front of a name. Many titles have short forms called **abbreviations.** Capitalize abbreviations of titles. Follow an abbreviation with a period.

Mister—Mr.   Mistress—Mrs.   Doctor—Dr.

The title *Miss* has no abbreviated form. Do not use a period after this title. *Ms.* has no long form.

Did **Mr.** **L**ee interview **Dr.** **S**mith or **M**ayor **G**entry?

Capitalize the word *I*.

Margaret and **I** walked to the library.

Exercises *Capitalizing Correctly*

A Copy the following sentences. Change small letters to capital letters wherever necessary.

1. A TV miniseries was based on books by lucy m. montgomery.
2. The name linda a. rigby was engraved on the plaque.
3. Some people think that thomas edison was a genius.
4. *Dachshund* is a german word meaning "badger dog."
5. A dentist, dr. w. t. g. morton, first used ether.
6. We watched coach burns give an award to j. kelly.
7. Stacy and i played tennis against mom and dad.
8. Mr. and mrs. torres have a cat named trigger.
9. The best teacher i ever had was professor eileen black.
10. Czar nicholas was a russian emperor.

B Copy the following sentences. Change small letters to capital letters wherever necessary.

1. Singer marian anderson was born in philadelphia in 1902.
2. In 1925 she won a contest that allowed her to sing in new york city with the new york philharmonic orchestra.

3. Then she made several european tours.
4. She was cheered by french, british, and italian audiences.
5. However some american audiences were not as kind.
6. Because of her race, she was forbidden to sing in a 1939 easter concert at constitution hall in washington, d.c.
7. The president's wife, eleanor roosevelt, was angered by this unjust act.
8. She arranged for ms. anderson to sing concerts at both the lincoln memorial and the white house.
9. Conductor arturo toscanini said, "i believe that a voice like anderson's comes only once in a hundred years."
10. In 1978 u.s. president jimmy carter honored anderson with a congressional medal.

c *Write Now* Write a movie review. Include the names of the main characters and the names of the actors or actresses who played these characters. Briefly tell what happened. Then tell why you think the movie was good or bad. Capitalize all proper nouns and adjectives.

2
More Proper Nouns

Focus Capitalize the names of places, races, languages, religions, days, months, and holidays.

Capitalize the names of particular places and things.

1. Capitalize cities, states, and countries.

   Laredo, **T**exas, is near **M**exico.

2. Capitalize streets, bridges, parks, and buildings.

   The tour guide showed us **W**all **S**treet, the **B**rooklyn **B**ridge, **C**entral **P**ark, and the **E**mpire **S**tate **B**uilding.

3. Capitalize geographical names. Do not capitalize *north, south, east,* or *west* when they refer to directions. Capitalize these words only when they refer to a particular section of the country or world.

   The Millers turned south and drove to **D**eath **V**alley.
   The **M**ason-**D**ixon line divided the **N**orth and **S**outh.

Capitalize the names of months, days, and holidays.

Do not capitalize the names of the four seasons: spring, summer, winter, and fall.

   We celebrate **F**ather's **D**ay and the first day of summer in **J**une.

Capitalize the names of races, religions, nationalities, and languages.

   Some **A**merican **I**ndian artists work in silver.
   Judaism and **C**hristianity share a belief in one God.
   The **R**ussians and the **C**hinese have border disputes.
   Does this junior high school offer **F**rench?

Capitalize words referring to God and to religious scriptures.

the **D**eity	the **B**ible	the **G**ospel
the **L**ord	the **T**almud	the **B**ook of **G**enesis
Allah	the **K**oran	the **N**ew **T**estament

Capitalize the names of clubs, organizations, and business firms.

Kate's dog is registered with the **A**merican **K**ennel **C**lub.
Have you heard of the **I**nternational **K**itefliers **A**ssociation?
Don's father works for **A**merican **P**lastics, **I**ncorporated.

Grammar in Action Carefully follow capitalization rules in your writing. Incorrect capitalization can be confusing.

Little Rock (Arkansas)
little rock (pebble)

I am going west. (direction)
I am going out West. (area of country)

Exercises Mastering Capitalization

A Copy the following sentences. Change small letters to capital letters whenever necessary.

1. The Romance languages include french, italian, and spanish.
2. Pope john paul II is the leader of the roman catholic church.
3. The first monday in september is labor day.
4. Gabriel joined the united states marine corps.
5. The richardsons will drive north to the great lakes.
6. On december 2, 1980, glacier bay became a national park.
7. Liz crossed brown's bridge and turned west on oak street.
8. The guggenheim museum is in new york.
9. Dolores tests computers for the digital equipment company.
10. The mesa garden club meets today in the carnegie library.

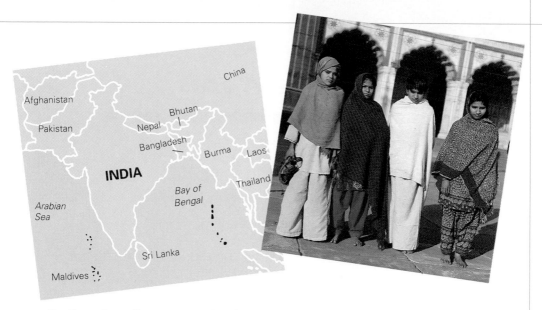

B Proofreading Copy the following paragraphs. Change small letters to capitals wherever necessary.

India, located in asia, is the seventh largest country in the world. It stretches from the indian ocean to the himalayas. Its largest cities are bombay, delhi, and calcutta. Calcutta lies east of bangladesh, a neighboring country. To the north, delhi lies near the ganges river. To the west, bombay rests between the mountains known as the western ghats and the arabian sea.

Many different cultures thrive in india. The majority of indians belong to the hindu religion. There are also many muslims who trace their faith to the sacred book called the koran. Fourteen major languages, including hindu and urdu, are recognized by the indian government. Each winter indians join together as a single people to celebrate republic day on january 26. This holiday honors the birth of india as an independent, democratic country.

C Write Now Imagine that you dreamed you were a crew member on a Viking ship. In your dream, you discovered an island tribe. Briefly describe the island, the tribe, its language, religion, and any other interesting details. Capitalize correctly.

First Words

Capitalize the first word of every sentence.

> **W**orkers digging the foundation found a mastodon bone.
> **W**hen will the eclipse begin?
> **L**ook out!

Capitalize the first word in most lines of poetry.

Even though a line of poetry may not begin a new sentence, it is usually capitalized.

> **I**'ll tell you how the sun rose,
> **A** ribbon at a time.
> **T**he steeples swam in amethyst,
> **T**he news like squirrels ran.
>
> From "I'll Tell You How the Sun Rose" by Emily Dickinson

Sometimes, especially in modern poetry, the lines of a poem may not begin with a capital letter.

> so much depends
> upon
>
> a red wheel
> barrow
>
> glazed with rain
> water
>
> beside the white
> chicken
>
> "The Red Wheelbarrow" by William Carlos Williams

Exercises Using Proper Capitalization

A Copy the following sentences. Capitalize wherever necessary.

1. the second sunday in may is mother's day.
2. is cotton still an important crop in the south?
3. last year, we had a dry summer and a rainy fall.
4. do you like italian food? have pizza at tina's restaurant.
5. there is a program on television tonight about japan.
6. dr. adams teaches english at alma college.
7. this month has five saturdays.
8. have you seen any movies by d. w. griffith?
9. carol and her family go out east in july.
10. a bird came down the walk:
    he did not know I saw;
    he bit an angleworm in halves
    and ate the fellow, raw.

> From "A Bird Came Down the Walk" by Emily Dickinson

B Rewrite each of these sentences. Use proper capitalization.

1. the atlanta symphony is playing a waltz by johannn strauss.
2. dad went to a lions' club dinner on saturday night.
3. on monday, i'll be late for dinner. our team has a game.
4. what is the spanish word for *table*?
5. our plane flew east over the atlantic ocean.
6. we celebrate flag day on june 14.
7. the canadians speak french in montreal, quebec.
8. have you ever seen the sears tower in chicago?
9. governor smith's mansion is on ninth avenue.
10. the Rhino is a homely beast,
    for human eyes he's not a feast,
    but you and i will never know
    why Nature chose to make him so.
    farewell, farewell, you old rhinoceros,
    i'll stare at something less prepoceros.

> "The Rhinoceros" by Ogden Nash

4
Outlines and Titles

Focus Capitalize the first words in outlines. Capitalize the first, last, and all important words in a title.

Capitalize the first word of each line of an outline.

Notice that the major divisions of an outline are marked with Roman numerals (I., II.). The next important divisions are identified with capital letters (A., B.). After that, Arabic numerals mark the divisions.

              Capitalization and Punctuation
   I. Use of capital letters
      A. Proper nouns and adjectives
      B. First words
         1. Sentences
         2. Poetry
         3. Outlines
         4. Titles
  II. Use of periods
      A. End of declarative and imperative sentences
      B. End of abbreviations

Capitalize the first word, last word, and all important words in a title.

Do not capitalize an article (*the, a, an*) or a short preposition (*in, for, from, by*) unless it comes first or last.

> *Raiders of the Lost Ark* (movie)
> *Gift from the Sea* (book)
> "The Walrus and the Carpenter" (poem)

Titles are also underlined or enclosed in quotation marks. Look on page 536 for rules on using these marks.

Exercises Capitalizing Titles and Outlines

A Number your paper from 1 to 10. Copy the following titles. Capitalize them correctly.

1. "highwire trapeze artist breaks record" (newspaper article)
2. *the peaceable kingdom* (painting)
3. "the brain is wider than the sky" (poem)
4. "mine strike in fifth week" (magazine article)
5. *pets of the world* (magazine)
6. *the return of the king* (book)
7. "what makes the aurora borealis?" (student's report)
8. "the world's deepest caves" (article)
9. "the kite-flying tournament" (pupil's report)
10. *where the red fern grows* (book)

B Rewrite the following outline using correct capital letters.

native americans of the northeast
  I. cultural groups
     a. lake tribes
     b. woodland tribes
 II. important foods
     a. lake tribes
        1. wild rice
        2. fish and shellfish
     b. woodland tribes
        1. corn, squash, and beans
        2. deer and other game

Chippewa Chief Okee Maakee Quid.

C *Write Now* A severe windstorm has knocked down power lines. You will be without electricity for three days. You do have oil lamps. Write a short paragraph telling what books, magazines, and newspapers you would read while waiting for the electricity to return. Capitalize correctly.

Linking Mechanics & Writing

A Imagine the excitement of being the first explorer to see the Pacific Ocean or set foot on the South Pole! In today's world the frontier of space offers similar challenges and conquests. Do some research about a famous "first" in exploration. Then imagine that you are the explorer and record the exciting events of this exploration "first" in your journal or ship's log. Be certain that you include the names of all the places and people who are involved. Check your log or journal entry for correct capitalization.

Francisco Coronado in search of Quivira, as painted by N. C. Wyeth.

B Using Mechanics in Writing You write the movie review column for your school paper. Choose a current movie that you feel is particularly well done or especially poor in quality. In two or three paragraphs tell your readers the best or worst points about your choice. Remember to include the names of the stars as well as a brief account of what happens and where the action takes place. You may want to also mention where the film is currently showing, but don't give away the ending. Moviegoers want to learn that for themselves. Check to see that you have followed the rules for correct capitalization.

Additional Practice

Parts 1–4 Using Capitalization Copy the following sentences. Capitalize wherever necessary.

1. salt lake city is in utah.
2. mr. sianis serves greek food in his restaurant.
3. early settlers moved west from virginia.
4. the name michigan comes from chippewa words meaning "great water."
5. the chinese have the world's oldest civilization.
6. arbor day is usually celebrated on the last friday in april.
7. benjamin franklin published the first *poor richard's almanac* in 1732.
8. my mother and i intend to visit the south this summer.
9. the main offices of the national football league are located in new york.
10. mary wollstonecraft shelley wrote *frankenstein*.
11. mrs. lopez teaches spanish at the college down the street.
12. tijuana, mexico, is close to san diego, california.
13. the parade on memorial day goes down state street.
14. the andes mountains run the entire length of south america.
15. *the war of the worlds* was written by h. g. wells.
16. the george washington bridge crosses the hudson river.
17. barbara jordan was born in houston, texas.
18. sequoyah developed an alphabet for the cherokee language.
19. the oldest religion in japan is shinto.
20. *steamboat willie,* the first cartoon to star mickey mouse, was made in 1928.
21. the columbus day celebration will be held in blair park.
22. *the house of dies drear* is set during the civil war.
23. the festival of lights is a swedish holiday.
24. dr. mary mcLeod bethune founded the national council of negro women.

25. uncle albert and i entered the three-legged race.
26. news reporters interviewed mayor fena and his advisors.
27. on tuesday, large crowds gathered in front of the lincoln memorial.
28. the picnic is in griffith park in los angeles on the first day of the month.
29. go north on colfax street to find carnegie library.
30. leaf burning is restricted on saturdays in october throughout the area.
31. the jewish temple will hold services for yom kippur.
32. the league of women voters endorsed bob smith for mayor.
33. on sunday, may 1, rev. tom lunde will give the sermon.
34. i don't know how often i've seen *the wizard of oz,* my favorite movie.
35. "i never saw a moor" is a poem by emily dickinson.
36. mark twain piloted a boat on the mississippi river and wrote about his experiences.
37. prospectors found gold in the mountains of the west.
38. the new testament of the bible has twenty-seven books.
39. the gateway arch in st. louis rises above the mississippi river.
40. the oakland a's won the 1988 american league pennant.
41. jack london's short story, "to build a fire," is suspenseful.
42. i want to study spanish before we visit mexico.
43. *treasure island* was written over one hundred years ago.
44. there was a Young Lady, whose Nose
    continually prospers and grows;
    when it grew out of sight,
    she exclaimed in a fright,
    "oh! Farewell to the end of my Nose!"

    "There Was a Young Lady Whose Nose" by Edward Lear
45. I. computer software
    a. word processing
    b. data base programs
    c. games

Application and Review

Lesson Review

A Capitalizing Proper Nouns and Adjectives Copy the following sentences. Capitalize wherever necessary.

1. The god apollo has the same name in both greek and roman mythology.
2. This week channel eleven is showing charlie chaplin movies every evening.
3. What are the three colors of the french flag?
4. At the oolong restaurant, i always order chinese fortune cookies.
5. The inventor of polio vaccine was dr. jonas salk.
6. Uncle ted and ms. yin waited anxiously for big ben to strike.
7. My neighbor, mr. liszt, makes delicious hungarian goulash.
8. The slavic languages use an alphabet different from ours.
9. The first hawaiian king was king kamehameha.
10. On valentine's day, gina and i made heart-shaped cookies.

B Capitalizing Poems Copy the following poems. Capitalize them correctly.

> brown and furry
> caterpillar in a hurry
> take your walk
> to the shady leaf or stalk.
>
> From "The Caterpillar" by Christina Georgina Rossetti

> so through the night rode Paul Revere;
> and so through the night went his cry of alarm
> to every Middlesex village and farm,—
> a cry of defiance and not of fear,
> a voice in the darkness, a knock at the door,
>
> From "Paul Revere's Ride" by Henry Wadsworth Longfellow

C Mastering Capitalization Copy the following sentences. Capitalize wherever necessary.

1. scientists worry that the sphinx, which guards the great pyramids at giza, egypt, is being damaged by the environment.
2. in some parts of ireland, street signs are written in the gaelic language.
3. the famous london bridge was moved from england and reconstructed in lake havasu city, arizona.
4. grandpa read us an interesting magazine article called "the origin of popcorn."
5. the mason-dixon line is a boundary between maryland and pennsylvania that divides the north and south.
6. *journey to the soviet union* is a book by samantha smith.
7. will halloween fall on a friday this year?
8. the koran, a sacred moslem book, is written in arabic.
9. every summer, over twenty thousand boy scouts of america attend a national camping jamboree.
10. in france, bastille day is like our fourth of july.

D Capitalizing Outlines Copy the following outline. Capitalize it correctly.

> reptiles
> I. extinct
>   a. dinosaurs
>   b. giant flying reptiles
>   c. giant swimming reptiles
> II. living today
>   a. turtles
>   b. snakes
>   c. alligators and crocodiles
>   d. lizards
>   e. tuatara

Chapter Review

A Capitalizing Correctly Copy the following sentences. Change small letters to capital letters wherever necessary.

1. just south of london, stands the mysterious stonehenge.
2. the gideon society places free bibles in hotel rooms.
3. french, flemish, and german are spoken in belgium.
4. dr. and mrs. blake attended a hawaiian luau in honolulu.
5. we met rabbi cohen before the service at the beth hillel synagogue.
6. skim the article "deserts" in *the world book encyclopedia*.
7. not all birds migrate south for the winter.
8. between the spanish and french border live the basques.
9. in canada, thanksgiving is on october tenth.
10. if i go to scotland, i want to find the loch ness monster.

B Capitalizing Outlines and Poems Copy the following groups of words on your paper. Change small letters to capital letters wherever necessary.

1.   the peanut butter story
   I. history of peanuts
      a. in the inca civilization
      b. in west africa
      c. their spread to america
  II. manufacturing peanut butter
      a. getting the nuts ready
         1. shelling, sorting, and roasting
         2. removing skin and splitting nuts
      b. grinding and adding other ingredients

2.   "to-night will be a stormy night—
     you to the town must go;
     and take a lantern, Child, to light
     your mother through the snow."
          From "Lucy Gray" by William Wordsworth

27

Punctuation

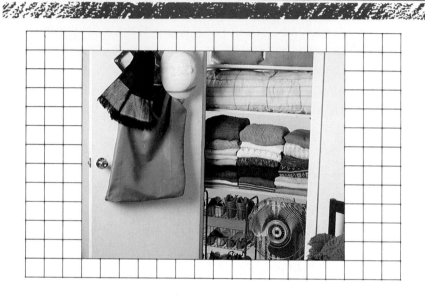

STOP! DON'T OPEN THE CLOSET!

Do you ever let your things pile up in corners or closets until there's no room for anything else? You always know that sooner or later you'll have to organize the jumble. Without organization it's difficult to find things. Your favorite sweatshirt or your autographed baseball could be lost forever.

Punctuation marks are the "organizers" of our written language. They signal when one thought stops and another begins. They show when a question is being asked or indicate the exact words of a speaker.

Without punctuation your writing would be a jumble of words. This chapter will help you learn to use punctuation correctly so that your writing will be organized and clear.

1
The Period

Focus Use a period in these situations: to end a declarative sentence; to end most imperative sentences; and after abbreviations, initials, and certain numbers.

Use a period at the end of a declarative sentence and most imperative sentences.

A **declarative** sentence makes a statement.

The next clue is hidden under that rock.

An **imperative** sentence states a command or request.

Look under that rock for the next clue.

Use a period after an abbreviation.

To save time and space we often use words in a shortened form. These forms are called *abbreviations*.

The names of states, days, and months are often abbreviated. Except for such abbreviations as *Mr., Mrs., Ms., A.M.,* and *P.M.,* avoid using abbreviations in formal writing.

P.O.	Post Office	in.	inch
U.S.A.	United States of America	doz.	dozen
St.	Street	ht.	height
Mt.	Mountain	wt.	weight
R.R.	Railroad	lb.	pound
D.C.	District of Columbia	oz.	ounce

Some special abbreviations are written without periods.

FM	frequency modulation	PBS	Public Broadcasting System
CB	citizens' band	USAF	United States Air Force
M	meter	ml	milliliter

The two-letter state abbreviations such as ME, OH, and CA are written with capital letters and no periods. See page 307 for a full list of state abbreviations. A dictionary will show whether an abbreviation is written with periods.

Use a period after an initial.

We often shorten a name to its first letter. This letter is called an initial.

> P. Travers—Pamela Travers
> J. C. Penney—James Cash Penney

Use a period after each number or letter that shows a division of an outline or that precedes an item in a list.

Punctuation (an outline)

I. End marks
  A. The period
    1. Declarative sentences
    2. Most imperative sentences
    3. Abbreviations and initials
    4. Outlines and lists
  B. The question mark
  C. The exclamation point
    1. Exclamatory sentences
    2. Some imperative sentences

Talent Show Act (a list)

1. tumblers
2. tap dancer
3. singer
4. band

Exercises Using Periods

A Copy these phrases, adding periods where necessary.

1. 4 ft 10 in
2. Washington, DC
3. PO Box 12
4. Bedford Ave
5. Aug 30
6. The Teevee Chair Co, Inc

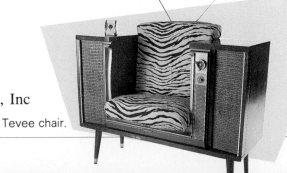

Teevee chair.

7. Dr H M Ritchie
8. 500 mi
9. Pine Tree Ln
10. Video Tape-Making (outline)

    I Recording equipment needed
      A Camera
        1 VHS
        2 VHS-C
        3 8-millimeter
      B Videotape
    II Viewing equipment needed
      A Video cassette recorder
      B Television

B Rewrite each of the following phrases, using abbreviations where possible.

1. East 126th Street
2. Reverend Marsh
3. Platte River
4. 4 gallons
5. December 9
6. New York
7. Raleigh, North Carolina
8. 10 square feet
9. Benader Game Company
10. Durapools, Incorporated
11. 13 pounds
12. Mount Everest
13. 450 milligrams
14. Columbia Broadcasting System
15. Post Office Box 1878

c *Write Now* Write a short note to a friend. Give directions from his or her house to a park or shopping center where you plan to meet on Saturday. Correctly punctuate abbreviations.

2
The Question Mark and the Exclamation Point

Focus Use a question mark after an interrogative sentence. Use an exclamation point after an exclamatory sentence, after some imperative sentences, and after an interjection.

Use a question mark after an interrogative sentence.

An **interrogative** sentence asks a question.

> Where are we?   When do the geese migrate?

Use an exclamation point after an exclamatory sentence.

An **exclamatory sentence** expresses strong feelings.

> Jackie struck out!   It's a home run!

Use an exclamation point at the end of an imperative sentence that shows surprise or another strong emotion.

> Look out!   Hurry!

Use an exclamation point after an interjection.

An **interjection** is a word or group of words used to express strong feeling.

> Oh! How beautiful!   Wow! What an ending!

Exercises Using End Marks

A Copy the following sentences. Add question marks and exclamation points wherever necessary.

1. Ouch This pan is hot
2. How many more play rehearsals do we have

3. Does Isaac Asimov write both fiction and nonfiction

4. Help I'm falling

5. Fire Move fast

6. Did Vanessa try out for the soccer team

7. Who was that on the phone

8. Oh, no You didn't forget the picnic, did you

9. Watch out That branch is breaking

10. Have you visited the Capitol in Washington, D.C.

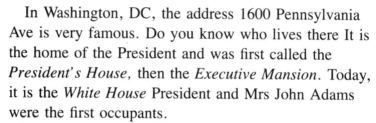

B Proofreading Rewrite the following paragraphs. Add periods, question marks, and exclamation marks as needed.

In Washington, DC, the address 1600 Pennsylvania Ave is very famous. Do you know who lives there It is the home of the President and was first called the *President's House,* then the *Executive Mansion.* Today, it is the *White House* President and Mrs John Adams were the first occupants.

"Fire" This cry caused James and Dolley Madison to flee as the British burned the mansion during the War of 1812. It was rebuilt, and in 1961, Mrs J F Kennedy supervised restoring the interior to its original appearance The public can visit certain rooms Tuesdays through Saturdays.

3
Commas That Separate Ideas

Focus Use a comma to separate items in a series. Use a comma when you use *and, but,* or *or* to join two sentences. Use a comma to avoid confusion.

Commas tell the reader to pause. This pause keeps the reader from running together words or ideas that are separate.

Use commas to separate the items in a series. There are always three or more words in a series.

> The pet store sells birds, lizards, turtles, and fish.

In a series, place commas after each word except the last. Notice how the meaning of this sentence changes when some of the commas are removed.

> The grocery clerk packed Anna's bag with soda, crackers, broccoli, soup, cream, cheese, and peanut butter.
> The grocery clerk packed Anna's bag with soda crackers, broccoli soup, cream cheese, and peanut butter.

When you use *and, but,* or *or* to combine two sentences, put a comma before these words.

> We ran fast. We nearly missed the bus.
> We ran fast, but we nearly missed the bus.

Use a comma whenever the reader might be confused.

Some sentences can be very confusing without commas.

Confusing	Going up the elevator lost power.
Clear	Going up, the elevator lost power.
Confusing	In the grocery bags were in demand.
Clear	In the grocery, bags were in demand.

Exercises Using Commas

A Copy the following sentences. Place commas where needed.

1. We saw the tracks and we knew there were raccoons nearby.
2. Catherine added garlic oregano and parsley to the sauce.
3. People left their farms and they moved to the city.
4. As Shelia wrote the teacher talked.
5. The meal includes sandwiches soup dessert and beverage.
6. You can use a typewriter or you can try a word processor.
7. According to the paper meat prices will soon go down.
8. In the story books were forbidden.
9. The typhoon brought high winds heavy rains and flooding.
10. The cab started forward and then it screeched to a halt.

B Copy the following sentences. Insert commas where needed.

1. Soccer rugby and football are somewhat similar games.
2. When I called my friend invited me to a movie.
3. A cold often means aches a fever chills and a runny nose.
4. You can tell me about the book but don't tell me the end.
5. In the forest trails for bikers have been marked.
6. They could close the mine or they could risk a cave-in.
7. After jumping the horse trotted to the next hurdle.
8. Tom had three items: macaroni salad and dessert.
9. When our team lost the players felt depressed.
10. The plumber fixed the faucet and he cleared the drain.

C *Write Now* Imagine that you are an expedition guide. You might lead hikers to the wilds of Alaska or guide climbers up Mt. Everest. Write instructions for your group. Use commas to list equipment needed and events scheduled.

4
Commas That Set Off Special Elements

Focus Use a comma to set off introductory phrases, the name of a person spoken to, and appositives. Use a comma to separate parts of dates and addresses.

Use a comma after *yes, no,* or *well* to begin a sentence.

Yes, we're walking.   Well, we'll meet you there.

Use commas to set off the name of a person spoken to.

One comma is needed when the name starts or ends the sentence. A comma is needed before and after a name in the middle of the sentence.

Pam, what is your favorite color? Which is yours, Tim? I think, Abigail, that you are taller than Sara.

Use commas to set off an appositive.

An **appositive** follows a noun and renames the noun. It is used to give more information.

Mr. Lopez, our swim coach, retired last week.

Use commas to separate the parts of a date. Use a comma after the last part of a date in the middle of a sentence.

Our field trip to the Bronx Zoo is on Friday, May 13. On November 7, 1962, Eleanor Roosevelt died.

Use a comma to separate the name of a city from the name of a state or country.

We once lived near Trenton, New Jersey. My parents traveled to Zurich, Switzerland, last year.

Exercises Using Commas

A Copy these sentences. Place commas where they are needed.

1. Albany New York is on the Hudson River.
2. Friday May 5 was our opening night.
3. Denmark Sweden and Norway are Scandinavian countries.
4. Beverly Cleary my favorite author addressed our book club.
5. January 12 1876 was the birthdate of Jack London.
6. Well what do you think?
7. We crossed a causeway to go to Key West Florida.
8. You know Adele I'll be away tomorrow.
9. On October 7 1943 my father was born in Portland Maine.
10. Dad this is Al Cresco a friend of mine.

B The following paragraphs are missing several commas. Copy these paragraphs, adding commas wherever they are needed.

The first bicycle the *draisienne* was built by Baron Karl de Drais. The German inventor first exhibited his *draisienne* or "dandy horse" on April 6 1818 in Paris France. It was made of wood and the rider made it go by paddling his or her feet along the ground. A Scottish blacksmith Kirkpatrick Macmillan added foot pedals.

A Frenchman Pierre Lallement was given the first patent for a bicycle in 1866. This bicycle also called the "bone shaker" had pedals attached to the front wheel. In the 1870's the *high-wheeler* or *penny-farthing* appeared. In 1893, the safety bike with wheels of equal size came to London England. Certainly bicycles have come a long way since the *draisienne*!

C *Write Now* Help a sheriff in the old "Wild West" make a "wanted" poster for a bank robber. Use direct address to get the attention of neighboring sheriffs. Include the city, state, and date the criminal was last seen. Give the robber's real name, using his nickname as an appositive.

5
Other Uses for Commas

Focus Use a comma to set off a direct quotation. Use a comma after the greeting and the closing of a friendly letter.

Use a comma to set off the explanatory words of a direct quotation.

Notice where the comma is placed in this direct quotation.

> Courtney announced, "The movie will begin in ten minutes."

The explanatory words *Courtney announced* come before the quotation. A comma is placed after the last explanatory word.

> "I want to go home," moaned Lisa.

The explanatory words come after the quotation. A comma is placed inside the quotation marks and after the last word of the quotation. Sometimes a quotation is separated into two parts.

> "One of you," the detective said, "is the murderer."

A comma is used after the last word of the first part. Another comma is used after the last explanatory word. You will learn more about punctuating quotations in part 6.

Use a comma after the greeting of a friendly letter and after the closing of any letter.

> Dear Agnes,   Sincerely yours,

Exercises Using Commas

A Copy these sentences. Add commas where they are needed.

1. Benjamin said "I'd like to visit Boston some day."
2. "This chili is delicious" said my father.

3. "It seems to me" Carol said "that this puzzle is too hard for a six-year-old child."
4. The note was signed: Sincerely Sherlock Holmes.
5. Dear Ms. Post I will gladly attend. Yours truly Mr. Todd.
6. Benjamin Franklin said "Honesty is the best policy."
7. "Who" the caterpillar asked Alice "are you?"
8. "Here" the salesclerk said "is the book you ordered."
9. "The radio is too loud" my mother complained.
10. "I'm up in the attic" Ned called.

B Rewrite these sentences using punctuation correctly. If a sentence has no errors, write *Correct*.

1. While Vicky painted Eric sanded the table.
2. "Friday's weather" the forecaster said "will be sunny."
3. Our team won but it was a very close score.
4. Ms. Gajda said, "The concert is at seven o'clock."
5. You will need sun lotion sun glasses and a beach towel.
6. Yes on May 2 our tour group will visit Savannah Georgia.
7. On your way out Helen close the windows.
8. Yvette asked, "What's on TV tonight?"
9. Our house has jalousies a kind of slatted window.
10. "Three weeks ago today" Meg said "I got my new bike."

c *Write Now* Samantha discovered a packet of letters in the attic. One letter was from Lydia Darragh to a colonel in the American Revolutionary Army. In the letter, Lydia reports overhearing British General Howe planning an attack on Washington's troops at Valley Forge. Write the letter. Include the letter opening, closing, and Howe's words quoted by Lydia.

Detail, *Washington Crossing the Delaware,* Eastman Johnson.

6
The Apostrophe and the Hyphen

Focus Use an apostrophe to show possession and to form contractions. Use a hyphen to divide a word at the end of a line and in compound numbers.

Use an apostrophe to show possession. To form the possessive of a singular noun, add an apostrophe and s.

city + 's = city's   Carlos + 's = Carlos's

To form the possessive of a plural noun that does not end in s, add an apostrophe and an s after the apostrophe.

gentlemen + 's = gentlemen's   geese + 's = geese's

To form the possessive of a plural noun that ends in s, add only an apostrophe.

birds + ' = birds'   cities + ' = cities'

Use an apostrophe in a contraction.

A **contraction** joins two words, omitting one or more letters. An apostrophe replaces the missing letters.

will + not = won't   he + had = he'd
you + will = you'll   she + would = she'd

Use a hyphen after the first part of a word at the end of a line. Then write the second part on the next line.

Before you choose a career, investigate many fields.

Never divide words of one syllable, such as *slight* or *bounce*. A dictionary shows how to divide a word into syllables.

Do not write a single letter at the end or beginning of a line. These divisions would be wrong: *a- mong, inventor- y.*

Use a hyphen in compound numbers from twenty-one through ninety-nine.

seventy-six trombones   Twenty-third Psalm

Exercises Using Apostrophes and Hyphens

A On your paper make contractions from the words in 1 to 4. Make the words in 5 to 8 show possession. Hyphenate the words in 9 and 10.

1. it is
2. she is
3. we would
4. had not
5. children

6. mechanics
7. Chris
8. cyclist
9. seventy nine
10. seventh

B Copy the following phrases. Decide whether you can divide the word in italics into two parts, each part having more than one letter. If you can, divide the word as you would at the end of a line. Add the necessary hyphens.

EXAMPLE   the thirty eight *cannons*   the thirty-eight cannons

1. forty five *minutes*
2. the fifty ninth *correction*
3. Twenty second *Amendment*
4. thirty four *years*
5. eighty one *trailers*

6. seventy nine years *ago*
7. ninety three *skateboards*
8. twenty nine *cents*
9. my sixty fourth *experiment*
10. forty *clarinets*

C *Write Now* Write an entry in a ship's log. Include the day's events, the number in your crew, and the ship's cargo. Write out all numbers. Use some possessive forms and contractions.

7
The Colon and the Semicolon

Focus Use a colon after the greeting of a business letter and to separate hours and minutes in expressions of time. Use a semicolon to join two related sentences.

Use a colon after the greeting in a business letter.

Dear Mrs. Winter**:**   Dear Sir**:**

Use a colon between the numerals that tell hours and minutes.

8**:**30 A.M.   3**:**30 P.M.

Remember to capitalize the letters and to use periods after each letter in the abbreviations A.M. and P.M.

Use a semicolon to combine two related sentences.

You can combine two related sentences into one by using a conjunction such as *and, but,* or *or* to connect the sentences. Use a comma before the conjunction.

The judge entered the courtroom, and everyone rose.

Another way to combine two related sentences is to use a semicolon (;). The semicolon takes the place of both the comma and the conjunction.

The judge entered the courtroom; everyone rose.

Grammar in Action Correct use of the semicolon will help you avoid writing run-on sentences.

Incorrect   The conductor raised her baton the concert began.
Correct   The conductor raised her baton; the concert began.

Exercises Using Colons and Semicolons

A Copy the following letter. Use colons, semicolons, and commas where they are needed.

June 14 19___

Dear Mr. Grant

Our puppet theater in Tyler Texas will present the story "Cinderella" this weekend. Please print the schedule in the Tuesday paper. The play will be shown on Saturday July 9 at 1100 A.M. and 300 P.M. furthermore it will be shown on Sunday July 10 at 1030 A.M. 230 P.M. and 700 P.M.

Sincerely yours
Toy Chest
Puppet Theater

B *Write Now* On "Up, Up, and Away Day" each student in your class wrote a message to be tied to a helium balloon. While holding onto the balloons, you were suddenly lifted into the air. You waved to shouting classmates as you began a five-day journey.

Write a diary. Start each entry with the date and time. Describe where you went that day and what you saw below you. What did people on the ground say as they saw you drift above them? Your last entry should describe how you landed safely and how you returned to school.

8
Quotation Marks

Focus Use quotation marks at the beginning and end of direct quotations.

When you write what a person has said, you are writing a **quotation**. A **direct quotation** is the restatement of the person's exact words. If you do not write the exact words, you are writing an **indirect quotation**. Study these examples.

Direct quotation   Steven whispered, "I'm hiding Dad's present."
Indirect quotation   Steven said that he was hiding Dad's present.

Put quotation marks before and after the words of a direct quotation.

Notice that Steven's exact words are set apart by quotation marks in the first sentence above. **Quotation marks** (" ") are two pairs of small marks that look like apostrophes. They tell the reader that the exact words of the speaker or writer are being quoted.

Separate the words of a direct quotation from the rest of the sentence with a comma or end mark in addition to quotation marks.

Julie exclaimed, "The band is marching!"
"The band is marching!" Julie exclaimed.

Place question marks and exclamation points inside quotation marks if they belong to the quotation itself.

Michael asked, "Did the bird's wing heal?"
"It's perfect!" answered Marianne.

In the first sentence, the question is quoted. Therefore, the question mark is placed inside the quotation marks. In the second sentence, the speaker is showing strong emotion. The exclamation point is also placed inside the quotation marks.

Place question marks and exclamation points outside quotation marks if they do not belong to the quotation. Capitalize the first word of a direct quotation.

Did Dad say, "Come home at seven o'clock"**?**
I was shocked to hear her say, "I'll go"**!**

Divided Quotations

Sometimes a quotation is divided. Explanatory words, like *she said* or *he asked,* are in the middle of the quotation.

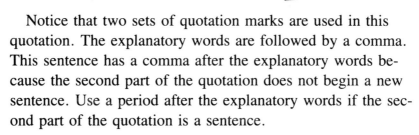

"My favorite movie," Lewis said, "is *King Kong.*"

Notice that two sets of quotation marks are used in this quotation. The explanatory words are followed by a comma. This sentence has a comma after the explanatory words because the second part of the quotation does not begin a new sentence. Use a period after the explanatory words if the second part of the quotation is a sentence.

"We wrote that**,**" said the class**.** "It is a group poem."

In this sentence, the second part of the quotation begins with a capital letter because it is the start of a new sentence.

Grammar in Action   *Said* is a common explanatory word used in writing. Try to use a variety of explanatory words when you write. Use some of these.

explained	announced	exclaimed	requested
commented	expressed	asked	noted

Exercises Using Quotation Marks

A Copy the following sentences. Add all the necessary quotation marks. Some sentences are correct.

1. Drop anchor, bellowed the captain.
2. The cashier asked, Will there be anything else?
3. Take the game home, Sally said. You can keep it.
4. What was that noise? asked my sister.
5. Dora said she'd come at about 8:30 on Saturday.
6. You can pat Prince, said Linda. He won't bite.
7. Last call for dinner, announced the train porter.
8. What would you do, Mr. Rocher asked, if the rope broke?
9. Mike suggested that we knot the tug-of-war rope.
10. No, answered Ethan. My jacket is maroon.

B On your paper, change the following indirect quotations to direct quotations.

1. Mom told us to be careful walking home.
2. Robin complained that she was getting cold.
3. Wendy asked where the kitten had hidden.
4. Sheila thought that the sunrise over the lake was the most beautiful she had ever seen.
5. The stranger asked where he could find a place to eat.
6. Hector insisted that the other way was shorter.
7. Dad told us to take our keys before locking the door.
8. Kevin said he'd like two eggs with bacon and toast.
9. Martin asked when the test would begin.
10. Mary wondered how she could help Mrs. Sundelius with the canned goods collection.

C *Write Now* Imagine that you are a musical instrument in a band or orchestra. The musicians are taking a brief break. You have a short conversation with the instrument next to you. Write the brief conversation you have. Use direct quotations.

9
Punctuating Titles

Focus Use quotation marks to set off the titles of short works. Underline the titles of longer works.

Put quotation marks around the titles of stories, poems, reports, articles, and chapters of a book.

"Spring Song"   "The Ransom of Red Chief"
   (poem)   (story)

Underline the title of a book, magazine, play, motion picture, or TV series. In print, these titles appear in italics.

Mary Jane   *Mary Jane*
   by Dorothy Sterling   by Dorothy Sterling

Underline the title of a painting or the name of a ship.

Washington Crossing the Delaware (painting)
Queen Elizabeth II (ship)

Exercises Punctuating Titles

A Copy the following titles. Add quotation marks and underlining as needed.

1. Rapunzel (story)
2. Fog (poem)
3. Ship Sinks (article)
4. The Muscles (chapter)
5. Cricket (magazine)
6. Back to the Future (movie)
7. Tom Sawyer (book)
8. Wonderworks (TV series)
9. Ramona Forever (book)
10. Salute to a Tree (poem)

B *Write Now* You wake one morning to find that it is the year 2020. Your town looks as if it has been deserted for about 35 years. In a brief paragraph, describe what you find in the town. Include the titles of books, magazines, and video tapes.

Linking Mechanics & Writing

A Suppose that two hundred years ago, someone was sitting right where you are sitting now. If you could talk to him or her, what would you ask about life in the eighteenth century? What would you like to tell that person about life today? Imagine the conversation you would have. Think of the questions both of you would ask and the answers you both would give. Then write the conversation. Use quotation marks, commas, question marks, and other punctuation marks properly in your conversation.

B You are about to take an Intergalatic Spaceways flight to another solar system. It's a long flight—several years—so you need to bring along things to read and to watch on your video screen. Think about the stories, articles, poems, books, magazines, movies, plays, and video cassettes of television shows you would like to take along. Then write a few paragraphs telling what titles you have selected and why you selected each one. Take care to use quotation marks and underlining correctly.

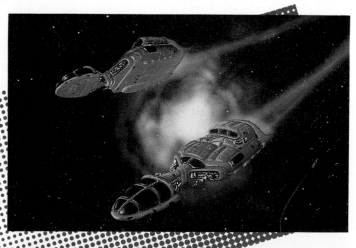

Additional Practice

Parts 1 and 2 End Marks Copy the following phrases and sentences. Add any missing periods and end marks.

1. The documentary by Mr Moyers was on the PBS station
2. Watch out for that step
3. When do the swallows return to Capistrano
4. 4 doz packages weighing 8 lb each
5. Request the catalog from Sod Busters, Inc, PO Box 2
6. Have you ever visited the Ozarks
7. What a great fireworks display that was
8. D N Gorski, Ames, IA, is the return address
9. Dr Chan is on the 4:45 flight to Washington, DC
10. Oh, no The bridge is out
11. Who played the violin solo with the orchestra
12. I have finished my report Have you
13. 144 sq in
14. Amazon R
15. The tour bus to Mt Shasta leaves at 8 AM daily

Parts 3, 4, and 5 Commas Copy the following sentences. Insert commas where needed.

16. That trio consists of a violin viola and cello.
17. No the ceremony is postponed until Wednesday February 12.
18. Moline Illinois is across the river from Bettendorf Iowa.
19. "Meet me at the library" Collen said.
20. In professional basketball games are forty-eight minutes long.
21. The address began "Four score and seven years ago. . . ."
22. Gwendolyn Brooks the poet was born in 1917.
23. While Sylvia cooked George set the table.
24. "Sprinters" said the starter "on your marks."
25. Meighan will you please answer the phone?
26. The curtain went up but no one appeared on stage.

27. Benito an exchange student comes from Florence Italy.
28. Yes I saw the Gauguin exhibit at the Art Institute.
29. It finally stopped raining and the sun came out.
30. Can we count on you John to do the necessary research?

Part 6 Apostrophes and Hyphens Rewrite the following sentences. In each sentence, change any italicized words to contractions. Add apostrophes and hyphens wherever necessary.

31. The cities mayors gathered for the annual political convention.
32. Todays high temperature was sixty four degrees.
33. *Do not* sign up for that class unless *you are* prepared to practice every evening.
34. The Colts quarterback completed a forty two-yard pass.
35. *They are* arriving at gate thirty three in approx imately one hour.

Part 7 Colons and Semicolons Copy the following sentences. Add colons and semicolons wherever necessary.

36. Dear Miss Allen
    Your appointment has been set for 945 A.M.
37. The light turned red the traffic halted.
38. Our flight to Denver leaves at 1205 P.M.
39. The gates opened the fans dashed to their seats.
40. Dear Mayor Davis
    Thank you for responding to our class's petition.
41. Because the game went into overtime, the 500 news was not on until 600.
42. Gwen picked the apples they were ripe.
43. At 1130 P.M. the meeting was adjourned it resumed the next day.
44. We close at 800 P.M. the doors are locked at 805.
45. Please read the enclosed notice fill in the response.

Part 8 Quotation Marks Rewrite the following sentences adding quotation marks where needed. Write *Correct* if no quotation marks are needed.

46. The umpire shouted, Play ball!
47. The candidate said that he would not raise taxes under any circumstances.
48. Give me liberty or give me death! cried Patrick Henry.
49. Ben looked at the map and inquired, Where is the country of Cameroon located?
50. Nora quietly asked where she could find a telephone for a private call.
51. Yesterday, Paul said, was the two-hundredth anniversary of the signing of the Constitution.
52. Did the officer say, Halt?
53. You can't park over there, the attendant said just as we found the perfect spot.
54. Did Hector say he was going to the library tonight or tomorrow night?
55. My favorite baseball team is the Tigers, Marie said. What's yours?

Part 9 Punctuating Titles Copy the following titles. Add quotation marks or underlining as needed.

56. The Highwayman (poem)
57. USS Constitution (ship)
58. All Summer in a Day (story)
59. Sports Illustrated (magazine)
60. The Princess Bride (movie)
61. The Bill Cosby Show (TV series)
62. Survival Training for Chimps (article)
63. Mona Lisa (painting)
64. And Then There Were None (book)
65. Romeo and Juliet (play)

Application and Review

Lesson Review

A   Using Commas and End Marks Correctly Copy the following sentences. Supply the missing commas, periods, question marks, and exclamation points.

1. It was wild The soccer game was still going on at 8:30 PM
2. Ashton are you going to the movie with us
3. "Satellites" Ms. Lee said "are used for communications weather reporting and navigation"
4. Do you mean Paris France or Paris Ontario
5. Well Tracy has money and she wants to buy the ring
6. Get help fast
7. Wow I never saw such a huge cave before
8. On July 20 1969 the United States landed two astronauts on the moon
9. Before broiling the cookbook says to season the meat
10. "Shouldn't you take an umbrella" Ned asked

B   Using Apostrophes and Hyphens Correctly Rewrite the following sentences. In each sentence, make a contraction of the words in italics. Change any underlined word to show possession. Add hyphens where necessary.

1. *He will* mail <u>Mother</u> thirty six invitations.
2. *They have* always bought cider at the apple orchard.
3. <u>Bret</u> dog *did not* wake up when the lightning hit.
4. The twenty two members of the band performed well.
5. <u>Isabelle</u> temperature was ninety nine degrees.
6. *We had* finished the game when it began to rain.
7. Alice *could not* see the <u>acrobats</u> performance.
8. I collected seventy five dollars for the Heart Association.
9. You *should not* phone <u>Cara</u> house again tonight.
10. Our seats are in section thirty one.

C Using Colons, Semicolons, and Commas Correctly
Copy the following letter using colons, semicolons, and commas where they are needed.

April 12 19___

Dear Ms. Walker

    We are glad you and your class have decided to visit the science museum in San Diego California. The museum opens at 930 A.M. There is an electricity demonstration at 1000 A.M., 130 P.M., and 400 P.M. there is also a program in the auditorium at 1115 A.M. and 330 P.M.

    We're looking forward to seeing you on Thursday May 3 and hope you'll enjoy your visit.

Very truly yours
Sarah Carlson

D Punctuating Quotations Correctly Copy the following sentences. Add all the punctuation marks that are needed.

1. Beat the eggs vigorously Julia said and pour them into a hot skillet.
2. I have some money but I'm saving it I told Alonzo.
3. Heather asked Where is my basketball Terence?
4. Which do you like asked Henry Is this photo better?
5. Paul have you ever read about old castles asked Ed.

E Punctuating Titles Correctly Copy the following titles. Use quotation marks or underlining as needed.

1. Frank's Place (TV show)
2. Paul Revere's Ride (poem)
3. It's Like This, Cat (book)
4. Rip Van Winkle (story)
5. Who Framed Roger Rabbit? (movie)

Chapter Review

A Copy the following sentences. Add the missing punctuation.

1. Mr and Mrs Gregory go to St Augustine every winter
2. Great We got the last four tickets
3. After Margo ate the squirrels gathered the crumbs
4. What circus did P T Barnum manage Carl asked
5. The banquet has been postponed until the twenty third
6. On March 4 we will move to 600 W 24th St
7. Marci shouted Dont touch that broken glass
8. Pete do you mean Athens Greece or Athens Georgia
9. Im coming Harry replied I wont be late
10. Wow Did we get sixteen inches of snow last night
11. The pebbles are cemented together by lime silica or clay
12. Skipper a mischievous puppy annoyed its new owner
13. The house is on fire shouted Rosalie
14. Adam asked if we were meeting at 700 PM
15. P G Wodehouse created comical characters for many books

B Rewrite the following letter. Add punctuation.

December 18 19____

Dear Ms de Angeli

The *Lapeer News* ran an article titled, Author Returns to Hometown. The article said you would be at the library from 300 to 500 on December 28. If possible Ms. de Angeli I would like to interview you for my school paper. My class just read your book The Door in the Wall and theyve all given me questions to ask you. I could meet with you on the twenty ninth if you are too busy on the twenty eighth.

Its exciting having an author come to Lapeer Michigan. Im hoping you will say that I may interview you.

Yours truly
Heidi Mann

Cumulative Review

A Capitalizing Correctly Rewrite the following sentences adding capital letters wherever necessary.

1. The spanish explorer coronado traveled to what is now the state of kansas in 1541 looking for gold.
2. In 1927 charles lindbergh flew the *spirit of st. louis* from new york to paris.
3. The orange bowl is in miami, florida, not pasadena, california.
4. The great salt lake valley is mostly desert.
5. In athens stands the parthenon, built to honor athena, goddess of wisdom.
6. The orinoco is a river in venezuela.
7. Many irish people wear green on st. patrick's day.
8. Please tell dad that uncle ernie called.
9. Ghost towns are reminders of the early days of the west.
10. The moslem name for god is *allah*.
11. Many people along the canadian border speak both french and english.
12. May i visit aunt harriet for a few days during christmas vacation?
13. The gobi desert lies north of beijing, china.
14. The poem begins, "this is my letter to the world."
15. The book was called *charlie and the chocolate factory*, but the movie was titled *willie wonka*.

B Understanding Punctuation Rewrite the following sentences and add punctuation where necessary.

1. W F Cody also called Buffalo Bill organized Americas first Wild West Show.
2. St Paul Minnesota is the capital of the state.
3. Is a bowling alley sixty ft long

4. On July 10 1890 Wyoming entered the union as the forty fourth state.
5. The region that makes up Lapland belongs to Sweden Denmark Norway and the Soviet Union.
6. Yes the tour includes a day in Sydney Australia so that we can visit the Opera House.
7. Mark we wont be picking you up until 830.
8. Good grief Is that tire flat again
9. Which movie introduced the song When You Wish Upon a Star
10. The lesson the chef said will begin with the sauce for the broccoli.
11. I answered the phone but apparently the caller had already hung up.
12. The lights dimmed the curtain went up.
13. Its beautiful Helen exclaimed.
14. After we ate the electricity went off.
15. The smile of the woman in the painting Mona Lisa is famous.

C Combined Review Rewrite the following paragraphs. Add necessary capitalization and punctuation.

Istanbul turkeys largest city began when the greeks colonized the area in about 600 bc. Later, constantine a roman emperor selected this city for his capital. The city then took the name constantinople or city of Constantine. In the 1400s, the ottoman turks captured the city and renamed it Istanbul.

Today, tourists visit istanbul to see its bazaars museums and mosques. They travel in *dolmus* special taxis that carry several passengers at once. During a taxi trip, a visitor may cross into another continent, because this is the only city located on two continents asia and europe. Who wouldnt want to see such a fascinating place

Writer's Handbook

Ideas for Writing

Ideas for writing are all around you. You need only to notice them and develop them. To help you get started, read the following lists of ideas. For other ideas, refer to Starting Points, pages 31–39. Then use the thinking skills you learned in Chapter 2 to turn these ideas into interesting writing topics.

Journal Starters

I wish I could trade places with:
  a friend
  someone in prehistoric times
  a famous movie star
I listen to music because . . .
By the time I'm 30 years old I will have . . .
I feel very lonely when . . .
Today I read that . . .
For me, the greatest honor would be . . .
Sometimes I worry about . . .
A best friend should . . .
A dream I always have is . . .
When I'm in high school . . .
A movie that really made me think was . . .

Narratives

Tell a story about:
a trip to _____
when _____ came to America
a time you were very proud
a lesson learned the hard way
how _____ became famous
a time when you couldn't believe your eyes
a second chance
a frightening experience
an embarrassing moment
a day that started like any other day, but ended in a very unusual way
someone who won't give up
a race with time
a day that wouldn't end
the best Saturday ever
waking up to find that your hair has turned purple

Descriptions

Describe one of the following:

a gnome
the view from the 67th floor of a skyscraper
how your favorite movie character walks
the taste, smell, appearance, and texture of any food
the sound of your favorite music
the sights and sounds of a shopping center
night sounds
a gremlin
the perfect brother / sister
your favorite place indoors
your favorite article of clothing
a sports event
a typical family celebration
a sunset
how an insect bite feels
the smell of tar and gasoline on a hot day
Paul Bunyan's Blue Ox

Explaining *How*

Explain how to:

make papier-mâché
do origami
make a combination pizza
study for a test
fix a flat bicycle tire
be a true friend
arrange flowers
tune a guitar
pack a backpack
pitch a tent
snorkel
play darts
design a zoo
purify water for drinking
recycle aluminum or paper

Explain how one of these items works:

a bagpipe
a fire alarm
a light bulb
a steam engine
a hang glider
a tape recorder
medieval armor

Explaining *Why*

Give reasons for or against one of the following:

believing in superstitions
TV time should be limited
a new fashion
winning is not important
movie ratings
intramural sports programs
conservation is everyone's responsibility

Give reasons why:
_____ is the best book
 you've ever read
a _____ is the best pet
_____ is your favorite
 music
everyone needs friends
you like to participate in a
 particular sport
_____ should be added to
 the lunch program
cooperation is important
you like to visit a museum

Reports

Write a report about:
the knights of the Round
 Table
a famous inventor
a famous sports figure
a famous explorer
a lunar eclipse
meteor showers
earthquakes
tidal waves
geysers
a famous pirate
the history of baseball
the story of photography
mummies
carrier pigeons
submarines
koala bears
the origin of Santa Claus

Creative Writing

an announcement that will
 change the way you live
an advertisement for a
 campaign poster—to
 elect you as President of
 the United States
a tall tale in which a sports
 star is the hero
a newspaper story about a
 strange event
your acceptance speech for
 an academy award

What if . . . ?
the wheel had never been
 invented
all clocks stopped
your pet could talk
you could see into the
 future
dragons ruled the earth

What happens to . . . ?
last year's calendar
an old tennis ball
your first toy

Write about:
sour
tired
confidence
wrinkled
blue
happiness

Outlines and Other Graphic Organizers

Graphic aids can help you to organize your ideas. You might use them to take notes or to plan a composition or speech. Outlines and other graphic organizers can help you record and arrange information in a logical way.

Correct Outline Form

A **formal outline** lists the main points of a topic. It shows the order in which these points are presented. It also shows the relationships between them.

Formal outlines may be either a sentence outline or a topic outline. In a **sentence outline,** each topic and subtopic is written as a complete sentence. A **topic outline** uses words or phrases for each point. Here is a portion of a topic outline.

Mazes, or Labyrinths

I. Modern mazes (First main point)
  A. Amusement (Subpoint)
    1. Materials used (Detail for A.)
      a. Hedges
        (1) Hampton Court, England   (Subdetails
        (2) Somerleyton Hall, England for a.)
      b. Bricks
      c. Tiles
    2. Shape
      a. Round
      b. Rectangular
  B. Scientific use
II. Ancient mazes
  A. Egypt
  B. Greece

Follow these steps when writing a topic outline.

1. Write the title at the top of the outline. The title is not considered part of the outline.
2. Arrange main points and subpoints as shown on the previous page. Main points are indicated by Roman numerals.
3. Indent each division of the outline.
4. Do not use a single subheading. Do not use a heading if it cannot be divided into at least two points. For example, if there is a *1* under *A,* there must be at least a *2.*
5. Keep items of the same rank in the same form. For instance, if *A* is a noun, then *B* and *C* should also be nouns.
6. Begin each item with a capital letter. Do not use end marks.

Writing an Informal Outline

An **informal outline** uses as few words as possible. Main ideas are listed as separate headings. Supporting details are written below each heading. You may use numerals, letters, or dashes for informal outlines.

Informal outlines are useful for quickly taking notes in class. They can also help you study and review material for tests. Here is an example of an informal outline on lightning.

I. How lightning occurs
—cloud's particles collide and become electrically charged
—positively and negatively charged particles separate
—positively charged particles in cloud collide with negatively charged particles on ground
II. Forms of lightning
—forked
—streak
—ribbon
—bead, or chain
—ball

Other Graphic Organizers

Chronological Organization Some ideas are related by time. These ideas can be arranged in chronological order. **Chronological order** is the order in which events happen. A good way to arrange details chronologically is to place them on a **time line**.

To make a time line, write the event that happened first at the far left of the time line. Then write the event that happened next. Continue in this way until you have listed all the events in order. Include when the events occurred. Here is an example of a time line. It organizes famous airplane flights chronologically.

Famous Airplane Flights

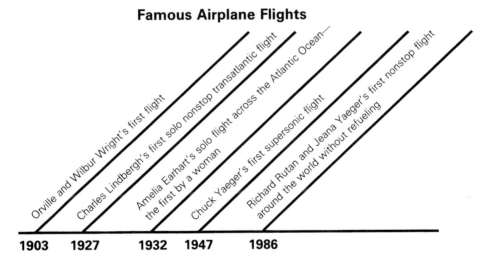

A **chart** is another way to organize and compare information. To make a simple chart, decide what types of information you want to collect. List each category in a column on the left. By filling in the chart, you can see where you have gaps in your information. In the chart on the next page, a student is collecting sensory details for a description. Notice the title at the top of the chart and the headings in the left column: *Sight, Sound, Smell,* and *Touch.*

Sensory Details: Man Restoring a Violin	
Sight	thin, gray hair of man; lined face with wire glasses resting on bridge of nose; rolled white shirt sleeves revealing tanned arms and hands
Sound	scraping of sandpaper against wood; "poof" sound of man blowing away loose particles of wood dust
Smell	dusty smell of sawdust in the air; sharp smell of wood stains in jars and bottles
Touch	rough edge of violin that needs refinishing; workman's hand glides over smooth polished surface

Charts can also be used to **compare** information at a glance. To do so, list the subjects you are comparing at the top of the page. On the left-hand side, list the characteristics that will change or vary. For example, suppose you needed to compare hurricanes and tornadoes for a science paper. You might create a chart like the one below.

Characteristics	Tornado	Hurricane
Strength	most powerful winds known; up to 500 kilometers per hour	winds of between 112–240 kilometers per hour
Most common path in U.S.	Midwest and South	Gulf and Atlantic coasts, Texas to Florida
Damage	Almost everything in its narrow path is destroyed.	Winds, rains, and floods cause great damage over a wide area.

Common Usage Problems

The following pages list problems experienced by many young writers. You will find them an excellent review and a useful guide when proofreading.

Abbreviations

In general, do not use abbreviations in formal writing. The following exceptions are permitted: titles (Mr., Mrs., Ms., Dr.), dates, and times (A.M., P.M., B.C., A.D.).

See also pages 518–519.

Clichés

A **cliché** is an overused expression. It sounds tired and old. Good writers avoid clichés because they make writing dull. Avoid the clichés listed below and any others you may think of. Instead, think of fresh ways to express your ideas in your own words.

over the hill	feeling under the weather
as sly as a fox	as slow as molasses in January
in over my head	as quiet as a mouse

Double Negatives

Words such as *no, not, nothing, no one,* and *never* are called **negatives**. Contractions that end in *n't* are also negatives. When two negatives are used in one sentence, a **double negative** occurs. Avoid double negatives in your writing.

Incorrect Rosa and Hirohito do*n't* have *no* pets.
Correct Rosa and Hirohito do*n't* have *any* pets.

See also page 450.

Jargon

Jargon is the special vocabulary of people in the same profession. For instance, carpenters use the words *doorjamb, casing, shoe,* and *shims.* Tennis players talk about *backhand, mixed doubles, lob,* and *break-point.* Real-estate agents use the terms *appraisal, closing,* and *earnest money.* These words have a special meaning for those within the same profession. However, jargon can be confusing to others. Always remember to use vocabulary that your audience will understand. Write your paper with your readers in mind.

Jargon   I planned to finish the Boston with a kick. Instead, I hit the wall at the twenty-mile mark and quit.

Clearer   I planned to finish the Boston Marathon, a twenty-six-mile race, with a burst of speed. Instead, I nearly collapsed at the twenty-mile mark and was unable to continue.

Modifiers

Adjective-Adverb Confusion Sometimes you may have trouble deciding when to use an adjective or an adverb. First, determine what word is being modified. Adjectives modify nouns or pronouns and tell *which one, what kind, how many,* or *how much.* Adverbs modify verbs, adjectives, or other adverbs and tell *where, when, how,* or *to what extent.*

Incorrect Rusty water trickled *slow* from the old pipe.
Correct Rusty water trickled *slowly* from the old pipe.

Incorrect That restaurant serves *real* spicy pizza.
Correct That restaurant serves *really* spicy pizza.

Incorrect I can wash the dishes *quick.*
Correct I can wash the dishes *quickly.*

See also pages 447–448.

Good-Well The words *good* and *well* are often confused. *Good* is always an adjective. It can only modify nouns or pronouns.

> We had a *good* breakfast. (adjective)
> That purple dress looks *good* on you. (predicate adjective)
> I feel *good* about my second-place finish. (predicate adjective—*feel good* refers to happiness or physical comfort)

Well is usually an adverb, modifying verbs, adjectives, or other adverbs.

> Annie performed her skating routine *well*. (adverb)

Well is an adjective when it describes a noun or pronoun and means "in good health."

> Matthew didn't feel *well* today. (predicate adjective—*feel well* refers to health)

See also page 448.

Comparative and Superlative Forms Use the comparative form of an adjective to compare two things. Use the superlative form to compare three or more things.

> Elise is *taller* than David.
> She is the *tallest* student in our karate class.

> That book is *funnier* than this one.
> It is the *funniest* book I have ever read.

Never use *-er* and *more* or *-est* and *most* together.

Incorrect   This is the *more sharper* of the two knives.
Correct   This is the *sharper* of the two knives.

See also pages 431–432.

Pronouns

Subject Pronouns The subject pronouns are *I*, *you*, *he*, *she*, *it*, *we*, and *they*. Use them as subjects of sentences.

> *He* and *I* helped to build the playground.
> *We* nurses voted to strike.

Also use subject pronouns after linking verbs.

> The winner is *she*.
> The doctor behind the surgical mask was *he*.
> It was *I* who called.

See also pages 405–406.

Object Pronouns The object pronouns are *me*, *you*, *him*, *her*, *it*, *us*, and *them*. Use them as objects of verbs or prepositions.

> The catcher tagged *her*. (object of verb)
> Jamie sat behind *me*. (object of preposition)

See also page 408.

Indefinite Pronouns **Indefinite pronouns** do not refer to a specific person or thing. Indefinite pronouns follow special rules of agreement. The following indefinite pronouns are always singular and use singular verbs.

each	neither	everyone	everybody
either	one	anyone	nobody

> <u>Either</u> <u>is</u> fine.
> <u>Everyone</u> <u>has</u> a bad day now and then.

Do not be confused when a prepositional phrase follows an indefinite pronoun. The verb must still agree with the subject. The verb does *not* agree with the object of the preposition.

> <u>Neither</u> of the envelopes <u>was</u> large enough.

The following indefinite pronouns are always plural.

several   few   both   many

Several of the fans have already left.
Few of the students were absent today.
Many are waiting in line.

The following indefinite pronouns may be singular or plural depending on their meaning in a sentence.

all   any   most   none   some   much

Singular All of the money is spent. (*Money* is singular.)
Plural   All of the tickets were sold. (*Tickets* is plural.)

Singular Most of the house is clean. (*House* is singular.)
Plural   Most of the potatoes were rotten. (*Potatoes* is plural.)

See also page 412.

Lack of Antecedents Do not use a pronoun without an antecedent, the word to which the pronoun refers. The meaning of the sentence will be unclear.

Unclear Anson couldn't stop thinking about his mistakes. It bothered him all day. (What bothered him?)
Clear   Anson couldn't stop thinking about his mistakes. His poor performance in the track meet bothered him all day.

Unclear Reference The reference of a pronoun is unclear when the pronoun may refer to more than one word.

Unclear Joshua pulled the cork out of the bottle and then washed it. (Did he wash the cork or the bottle?)
Clear   Joshua pulled the cork out of the bottle and then washed the bottle.

See also pages 402–403.

Sentence Errors

Fragments   A **sentence** expresses a complete thought. A group of words that does not express a complete thought is a **fragment**. A fragment is missing a subject, a predicate, or both.

Fragment   Climbed the telephone pole. (missing subject)
Sentence   *The telephone installer* climbed the telephone pole.

Fragment   Three seals at the zoo. (missing predicate)
Sentence   Three seals at the zoo *slept in the sun*.

Fragment   Across the tightrope. (missing subject and predicate)
Sentence   *The acrobat walked* across the tightrope.

See also page 316.

Run-on Sentences   A **run-on sentence** is two or more sentences written as though they were one sentence. To correct a run-on, put a period at the end of the first sentence. Begin the second sentence with a capital letter.

Run-on   The leaves are changing colors autumn is here.
Correct   The leaves are changing colors. Autumn is here.

Stringy Sentences   A **stringy sentence** strings too many ideas together with the word *and*. To correct this sentence error, write each complete thought in a separate sentence.

Stringy Sentence   Andrew cleared the garden of rocks and twigs and he raked the soil and he dug several small holes and then he planted tomatoes, carrots, and strawberries.
Correct   Andrew cleared the garden of rocks and twigs. He raked the soil and dug several small holes. Then he planted tomatoes, carrots, and strawberries.

See also pages 74-75.

Verbs

Agreement with Subject   The verb in a sentence must agree in number with its subject. A verb and a subject agree in number when they are both singular or both plural. The verb agrees with its subject in number even if the subject is separated from the verb by a prepositional phrase.

Singular   The <u>road</u> through the mountains <u>looks</u> icy.
Plural   The <u>clocks</u> on the mantle <u>chime</u> every hour.

When two or more parts of a compound subject are joined by *and*, use the plural form of the verb. When the parts are joined by *or, either-or,* or *neither-nor*, the verb agrees with the nearer subject.

> <u>Books</u> and <u>puzzles</u> <u>are</u> on those shelves.
> The <u>radio</u> or the <u>television</u> <u>is</u> on.
> Either <u>James</u> or his <u>sisters</u> <u>have</u> that album.
> Neither the <u>swimmers</u> nor the <u>coach</u> <u>has</u> the key.

See also pages 480–495.

Avoiding Tense Changes   Tense means "time." Most verbs change their forms to show present, past, and future time. Avoid changing the verb tense in the middle of a sentence.

Incorrect   We *mow* the lawn and then *washed* the car.
Correct   We *mowed* the lawn and then *washed* the car.

See also pages 376–377.

You, *Use of*

Do not write the pronoun *you* unless you mean the reader.

Incorrect   *You* must wait in long lines during the holidays.
        (The writer does not mean *you* personally.)
Correct   *Customers* must wait in long lines during the holidays.

Word Usage

Sometimes problems are caused by words that are easily confused. These words sound the same, or nearly the same, but are spelled differently and have different meanings. Words of this type are called **homonyms**. These are homonyms.

horse—hoarse   pare—pear—pair   do—dew—due

When you have problems with homonyms, the only solution is to memorize which spelling goes with which meaning.

Here is a list of homonyms and other words frequently used and frequently confused in writing. Study the sets of words, and try to connect each word with its correct meaning.

accept means to agree to something or to receive something willingly.

except means to keep out or leave out. As a preposition, *except* means "but" or "leaving out."

> My brother will *accept* the job at the grocery store.
> Michelle likes every flavor of yogurt *except* lemon.

capital means chief, important, or excellent. It also means the city or town that is the official seat of government of a state or nation.

capitol is the building where a state legislature meets.

the Capitol is the building in Washington, D.C., in which the United States Congress meets.

> The *capital* of Illinois is the city of Springfield.
> The *capitol* of Illinois is a stately building in Springfield.
> The senators arrived at the *Capitol* in time to vote.

hear means to listen to.
here means in this place.

> Every time I *hear* this song, I feel happy.
> Reference books are found *here* in the library.

it's is the contraction for *it is* or *it has*.
its shows ownership or possession.

> *It's* nearly midnight.
> The boat lost *its* sail during the storm.

lead is a heavy, gray metal.
lead means to go first, to guide.
led is the past tense of *lead*.

> Water pipes are often made of *lead*.
> These signs will *lead* us to the hiking trail.
> Bloodhounds *led* the detectives to the scene of the
> crime.

loose means free or not tight.
lose means to mislay or suffer the loss of something.

> The rider kept the horse's reins *loose*.
> If you *lose* your book, report the loss to the library as
> soon as possible.

peace is calm or stillness or the absence of disagreement.
piece means a portion or part.

> After two years of war, *peace* was finally achieved.
> This statue was carved from a *piece* of jade.

principal means first or most important. It also refers to the
head of a school.
principle is a rule, truth, or belief.

> A *principal* export of Brazil is coffee.
> Our school *principal* organized a safety council.
> One *principle* of science is that all matter occupies
> space.

quiet means free from noise or disturbance.
quite means truly or almost completely.

> The only time our classroom is *quiet* is when it's empty.
> The aquarium tank is *quite* full.

their means belonging to them.
there means at that place.
they're is the contraction for *they are*.

> Our neighbors sold *their* house and moved to a farm.
> Please take the squirt guns over *there*.
> My sisters have never skied, but *they're* willing to learn.

to means in the direction of.
too means also or very.
two is the whole number between one and three.

> The surgeon rushed *to* the operating room.
> The lights went off, and then the heat went off *too*.
> Only *two* of the four climbers reached the peak.

weather is the state of the atmosphere referring to wind,
  moisture, temperature, etc.
whether indicates a choice or alternative.

> Australia has summer *weather* when Canada has winter.
> *Whether* we drive or take the train, we will arrive late.

who's is the contraction for *who is* or *who has*.
whose is the possessive form of *who*.

> *Who's* been chosen to be a crossing guard?
> *Whose* skateboard was left on the sidewalk?

you're is the contraction for *you are*.
your is the possessive form of *you*.

> *You're* going to the costume party, aren't you?
> Please bring *your* sheet music to choir practice.

Quick Guide to Capitalization

Proper Nouns and Proper Adjectives

1. Capitalize the names of people and pets.

2. Capitalize a title used with a person's name.

3. Capitalize the word *I*.

4. Capitalize cities, states, and countries.

5. Capitalize streets, bridges, parks, and buildings.

6. Capitalize geographical names that refer to a particular section of the country. Do not capitalize *north, south, east,* or *west* when referring to directions.

7. Capitalize the names of months, days, and holidays. Do not capitalize the names of the four seasons.

8. Capitalize the names of races, religions, nationalities, and languages.

9. Capitalize words referring to God and to religious scriptures.

10. Capitalize names of clubs, organizations, and businesses.

First Words, Outlines, and Titles

1. Capitalize the first word of every sentence.

2. Capitalize the first word in most lines of poetry.

3. Capitalize the first word of each line of an outline.

4. Capitalize the first word, last word, and all important words in a title.

See also pages 498–515.

Quick Guide to Punctuation

The Period

1. Use a period at the end of a declarative sentence and most imperative sentences.

2. Use a period after an abbreviation. Some special abbreviations are written without periods, such as metric units of measure. The two-letter state abbreviations, such as *CA* for *California*, are written with capital letters and no periods.

3. Use a period after an initial.

4. Use a period after each number or letter that shows a division of an outline or that precedes an item in a list.

The Question Mark and the Exclamation Point

1. Use a question mark at the end of an interrogative sentence.

2. Use an exclamation point at the end of an exclamatory sentence and after an imperative sentence that shows surprise or another strong emotion.

3. Use an exclamation point after an interjection.

The Comma

1. Use commas to separate three or more items in a series. A series always includes at least three items. Place commas after each item except the last.

2. Use a comma after *yes*, *no*, or *well* if these words begin a sentence.

3. Use a comma to combine two sentences with *and*, *but*, or *or*.

4. Use commas to set off the name of a person spoken to.

5. Use commas to set off an appositive. An appositive follows a noun and renames the noun.

6. Use commas to separate the parts of a date. If a date is in the middle of a sentence, use a comma after the last part.

7. Use a comma to separate the name of a city from the name of a state or country.

8. Use a comma to set off the explanatory words of a direct quotation.

9. Use a comma after the greeting of a friendly letter and after the closing of any letter.

10. Use a comma whenever the reader might be confused.

The Apostrophe and the Hyphen

1. Use an apostrophe to show possession.

2. Use an apostrophe in a contraction such as *can't*.

3. Use a hyphen after the first part of a word at the end of a line. Write the second part of the word on the next line. Never divide words of one syllable.

4. Use a hyphen in compound numbers from twenty-one through ninety-nine.

The Colon and the Semicolon

1. Use a colon after the greeting in a business letter.

2. Use a colon between the numerals that tell hours and minutes.

3. Use a semicolon to combine two related sentences.

Quotation Marks

1. Put quotation marks before and after the words of a direct quotation. Do not use quotation marks with an indirect quotation, a quotation that does not use the speaker's exact words.

2. Separate the words of a direct quotation from the rest of the sentence with a comma or end mark in addition to quotation marks.

3. Place question marks and exclamation points inside quotation marks if they belong to the quotation itself.

4. Place question marks and exclamation points outside quotation marks if they do not belong to the quotation.

5. Sometimes a quotation is divided. Use a period after explanatory words only if the second part of the quotation is a sentence.

Punctuating Titles

1. Put quotation marks around the titles of stories, poems, reports, articles, and chapters of a book.

2. Underline the title of a book, play, magazine, motion picture, or TV series. In print these titles appear in italics.

3. Underline the title of a painting or the name of a ship.

   For more information on punctuation and examples on how to use each of these rules, *see also* pages 516–543.

Spelling

Almost everyone has occasional trouble with spelling. Several strategies can help you become a better speller.

How to Become a Better Speller

1. **Make a habit of looking at words carefully.** Practice seeing every letter in a word. When you see a new word or a tricky word, like *library,* look at all the letters. Write the word several times to remember it.

2. **When you speak, pronounce words carefully.** Sometimes people misspell words because they say them incorrectly. Be sure that you are not blending syllables together. For example, you may write *probly* for *probably* if you are mispronouncing it.

3. **Identify your own spelling enemies and attack them.** Look over your assignments and make a list of the misspelled words. Also, list new words that are difficult for you.

4. **Find memory devices to help with problem spellings.** A memory device is a trick, or a catchy sentence, that helps you remember how to spell difficult words. Here are three examples:

principal	The princi*pal* is my *pal*.
tragedy	Every *age* has its tr*age*dy.
embarrass	I turned *r*eally *r*ed and felt *s*o *s*illy.

5. **Proofread what you write.** Reread your work carefully, word for word. Don't let your eyes race over the page and miss incorrectly spelled words.

6. **Use a dictionary.** You don't have to know how to spell every word. Instead, form the habit of using a dictionary whenever you need help with spelling.

When you notice that you are having trouble with a certain word, take a few minutes to study it carefully. Give the word all your attention. If you spend the time and energy to learn it correctly once, you will save yourself all the trouble of correcting it many times.

Follow these five steps to master the spelling of a specific word.

Steps for Mastering Specific Words

1. **Look at the word and say it to yourself.** Pronounce the word carefully. If the word has two or more syllables, say it again, one syllable at a time. Look at each syllable as you say it.

2. **Look at the letters. Spell the word aloud.** If the word has two or more syllables, pause between each syllable as you say the letters.

3. **Without looking at the word, write it.** Picture the word in your mind as you write it. Be sure to form each letter properly. Take your time. Really concentrate as you write the word.

4. **Now look at your book or list to see if you have spelled the word correctly.** Take note of any words you spelled incorrectly. These words will need further drill and study.

5. **If you have misspelled the word, notice where the error was.** Identify the mistake you made. You will be less likely to repeat the mistake again. Repeat steps 3 and 4 until you have spelled the word correctly three times in a row.

Many common spelling errors occur with words that have the same, or nearly the same, sound but are spelled differently, such as *who's* and *whose*. For a list of these words, see pages 561–563.

Rules for Spelling

In addition to the spelling strategies on pages 568–569, there are certain rules that can help you become a better speller.

Prefixes

A prefix is a word part added to the beginning of a word to change its meaning.

When a prefix is added to a word, the spelling of the word stays the same.

Prefix	Base Word	New Word
un- (not)	+ named	= unnamed (not named)
re- (again)	+ enter	= reenter (enter again)
pre- (before)	+ set	= preset (set before)

The Suffixes -ly and -ness

A suffix is a word part added to the end of a word to change its meaning.

When the suffix -ly is added to a word ending with l, both l's are kept. When -ness is added to a word ending in n, both n's are kept.

Base Word	Suffix	New Word
mean	+ -ness	= meanness
practical	+ -ly	= practically

The Final Silent e

When a suffix beginning with a vowel is added to a word ending with a silent *e*, the *e* is usually dropped.

make + -ing = making   believe + -able = believable
fame + -ous = famous   expense + -ive = expensive

When a suffix beginning with a consonant is added to a word ending with a silent *e*, the *e* is usually kept.

hate + -ful = hateful   hope + -less = hopeless
bore + -dom = boredom   sure + -ly = surely

The following words are exceptions to this rule:

truly   argument   ninth   wholly

Words with ie *or* ei

When the sound is long *e* (ē), the word is spelled *ie* except after *c*.

The following rhyme provides some rules that will help you spell better.

I before *E*
Except after *C*,
Or when sounded like *A*
As in n*ei*ghbor or w*ei*gh.

I before *E*

belief   relievc   yield   fierce   achieve
niece   brief   field   chief   shield

Except after *C*

receive   ceiling   perceive   deceit
conceive   conceited   receipt

Or when sounded like *A*

weight   eight   neigh

These words are exceptions:

either   weird   species
neither   seize   leisure

Words with the "Seed" Sound

Only one English word ends in *sede: supersede*. Three words end in *ceed: exceed, proceed, succeed*. All other words ending in the sound of "seed" are spelled *cede*.

concede   precede   recede   secede

Words Ending in y

When a suffix is added to a word that ends with y following a consonant, the y is usually changed to *i*.

noisy + -ly = noisily   carry + -age = carriage
happy + -est = happiest   fifty + -eth = fiftieth
ruby + -es = rubies   wavy + -er = wavier

Note this exception: When *-ing* is added, the *y* remains.

bury + -ing = burying   cry + -ing = crying
deny + -ing = denying   apply + -ing = applying

When a suffix is added to a word that ends with y following a vowel, the y usually is not changed.

relay + -ed = relayed   pay + -ment = payment
joy + -ful = joyful   annoy + -ed = annoyed
stay + -ing = staying   gray + -ness = grayness

The following words are exceptions: paid, said.

Doubling the Final Consonant

Words of one syllable, ending with one consonant following one vowel, double the final consonant before adding *-ing, -ed,* or *-er*.

sit + -ing = sitting   sad + -er = sadder
hop + -ed = hopped   let + -ing = letting
ship + -ing = shipping   run + -er = runner

The final consonant is **not** doubled when it follows two vowels.

meet + -ing = meeting   loan + -ed = loaned
break + -ing = breaking   train + -er = trainer

Exercise Spelling Practice

Find the misspelled words. Spell them correctly.

1. Luis was imobile in a plaster cast.
2. Some fameous people are lonly.
3. Why are we haveing this silly arguement?
4. Anna recieved an award for her painting.
5. Carolyn likes this meat for its leaness.
6. In all the confusion, Lance droped his wallet.
7. The tide receeds twice a day.
8. Mistreating animals should be ilegal.
9. People who write carefuly don't often mispell words.
10. Mr. Johnson gave his neice a wierd mask.
11. I beleive this meeting should be postponed.
12. Our coach was giveing us guideance in shooting baskets.
13. In an earlyer film, she portrayed a reporter.
14. Marla feircly defended her beleif in UFO's.
15. During the winter, bears are generaly innactive.
16. Some people who achieve fame become concieted.
17. The painting featured an iregularlly shaped blue spot.
18. The animal keepper fed the biger of the two cats first.
19. The summer night was strangly peacful.
20. The signature on the check was ilegible.
21. Last summer, our nieghbor's loud parties often annoied us.
22. We hopped that the cheif justice would get well quickly.
23. This is our nineth game of the season.
24. The South tryed to sesede from the union.
25. I truely think that your judgment was correct.

Thesaurus

What Is a Thesaurus?

A strong vocabulary adds power to your speaking and writing. It allows you to express your ideas clearly. This thesaurus can help you to develop a strong vocabulary.

A thesaurus is a tool writers use to improve their writing. In a thesaurus, words with similar meanings—synonyms—are listed in groups. These groups of synonyms can help you find the best word to express an idea. They can also help you add variety to your speaking and writing.

Using This Thesaurus

To find synonyms for a word, first find the word in the index on pages 586–588. The index lists, in alphabetical order, every synonym that appears in the thesaurus. Look at the following portion of the index.

> **finish** *see* END
> **fit** *see* RIGHT
> **frightened** *see* AFRAID
> **FUNNY**
> **furious** *see* ANGRY

Some of the words in the index are printed in capital letters. These words are called **entry words**. *Funny* and *angry* are entry words. An entry word has a general meaning. It is the word under which one group of synonyms is organized.

The words in small letters in the index are synonyms for entry words. *Frightened* is a synonym for *afraid*. *Furious* is a synonym for *angry*.

Suppose you wanted to find a synonym for the word *glowing*. First you would look up *glowing* in the index. The index would tell you to look at the entry for *bright*. Here is what you would find.

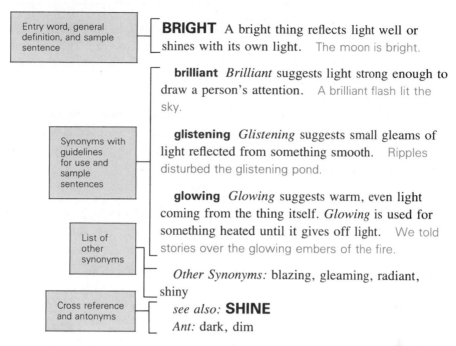

Entry word, general definition, and sample sentence

BRIGHT A bright thing reflects light well or shines with its own light. The moon is bright.

Synonyms with guidelines for use and sample sentences

brilliant *Brilliant* suggests light strong enough to draw a person's attention. A brilliant flash lit the sky.

glistening *Glistening* suggests small gleams of light reflected from something smooth. Ripples disturbed the glistening pond.

glowing *Glowing* suggests warm, even light coming from the thing itself. *Glowing* is used for something heated until it gives off light. We told stories over the glowing embers of the fire.

List of other synonyms

Other Synonyms: blazing, gleaming, radiant, shiny

Cross reference and antonyms

see also: **SHINE**
Ant: dark, dim

Understanding the Entries

The entry begins with the entry word, *bright*. This general word is then defined and used in an example sentence. Following the definition and sentence are synonyms for *bright*. These synonyms include *glowing,* the word you looked up in the first place, *brilliant,* and *glistening.* Each synonym is followed by a sentence or two that tells how the word should be used and an example sentence. Read all the synonyms before you decide which one best expresses your idea.

At the end of some entries, there is a list of other synonyms. These words are not defined and not used in example sentences. Be careful about using these words. Before you choose one, look it up in a dictionary. Study its meaning. Then decide whether it is really the right word for you to use.

Often antonym *(Ant.)* listings are given at the end of entries. Sometimes there are even cross-references to related words. These cross-references are indicated by the words *see also*.

AFRAID The words in this group mean "feeling fear." *Afraid* shows that the fear has lasted for a while and will probably last longer.   Tony is afraid of cats.

alarmed Use *alarmed* to show that fear came on suddenly and was caused by danger.   Everyone was alarmed by the tornado warnings.

fearful Use *fearful* to show fear of something that may happen.   I'm fearful that the river will flood.

frightened A frightened person feels fear because something has happened.   The earthquake frightened the people in the city.

scared *Scared* is like *frightened*. However, *scared* is less formal than *frightened*. A scared person is not as afraid as a frightened one.   A loud noise scared us.

wary A *wary* person is being careful because something dangerous may happen.   Parents teach children to be wary of strangers.
   Ant: unafraid, calm
      see also: **BRAVE**

ANGRY *Angry* means "upset by something that hurts or is against one."   The rumors about me made me angry.

annoyed An annoyed person isn't very angry. The annoying thing usually has lasted for a while.   A barking dog annoyed Carla all night.

enraged An enraged person is extremely upset and may be shouting.   We were enraged by the vandalism.

furious A furious person is so enraged that he or she is out of control.   Senator Wilson was so furious that he couldn't speak.

upset Use *upset* to show that a person feels nervous and troubled. This is a mild word.   I was so upset that I couldn't eat.
   Ant: glad, happy, pleased

ANSWER To answer is to say or do something as a way of reacting to a question or request.   Will you answer my question?

reply *Reply* is more formal.   Mr. Summers will reply to your letter.

respond *Respond* suggests cooperation.   When we asked for volunteers, dozens responded.

retort To retort is to answer in an angry or clever way.   "That's none of your business," Anderson retorted.
   Ant: see **ASK**

ASK To ask is to request something that a person wants. A person may ask for information or for help.   We asked for directions to the aquarium.

demand To demand is to ask for what a person thinks he or she deserves.   The reporter demanded an answer from the mayor.

inquire *Inquire* suggests that the person has a serious reason for asking. It is more formal than *ask*.   Call the hospital to inquire about Dan's condition.

request To request is to ask in a formal, courteous way.   "We request a recess, your honor," said the lawyer.
   Ant: see **ANSWER**

BAD The word *bad* has two main meanings: "not satisfactory," and "evil."   Dan did a bad job of fixing the leak. Stealing is bad. **Caution:** Many people use *bad* carelessly. Before you use *bad* or a synonym, think. Decide what is wrong with what you are describing. You may not need any of these words.

careless *Careless* describes a thing done without caring about doing a good job. Careless drivers should not be on our roads.

evil *Evil* suggests deliberately doing wrong. Badness shows in nearly everything an evil person does. Evil rulers imprisoned people without a trial.

poor A poor thing makes us wonder if it could ever be any better. The show closed because of poor attendance.

vicious A vicious thing is cruel. It may be done to hurt someone. He spread vicious rumors about her.

wicked A wicked thing is wrong in thought and deed. They had a wicked plan to cheat elderly people.

see also **MEAN**
Ant: see **GOOD**

BEAUTIFUL *Beautiful* and its synonyms mean "pleasing and nice to look at." *Beautiful* suggests that a thing is perfect in some important way. A beautiful vase held a single rose.

attractive Use *attractive* to show that a thing's beauty draws attention. He wore an attractive sweater.

elegant Use *elegant* to show good taste, grace, and excellence. The Taj Mahal is an elegant palace.

gorgeous A gorgeous thing is brilliant or dazzling. It may almost be gaudy. Darlene has a gorgeous new red convertible.

lovely *Lovely* suggests beauty that is

cozy or comforting. We pitched our camp beside a lovely lake.

stunning A stunning thing has striking beauty. Its beauty can astonish a person. From the mountain peak, we saw a stunning sunrise.

Other Synonyms: fair, handsome, pretty
Ant: homely, hideous, ugly

BIG *Big* and the other words in this group mean "great in size or amount." A big shopping mall will be built here.

colossal A colossal thing is "bigger than life." It seems much bigger than things like it usually are. At our family reunions, we have colossal meals.

enormous An enormous thing is bigger than the norm for things like it. The meaning is nearly the same as the meaning of *colossal*. Alissa grew some enormous tomatoes in her vegetable garden last summer.

immense Long ago, *immense* meant "not measurable." An immense thing seems too great to measure. The amount of sand in the world is immense. A large car is not. It's hard to imagine the immense size of the universe.

mammoth *Mammoth* is the name of a prehistoric animal similar to an elephant. It suggests something big and heavy. The ship struck a mammoth iceberg.

Other Synonyms: gigantic, huge, large, monumental
Ant: see **SMALL**

BRAVE All the words in this group have the meaning of *brave:* "facing up to dangers or troubles." Brave drivers delivered the medicine in the storm.

bold *Bold* may suggest cockiness. A bold person is quick to meet a challenge. Perry was a bold explorer.

courageous A courageous person not only faces up to trouble but welcomes the challenge. Courageous men and women volunteered to rescue flood victims.

daring *Daring* suggests taking risks. A daring person may look for dangerous situations. The astronauts made a daring attempt to fix the satellite.

fearless *Fearless* means "without fear." A fearless person doesn't think about personal safety. One fearless doctor dashed into the burning building.

Other Synonyms: plucky, valiant
Ant: see **AFRAID**

BREAK *Break* and its synonyms all mean "to divide into pieces." Tree branches broke in the storm.

shatter To shatter is to break so that pieces scatter. The glass shattered on the floor.

smash To smash is to break something into small pieces, making noise by doing it. *Smash* is a blend of *smack* and *crash*. The car smashed through the window of a shop.

wreck *Wreck* means "destroy." Use *wreck* for large things, especially vehicles. Do not use it for the breaking of small things, such as a glass. Pounding waves wrecked the dock.

Other Synonyms: crack, crumble, crush, snap

BRIGHT A bright thing reflects light well or shines with its own light. The moon is bright.

brilliant *Brilliant* suggests light strong enough to draw a person's attention. A brilliant flash lit the sky.

gleaming *Gleam* comes from an old Germanic word meaning "glowworm." *Gleaming* suggests light like the light from a firefly. On each petal were gleaming drops of dew.

glistening *Glistening* suggests small gleams of light reflected from something smooth. Ripples disturbed the glistening pond.

glowing *Glowing* suggests warm, even light coming from the thing itself. *Glowing* is used for something heated until it gives off light. We told stories over the glowing embers of the fire.

Other Synonyms: blazing, radiant, shiny
see also: **SHINE**
Ant: dark, dim

END To end something is to stop it. The movie ended sooner than I thought it would.

bring to a close Use the phrase *bring to a close* to suggest ending something in a planned way. A person may bring a meeting to a close, for example. We brought the meeting to a close by introducing the new officers and singing the club song.

finish To show that a person has completed something, especially a job, use *finish*. We finished decorating the school lobby.

halt Use *halt* for a sudden stop. *Halt* suggests that the end was not planned or expected. Work on the bridge was halted by a blizzard.

Other Synonyms: close, conclude, stop
Ant: continue, keep up, persist

EXPLAIN To explain means "to make understandable." Can you explain this math problem?

clarify *Clarify* means "to make clear." Use it to emphasize that something was "foggy" or "murky" before it was explained. Jack clarified the reasons for his disappearance.

demonstrate When explaining includes showing how something works or why something is so, use *demonstrate*. Phyllis demonstrated how locks in a canal work.

describe *Describe* emphasizes giving a picture in words. Please describe the countryside in Scotland.

interpret Use *interpret* to stress putting something in other words to explain it. Jack interpreted Professor Held's theories for us.

FUNNY *Funny* and its synonyms describe things that make a person smile or laugh. I have a funny story to tell you.

amusing *Amusing* suggests smiles or chuckles more than loud laughs. Ms. Larkin gave an amusing talk about birds and their habits.

comical *Comical* suggests funny action rather than words. Lena put on a comical show as a clumsy juggler.

hilarious Use *hilarious* for something lively and merry. *Hilarious* may suggest too much noise and action. The Three Stooges specialized in hilarious slapstick comedy.

humorous Something humorous is funny in a friendly and gentle way. This film is a humorous look at frontier life.

Other Synonyms: laughable, silly, witty

GET The words in this group have the general meaning of *get:* "to come to have." Ann got tickets for the play.

acquire Use *acquire* to show that getting a thing took a long time. *Acquire* also suggests collecting or accumulating things. Nancy has acquired a large coin collection.

gain *Gain* shows that a person worked to get something valuable. From helping in the hospital kitchen, Rico gained skill as a cook.

obtain *Obtain* suggests work and desire. At last we obtained the funds.

receive *Receive* does not suggest that a person worked for a thing or even wanted it. I received a catalog in the mail.

Other Synonyms: amass, buy, collect, earn, procure, purchase, realize, reap, secure, win

Ant: see **GIVE**

GOOD The word *good* has two general meanings: "okay; meeting standards," and "morally right." You did a good job. It is good to help needy people. **Caution:** Do not use *good* carelessly. If you use *good* or a synonym, think. Decide what you like about what you are describing.

honorable An honorable person knows what is right and behaves in the right way. Ms. Gordon had an honorable career in the Senate.

pure A pure person or thing is free from guilt or badness. A person may have pure reasons for doing something, even if it turns out wrong. His motives were pure.

satisfactory A satisfactory thing meets a person's needs or wishes. It is no more or less than what was expected. Your work is satisfactory.

Ant: see **BAD**

GROUP A *group* is a number of people, animals, or things that are together. Every afternoon, we run in a group.

band A band is a group joined for a purpose. One purpose may be to make music, and that is a common use of *band*. A band of rebels controls the mountains.

crew A crew is a group brought together by their work. *Crew* doesn't suggest that they chose to get together, as *band* does. A crew of electricians arrived today.

crowd A crowd is a large group. *Crowd* suggests people squeezed together. It may suggest disorder. A crowd waited outside the theater.

gang *Gang* can mean workers who do a job as a group. The construction gang worked on the foundation. It can mean a group of lawbreakers. A gang of hoodlums committed the crime.

mob A mob is disorderly and may be lawless. Do not use *mob* just to mean "a large crowd." "Sheriff," he warned, "there's an angry mob outside."

ANIMAL GROUPS Specific words are used for groups of animals; for example: bevy of swans, brood of chicks, colony of ants, drove of cattle (or oxen), flight of birds, flock of sheep (or camels), gag-gle of geese, herd of elephants, horde of gnats, pack of dogs (or wolves), pride of lions, school of fish, swarm of bees (or eels), troop of kangaroos.

HELP To help is to do something to make things easier or better for others. Jack helped with the chores.

aid *Aid* is more formal than *help*. Use *aid* when the help is serious. Hundreds aided the flood-relief effort.

assist *Assist* is also more formal than *help*. Use *assist* to show that what the helper does is much less important than what the other does. Ted assisted a scientist in her experiments.

rescue To rescue is to save from danger. Dan rescued Carl from the fire.

support *Support* may mean "to give approval or understanding." However, it may mean "meeting a person's needs, either by giving money or what is needed." We support Senator Giles's stand on taxes.

Ant: interfere, hinder

IMPORTANT Something important has great meaning or great influence. have important news.

grave Something grave is important and serious. It may be threatening. Every volunteer knows that there are grave risks in this mission.

serious *Serious* suggests something very important. I have to make a serious decision.

urgent Use *urgent* for something that is important and should get immediate attention. The show was interrupted by an urgent bulletin.

vital Do not use *vital* just to mean "important." Something vital is absolutely necessary. A compass is handy on a hike, but vital on a boat.

Ant: unimportant

LAUGH To laugh is to make sounds that show happiness or ridicule. Everyone laughed when Tina told her story.

chuckle To chuckle is to laugh softly in low tones. A person may chuckle when something is mildly amusing. Lisa chuckled when she saw that she would finish in time.

giggle A giggle is a high-pitched laugh. An embarrassing or silly thing may make a person giggle. I giggled at Andy's ridiculous hat.

roar To roar is to laugh loudly or boisterously. The crowd roared when I imitated a chicken.

snicker To snicker is to make a sly laugh, often at someone else's confusion. When I forgot my lines, a few of my "friends" snickered.

Other Synonyms: cackle, chortle, crow

LIKE *Like* and its synonyms all have the general meanings "to be pleased with, to enjoy." Is there anyone who doesn't like summer?

admire To admire is to like something because it impresses. A person looks up to what he or she admires. I admire the shuttle astronauts' skill and courage.

adore To adore is to like something so much that you honor it. Don't waste *adore* by using it just to mean "like very much." Hiking and camping taught me to adore nature.

enjoy To enjoy means "to get pleasure from." People enjoy comedy movies.

love To love is to feel a strong, deep, and tender affection. People sometimes use *love* to exaggerate their likes. I love hamburgers with onions! In writing, avoid using *love* that way. I love my parents.

MAKE To make is to bring into being. We'll make omelets for lunch.

construct *Construct* suggests putting together according to a plan. With this kit, you can construct a model plane.

create To create is to bring into being something that did not exist. Computer companies created new jobs.

manufacture *Manufacture* originally meant "make by hand." Now, *manufacture* means made by machine. The factory will manufacture farm equipment.

Ant: demolish, destroy, dismantle

MANY *Many* means "a great number of." **Caution:** Whenever you can, tell how many, instead of using *many* or one of its synonyms. Many people returned the dangerous toy. Over forty people returned the dangerous toy.

a lot The phrase *a lot* is used in casual speech to mean "very many" or "very much." Avoid it in most writing and speaking.

a number of Many people use *a number of* to mean "many." This phrase is more formal than *a lot,* but it is just as vague. Try to use a more precise synonym or use a figure.

countless *Countless* means "too many to count." It may give emphasis by exaggerating. I've been to Jean's house countless times.

numerous *Numerous* is more formal than *many*. It suggests many more than expected. We received numerous requests for tickets.

several *Several* means "more than two but not many." Many people called, and several sent letters.

MEAN One meaning of *mean* is "bad-tempered or unkind." It was mean of you not to answer my letter.

bad-tempered A bad-tempered person is irritable or cranky. You're bad-tempered this morning!

nasty A nasty person is very unpleasant or harmful. The word suggests that people are disgusted by the person's meanness. He was so nasty that I left.

selfish A selfish person cares too much for his or her own interests. He or she gives little thought to others. Carol is too selfish to lend me her ruler.

unkind *Unkind* means "not kind." It is stronger than *bad-tempered*. An unkind person treats others harshly or cruelly. You were unkind not to invite Janet.

QUIET All the words in this group mean "without sound." *Quiet* suggests freedom from excitement or confusion. We stayed at a quiet country inn.

hushed *Hushed* suggests that sound a person might expect is missing or softened. The crowd was hushed before the curtains opened.

noiseless *Noiseless*, of course, means "without noise." *Noiseless* stresses that there is no noise and often suggests move-ment without sound. A noiseless spider spun a web in the morning sun.

silent *Silent* means "without any sound of any kind." Space is utterly silent.

still *Still* usually means "without sound or movement." In the time before dawn, the forest was still.

RIGHT *Right* has two general meanings: "correct" and "proper." Your answer was right.

correct *Correct* means "fitting the facts," or "matching a standard." It may suggest that there are no errors: You have the correct answer. It may suggest that a thing is proper: I want to see correct behavior.

fit *Fit* is used for something that is just what is needed in some situation or for some purpose. We bought equipment fit for an Arctic expedition.

proper *Proper* is used for a thing that good judgment says is right. She always shows proper respect for her parents.

Other Synonyms: accurate, exact, fitting

Ant: see **WRONG**

RUN All the words in this group share the meaning of *run:* "to go by moving the legs faster than in walking." We ran for cover when rain began to fall.

dash Use *dash* for a sudden quick run over a short distance. Janet dashed from the room.

gallop *Gallop* is used for a horse's fastest running. It suggests running without thinking. A horde of shoppers galloped into the market.

race Use *race* to suggest moving extremely fast or too hastily. We raced through the house, dusting and vacuuming.

scamper *Scamper* suggests small, quick movements, like those that a squirrel would make. Dozens of tots scampered in the field.

Other Synonyms: jog, trot

SAY The words in this group share the general meaning of *say:* "to utter words; to speak." "We'll begin work tomorrow," he said.

announce *Announce* is a more formal word than *say*. Henderson announced that he will not run for mayor.

cry To cry is to speak loudly or boldly. "I found the treasure!" he cried.

exclaim To exclaim is to speak with excitement, as in surprise or anger. "You're Ted Atwood!" she exclaimed.

roar To roar is to speak in a blustering or boisterous way. "We're number one!" roared Rita.

Other Synonyms: assert, blurt, boast, comment, declare, growl, grumble, remark, shout, state, whisper

SEE To see is to get information through the eyes. We saw a boat on the horizon.

glimpse To glimpse is to see briefly. Through the fence, I glimpsed a garden.

inspect To inspect is to look at carefully, to examine. We inspect each part of the engine for tiny cracks.

observe To observe is to pay special attention to something. Satellites observe weather on the earth.

sight To sight is to see something for which one has been looking. Astronomers have sighted the comet.

spot To spot is to pick out something that is hard to find. We spotted Hank in the crowd.

watch To watch is to observe something closely to find out something. If you watch Martina serve, you'll learn something. However, it is also used to mean looking at something without close attention. They spent the evening watching television.

SMALL Something small is little in size or value. It is less than things like it usually are. Mr. Carson drives a small car.

little Use *little* to show that something is small without comparing it to other things. We have a little time left.

miniature Use *miniature* for a copy or model that is much smaller than the original. In the box was a set of miniature tools.

tiny Use *tiny* for something so small that it can only be noticed by looking carefully. There is a tiny scratch on this table.

Ant: see **BIG**

SMART *Smart* and the other words in this group mean "intelligent, alert, clever." *Smart* is an informal word. She is a smart girl.

bright *Bright* is also an informal word. It emphasizes alertness. It suggests a lively mind. Andy is so bright that he is already learning to read.

clever *Clever* suggests a mind that comes up with new or unusual ideas. Clare's idea is clever.

gifted *Gifted* emphasizes an inner intelligence or talent rather than learning or experience. Carl is a gifted musician.

intelligent *Intelligent* emphasizes the ability to learn or to deal with new situations. We need intelligent leaders for the hard times ahead.

STRANGE Something strange is out of the ordinary, peculiar, or odd. I have a strange story to tell you.

fantastic Use *fantastic* for a thing so wildly different from experience that it seems to have come from a dream. The ship was attacked by fantastic creatures.

mysterious Use *mysterious* for a thing that is unknown, unexplained, or secret. Duane is behaving in a mysterious way.

peculiar Use *peculiar* for a thing that is puzzling or difficult to explain. Dr. Christie had a peculiar machine with her.

weird Use *weird* for a thing so strange that it doesn't seem to be real. A weird green light filled the sky.

Other Synonyms: extraordinary, odd, unfamiliar, unusual

Ant: familiar, ordinary, usual

TEACH To teach is to show someone how to do something or help someone learn something. Teach me to play the guitar.

coach *Coach* combines the meanings of *instruct* and *train*. Coaching involves step-by-step guidance. Before the club dance, Carl coached me in the latest steps.

instruct To instruct is to teach according to some system, usually in a particular subject. Lois will instruct you in the use of the computer.

train To train is to develop a particular skill, or to teach a person to do a particular job or follow a particular career. Renata has been trained in first aid.

Other Synonyms: drill, educate, school

TERRIFIC The words in this group are often used in casual speech to mean "unusually fine or enjoyable." This is not the best use for these words. Each has a specific meaning of its own. *Terrific* actually means "terrifying, dreadful." A terrific fire raged through the village.

fabulous *Fabulous* means "incredible, astounding." It refers to things that might be in a fable rather than in real life. They described a fabulous city of glass.

remarkable A remarkable thing is one that people notice because it is exceptional for its type. She has remarkable strength.

sensational A sensational thing usually causes strong feeling or great excitement. The end of the game was sensational.

wonderful Something that is wonderful causes wonder or amazement. Toni put on a wonderful display of magic.

TRAVEL The words in this group share the general meaning of *travel:* "to go from one place to another." Someday I'm going to travel to China.

journey *Journey* once meant "a day's travel." Now, it suggests a long and difficult trip. They journeyed through the jungles of the Amazon.

roam *Roam* suggests freedom and pleasure. I could spend hours roaming through a hardware store.

wander *Wander* emphasizes aimlessness or lack of purpose. We wandered through the mall until the rain stopped.

WALK To walk is to go on foot at a normal pace, not running. We can walk to the store from here.

pace Use *pace* for walking back and forth. Often, pacing suggests nervousness or boredom. I paced the hallway, waiting to see Dr. Hirsch.

stride Use *stride* for walking with long steps, in a vigorous or bold way. Dan strode to the counter and demanded a refund.

strut Use *strut* for walking in a proud or showy way. The winners strutted off the field.

trudge Use *trudge* for the way a tired or unhappy person would walk. The losers trudged off the field.

Other Synonyms: hike, march, parade, saunter, step, stroll, tramp, tread

WRONG *Wrong* has several meanings. The one shared by the words in this group is "not what is true, correct, or wanted." We made a wrong turn.

inaccurate Something inaccurate is wrong because it is not exact or precise. Your count of tickets was inaccurate.

incorrect *Incorrect* simply means "not correct." It is more formal than *wrong*. Many people consider it more polite. Your information is incorrect.

mistaken *Mistaken* suggests being wrong by accident. I was mistaken about the bus schedule.

Index

A

acquire *see* GET
admire *see* LIKE
adore *see* LIKE
AFRAID
aid *see* HELP
alarmed *see* AFRAID
a lot *see* MANY
amusing *see* FUNNY
ANGRY
animal groups *see* GROUP
announce *see* SAY
annoyed *see* ANGRY
ANSWER
a number of *see* MANY
ASK
assist *see* HELP
attractive *see* BEAUTIFUL

B

BAD
bad-tempered *see* MEAN
band *see* GROUP
BEAUTIFUL
BIG
bold *see* BRAVE
BRAVE
BREAK
BRIGHT
bright *see* SMART
brilliant *see* BRIGHT
bring to a close *see* END

C

careless *see* BAD
chuckle *see* LAUGH
clarify *see* EXPLAIN

clever *see* SMART
coach *see* TEACH
colossal *see* BIG
comical *see* FUNNY
construct *see* MAKE
correct *see* RIGHT
countless *see* MANY
courageous *see* BRAVE
create *see* MAKE
crew *see* GROUP
crowd *see* GROUP
cry *see* SAY

D

daring *see* BRAVE
dash *see* RUN
demand *see* ASK
demonstrate *see* EXPLAIN
describe *see* EXPLAIN

E

elegant *see* BEAUTIFUL
END
enjoy *see* LIKE
enormous *see* BIG
enraged *see* ANGRY
evil *see* BAD
exclaim *see* SAY
EXPLAIN

F

fabulous *see* TERRIFIC
fantastic *see* STRANGE
fearful *see* AFRAID
fearless *see* BRAVE
finish *see* END
fit *see* RIGHT

frightened *see* AFRAID
FUNNY
furious *see* ANGRY

G

gain *see* GET
gallop *see* RUN
gang *see* GROUP
GET
gifted *see* SMART
giggle *see* LAUGH
gleaming *see* BRIGHT
glimpse *see* SEE
glistening *see* BRIGHT
glowing *see* BRIGHT
GOOD
gorgeous *see* BEAUTIFUL
grave *see* IMPORTANT
GROUP

H

halt *see* END
HELP
hilarious *see* FUNNY
honorable *see* GOOD
humorous *see* FUNNY
hushed *see* QUIET

I

immense *see* BIG
IMPORTANT
inaccurate *see* WRONG
incorrect *see* WRONG
inquire *see* ASK
inspect *see* SEE
instruct *see* TEACH
intelligent *see* SMART
interpret *see* EXPLAIN

J

journey *see* TRAVEL

L

LAUGH
LIKE
little *see* SMALL
love *see* LIKE
lovely *see* BEAUTIFUL

M

MAKE
mammoth *see* BIG
manufacture *see* MAKE
MANY
MEAN
miniature *see* SMALL
mistaken *see* WRONG
mob *see* GROUP
mysterious *see* STRANGE

N

nasty *see* MEAN
noiseless *see* QUIET
numerous *see* MANY

O

observe *see* SEE
obtain *see* GET

P

pace *see* WALK
peculiar *see* STRANGE
poor *see* BAD
proper *see* RIGHT
pure *see* GOOD

Q

QUIET

R

race *see* RUN
receive *see* GET
remarkable *see* TERRIFIC
reply *see* ANSWER
request *see* ASK
rescue *see* HELP
respond *see* ANSWER
retort *see* ANSWER
RIGHT
roam *see* TRAVEL
roar *see* LAUGH, SAY
RUN

S

satisfactory *see* GOOD
SAY
scamper *see* RUN
scared *see* AFRAID
SEE
selfish *see* MEAN
sensational *see* TERRIFIC
several *see* MANY
serious *see* IMPORTANT
shatter *see* BREAK
sight *see* SEE
silent *see* QUIET
SMALL
SMART
smash *see* BREAK
snicker *see* LAUGH
spot *see* SEE
still *see* QUIET

STRANGE
stride *see* WALK
strut *see* WALK
stunning *see* BEAUTIFUL
support *see* HELP

T

TEACH
TERRIFIC
tiny *see* SMALL
train *see* TEACH
TRAVEL
trudge *see* WALK

U

unkind *see* MEAN
upset *see* ANGRY
urgent *see* IMPORTANT

V

vicious *see* BAD
vital *see* IMPORTANT

W

WALK
wander *see* TRAVEL
wary *see* AFRAID
watch *see* SEE
weird *see* STRANGE
wicked *see* BAD
wonderful *see* TERRIFIC
wreck *see* BREAK
WRONG

Index

Anecdotes, in developing topic, 46–47
Antecedent, 402–3, 558
  agreement with pronoun, 402–3, 412, 558
  for indefinite pronouns, 412
Antonyms, 272–73
  in thesaurus, 576
Apostrophe, 529–30
  in contractions, 529, 566
  to show possession, 355–56, 529, 566
Appositives, use of comma to set off, 525, 566
Articles
  encyclopedia, 248
  titles of, 536, 567
Articles (*a, an, the*), 426
Articulation, 223
Assignments
  long-term, 279
  managing, 278–79
  short-term, 279
Atlases, 249
Audience, 45
  choosing language for, 50–51
  for descriptive writing, 92, 93
  for explanatory writing, 140, 142–43
  for narrative writing, 115, 116, 117, 118
  for persuasive writing, 164
Author cards, 243–44
Autobiography, 241

B

bad, badly, 448
Base words, 210–11
between, among, 468
Bias, 231
Bibliography, in report, 176–77, 187
Biography, 241

Blended words, 201
Body
  in business letters, 305
  in friendly letters, 299
  in narrative writing, 114
  in reports, 182, 184–85
Book(s)
  in bibliography, 176, 187
  call numbers for, 240–41
  classification of, 238–41
  fiction, 192
  glossary in, 286
  index in, 286
  nonfiction, 192
  science fiction, 126
  table of contents in, 286
  titles of, 508, 536, 564, 567
Booklets, writing, 56
Book reports, 192
Borrowed words, 198, 204
Brainstorming, 20, 46, 110–11
Bridges, capitalizing names of, 503, 564
Buildings, capitalizing names of, 503, 564
Bulletin boards, 56
Business firms, capitalizing names of, 504
Business letters, 303–5
  body of, 305
  closing of, 305, 566
  colon in, 303, 531, 566
  complaint letter, 305
  greeting in, 303, 531, 566
  heading in, 303
  inside address in, 303
  order letters, 305
  request letters, 305
  salutation in, 303
  signature in, 305
Business names, capitalizing, 564
but, in sentence combining, 76–77, 523

C

Call number, 240–41, 243
can, may, 384
capital, capitol, 561
Capitalization
    of abbreviations, 501
    in direct quotations, 534
    of first words in lines of poetry,
        506, 564
    first words in outlines, 508,
        564
    of first words in sentences, 506,
        564
    in friendly letters, 300
    of initials, 500
    of proper adjectives, 422, 500,
        564
    of proper nouns, 350, 500,
        503–4, 564
    of titles, 508, 536, 564, 567
    of personal titles, 501
capitol, capital, 561
Card catalog, 243–45
Catalog cards
    author cards, 243–44
    cross-reference cards, 245
    subject cards, 243, 245
    title cards, 243–44
Chapters of books, titles of, 536,
    567
Characters
    in narratives, 109
    in plays, 124
Charts, 148, 552
    getting information from,
        256–57
Checklists
    for revising and peer editing
        explanations, 142
    for revising and peer editing
        narratives, 121
    for revising and peer editing
        persuasive writing, 164

for revising and peer editing
    reports, 188
see also Guidelines
Chronological order, 48–49, 112,
    137, 552
Cities, capitalizing names of, 503,
    564
Clichés, 554
Climax, in narrative writing, 109,
    114
Clipped words, 200
Closing
    in business letters, 305
    in friendly letters, 299
Club names, capitalization of, 504,
    564
Clustering, 21
Collective biography, 241
Colons, 531–32
    after greetings in business letters,
        303, 531, 566
    in time expressions, 531, 566
Combining sentences. *See*
    Sentences, combining
Commands. *See* Imperative
    sentences
Commas
    in addresses, 525, 566
    to set off appositives, 525, 566
    after closings in letters, 527, 566
    to avoid confusion, 523, 566
    to set off explanatory words in
        direct quotations, 527, 566
    after greetings in friendly letters,
        527, 566
    after introductory words, 525, 565
    in dates, 525, 566
    to set off direct quotations, 527
    in friendly letters, 300
    to separate ideas, 523–24
    with nouns of direct address, 525,
        565
    in sentence combining, 76–82,
        470, 523, 565

informal, 51
Standard, 50–51
see also Language
Entry words
in dictionaries, 262, 267
in thesauruses, 575
Envelopes, addressing, 306–7
-er, 214
Essay questions, 293
Evaluating. *See* Analyzing
Examples
in developing topics, 46–47
key words signaling, 209
except, accept, 561
Exclamation points
after exclamatory sentences, 328,
521, 565
after imperative sentences, 328,
521, 565
after interjections, 521, 565
with quotation marks, 533–34
Exclamatory sentences, 328
exclamation points after, 328,
521, 565
fining subjects in, 330
Explanation in Literature, 132–34
Explanatory words, use of commas
to set off, 527, 566
Explanatory writing, 128–49
adverbs in, 140
analysis of, 130–34
arranging details, 137, 138
choosing topics, 135
details in, 137–38
drafting, 139–41
gathering information, 135
ideas for, 36–37, 548–49
listing steps in, 136
organization in, 136, 137–38
presenting, 145
prewriting, 135–38
proofreading, 144
publishing, 145
revising, 142–44

signal words in, 140
writing plans for, 137–38

F

Facts, 225
distinguishing from opinions,
157–58
in developing topics, 47
recognizing, 157
Fiction, 192, 238
science, 126
Figurative language
metaphors, 97
similes, 97
Fill-in-the-blank questions, 292
Flow charts, 148
Formal English, 51
Formal outlines, 550
Forms, filling out, 308
Fragments, 316, 559
Freewriting, 20
Friendly letters, 298
capitalization in, 300
closings in, 527, 566
commas in, 527
greetings in, 527, 566
parts of, 299
punctuation in, 300
-ful, 214
Future tense, 376
forming, 377

G

Generalizations, 225
Geographical names, capitalizations
of, 503, 564
Gestures, use of, in talk, 222
Glossaries, 286
God, capitalizing words referring to,
504, 564
good, well, 448, 556
Grammar in Action, 95, 117, 140,

contests, 56
posters, 56
writing booklets, 56
see also Presenting
Punctuation, 516–43
  apostrophes, 529–30
  colons, 531–32
  commas, 209, 523–28
  dash, 209
  exclamation points, 521–22
  in friendly letters, 300
  hyphens, 529–30
  italics, 536
  parentheses, 209
  periods, 518–20
  question marks, 521–22
  quotation marks, 533–36
  semicolons, 531–32
  signaling definition or restatement
    with, 209
Purpose, 45

Q

Questioning, 24–25, 30, 45
Question marks, 521
  after interrogative sentences, 328,
    565
  with quotation marks, 533
quiet, quite, 562
Quotations
  direct, 117, 527, 533–34, 566,
    567
  divided, 533, 534, 567
  indirect, 533
Quotation marks
  for direct quotations, 117,
    533–34, 567
  exclamation points with, 523–24,
    567
  question marks with, 523–24,
    567
  with divided quotations, 567
  for titles, 508, 536, 567

R

Races, capitalization of, 503,
  564
raise, rise, 386
Rate, of speech, 223
re-, 212
Readers' Guide to Periodical
  Literature, 176, 250
Reading skills
  context clues, 208–9
  scanning, 281
  skimming, 281
Reasons, in developing topics,
  47
Reference materials
  almanacs, 250
  atlases, 249
  dictionaries, 249, 262–71
  encyclopedias, 246–48
  magazines, 250
  newspapers, 250
  thesauruses, 272–73
  vertical files, 250
  yearbooks, 250
Reflecting, 19, 20–21, 30
Regret, notes of, 302
Religious terms, capitalization of,
  504, 564
Reports
  bibliography in, 176, 187
  body in, 182, 184
  conclusion in, 182, 186
  crediting sources in, 187
  drafting the body, 184
  introduction in, 182–83
  ideas for, 549
  peer editing, 188
  presenting, 189
  prewriting, 174–81
  proofreading, 189
  revising, 188–89
  signal words in, 184
  titles of, 536, 567
  writing, 172–93

Request letters, 305
Research skills
  gathering information, 135
  getting information from graphic
    aids, 256–57
  interviewing, 254–55
  note taking, 252–53
  see also Libraries
Restatement, using context clues for,
    208–9
Revising, or Editing, 43,
    52–55
  descriptive writing, 96–97
  explanatory writing, 142–44
  guidelines for, 52
  narrative writing, 119–22
  persuasive writing, 164–66
  reports, 188–89
  symbols for, 54
Revision and Peer-Editing Checklists
  for explanations, 142
  for narratives, 121
  for persuasive writing, 164
  for reports, 188
rise, raise, 386
Run-on sentences, 74–75, 559

S

Salutations
  in business letters, 303
  in friendly letters, 299
Scanning, 281
Science fiction, 126
"Seed" sound, spelling words with,
    572
Semicolons, 531–32
  to combine sentences, 531, 566
Senses
  in descriptive writing, 94, 98
  in writing, 8–15, 46
    hearing, 8–9, 98
    sight, 8–9
    smell, 10–12

taste, 10–12
touch, 10–12
Sensory details
  in descriptive writing, 86, 91
  in developing topics, 46–47
Sensory word lists, making,
    11–12
Sentences, 314–45
  adding words to, 78–82
  beginning with *here, there,* and
    where, 326
  capitalization of first words in,
    506, 564
  combining, 76–82, 470, 523,
    531, 565
  compound predicates in, 334
  compound subjects in, 332
  declarative, 328, 330, 518,
    565
  definition of, 316
  exclamatory, 328, 330, 521,
    565
  fragments, 316, 559
  imperative, 328, 330, 518, 521,
    565
  interrogative, 328, 330, 521,
    565
  predicates in, 318, 320–21
  run-on, 74–75, 559
  stringy, 74–75, 559
  subjects in, 318, 323–24, 330
    different positions, 326
  topics, 67–69
Sentence outlines, 550
Series, commas in, 332, 334, 523,
    565
set, sit, 386
Setting
  in narratives, 109
  in plays, 124
Ships, capitalizing names of, 536,
    567
Short answer questions, 292
Short-term assignments, 279

in different positions, 326
finding, in different types of
    sentences, 330
simple, 323–24
Subject cards, 243, 245
Subject pronouns, 405–6
Suffixes, 214–15
spelling words with, 570
Summary statements, 190
Superlative forms
of adjectives, 431, 556
of adverbs, 444–45
Synonyms, 269, 272–73, 575
in dictionaries, 269
in thesauruses, 576

T

Table of contents, 286
Tables, getting information from, 256
Talks
Guidelines for Evaluating,
    227
Guidelines for Listening to,
    226
listening to and judging,
    226–27
practicing, 221
preparing, 220
presenting, 222–23
using note cards for, 220
using visual aids in, 222
see also Speaking and
    Listening
Taste, using sense of, in writing,
    10–12
teach, learn, 386
Television series, titles of, 536,
    567
Tenses
avoiding changes in, 560
future, 376, 377
past, 376, 377
present, 376

Test-taking skills
preparing for classroom tests,
    290–91
preparing for standardized tests,
    291
types of test questions,
    292–93
Thank-you notes, 301
the, 426
their, there, they're, 563
there, sentences beginning with,
    326
there, they're, their, 563
there is, verb agreement with,
    484
Thesaurus, 574–85
entry words in, 574
index for, 586–88
using a, 272–73
they're, there, their, 563
Thinking skills, 19
analyzing, 13–15, 19–30, 86–90,
    104–8, 130–34, 152–56
brainstorming, 20, 46,
    110–11
clustering, 21
creative thinking, 26–27, 30, 43,
    100
freewriting, 20
inquiring, 30
observing, 19, 22–23, 30
questioning, 24–25, 30, 45
reflecting, 19, 20–21, 30
seeing relationships in math, 29
see also Organizing ideas; Study
    skills
Time expressions, colon in, 531,
    566
Time lines, 552
Time words, in narrative writing,
    115
Title cards, 243–44
Titles, capitalization of personal,
    501, 564

Titles, of works
  capitalization in, 508, 564
  italics for, 536
  quotation marks in, 536
to, too, two, 563
Topics
  choosing and limiting, 44–45, 61,
    68, 135, 174–75
  developing, 46–47
  finding, 110, 174–75
Topic outlines, 550–51
Topic sentences, 67–69
Touch, using sense of, in writing,
  10–12
True-false questions, 292
two, too, to, 563

U

un-, 212
Unabridged dictionaries, 249
Underlining
  ship names, 536, 567
  titles of works, 508, 536,
    567

V

Verbs, 320–21, 364–98
  action, 96, 321, 366, 408
  agreement with subjects, 482,
    484, 486, 488, 560
  avoiding tense changes in, 560
  confusing pairs of, 384, 386
  definition of, 366
  direct objects of, 372
  helping, 369–70
  irregular, 381–82
  linking, 321, 366, 367, 374
  main, 369–70
  principal parts of, 379–80
  separated parts of, 370
  state-of-being, 96, 321, 366,
    367

  strong, in descriptive writing,
    96
  tenses, 376–77
Vertical files, 250
Visual aids. *See* Graphic aids
Vocabulary
  acronyms, 203
  antonyms, 272–73
  base words, 210–11
  blended words, 201
  borrowed words, 198, 204
  clipping, 200
  compound words, 201
  homophones, 561–63
  prefixes, 212–13
  sensory words, 11–12
  suffixes, 214–15
  synonyms, 269, 272–73
  using context clues, 207–9
  words from initials, 203
  words from names of people and
    places, 202–3
Voice, effective use of, 222, 223
Volume, of voice, 223

W

weather, whether, 563
well, good, 448, 556
where, sentences beginning with,
  326
where is, verb agreement with,
  484
whether, weather, 563
who's, whose, 563
whose, who's, 563
Word division, hyphens in, 529–30,
  566
Word origin, in dictionaries,
  268
Word parts
  base words, 210–11
  prefixes, 212–13
  suffixes, 214–15

Editorial Credits

Executive Editor, Secondary Language Arts: Julie A. Schumacher
Editors: Diane E. Carlson, Marcia Crawford Mann
Associate Editor: Richard Elliott
Assistant Editor: Peter P. Kaye
Project Assistance: Ligature, Inc.

Acknowledgments

Sources of Quoted Materials

13: Holiday House: For excerpts from *My Prairie Year* by Brett Harvey; copyright © 1986 by Brett Harvey, all rights reserved. **37:** Curtis Brown Ltd: For "December" by Lucille Clifton, from *Everett Anderson's Year;* text copyright © 1974 by Lucille Clifton. **64:** Harper & Row Publishers, Inc.: For a brief excerpt from *Sounder* by William Armstrong; copyright © 1969. **87:** Random House, Inc.: For a brief excerpt from "A Christmas Memory" by Truman Capote from *Selected Writings of Truman Capote;* copyright © 1956 by Truman Capote. **88:** Macmillan Publishing Company: For excerpts from Chapter 12, from *M.C. Higgins, the Great* by Virginia Hamilton; copyright © 1974 by Virginia Hamilton. **101:** Charles Scribner's Sons: For an excerpt from "Bull Fighting: A Tragedy," reprinted from *By-Line: Ernest Hemingway,* edited by William White; copyright © 1967 By-Line Ernest Hemingway, Inc. **105:** The Dial Press: For a brief excerpt from *The Unicorn and the Lake* by Marianna Mayer; copyright © 1982 by Marianna Mayer. **106:** Dodd, Mead & Company: For "The Sleeve Trick" by Stephen Leacock, adapted from *Literary Lapses* by Stephen Leacock; copyright © 1963 Dodd, Mead & Company. **131:** Scholastic, Inc.: For an excerpt from "The Science of Fighting Fires" by James A. Baggett, from *Science World* (November 1, 1985). **132:** Farrar, Straus & Giroux, Inc.: For excerpts from *Flying to the Moon and Other Strange Places* by Michael Collins; copyright © 1976 by Michael Collins. **148:** Tricia Connor: For "How to Blow Your Nose" by Tricia Connor, from *Enter* Syndicated Strip, Children's Television Workshop, New York. **154:** William Morrow & Company, Inc. (Lothrop, Lee & Shepard Books): For excerpts from *Our Fragile Earth* by Elizabeth S. Helfman; copyright © 1972 by Elizabeth S. Helfman. **177, 247, 253:** World Book, Inc.: For an article on "Arthur Mitchell" by Dianne L. Woodruff, an entry from the Index, and an article on "Annie Oakley" by Howard R. Lamar, from *The World Book Encyclopedia;* copyright © 1986 by World Book, Inc. **193, 284:** World Book, Inc.: For excerpts from "Maya" and "Roller Skating," from *The World Book Encyclopedia;* copyright © 1988 by World Book, Inc. **265, 271:** Simon & Schuster, Inc.: For p. 737 and the entry "dip" of *Webster's New World Dictionary,* Student Edition; copyright © 1981 by Simon & Schuster, Inc. **440:** Houghton Mifflin Company: For "Grizzly Bear," from *The Children Sing in the Far West* by Mary Austin; copyright 1928 by Mary Austin. Copyright renewed 1956 by Kenneth M. Chapman and Mary C. Wheelright. **480, 507:** Little, Brown and Company: For "The Octopus," from *Verses From 1929 On* by Ogden Nash; copyright 1942 by Ogden Nash, first appeared in *The New Yorker.* For "The Rhinoceros" by Ogden Nash; copyright 1933 by Ogden Nash, first appeared in *The New Yorker.* **506:** New Directions Publishing Corporation: For "The Red Wheelbarrow" by William Carlos Williams, from *Collected Poems Vol. I,* 1909–1939; copyright 1938 by New Directions Publishing Corporation.

Every effort has been made to trace the ownership of all copyrighted material found in this book and to make full acknowledgment for its use.

Title Page Photography

Craig Aurness—West Light/Masterfile; J.A. Kraulis/Masterfile; David W. Hamilton/Image Bank

Unit Opener Art

Composition Unit Opener, 2–3: Newspaper Rock, Michael Bright, Stock Imagery; **Resources and Skills Unit Opener, 194–195:** (Detail) *Tropical Storm with a Tiger,* Henri Rousseau, Three Lions, Superstock; **Grammar, Usage, and Mechanics Unit Opener, 312–313:** Mural by Thomas Hart Benton in the Country Music Hall of Fame & Museum

Photographs

Assignment Photographs: 40: Renny Mills; **80:** Gary Ganert; **91:** Rich Helleyer; **93:** Renny Mills; **108:** Gary Ganert; **128:** Scott Wanner, Journalism Services; **136:** (t) Gary Ganert; (b) Gary Ganert; **162–163:** Gary Ganert; **227:** Renny Mills; **245:** Siede Preiss; **246:** (b) Paul Rotton; **263:** Siede Preiss; **270:** (b) John Payne; **272:** John Payne; **276:** Renny Mills; **297:** Renny Mills; **304:** Siede Preiss; **314:** Rich Helleyer; **351:** Renny Mills; **380–381:** Siede Preiss; **387:** John Payne; **401:** Stewart Halperin, Thanks to Fashion Merchandising, Home Economics Dept., St. Louis Community College at Florissant Valley. **420:** Gary Ganert; **421:** Ross Ehlert; **424:** Gary Ganert; **440:** Renny Mills; **444:** Greg Gillis; **480:** Greg Gillis; **506:** Frank Loose; **516:** Renny Mills; **517:** Renny Mills; **520:** Greg Gillis

Stock Photographs: 4: Jeff Reed, The Stock Shop; **5:** Tony Schanuel, Photographic Resources; **7:** Joe Viesti, Viesti Associates, Inc.; **10:** Les Van, Nawrocki Stock Photo; **13:** Janet Foster, Masterfile; **15:** (tl) Russell Schleipman; (tr) Lou Jones; **16:** Gerard Vandystadt, Photo Researchers; **18–19:** Photos by George Nissen (Hand-tinted by Lynne Fischer); **23:** Dennis W. Trowbridge, Journalism Services; **25:** Morton Beebe, Image Bank; **27:** Aaron Rapoport Photography; **28:** Guido Alberto Rossi, Image Bank; **32:** (tl) Wernher Krutein, Jeroboam; (tr) Larry Tackett, Tom Stack & Associates; (br) Spencer Swanger, Tom Stack & Associates; **33:** (tl) Artist: Bill Harding, Photographer: Loren Santon; (tr) Stephen Rosser, Prairie Lee Gallery; (br) Steve Colletti; **34:** (cl) Calvin & Hobbes, © 1986, Universal Press Syndicate. Reprinted with permission. All rights reserved.; **35:** (tl) Dan McCoy, Rainbow; (tr) Bob McKeever, Tom Stack & Associates; (br) Gene Staver, Gas Company; **36:** (b)

Stephen Dalton, Animals Animals; (c) Paul Slaughter, Image Bank; **37:** (tl) Jim Gary, Twentieth Century Dinosaurs; (tr) Jim Gary, Twentieth Century Dinosaurs; (cr) David M. Doody, Tom Stack & Associates; (bl) Frank Oberle, Photographic Resources; **38:** (tl) Carson Baldwin, Jr., Animals Animals; (cr) Jim Olive, Uniphoto; (bl) Dick George, Tom Stack & Associates; **39:** (tl) Elizabeth Crews, Stock, Boston; (br) Stewart Halperin; **41:** Ted Horowitz; **47:** J. Nettis, H. Armstrong Roberts; **53:** Peter Wong, Frozen Images; **59:** Eric Meola, Image Bank; **62:** Bob Daemmrich, Tony Stone Worldwide; **63:** Bob Daemmrich, Stock, Boston; **66:** Frank Phillips Foundation, Inc., Woolaroc Museum, Oklahoma; **72:** Star Tribune; **73:** Everett C. Johnson, Uniphoto; **74:** Reprinted by permission: Tribune Media Services; **79:** Dan Morrill; **84:** H. Wendler, Image Bank; **85:** Gallery Moos Ltd., Toronto; **87:** Elyse Lewin, Image Bank; **89:** (tl) Rod Walker, The Stock Broker; (tr) Bobbe Wolf; **95:** Calvin & Hobbes, © 1987, Universal Press Syndicate. Reprinted with permission. All rights reserved.; **98:** Bob Daemmrich; **99:** Joe Viesti, Viesti Associates, Inc.; **102:** Horst Wackerbarth, *The Red Couch: A Portrait of America,* Alfred Van Der Marck Editions; **103:** Kevin Clarke, *The Red Couch: A Portrait of America,* Alfred Van Der Marck Editions; **107:** George Obremski, Image Bank; **113:** Rod Walker, The Stock Broker; **116:** Joanna McCarthy, Image Bank; **118:** Tom Tracy, The Stock Shop; **121:** Kurt Stier; **122:** Joe Baraban; **124:** Bob Daemmrich; **125:** (l) Gary Irving, Tony Stone Worldwide; (r) William Stage, Photographic Resources; **126:** Gregory Heisler, Image Bank; **129:** Neon sculpture by Lili Lakich from Museum of Neon Art, Jeff Atherton Collection; **131:** D. Klumpp, Image Bank; **133:** Allen Green, Visual Departures, Ltd.; **134:** NASA; **144:** F. Salmoiraghi, Stock Market; **147:** Rene Burri, Magnum Photos; **150:** Fotomarket-Zefa, Masterfile; **151:** Caroline Kroeger, Animals Animals; **153:** UPI/Bettmann Newsphotos; **155:** C.C. Lockwood, Animals Animals; **161:** Reprinted with permission of UFS, Inc.; **166:** Reprinted with permission of UFS, Inc.; **169:** Culver Pictures; **172:** John Elk III, 1985, Stock, Boston; **173:** Abe Rezny, Laserlight; **175:** Michael Medford; **177:** Jonathon Atkin; **178:** The Bettmann Archive; **181:** Bridgeman, Art Resource; **187:** Culver Pictures (Hand-tinted by Lynne Fischer); **191:** Tim Street-Porter; **196:** Steve Elmore, Tom Stack & Associates; **197:** Thomas Kitchin, Tom Stack & Associates; **199:** Dan McCoy, Rainbow; **200:** Bob Daemmrich, Uniphoto; **204:** Thomas Kitchin, Tom Stack & Associates; **206:** Charles Krebs, Aperture; **207:** David Madison; **210:** Charles Feil, FPG; **213:** Gene Staver, Gas Company; **218:** Gene Staver, Gas Company; **219:** Red Morgan; **228:** Chuck O'Rear, Masterfile; **230:** David Klutho, Allsport USA; **233:** Jeffrey W. Myers, FPG; **236:** Photo by Henry Wolf. Permission of Fieldcrest Cannon, Inc., Carpet and Rug Division; **237:** John Martin; **238:** Reprinted with special permission of King Features Syndicate, Inc.; **240:** Courtesy Roy Boyd Gallery; **246:** (t) 1982 Universal City Studios, Inc., Movie Still Archives; **250:** (l) Kathy Willens, Wide World Photos; (r) Jeff Robbins, Wide World Photos; **253:** Buffalo Bill Historical Center; **255:** Breck P. Kent, Animals Animals; **260:** Hank Morgan, Rainbow; **261:** Harold Sund, Image Bank; **264:** Los Angeles County Museum of Art; **270:** (t) Reprinted with special permission of King Features Syndicate, Inc.; **274:** Stephen Dunn, Allsport USA; **277:** Albert Normandin; **285:** (l) Photoworld, FPG; (r) Robert Landau, West Light; **289:** F. Stuart Westmorland, Aperture; **293:** Reprinted by permission: Tribune Media Services; **294:** Lisl Dennis, Image Bank; **296:** Paul Chesley, Photographers/Aspen; **301:** Gerard Vandystadt, Photo Researchers; **315:** Joe Viesti, Viesti Associates, Inc.; **316:** Joe Viesti, Viesti Associates, Inc.; **318:** Ron Kimball; **322:** Kenneth Hayden, Tony Stone Worldwide; **325:** (c) Larry Tackett, Tom Stack & Associates; (br) Anthony Bannister, © Barbara Bannister, Animals Animals; **328:** Frank Loose; **332:** Mel Diagiacomo, Image Bank; **335:** M. Qualetiman, Animals Animals; **336:** Enrico Ferorelli, DOT; **346:** (cl) Dan McCoy, Rainbow; (cr) Luis Castaneda, Image Bank; **347:** Dan Morrill; **348:** Jayme Odgers; **352:** (l) Gene Staver, Gas Company; (r) Stewart Halperin; **354:** Lael Morgan, Tony Stone Worldwide; **355:** Chuck O'Rear, West Light; **357:** Giraudon, Art Resource; **364:** Larry Ditto, Tom Stack & Associates; **365:** The Bettmann Archive; **366:** (l) Keystone Pictures, FPG; (r) Photoworld, FPG; **367:** Giraudon, Art Resource; **371:** Clint Clemens; **375:** Richard and Mary MacGruder, Image Bank; **377:** Doug Lee, Tom Stack & Associates; **383:** AP, Wide World Photos; **388:** The Bettmann Archive; **400:** Mark Segal, Tony Stone Worldwide; **404:** The Bettmann Archive; **411:** Elizabeth Crews, Stock, Boston; **414:** The Far Side cartoon by Gary Larson is reprinted by permission of Chronicle Features, San Francisco, CA.; **422:** Bruce Davidson, Animals Animals; **427:** Zig Leszczynski, Animals Animals; **428:** Joseph Jacobson, Journalism Services; **430:** David Stoecklein, Uniphoto; **432:** Ken Wyner, Uniphoto; **434:** Superstock; **441:** Charles Palek, Animals Animals; **446:** Brian Parker, Tom Stack & Associates; **449:** Zig Leszczynski, Animals Animals; **451:** The Bettmann Archive; **452:** Kevin Vandivier, Viesti Associates, Inc.; **460:** (l) Thomas Zimmerman, FPG; (c) E. Manewal, FPG; (r) Ken Lax, The Stock Shop; **461:** NASA; **464:** Sobel/Klonsky, Image Bank; **467:** Alpha, FPG; **471:** Jeff Schultz; **481:** Dave B. Fleetham, Tom Stack & Associates; **498:** (l) Bill Gillette, Stock, Boston; (r) Ron Kimball; **499:** G. Heisler, Image Bank; **502:** UPI, The Bettmann Archive; **505:** Kugien, FPG; **509:** The Bettmann Archive; **510:** The Bettmann Archive; **519:** Aaron Rapoport Photography; **522:** Robert Shafer, Folio, Inc.; **528:** Art Resource; **532:** Vito Palmisano, Nawrocki Stock Photo; **537:** F. Reginato, Image Bank

Illustrations

49, 100, 256, 259: JAK Graphics; **141, 282:** Joe LeMonnier; **143:** Linda Kelen; **169, 183:** Precision Graphics; **474:** Floyd Cooper; **Handwriting:** Valerie Weilmunster, Pen Graphics, Inc.